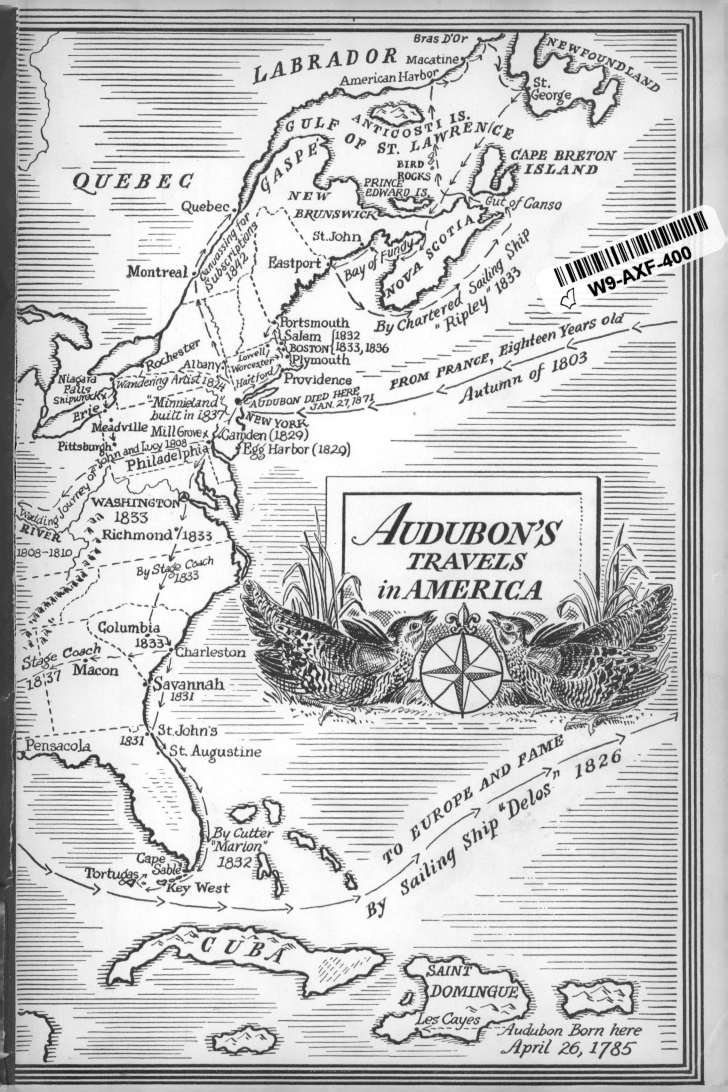

NEWFOUNDLAND

LABRADOR Bras D'Or
Macatine
American Harbor
St. George

GULF ANTICOSTI IS.
OF ST. LAWRENCE
GASPÉ BIRD CAPE BRETON
ROCKS ISLAND
PRINCE
EDWARD IS.
Gut of Canso

QUEBEC NEW
BRUNSWICK
Quebec Canvassing for Subscriptions 1842
St. John Bay of Fundy NOVA SCOTIA
Montreal Eastport By Chartered Sailing Ship "Ripley" 1833

Rochester Portsmouth
Salem 1832
Albany Lowell BOSTON 1833, 1836
Worcester Plymouth FROM FRANCE, Eighteen Years old
Niagara Wandering Artist 1824 Hartford Providence
Falls Shipwreck Autumn of 1803
Erie "Minnieland" AUDUBON DIED HERE
built in 1837 JAN. 27, 1871
Meadville Mill Grove NEW YORK
Pittsburgh John and Lucy 1808 Camden (1829)
Philadelphia Egg Harbor (1829)

Wedding Journey of
WASHINGTON
RIVER 1833
1808-1810 Richmond 1833

By Stage Coach
1833

Columbia
1833
Stage Coach Charleston
1837 Macon
Savannah
1831

St. John's
Pensacola 1831 St. Augustine

By Cutter
"Marion"
Cape 1832
Sable
Tortugas
Key West

AUDUBON'S
TRAVELS
in AMERICA

TO EUROPE AND FAME
By Sailing Ship "Delos" 1826

CUBA

SAINT
DOMINGUE

Les Cayes Audubon Born here
April 26, 1785

AUDUBON'S

AMERICA

John J. Audubon

A SELF-PORTRAIT IN OILS, MADE AT BEECH WOODS,
FELICIANA PARISH, LOUISIANA, IN 1822, AT THE AGE OF 37
REPRODUCED THROUGH THE COURTESY OF
MR. ALAN G. RINEHART

AUDUBON'S AMERICA

THE NARRATIVES AND EXPERIENCES OF

JOHN JAMES AUDUBON

Edited by Donald Culross Peattie

Illustrated with facsimiles of Audubon's prints and paintings

HOUGHTON MIFFLIN COMPANY · BOSTON

The Riverside Press Cambridge

1940

The Riverside Press
CAMBRIDGE · MASSACHUSETTS
PRINTED IN THE U.S.A.

ACKNOWLEDGMENTS

GRATEFUL acknowledgment is made to the Club of Odd Volumes for permission to reprint from the *Journal of John James Audubon made while obtaining subscriptions to his Birds of America, 1840–1843* (1929), and from Audubon's *Letters, 1826–1840* (1930), both edited by Howard Corning; and to the Field Museum of Chicago for permission to quote from 'The Wild Turkey,' by John T. Zimmer, *Zoölogical Leaflet No. 6*, Field Museum of Natural History, Chicago, 1924.

The editor further acknowledges his great indebtedness to the researches of some of Audubon's distinguished contemporary biographers. First he must mention Doctor Francis H. Herrick in his *Audubon the Naturalist* (D. Appleton and Company, New York, 1916), and *Audubon and the Dauphin*, in *The Auk*, vol. 54, October, 1937, pp. 476–499. Another work of great value, *Audubon: An Intimate Life of the American Woodsman*, by Stanley Clisby Arthur (Harmanson, New Orleans, 1937), by its researches places this editor in its debt.

CONTENTS

Contents

ILLUSTRATIONS

The illustrations in this book are produced by offset lithography,
by The Lakeside Press, Chicago, and The Tudor Press, Boston

WHAT AUDUBON KNEW

Show us gold plate of the sea kings of Crete, Ashoka's throne or the mace of Charlemagne, and some awe may mingle with our far-off curiosity. Such splendor, we think, and so long ago! That is history in its heraldic and colorful pageantry, dramatized by majestic personalities, star-crossed with tragic destinies whose tragedy we cannot really feel.

But to an American a faded flag from Saratoga is not just a relic of history, and neither is a wagon wheel from the Oregon Trail, nor an old fowling piece carried over the Wilderness Road, where Lucy Hanks carried her baby. When you say to an American, Appomattox or Yorktown, Fredericksburg or Marblehead, Fallen Timbers, Mountain Meadows, New Salem — more than pride wells up in him. Something within him hurts, as only the adventure of living can. For he does not call these thoughts and deeds history. He says, '*We lived this.*'

Not 'they lived that,' but we lived it, and 'we' means many people, not necessarily ancestral to the speaker. We may mean more than pioneer ancestors of English descent. We may refer even to some not born American. Say, La Salle, De Soto, Marquette. They too are *we* because they came here with the American dream already in their hearts before ever they left their native countries. And they died here with the gleam of it still in their eyes. La Salle's body was left upon the Texas plain, De Soto's lowered into the Father of Waters, Marquette's buried under the burr oaks and hickories of Illinois. America still holds them; their own lands scarcely claim them. So they are we.

And we, as we stare across the August shimmer of the Indian corn, at the cool trail of the river woods, feel that we see it all as they did.

We feel their old unrest; we see the great high hope of the October skies, and the baffling horizon; we are always hunting some impossible Northwest Passage, and what we meet, instead, is the 'shining mountains,' the snowy front wall of Rockies lifting out of the old buffalo country, just as the Verenderyes, first of all white men, beheld them. And you can never hear the chuckle of lake waters at your paddle without remembering the Indians and feeling one with them, or the storm of the crows in a wild autumn sky, or the clash of the corn blades. So that they, too, are we.

We say we built the Union Pacific, when we mean that Chinese coolies built it, starting from Sacramento, and Irish paddies built it, starting from Omaha, till they stared at each other across the Golden Spike in Mormon country. We built the *Constitution*, yes — out of Maine pine and Georgia oak, and we caulked it with North Carolina pitch and manned it with seafaring men of Massachusetts. So that it is not by one blood or language, one culture or religion, that we are unified. Something else than these has moulded us, in the clenching of a great palm.

And that something is America. It is the air we breathe and some horizon we see. It is the great grass plains, and the long lake waters, the arc of the sky, and the depth of the loam; it is the timber that made our cradles and musket butts; it is the flying birds, and the herds snuffing and stamping.

These are America, as it was, as we remember it, as, in some measure, it still is. Who can say why our sky is not the same as Europe's? Why our soil is not like China's good earth, why are the prairies not the steppes? Perhaps we cannot answer, but we feel the difference in our bones. The canyons are carven deep in us, and the broad rivers run in our blood.

Not that any one of us is by the smallest fraction equal to the land we inhabit. It is America, the continent, which has been decisive in the story of Americans. It has, violent and beautiful, spacious and demanding, brought out the best and the worst in the men who came to it. To describe it is to recount our history.

And the materials of history are, in the last analysis as in the first place, the accounts of eye-witnesses. Hearsay, second-hand accounts, are not evidence. The source of history is the narratives of those who lived it. Every written word of the settlement of Virginia, the exploration of the Northwest Territory, the saga of Texas or the Santa Fe

What Audubon Knew

Trail, is precious to us. And anyone who could turn up the missing journals of the Lewis and Clark expedition would have American treasure.

Now of all those who ever lived here, traveled and greatly adventured, none could bear more fascinating testimony than John James Audubon. He had the advantage of being a foreigner (as Crèvecoeur and Tonti and Marquette and Lord Bryce were foreign commentators). So that he took nothing for granted, and in the perspective of a more mature culture, all things American struck him as fresh. He had the further advantage that he was a genius, and a genius of art at that, so that to observe, to depict what he saw, was habitual and instinctive.

But Audubon had, too, a genius for the art of living. He lived with zest for the adventure, and with personal ardors. He savored everything, even the unsavory. He saw almost everything, from 1803 to 1849, from Florida to Labrador, from New York City to Fort Union on the borders of Montana. He lived among Pennsylvania Quakers, in Kentucky among pioneers from Virginia, in New Orleans among Creoles, in Mississippi among planters, in North Dakota among Indians. He explored Maine and South Carolina, Texas and Florida. He knew all types; he was the friend of Daniel Boone and Daniel Webster.

In the nearly fifty active American years of Audubon's life what other individual had such a variety of experience? No one, certainly, who was at once so sensitive and so lusty. No one with his pen and his brush. One thinks of Mark Twain. But Clemens was a child when Audubon was old. Clemens went down the Mississippi in a gilded steamboat, as a light-hearted adventure. But Audubon made the same journey years before, in a flatboat, and his life's success seemed to depend on the venture.

One thinks perhaps of Lincoln. But Lincoln left no personal narrative. Of Whitman, who certainly left plenty of self-exposition, but it was the work of an introspective, an impressionist. No one would dream of suggesting that Emerson knew his America as Audubon knew it, or that Thoreau did, or Cooper or Parkman. The only comparable character I can think of is André Michaux, a man whose nationality, adventures and gifts parallel Audubon's. Beside Audubon, Michaux is a short shadow.

Fame as an ornithologist has obscured Audubon's value as a witness to our heroic age. His painter's art has overshadowed his abilities as a writer. For besides being a detailed diarist and an inveterate correspondent, Audubon was a professional writer. He wrote to sell, and did sell. I am not saying that he knew how to write history like the learned Parkman, or style like the choice Thoreau, or that he thought as an equal with Emerson. I am asserting only that while Cooper went to England while he wrote *The Prairie* (an unreadably dull book, to my ears), Audubon was *on* the prairies. That where Emerson knew his Carlyle, Audubon knew his Mississippi squatters, that while Thoreau was traveling around Concord, Audubon was traveling around North America. While Parkman was writing history, Audubon was making and witnessing it.

And yet there has never before been collected into any one volume a general selection of the first-hand narratives of this shrewd and eager observer of all conditions and aspects of American men, manners, and scenes. He is seldom even quoted save in evidence for the unbelievable numbers of the passenger pigeons, or the destruction of the buffalo, or on some other point in natural history. This is due in part to the fact that his writings have remained scattered through a wide assortment of volumes, many of them accessible only in a few great libraries. Others of them, notably his unaltered diaries and journals, have but recently been published and only in limited and costly editions.

This volume is intended to make up in some measure for neglect of Audubon's precious testimony. As editor I have preferred to bring him forward less as the naturalist than as one who knew river captains and roustabouts, pioneers and men of letters, Indians and scientists. This without, of course, slighting his natural history writings, but reducing them to some reasonable proportion to the whole. That whole is the America of his day, America as he, and perhaps only he, knew it. Audubon's America.

BIOGRAPHICAL NOTE

JOHN JAMES AUDUBON gave many accounts of his own birthplace and parentage, and the date of that birth. Any one of them might have been fairly convincing, if they were not all more or less in contradiction, except on one point. And that point is his repeated assertion and inference that he was born in the New World, the Western Hemisphere.

This should set at rest the preposterous claim that has recently (and only recently) been set up for him, that he was none other than the lost Dauphin, Louis XVII, majesty disguised as a wandering artist! This legend would be too far-fetched for notice if it were not, unfortunately, the one story about Audubon that sticks in many minds. Two women biographers of Audubon have recently taken it quite seriously, and thousands of words have been written in debate on this point. They can all be cut short by laying down a fact denied by nobody. The unfortunate little Bourbon prince had a deformed ear, while Audubon's ears were both quite normal. Who will seriously argue the point beyond this?

All the documents in the case prove, to the satisfaction of most who have examined them, that the great bird painter was born April 26, 1785, at the port of Les Cayes or Aux Cayes on the south coast of what is now the republic of Haiti, though it was then called by the French, who were in possession of it, Saint-Domingue. The father, Jean Audubon, was a lieutenant in the French navy, with a record of distinguished courage and ability in battle. He was a rich sugar planter, a careful and successful business man, and an owner of properties in the West Indies, France, and Pennsylvania.

But the mother of the future artist remains a mystery. She was a native of the island, a Creole of good birth. Her family name may have been either Rabin or Fougère; there is equal evidence for both, and the Fougères and Rabins were and still are distinguished families in Haiti. Probably somewhere in this woman's ancestry was the then locally well-known name of Laforest. She bore the lieutenant (so it seems in the light of latest researches) four sons, of whom Jean Jacques Audubon was the youngest. Two of the others died. One still has descendants in Haiti.

The infant was not, however, then called Jean Jacques Audubon, but, probably, Fougère Rabin. The reason for this was the bald fact that the seafaring planter could not marry his island love. He had a wife in France, a woman older than he, a woman of property. When the little Fougère was about one year old his mother died. Her place at the plantation was taken by another, by whom the lieutenant had a daughter, Muguet. From her mother he seems to have become separated, but the girl child remained with her father. So there, when at last he was obliged to return to France, was the sailor with a brace of tiny love children, babes-in-the-jungle who might reasonably have expected no other fate than to be abandoned there, at best to hired care.

But Jean Audubon was conscientious. He took his children back to France, in 1789, probably crossing the United States on his way, and placed them in the tender arms of his childless wife in Nantes. Five years later Lieutenant Audubon legally acknowledged the paternity of 'a male child, Fougère,' as well as of the small girl, and formally adopted both. Subsequently the boy's name seems to have changed at home, and his half-sister's too, perhaps to relieve the children from reminders of their illegitimacy, so that when fifteen years old the boy was baptized under the name of Jean Audubon-Rabin. When quite young he had a whimsy for signing drawings Laforest Audubon, but he dropped it into oblivion when he became famous. For a while he styled himself Jean Jacques Fougère Audubon, but the names Fougère and Rabin were hateful to him; in later life he practically denied that he had ever borne them, for it seems certain, from his actions, that he understood their significance. Bit by bit his name evolved from Fougère Rabin to John James Audubon, with intermediate links attested in his own writing. His signatures tell a story of strange destiny, from a secret and luckless birth in dark Haiti to golden triumph in America.

The lad was brought up in Nantes and at his father's country estate down on the estuary of the Loire, and was educated irregularly in school and at home. Audubon, like many artists, was poor at mathematics — a defect that was to plague him for years. But his father taught him, or had him taught, English, fencing, dancing, and music, and the day was to come when his career depended upon them. His father was exacting, just, stern, bracing; his foster mother praised his beauty to his face, filled his pockets with coins, and abetted him in skylarking. Between them, like a little tree played upon by opposing tropisms, grew the child of genius, governed by mysterious inner promptings to be only its sole self; for his destiny had been predetermined in the seed. Willful, ardent, cocky, clever, tremulously sensitive, determined to be nothing but what he wished, with that ruthlessness appalling to parents, he got his young roots into life and shot up his sapling identity.

From early childhood Audubon began to draw birds. He was also a hunter, a distressingly active home taxidermist, a persistent collector of nests and a blower of eggs. But drawing birds was his passion, and rather surprisingly his father seems to have indulged and assisted this passion up to a certain point. When it seemed that natural history was interfering with the boy's serious studies, the father put him in a naval training school. But the now caged young eagle immediately went frantic at restraint and broke free without leave. His father surrendered and sent him to Paris to study in the *atelier* of David, the best drawing school of the day. If Audubon had been a mediocrity he would probably have done well, as teachers gauge achievement. But he had no patience with elementary routine, and no interest in drawing anything but birds. In a short time he was at home again, the despair of his family.

As Lieutenant Audubon had left Haiti just in time to escape the frightful massacres of the race war that had its beginnings at Les Cayes, so now he got his son out of France just in time to escape the wholesale conscriptions of Napoleon. Young Audubon was sent to America, to his father's estate near Norristown, Pennsylvania, in 1803; and it is there and then that the curtain, for purposes of this book, really rises.

'Mill Grove,' the Audubon estate, was a manor house situated in what we might call the Valley Forge country, and connected with some lead mines which the lieutenant had bought as a speculation. It was secluded deep in the country, that eastern Pennsylvania countryside which has some of the qualities of English scenery — gentle, tranquil, aristocratic. At the opening of the nineteenth century it must still have possessed what it has never completely lost, an eighteenth-century charm, that colonial seaboard atmosphere of a temperate New World tingling with wildness in which are set an Old World elegance and leisure. The inhabitants, with exceptions important to Audubon, were Quakers, a peaceful and industrious lot quite without sympathy for Audubon's hobbies of shooting, music, bird-watching, drawing, and fine dress. Not far away, as distance seems to us today, was Alexander Wilson, teaching school, playing his melancholy flute, unsuccessfully courting, and beginning to draw and study birds. But destiny had not yet drawn their paths to cross; back to back, they looked still in opposite directions.

Perhaps the most carefree year of his life was that when Audubon lived at Mill Grove, self-styled lord of the manor. His father had intended him to look after the lead mine, in company with an older and hostile partner. But the mine, which never had paid and never would pay, was only a source of distress to Audubon; he shook off unpleasant duties lightly in those days and, clad in elegant pumps and ruffled shirt, he roamed his woods with the finest fowling piece he could purchase, shooting grouse like an English lord.

Of the Pennsylvania period of his life Audubon has left us a narrative, and if the purpose of this book were another biography of Audubon, it would be quoted in the pages that follow. But as that purpose is to permit Audubon to describe the American scene, it is not quoted, for the eighteen- and nineteen-year-old Audubon was entirely taken up with himself. He views nature as a hunting preserve, and judges everyone as friend or enemy, by which he means one who liked him, or one who did not let him have his way. Few managed to enter the self-indulgent boy's good graces except for a fellow hunter and landed neighbor, the Englishman William Bakewell. Calling upon him one memorable day, John James found at home only his neighbor's daughter, Lucy, and in spite of her tender years, he at once fell utterly in love with her. However he misjudged others at this time, he made no mistake about his future mate, and in the innocent and unwritten features of a girl of fifteen he read the woman aright.

But Mr. Bakewell had no intention of giving his daughter to a lad who had not yet come into his fortune, either by inheritance or dint of effort, and the young Audubon went to France to obtain the consent and financial assistance of his father. The practical lieutenant set about planning for his son a business partnership with Ferdinand

Biographical Note

Rozier, a young merchant to whose capital Audubon *père* joined a substantial amount, which was to be his son's anticipated heritage. While his future was thus arranged for him, Jean Jacques was rambling the woods with the gifted naturalist Charles D'Orbigny, an excellent systematist who probably put into some sort of order the boy's undirected and now forbidden passion for birds. Back in New York, drudging obediently as a clerk in a business house to gain experience, he found or stole the time to work on the side in the private museum of Doctor Samuel Mitchell, where he learned taxidermy. He haunted the New York markets where were exposed, in all seasons then, waterfowl and game birds of every sort, and these he used to buy up for dissection and drawing. His drawings of this period (the earliest extant being made on his return to France) are always carefully studied by Audubon's biographers. For they begin to show finish and individuality of style. From Mitchell and D'Orbigny, apparently, he has learned to include on the drawing measurements and weights of parts; enlarged details of critical points like bill and feet are often added, and eggs are frequently figured too.

Here, then, is the great ornithologist, the dual genius of art and science, already in the making. But this genius has just lost a handsome sum in speculation on a collapsing indigo market, and with this as the best of his preparation for business, he now (1807) sets off, in company with the solid and sober young Rozier, for Kentucky, there to open a frontier store. From now on, for eleven years, from the age of twenty-two to thirty-three, the great adventure of his youth is to be bound up with the men of the frontier, with the woods and swamps, the sparse cities, the plantations, the rivers, and above all with the wilderness bird life of that great system of waterways that is the Mississippi Basin.

There were then a million white people living between the Appalachians and the Rockies. This included only one considerable town, New Orleans with eight thousand souls. The rest of the population might be anywhere, even trading with the Sioux almost within sight of the Big Horns. But most of them were still localized in two separate centers united by the great waterways. One, on the lower Mississippi, was a mixed group of subtropical planters of French and American (chiefly Southern) origin. The other, along the Ohio and its tributaries, was rapidly filling with a wholly American stock, where Virginian gentry, with slaves and silver plate, children and Chippendale, mingled somewhat disdainfully with small farmers, traders, speculators, homeseekers, land sharks, Indian missionaries, Indian cheaters, outlaws, school teachers, editors, debtors, evangelists, eloping couples, founders of fantastic ideal communities, and the whole mass of old-style pioneers who had left the stabilities and the restrictions of Atlantic seaboard life. They left either because of superior initiative and courage, or from inherent shiftlessness and a tendency to run away from life's responsibilities. They left because they hoped to find a place to live under better conditions, or because conditions back East were too good, and they sought a place where they could be idle, drunk, immoral, and habitually defaulting without the restraint of neighbors. They came from all states: Johnny Appleseed was from Springfield, Massachusetts; Aaron Burr was Hudson River. Daniel Boone was a North Carolinian. Henry Clay was buckled-shoon Virginia, Lucy Hanks was barefoot Virginia; George Rapp was Pennsylvania Dutch, and he came to found, on the banks of the Wabash, the kingdom of heaven, where the sexes never cast eyes on each other and you got forty per cent on your money. Nicholas Roosevelt was New York Dutch, and he came to look over the possibilities of a fleet of these new steamboat things, something to link Pittsburgh with New Orleans, to carry the new commonwealth's corn and fur, timber and meat, to market.

For though they had little in common in origin and tastes, these people, these self-styled 'men of the western waters,' did form a commonwealth. The market price in New Orleans mattered more to Cincinnati than the market price in New York. For the West could not ship to the East and sell at a profit: no railroads, no rivers, no canal, no highroads. Appalachians looked high in those days. No, you had to sell down-river. New Orleans was the market; also the importing and exporting point for the West Indies and Europe. That was why President Jefferson bought Louisiana in 1803 — everything from New Orleans to the headwaters of the Missouri. Everything west of the Mississippi, east of the Rockies. He bought the Father of Waters to run, duty free, from the source to the mouth. He made the West, the Middle West of today, possible.

Then he seemed to do his best to break it. That was in 1807 when he passed the Embargo Act, which, to punish England and France, forbade America to sell to Europe. New England and Virginia and New York went into collapse. Their banks had financed the 'Ohio fever,' the land purchase and the farm materials; now they called for their loans, and the West couldn't pay. New Orleans and Natchez were broken too. They couldn't buy, because they couldn't export.

It was on the eve of just this disaster that Rozier and Audubon with his bride Lucy went into business in Louisville, Kentucky, a village of one thousand souls. Not for eight years was the country again to know real prosperity. Eight years is soon over, in a nation's life. In Audubon's life it was the critical period of his young manhood and it sufficed to break him as a business man. That was precisely what had to happen before he could become an ornithologist and an artist.

It is certainly doubtful if the Audubon-Rozier venture, which was transferred from Louisville to Henderson in the vain hope of better trade, could have succeeded even in times of prosperity. Imagine Rozier's despair at a partner who, with a boy to help, was supposed to tend store, and not only went birds'-nesting and generally skylarking instead, day after day and weeks on end, but took the boy with him to help him shoot, retrieve, and carry back the ornithological specimens. True, his gun kept the table supplied with grouse, turkey, and duck. But his accounts were never in order, and what was worse, he was not made miserable by the fact. He needed and wanted, and knew how liberally to spend, money. But he seemed to think that where it came from was the business of Rozier or his father, or his father-in-law. His own was that portfolio of drawings — a wallet that never got thinner.

Indeed by the year 1810 Audubon's collection contained more than two hundred pictures. They were far inferior to the finished product of later years, but they were the nucleus of his great work, and it is important to note that they were, like the first edition of *The Birds of America*, which was issued in elephant folio dimensions, all life-size drawings, whether of eagles or titmice. This was Audubon's unique idea, and, though it proved so difficult of realization when it came to publication, it was also one of the most novel and telling points for the sale of his book. Thus early did *The Birds of America* take shape. What hours of labor, what days and even weeks of wood rambling, what a stored wealth of field experience the drawings already represented, Lucy and Rozier could have told. 'I have a rival in every bird,' Lucy laughed and sighed to her sister.

Rozier, who returned Lucy's dislike, determined to strike out again, and got Audubon to go with him, leaving Lucy for the time behind. They made their way toward the old French settlement of Ste. Gene-

vieve on the Mississippi, in Missouri, where they hoped to find better
customers than the American pioneers. On the way they became ice-
bound, and while their boat was jammed in the floes, and Rozier the
business man slept day and night to forget his gloomy thoughts, Audubon was in his glory. His famous passage on the wild swan owes its
origin to these snow-blanketed days and nights. He fraternized with
the Osages. He roamed the woods, tracking beasts and following birds,
his own master, breathing his own element — the wilderness air. When
the ice broke up, and they had again to stagger and strain at the tow
rope, pulling three hundred barrels of whiskey cargo against the
thawing Mississippi's might, Rozier took up heart, but the heart of
John James Audubon was again the rebellious heart of a slave who
searches this way and that for escape.

At Ste. Genevieve Audubon and Rozier dissolved their partnership.
Rozier bought Audubon's interest, and with the money Audubon returned to the store in Henderson.

In 1810 Henderson, Kentucky, was a log-cabin town eighteen years
old, set in the midst of great canebrakes alive with birds and game.
Here Audubon brought his little family, and the finest piece of furniture in the house, he said, was the cradle. This has been taken to mean
destitution, which was not the case. There was plenty of furniture;
there were Lucy's silverware and china. He merely said the cradle
was the finest thing in the house. It is the finest thing in any house, as
long as it is filled. When little Victor was lifted from it for the last time,
it was to make room for his brother John, who, like his elder brother,
was to be his father's faithful helper many years later. At the moment
he was but a source of anxious pride.

From the age of twenty-seven to thirty-five, Audubon lived at
Henderson, Kentucky. Those are core years in a marriage, when early
love is welded into enduring strength by the fires of living, when
children are born, and sometimes lost (Lucy bore four and lost two),
and dreams are begotten, and tried, and go begging at any price,
without believers. These years, 1812 to 1820, furnished forth materials
for many of Audubon's most stirring adventures, told years later in
the *Episodes of Western Life*, so liberally quoted in this book. In the
telling, they sound wonderful; hardships seem in them merely to be
forging our hero; mishaps are prod to a laugh. In a backward look,
such tribulations gleam like treasure.

But at the time we call them those troubles that never come singly.

Biographical Note

The best of businesses failed then. Audubon failed conspicuously even in a panic. A store, a mill, a commission business, all met with lack of success. Audubon was sued, and instituted futile suits. He was reviled, attacked, sought by a mob, assaulted by a business enemy, brought to trial for defending himself, and finally taken to jail for debt. When he declared bankruptcy, the sheriff took everything, all Lucy's silver and china, his house, his furniture. Everything but his clothes and gun. Oh, yes, and his drawings, which of course would not fetch a cent; they were worthless; those he might keep.

Without a dollar in his pocket he set out to walk to Louisville alone. 'This,' he said, remembering it long after, 'was the saddest of all my journeys, the only time in my life when the wild turkeys that so often crossed my path, and the thousands of lesser birds that enlivened the woods and the prairies, all looked like enemies, and I turned my eyes from them, as if I could have wished that they never existed.'

Every resource was now exhausted — Lucy's patrimony, Audubon's last asset. But he hit upon the talent that was to change the course of his life. He began to draw portraits. For a few dollars he promised, like a boardwalk artist today, a striking likeness while you wait. Soon he could charge more, and take more time. Swiftly he evolved a talent that, if he could hardly make it support himself and his family, saved him again and again from utter destitution.

It is for some critic to tell how good a portraitist Audubon was. He certainly seems to me to have had a strong gift for seizing character. True that he had no knowledge of anatomy; he never learned how to handle oils with confidence; he worked much too rapidly and never respected the portraitist's art in himself. Admit all this and more. But he had vitality, a real, electric current of young vitality, and whether it was his natural gusto for life and people, or whether it was the wolf snapping at his heels, he did the wolf-scarers with a dash and swing that, in spite of bad drawing, brings men and women right off the page, alive. Whatever rank his portraits may take as art, there is not one of them still extant whose owners are not as proud to boast it as if it were the finished flattery of Sir Thomas Lawrence. The Middle West, or rather the Middle South, today is filled with ancestral portraits attributed to Audubon. Rightly or wrongly so, but proudly.

Through the influence of friends, Audubon received an appointment in 1819–20 in the private natural history museum of Doctor Daniel Drake of Cincinnati, himself an excellent naturalist. The salary was

good, and the task consisted of taxidermy and classification, invaluable
to the future ornithologist. And more than that, he now tasted the
fountain of science again. Combined with the rich store of his Kentucky wood wanderings, and his maturing talent for drawing, this one
taste was enough to set him off at last upon his great adventure, his
project to become the portraitist of all the birds of America, to be
drawn life-size, in living attitudes and in the full color of their fresh
plumage. It was a venture without precedent in the history of American
ornithology. Without historic parallel, indeed, in the business of publishing. (Hadn't Wilson worked himself to death trying to sell his
modest efforts?)

The world to which he was coming, the world of birds and great
trees, belongs to an era when the Mississippi Valley would have been
unrecognizable for us. It was then still a wilderness, with no more
than farmed clearings here and there. Many of the settlers were back
completely in the hunting stage, in the Daniel Boone period when the
life of a man was built around the life of the black bear, his natural
food, robe, and sport. Men hunted the bear and the deer and the coon
for a living, as they hunted cougars and Indians out of enmity for
natural foes. God had put robins and thrushes in the forest to be
eaten as surely as He had passenger pigeons and wild ducks, though
why in His wisdom He had made the wild parakeet, which came out
of the thickets to devour the farmer's scratched corn patch, nobody
knew, and so a blast of birdshot for them, and might it bring down
every one of the marauders!

All this bespeaks a vanished abundance, and never in historic times
was there in the temperate zone such prodigality of life. The Mississippi was — it still is — the principal interior flyway of most of the
migrating birds of North America, on their way to the breeding grounds
in the North, and back in autumn, to the South. It was, then at least,
a far richer ornithological field than the Atlantic coast flyway, a little
richer in species especially of big and strange birds, and far richer in
numbers. Whooping cranes and pelicans, passenger pigeons and loons,
whistling swans and golden plovers and wild geese swept through this
kingdom of forests and prairies. Grouse and prairie chickens, meadow-
larks and horned larks were found in the North, anhingas and blue
grosbeaks and orchard orioles and summer tanagers in the South.
Coots and gallinules and curlews and sandpipers minced along the
shores, and in the woods the wild turkey lorded it over his hens. It

PURPLE GRACKLE

'With his own hands Joseph Mason painted perhaps a hundred of the marvelous details of vegetation that illuminate the earlier *Birds of America*. In the technique of perspective and naturalism, Mason's flowers and fruits and leaves are just as bold and successful as Audubon's living birds . . . See the wonderful corn plant in Plate 7 being ravaged by grackles.' — P. 135.

The Purple Grackle is one of the first ten plates of *The Birds of America*, engraved by William H. Lizars of Edinburgh. Later these plates were retouched and reprinted by Robert Havell & Son of London, who completed the work which Lizars began. The reproduction here is from an original impression of the plate as engraved by Lizars before being retouched by Havell.

Purple Grackle

QUISCALUS VERSICOLOR.

1. Male. 2. Female.

Plant Vulgo, Indian Corn.

Drawn from Nature by John J. Audubon F.R.S.E. M.W.S.

Engraved by W. H. Lizars Edin.r

Printed & Coloured by R. Havell Sen.r

was a paradise of birds, never before seen by a great ornithologist, save for a swift journey of Alexander Wilson.

Audubon followed Wilson down the Mississippi ten years behind him. During this time steamboats had become common, and many the plantations which sprang up on the crop-lands, well back from the river and its malarial flood plains. The account of that journey, being quoted extensively in the pages that follow, need not be retraced here. Absolutely without funds, leaving his brave wife to support herself and the two children by teaching, Audubon set forth with his dog, his gun, his crayons, and his paper, to see the world — of birds.

He took with him as his assistant young Jo Mason, a Cincinnati boy of thirteen, of whom much will be found in the quotations that follow, and of his life and remarkable talents more will be said. Here it is only to be mentioned that the debt Audubon owes to this gifted boy is little understood. He was a botanist, and a good one, and taught that science to Audubon as they went down-river. More, he taught Audubon to observe plants minutely, and to develop a delicate feeling for wild vegetation. But best of all he actually painted in scores or perhaps a hundred or so of the gorgeous flowers and fruits and leaves that give to the early period of *The Birds of America* much of their naturalism and their value as complete habitat groups. The idea of such an addition to ornithological illustration (previously almost unheard of) was probably Audubon's, but the work, in the earlier plates, was the boy's. Later, Audubon mastered the trick himself completely, but the mannerism was always Mason's.

So they set forth in a flatboat, in October of 1820, and we find Audubon for the first time in his life keeping what it is a pity he did not keep long before, a journal of his daily observations. We find him, this time, determined to draw not only what took his fancy, but everything with wings. Nothing now must escape his observation; every bird must be identified. The Mississippi with its ox-bow lakes and bayous and tributaries was then a great resort of multitudes of waterfowl and shore birds and birds of prey. Above all is this true during the fall migration and winter season, at which time he found himself traveling, and he neglected not one of his opportunities.

The first sojourn in New Orleans has also been quoted in this book, and speaks for itself of Audubon's starvation, loneliness, and defeats, the snubs he endured, the indifference he encountered. These he may sometimes be exaggerating, for he was conscious of his genius before it had displayed itself, was touchy as a D'Artagnan, and saw no reason (as indeed there was none) why he should not at once be received in all the best houses and become the leading drawing master of the Creole capital. There is no doubt that he was unappreciated, or that he was often scurvily treated. Particularly in the matter of payment for his work he was, if he is speaking truly, often unable to collect certain parts, or any, of his recompense. New Orleans was not more faulty than other places in this regard. Many people in later years subscribed to *The Birds of America* and received plate after plate without paying for them.

Unfortunately for Audubon as a new-come teacher and portraitist, there were rival artists in the city already established. But Audubon was never idle. He haunted the markets for specimens of birds, went out with the shooting gentry, employed hunters to bring him specimens from distant lakes and swamps, and formed projects, never to bear fruition, for joining some government party of exploration to the west.

My selection from Audubon's New Orleans journal ends with his departure for 'Oakley,' the plantation of Mr. James Pirrie in West Feliciana Parish, Louisiana. Mrs. Pirrie had taken a liking to the man; he was the sort that immediately makes an impression on women. Handsome, vivacious, gallant, he had the charm which American women feel so strongly in a foreign artist of any sort; he was the exact opposite of the average male with which American women are acquainted. And Mrs. Pirrie, newly come to prosperity, probably had in mind his painting her portrait. Audubon was employed, however, as the tutor of her daughter Eliza, 'My lovely Miss Pirrie,' as Audubon tenderly calls her, and when not engaged in teaching the lass, he was wood-wandering with Joseph, or drawing, drawing, in his rooms.

West Feliciana Parish was the resort of great numbers of warblers, those most difficult and fascinating of all the small North American birds. It is within the range of many species little known outside the South, such as orchard orioles, summer tanagers, blue grosbeaks, and chuck-will's-widows. And the whole environment and countryside were new to Audubon. He had known Pennsylvania and Kentucky woods, and cypress swamps and canebrakes. But never before had he beheld the upland South, with its red hills and pine groves mixed with flowering trees and evergreen shrubs. Before long he realized that birds he had seen on his trip, and others he was seeing now, were not in Wilson's *Ornithology*, nor in Linnaeus, and for the first time he began

Biographical Note

to venture as a systematic ornithologist — not in a hurry to publish new Latin binomials, but eager to master new life histories, and make portraits of the never before figured. Among these first original ornithological discoveries of his are the stately king rail, the beguiling little Bewick's wren, and the rough-winged swallow. From this period date such famous plates as the mockingbirds defending their nest against a rattlesnake, the lavish painting of Carolina parakeets, the Baltimore orioles and their pensile nest, and the great ivory-billed woodpeckers.

In his personal relations, Audubon was seldom at a standstill with anybody; he either loved or hated, he either enchanted people or wearied them. So it was with the Pirries. At first he pleased everyone and was pleased by all. Inside of four months the mutual pleasure had reached the bounds of its possibilities and was over. Mrs. Pirrie was perhaps annoyed that Audubon had not taken more interest in doing her portrait and that ornithology came first among his duties. And his devotion, full of delicacy and solicitude, went all to his little pupil who returned it to her teacher with innocent ardor. There was no question of love between them; Audubon was always utterly faithful to his Lucy and would have thought with horror of making love to his pupil. The girl had young suitors who interested her amply, and on one of them her mother was determined to bestow her. The suitor was jealous of the drawing master; Mrs. Pirrie was tired of him; her sister loathed him; his moody and brilliant personality was more than the family circle could take; and the whole arrangement broke up in a blazing quarrel.

Returned to New Orleans, Audubon rented a house on Dauphine Street, and set about looking for work once more, constantly writing to Lucy to come with the children and join him. His first act was to order a new suit of clothes, his others being ragged and shapeless, and to get his hair cut, an event long overdue. Though he felt like a shorn lamb after this was done, his locks still fell to his shoulders!

While waiting for Lucy he sought, generally in vain, for work as a teacher or portraitist, and beguiled his time with adding to his swelling portfolio of drawings. He kept a hunter in the field, bringing him rarities. One of them was the white-fronted goose which he had not seen before in the South, and Wilson had not figured; others were the trumpeter swan, and the whooping crane. Bit by bit, the momentous task was progressing, when Lucy arrived with the boys and all Audubon's Kentucky drawings and the splendid harvest of his Mississippi journey. That Christmas, 1821, viewing his own work, he was jubilant over his future. But the cupboard was bare.

We next find Audubon in Natchez where Jo Mason left him to return to his widowed mother in Ohio. Audubon gave him his gun and crayons, to work and hunt his way. It was in Natchez that Audubon received his first lessons in the use of oils, from the itinerant portrait painter, John Steen. And though oils were never to be the real medium of his bird paintings, the skill that he gained from Steen stood him in good stead in years to come, and in many a tight place. Mrs. Audubon had gone meantime as a governess to 'Beechwoods,' the estate of the Percys in West Feliciana Parish, and here Audubon visited her. The Percys were delighted with him, and he stayed through the summer teaching the Percy girl children music and drawing and dancing, and even (it was the talk of the countryside) how to swim, in a big spring-house.

The tradition is that Audubon spent most of his days roaming the woods in search of birds, and there is no reason to doubt it. All the time he was perfecting himself in oils, and he had independent ideas about the faithful use of color. So that when he painted the Percy children with the sallow cheeks they probably had, Mrs. Percy was furious. Pleasant relations once again had passed the point where they could expand without rupture, and a crashing quarrel ensued, in which Lucy did not side with her husband.

He left, with the boy Victor, for Natchez, where both fell ill of yellow fever. Lucy brought them back to 'Beechwoods,' where Mrs. Percy generously buried their quarrel. Recovered, he and Victor made their way to Kentucky, where the fourteen-year-old boy was offered a position in his uncle's office.

Next spring Audubon set off to Philadelphia to seek a publisher for his great work. There Wilson's *American Ornithology* had been printed. It was at the time the cultural capital of the country both in science and art, and it numbered among its citizens George Ord the zoologist, who was dead Wilson's friend and biographer, Thomas Say the entomologist and conchologist, Richard Harlan the mammalogist, Alexandre Le Sueur the artist and zoologist, Thomas Sully the portraitist, and the brothers Peale: Rembrandt, Titian, and Robert. Wilson's old engraver, Alexander Lawson, lived there too, and there was visiting at the time that international ornithologist, Charles Lucien Bonaparte, Prince of Canino and Musignano.

Biographical Note

Audubon's disappointment was sharp. Ord's jealousy for his friend Wilson went to lengths well-nigh insane; further, he had a financial interest in Wilson's book and was projecting the execution of a new edition. Titian Peale, himself an ornithological painter in the old-fashioned style of profiles of stuffed specimens on a perch, was hostile to Audubon's living birds. Lawson foresaw that the sale of Wilson's work would be ruined if such magnificent drawings came to the notice of the public, and pronounced Audubon's birds out of drawing and untrue to nature. Ord objected to the mingling of flowers and fruits and leaves — the natural habitat, in short — with birds. Peale even refused to let Audubon view a certain specimen in his collection. No doubt that there was a conspiracy. Audubon used every grace, every flattery in vain. No one befriended him except Sully, who gave him free lessons in oils, and Le Sueur and Bonaparte, who pronounced the drawings magnificent and urged him to take them to Europe both to find a good engraver and the requisite number of subscribers. Audubon asked Bonaparte to advance him the money to go to Europe, but was 'coldly refused.' Nevertheless Bonaparte remained the artist's friend and defender; and financial aid to tide him over was at hand. Edward Harris, the future entomologist, called to inspect some drawings Audubon had placed on sale. 'Young Harris, God bless him,' Audubon records, 'looked at the drawings and said he would take them all, at my prices. I would have kissed him, but that is not the custom in this icy city.' As he was leaving, Harris pressed an extra hundred in his hand. Audubon thereupon gave him all his drawings of French birds, which were to come to light so long afterward.

In pocket now, Audubon pressed on to New York, where he was elected to its Lyceum of Natural History. The records of the Lyceum state of Audubon:

> This gentleman, with an enthusiasm equalled by that of our late lamented Wilson has devoted nearly twenty years to American Ornithology. He has followed the birds into their most secret haunts, and traversed the United States in almost every direction. To the learnings of a naturalist, he unites the skill of an artist, and his magnificent collection of drawings, representing four hundred species, excels anything of the kind in this country and has probably never been surpassed in Europe.

Audubon made his debut as an ornithologist by reading to the Lyceum a paper disproving the theory of 'torpidity' of swallows in winter. But no New York publishers would consider the venture of his work, and so with the money Harris had given him he decided to travel back south by way of Niagara and Lake Erie. Soon light of purse again, the artist worked his way, painting curb portraits, to Pittsburgh, where he met a landscape artist, a Swiss, George Lehman, who in later years was to contribute the delicate distances that are seen in so many of the famous plates done in the middle period of *The Birds of America*. In Cincinnati he borrowed money to pay his deck passage to Louisville where he arrived with portfolio, gun, ragged clothes, and empty pockets. Louisville, including his wife's relatives, shook knowing heads. They could not see that in all these years he had got on very far. One brief embrace of his son Victor, and he was off again, arriving one morning at his wife's school at the Percy plantation with rent apparel and unkempt locks, no nearer his fame, it would seem, nor his accomplishment, than ever.

But he was back with his Lucy and back 'in the woods, the woods of Louisiana . . . my heart was beating with joy.' Here more than a year fled by, while he collected and painted, and taught dancing and fencing, French and the violin. Suddenly he had become the rage in two states, and must go from plantation to plantation, giving lessons and leading cotillions. For the first time in many years he had money in his pocket; he had savings, and these, with Lucy's own, enabled him at last to set sail from New Orleans in May of 1827 for Liverpool. Even in mid-ocean he found birds to draw — the petrels, which he had never before had the chance to study.

Successively Audubon took by storm Liverpool and Edinburgh, London and Paris. In each case he had three deeply entrenched bastions to carry simultaneously. There was first the world of art, to which he was bringing such wares as no one had ever asked it seriously to consider before — bird paintings, forsooth! The second was the rampart of science, and a stay-at-home, museum or 'closet' science at that, in which his wealth of field experience barely outweighed his unorthodox lack of formal training, while his eccentric dress, his gracile personality, his naïve vanity all told against him. And finally there was the redoubt of wealth and social influence, without which he could not secure the proper subscribers. But when we say that his friends and supporters soon numbered among them Sir Walter Scott, Sir Thomas Lawrence, Thomas Bewick, 'Christopher North,' William Swainson, George Children, Baron Cuvier, Louis Philippe, Duke of Orleans, the wealthy William Rathbone, Lord Stanley, afterwards Earl of Derby,

Biographical Note

Lord Elgin, Sir William Jardine, Professor Robert Jameson, Selby the ornithologist, Geoffroy Saint-Hilaire, and Redouté the great flower painter, we see that he was successful on every front, in three capitals.

Enemies, it is true, he found. George Ord had written to Charles Waterton, the well-known English naturalist, and Waterton, with vindictiveness and petty intrigues rare in a man of science, openly tried to ruin the newcomer. Audubon made a rather unfavorable impression on Darwin (then a pottering amateur) because of his eccentricity and vanity. He made some mistakes; he lost one or two of his friends. He was often near bankruptcy, but staved it off time and again with spirited wolf-scarers that fetched him handsome sums.

But the great event of his first European trip was the launching of *The Birds of America*, which Lizars of Edinburgh began to publish, and Havell of London completed. The prospectus was issued in March of 1827, and after all that has been said of Audubon's failures as a business man, it should be recorded of him that he carried through a titanic publishing venture, securing the subscribers and collecting from them by his own efforts, paying his engravers and colorists in cash, and managing the complete sale of a thousand sets of a work which was to cost each subscriber a thousand dollars. I venture to assert that it would take a very large sales force, great initial capital, extensive advertising, and several trained accountants as well as a corps of editors to equal that performance today.

The original plan of *The Birds of America* was to issue it in parts of five plates each, at two guineas a part, to the total of eighty parts, and the project was to require fourteen years for completion. The plates were copper engraved and then had to be colored, and as there were to be a thousand copies of the edition, this required the hand-coloring of something like one hundred thousand plates. Actually the number of parts increased through the years to eighty-seven, or four hundred and thirty-five plates, representing over a thousand individual birds, besides all the other animals and plants. The first pictures went to the subscribers in 1827, but the final plate reached them in 1838, or three years sooner than Audubon had hoped.

The first European sojourn occupied almost three years; they had seen Audubon elected to the learned and scientific honorary societies of Edinburgh, London, and Paris; his work had been acclaimed in superlatives that the surfeited capitals are quite unaccustomed to bestow; he had noble and royal patronage, and a host of subscribers.

And above all the great work was actually coming off the presses, and a whole engraving establishment had been turned over to him and was producing work that, for the moment, he could now safely leave.

It was plainly time to return to America to study, collect, and paint the birds he had never yet encountered, and take a second look at those he knew too slightly.

And he must return to America for that rare bird, the subscriber. His only funds were still those derived from the subscriptions, most irregularly paid. Yet this did mean money in the pocket, at times, and occasionally large sums of it. His return to America in the spring of 1829 was an unexpected triumph. Of all things Americans love with a sudden fanaticism it is one they have neglected to honor or even understand, who has gone abroad and won acclaim from the severest of critics. Suddenly Audubon was a native son, in whom everybody had believed all along, and when a man of Edward Everett's stamp came forward to enroll himself as one of the first American subscribers, the tide was turned.

Audubon first visited Great Egg Harbor on the New Jersey coast, occupying the same cabin where Wilson had once stayed, while he sought for marsh and shore birds. Next he visited the Great Pine Swamp of Pennsylvania for arboreal birds, and then hastened down the Ohio, seeing his sons in Louisville, to Louisiana where he rejoined Lucy.

On his return to England in 1830 he took his mate with him upon this triumphal flight. Fresh subscriptions were now sought abroad, but the greatest find of all was William MacGillivray of Edinburgh, an excellent ornithologist who was well qualified to draw up the formal descriptions of birds, research their systematics, make dissections and do comparative anatomy. More important still, the sympathetic Mac-Gillivray was, if not an inspired nature writer, at least a very sound and faithful editor, who knew how to put Audubon's whimsical English into acceptable prose which still kept much original flavor.

And Audubon needed just such a man. For, though no text had accompanied *The Birds of America*, except for the legends identifying the birds, Audubon had now resolved to publish life histories of his subjects, under the title *Ornithological Biography*, from which there are such frequent quotations in this book. The *Ornithological Biography* began to appear in Edinburgh in 1831, ran to five volumes (till 1839) and greatly assisted in the sale of *The Birds of America*, since they followed closely the illustrations, the author presuming that in each case the reader was a subscriber to *The Birds* and had a designated plate before him. To the glory of his colors, then, he adds the story of the bird's life, his impressions of its music or its cries, the very breath and feel of the scenes amid which it lives.

Interspersed with the bird life histories were scattered sketches of the American woodsman's adventurous life. These last were later separated out as *Episodes of Western Life* and enjoyed, in themselves, a good sale. From none of Audubon's writings have I drawn more freely than from these eye-witness accounts of the American scene. And, in passing, let us acknowledge that if the materials, the zest in the telling, and the whole inspiration are Audubon's, the editorship and some of the style are MacGillivray's.

In 1831 the Audubons were back in America. This time John James was resolved to see the bird life of Florida, probably the richest, certainly the most resplendent, in America. On his way south, stopping at Charleston, he met John Bachman, pastor of the Lutheran Church. A man of upright and generous character, firm alike in his duty to religion and to the truth that is science, John Bachman was also a learned zoologist. He was to play a great part in Audubon's life and works, in the years to come. Already he was able to introduce Audubon to the leading scientists of the South, to show Audubon birds he had never before beheld, and greatly to expedite the impending Florida sortie.

Audubon's importance was now recognized, and he had no difficulty in obtaining passage on a revenue cutter from St. Augustine to Key West and return, with flamingoes and caracaras in his bag, and the great white heron added to the list of new and original species. Back then through Charleston to Philadelphia and to Boston and up the coasts of Maine and New Brunswick after northern birds. Meantime business affairs in England were calling, and the boy Victor was dispatched to attend to them. This was the first of that long and loyal collaboration given by both sons, who learned to collect, mount, and draw specimens, copy or color drawings, and handle the affairs of what had now become a family business.

From Boston, Audubon set out in 1833 for Labrador, taking with him the younger boy John, in the schooner *Ripley*, chartered at his own expense. He returned laden with spoils, and though the number of new species was small, the drawings were many and splendid. On his return we find him visiting the Atlantic seaboard cities for subscribers, and at the Capital he is befriended by Washington Irving. That winter he and Lucy and John spent at the Bachman home, where Bachman had two new species of warblers to show him, that the good pastor himself had discovered and Audubon published under the names of Swainson's Warbler and Bachman's Warbler. Once again Lucy and Audubon visited England. The two boys were now touring the Continent, canvassing for subscriptions, and studying specimens, while Audubon hastened back to America to get a glimpse of the first great series of western birds, which had just been sent to Philadelphia from the Nuttall-Townsend collection. New species, indispensable for *The Birds of America*, were among them, and Audubon was eager to study them, but the old opposition to Audubon was not dead in Philadelphia and he was refused even a sight of the coveted skins. Edward Harris tried to buy the collection outright to give to Audubon, but without avail. In Boston good old Nuttall himself promised him duplicates of all the new birds he had brought from the West. Eventually Audubon was able to purchase a set of his own. This completed, so far as was possible in those days when the West was scarcely accessible to anyone, the rollcall of American birds.

In 1837 Audubon and John and Edward Harris explored the Texas coast bayous in the schooner *Crusader* as far as Galveston, where Audubon met President Sam Houston. Back to Charleston now for John's marriage to Maria Bachman. Off to London then, just when the panic of 1837 is causing the loss of many subscribers. Yet Audubon is enlarging *The Birds of America* to admit the addition of the last of these new western species. The following year the great work was completed, and the year after, the last of the *Ornithological Biography* was sent forth.

This is the moment, perhaps, to summarize his great work. As art the pictures must be judged as illustration, a form of art with certain duties and even trammels. Accepting them as illustration, and not imaginative creation, they were then the greatest bird pictures that had ever come from the brush and crayon. But he invented his own style — the living bird in action, and in its natural habitat. Since then he has had imitators, perfectionists upon his invention whose way was not too difficult — after he showed it. But nobody ever painted birds with his dash and verve, his swing and rapture.

The Birds of America falls into three phases. First there is the early one, of the first hundred and fifty plates or so, full of an ebullience that at times is overwrought, overladen, but instinct on every page with original genius. In the second phase, up to about Plate 370, Audubon is at the height of his mature powers; he has his technique perfectly under control and makes few mistakes and fails seldom. In this period we do not have Mason's marvelous floral decorations, but Lehman's middle-grounds and backgrounds are exquisitely done. The last third of the plates seems to me to fall off, with of course sudden and glorious exceptions. But there is a repetition of scenes, a sort of self-imitation. Sometimes several different birds are grouped together in one plate. The scenic effects, filled in sometimes by the engravers or hack substitutes, are artificial and unlifelike, and sometimes all background is hastily omitted. For the western birds which Audubon knew only as skins he lacked feeling, as necessarily he did for the western scenery he had not looked upon.

Judged as science, *The Birds of America* is likewise uneven. Sometimes every pinion is distinct, every attitude invaluably lifelike. Again there is evidence of haste and even lack of great interest. But if we take *The Birds* in connection with the *Ornithological Biography*, we have a monumental work whose like has never been surpassed. Both as painter and writer, Audubon was an eye-witness of the heroic age of American bird life. He saw sights that will never be beheld again. He painted and described them in heroic vein. So that they too are part of Audubon's America. They were our world as we had it in the days of the whooping crane and the trumpeter swan, the ivory-billed woodpecker and the passenger pigeon. Of the paintings as they struck the eye of a French critic who saw them in Edinburgh in 1827 we have the following impression:

> Imagine a landscape wholly American, trees, flowers, grass, even the tints of the sky and the waters, quickened with a life that is real, peculiar, trans-Atlantic. On twigs, branches, bits of shore, copied by the brush with the strictest fidelity, sport the feathered races of the New World, in the size of life, each in its particular attitude, its individuality and peculiarities. Their plumages sparkle with nature's own tints; you see them in motion or at rest, in their plays and their combats, in their anger fits and their caresses, singing, running, asleep, just awakened, beating the air, skimming the waves, or rending one another in their battles. It is a real and palpable vision of the New World, with its atmosphere, its imposing vegetation, and its tribes which know not the yoke of man. The sun shines athwart the clearing in the woods; the swan floats suspended between a cloudless sky and a glittering wave; strange and majestic figures

keep pace with the sun, which gleams from the mica sown broadcast on the shores of the Atlantic; and this realization of an entire hemisphere, this picture of a nature so lusty and strong, is due to the brush of a single man; such an unheard of triumph of patience and genius! — the resultant rather of a thousand triumphs won in the face of innumerable obstacles!

In 1839, Victor Audubon married Mary Eliza Bachman, and Audubon and Bachman began work upon the *Quadrupeds of America*, the third and last of Audubon's great productions. As MacGillivray had collaborated on the style and formal descriptions of the *Ornithological Biography*, so Doctor Bachman made the dissections, researched the systematics, and edited the text, as well as contributing many of the field notes upon the life histories of our native mammals. The two Audubon sons collected, assisted in the taxidermic work, in the painting and in publication, and securing of subscriptions. Once again the great Audubon industry is in full swing, and into the new project the old master entered with all the zest, so he wrote his young friend Spencer Baird, that he had once felt for birds.

As a home and workshop, Audubon purchased land above the Hudson, at what is now 157th Street, which he called 'Minnie's Land.' Minnie was the children's name for their mother. At fifty-eight he set forth up the Missouri, with four assistants, to reach the Rockies. In this he was to be disappointed, as the quotations in the following pages show, but he reached the buffalo country of North Dakota on the borders of Montana, the amplest virgin territory for the study of great beasts that remained in North America. Here bison and wolves and Indians still made, literally, a howling wilderness. The first of *The Quadrupeds* began to appear in 1845, and in this work Audubon was engrossed for years.

During them, his magnificent powers gradually waned. More and more his sons substituted for him. It would be hard to say whether it was he or they who sometimes overcolored the subjects; *The Quadrupeds*, as pictures, are certainly not, as a whole, up to *The Birds*. Yet there are magnificent exceptions — moments when the old power must have returned. Only one volume was actually completed in Audubon's lifetime. His mind wandered, though he was only in his sixties. It was as if his tremendous exertions had worn him out before his time. At the end he would ask nothing but to hear an old French nursery song, from the lips of his beloved Lucy. In 1851, being then sixty-six years old, his spirit took wing.

AUDUBON AS A WITNESS

IN THIS BOOK John James Audubon is called forth as an eye-witness of a vanished America. It is proper to ask then what sort of witness he was. Is he reliable? The question must be met, for it was asserted in his lifetime, and it has been whispered since, that he was not. He did not tell a straight story about his illegitimate birth, though perhaps he did not know the true one. But, more, his reputation as an authentic naturalist has been often attacked.

The claims against him rest chiefly on the malignant hatred of Ord and Waterton. They took, for example, his picture of mockingbirds defending their nest against a rattlesnake, and asserted that the snake's recurved fangs were untrue to nature. Actually just such fangs are found in the species of rattler he drew. True, Audubon printed the story of a rattlesnake which he said he saw constrict its prey to death, and here he was definitely in error, but with no intention of deceiving the public. What he gives is an excellent description of the way in which the American black snake kills its prey, though by an error of memory, long after the event, he assigned the deed to the venomous serpent.

When he asserted that vultures cannot smell their carrion food, but locate it by sight, his critics conducted experiments to prove that he was wrong. But John Bachman, in Charleston where black vultures used to haunt the markets for offal, took a putrescent deer and covered it with a cloth. Not a vulture approached; when it was uncovered, they flocked at once. This controversy between the 'Nosarians' and 'Anti-Nosarians' is still going on among ornithologists.

One of Audubon's paintings contained a flower which enemies insisted never grew. After his death this water lily was discovered again in Florida, and authenticated by Asa Gray. Ord asserted that Audubon plagiarized one of Wilson's drawings. It is true that a figure of a hawk in one of Audubon's plates is actually one of Wilson's printed backward, with one toe missing and the name of the sex changed. But the work was certainly not done by Audubon, but by someone in the engraving establishment during his absence.

Nothing, in short, has stood up as evidence against Audubon as a man of science reliable in his intentions. As to his character, it has never, to my knowledge, been questioned but once. The curious will find in the letters of John Keats a reference to Audubon in unflattering terms. George Keats, the poet's brother, then settled in Kentucky, asserted that Audubon had sold him the cargo of a boat which Audubon at the time knew to be at the bottom of the Mississippi. The Keats brothers exchanged their indignation, and the poet then goes on to express his feelings about Americans in general, not sparing George Washington or Benjamin Franklin. They are the regulation British caricatures of American character, and for those who love Keats with reverence, this passage is a painful cliché. In any case, the loss was made up to George Keats by Lucy's brother, and I cannot find reason to believe that Audubon was capable of business dishonesty.

Further to examine his character as a witness, one might assemble a long list of his known traits, such as the fact that he was indubitably an extreme individualist, an eccentric, a man accustomed to, and liking to hold, the attention of an audience. That in his youth he lived on the American frontier where humor and entertainment took the form of topping, with a straight face, the tall tale just concluded. That he was fond of playing pranks on the credulous (as witness his treatment of Rafinesque in the quoted episode entitled 'The Eccentric Naturalist'). When the psychoanalytic biographers get hold of a man, they can see predetermining factors in such details as that he owned slaves, took snuff, swore roundly on occasion, was subject to seasickness, and belonged to the Masonic order. Incidentally, Audubon answers to all these details. And none of them, nor any like them, have in my view any material bearing on the essential character of the man.

This book, of his own writing, is our most unimpeachable testimony as to what manner of man was John James Audubon. And the evidence of his pen repeats what his brush attests. Here is the same vivacity of first impression, the swiftly caught attitudes of life still glowing with

Audubon as a Witness

color and movement, which are the soul of the great bird pictures. His writing, of course, is but the shadow of his painting, but every page of it is a glimpse of America through the eyes of a great American.

The quotations of which this volume is composed are of two sorts: Audubon's journals and letters as they came from his pen, untouched, and the more studied work which others edited for him. This editing, done by his wife, his granddaughters, by MacGillivray, by Bachman, and by the eminent naturalist Elliott Coues, was all well intentioned. The idea was to smooth asperities of style, to eliminate the prolix or the highly personal, to correct contradictions and to trim from the hero all that might be unheroic. The result is in one way excellent, though it is a matter of the utmost regret that one of his descendants saw fit to destroy all the originals. But the unedited material is, for all its faults of haste and unfamiliarity with the language, peculiarly precious, and we owe its existence to the fact that his descendants could not lay their hands upon it. It tells us, incidentally, that Audubon never learned to pronounce the English language, that he used plain words about matters once, at least, considered highly indelicate. And that he was, in short, a much more ruggedly honest man than his editors, bent on giving him wings, have allowed us to realize.

Among the selections here gathered, whether edited or not, every one, I have come to believe, is a narrative distinguished by truth and abundantly corroborated by contemporary witness. Of necessity I have had to cut them, but I have particularly cut out all passages in which Audubon is repeating hearsay. It may be interesting to read some old hunter's account of a battle with a bear, but it is not Audubon's own evidence. In my selections from *The Quadrupeds of America*, I have eliminated, so far as I could judge, everything that came from the experiences of the joint author, Doctor Bachman. I entertain the warmest affection and respect for Bachman, but this is not his book.

It is all Audubon's book, and for my part I take his word for it, whether he is speaking of Indians or lynch law, of negro slaves or Creole aristocrats. A very sensitive man about himself, he was equally sensitive to every stranger who approached him. He never, his whole life long, looked at anyone with opaque or preoccupied eyes. His sense of humor, his perceptions of tender relationships, his hatred of injustice, his personal fastidiousness that never lessened a zest for roughing it, made him keen as a watchdog. He had an eye for dress, for a beautiful woman, for a gay child, and for all sorts of men — knaves, roustabouts, popinjays, adventurers. He knew a man when he met one, whether the soul inhabited a fugitive slave or Sam Houston. He had, it seems to me, both what we call a man's perceptions and a woman's intuitions. He loved a big horse and a clever dog, a sword and a gun and a ballroom floor. He enjoyed the worldly great (when they recognized his greatness), and yet amid the simple he asked only to be accepted as a man among men. With such varied personalities his pages are crowded. I invite you now to meet him and his friends.

MINK

'The Mink is a constant resident of nearly every part of the continent of North America . . . we have seen it in every State of the Union.

'This species prefers taking up its residence on the borders of ponds and along the banks of small streams, rather than along large and broad rivers. It delights in frequenting the foot of rapids and waterfalls.

'Next to the ermine, the Mink is the most active and destructive little depredator that prowls around the farm-yard, or the farmer's duck-pond.' — *The Quadrupeds of North America* by John James Audubon and John Bachman, vol. 1, pp. 253, 257, 259.

PUTORIUS V

NIN

MALE & FE

VISON, LINN.

K.

ALE.

Lith. Printed & Col.d by J.T.Bowen, Phila. 1844.

KENTUCKY
DAYS AND NIGHTS

LOUISVILLE IN KENTUCKY

(Audubon meets Alexander Wilson)

INTRODUCTION

O F ALL Audubon's pictures of American life and manners, his account of Louisville, Kentucky, then a town of one thousand population, is the earliest. More exactly it relates to the earliest period of his life, aside from purely autobiographical material, of which he has left us any formal description. It is not the earliest from the point of view of the date when written, for that honor goes to a later excerpt in this book, entitled 'Down the Ohio and Mississippi.' The following account was actually written long after the events that took place, and appeared for the first time in 1831, in volume one of the *Ornithological Biography*, where it was inserted in order to give Audubon's version of the famous meeting of the rival ornithologists, Alexander Wilson and himself.

Our author opens with an enthusiastic description of the country around Louisville and its pioneers, among whom he particularly mentions Major George Croghan (1791–1849), a native of Louisville, hero of the war of 1812 and later of the war with Mexico, and Colonel George Rogers Clark (1752–1818), the famous explorer, Indian fighter, and hero of the Revolution. But Audubon is really hurrying on to his meeting with Wilson in the shop of the firm of Audubon and Rozier on March 7, 1810.

Alexander Wilson, when he sought the French storekeeper's subscription to his *American Ornithology*, had no more heard of Audubon than Audubon of him. Wilson was then forty-four years old, a native

[33]

of Paisley, Scotland, a weaver by trade, a poet of some merit, an ex schoolmaster and, having also been a peddler, an old hand at selling upon the road. He had been studying ornithology for seven years at this time, and three years previously he had issued an elaborate prospectus of his proposed *American Ornithology*. This work was planned to comprise ten volumes of bird life histories and illustrations, and to cost the sum of one hundred and twenty dollars, an amount unheard of in America for a local work upon natural history. The first volume, published by Lawson of Philadelphia, appeared in 1808, in an edition of two hundred copies, and its author then set out first for New York and New England, and later through the south Atlantic seaboard, in search of subscribers. In spite of rebuffs and disappointments, Wilson managed to secure a great many subscribers, far more than one would realize from his plaints. There existed at the time no other work devoted exclusively to American birds. All previous descriptions had appeared in Europe, whether systematic works upon new species from the New World, like those of Linnaeus and Gmelin, or fragmentary sketches of the life histories of our birds, such as one derives from Mark Catesby and Peter Kalm.

So that Wilson's *American Ornithology* entered a virgin field, and had a head start of many years over Audubon's *Birds of America* and *Ornithological Biography*. (Indeed when Audubon and Wilson met, it had apparently never entered Audubon's head to publish.) And Wilson's field for the discovery of new species was still but half gleaned. Thus, in the ten brief years of his life as an ornithologist, he carefully traced the life histories of two hundred and seventy-eight species of American birds, and added more than forty species which were new to science. Among them are such well-loved familiars as the black-billed cuckoo, the long-billed curlew, the canvas-back and ruddy ducks, the solitary sandpiper, the song sparrow and field sparrow, the pine siskin, goshawk, raven, magpie, whip-poor-will, and many warblers — the Tennessee, the Nashville, magnolia, cerulean, bay-breasted, northern parula, the northern pine warbler, and the Kentucky, Connecticut, mourning, and Wilson's warblers. The *American Ornithology*, which Wilson did not complete (the task was finished by George Ord and Bonaparte), was the first great ornithological work to come out of the young United States, and it is distinguished not only by its originality and thoroughness but by the stylistic ability of a born writer.

In one respect only it was a comparative failure; it was not well illustrated. Wilson was not a natural artist at all, but one self-taught who accomplished much by sheer industry. The engraving, done by Lawson of Philadelphia, was, in spite of Lawson's and Ord's opinion of it, distinctly mediocre, and the coloration childish. Or so we can see now; at the moment it was remarkable that even such plates existed; they were probably, since they made instantaneous optical appeal, Wilson's strongest selling point, and they had no rivals — until Audubon, the backwoods storekeeper, spread out his drawings that March morning in Louisville.

From that instant the two men no doubt felt rivalry. But that rivalry was not fanned to the point of heated words until years later — until, indeed, George Ord published Wilson's diary in the ninth (and posthumous) volume of the *American Ornithology*, in 1814.

Audubon was at that time still deep in lamentable business entanglements in Kentucky. It was only years later, when indeed he was first rising to fame, that he discovered what was obviously a reference, and a most slighting reference, to himself in Wilson's account of their meeting in March, 1810. By this time Ord and Lawson, fearful that Audubon's work would stop the sale of Wilson's, in which they were both financially interested, had already begun a whispering and poison-pen campaign against Audubon. Very naturally the victim wished to reply, and to tell his own version. Before we read it, let us hear Wilson's, as edited and underscored by his champions:

> *March* 17. Take my baggage and grope my way to Louisville — put up at the Indian Queen tavern, and gladly sit down and rest myself.
> *March* 18. Rise quite refreshed.
> *March* 19. Rambling round the town with my gun. Examined Mr ——'s drawings in crayons — very good. Saw two new birds he had, both Motacillae.
> *March* 20. Set out this afternoon with the gun — killed nothing new. (People in taverns here devour their meals. Many shopkeepers board in taverns — also boatmen, land-speculators, merchants &c.) *No naturalist to keep me company.*
> *March* 21. Went out shooting this afternoon with Mr A. Saw a number of Sandhill Cranes. Pigeons numerous.
> *March* 22.
> *March* 23. Packed up my things which I left in the care of a merchant here, to be sent on to Lexington; and having parted with great regret, with my paroquet, to the gentleman of the tavern, I bade adieu to Louisville, to which place I had four letters of recommendation, and was taught to expect much of everything there, but neither received one act of civility

from those to whom I was recommended, one subscriber, *nor one new bird;* though I delivered my letters, ransacked the woods repeatedly, and visited all the characters likely to subscribe. *Science or literature has not one friend in this place.* (Everyone is so intent on making money, that they can talk of nothing else; and they absolutely devour their meals, that they may the sooner return to their business. Their manners correspond with their features.)

I have quoted this as Ord gave it to the world. It is too much to assume that it is just what Wilson wrote; and indeed it sounds a great deal more as though it is Wilson, plus some spiteful interpolations by Ord, plus some slurs upon American manners in general by Waterton. For Ord destroyed Wilson's originals, thereby preventing any future comparison of the genuine documents with what he chose to give out. The passages in parentheses were added by Waterton, who merely asserts that he remembers seeing them. There is no particular reason to take his word for it, and they are so un-Wilsonian, so like the prevalent notions of America held by Englishmen who had never seen it, that they are suspect until proved genuine.

Can it be wondered that Audubon wished to reply to such aspersions? His reply indeed is forbearing and courteous, and takes upon himself much blame for not having subscribed to Wilson's work. He gives a reason — vanity; but this was certainly not the only reason. Audubon, though he does not admit it here, simply did not have one hundred and twenty dollars to subscribe. He was on the verge of failure, his wife and children were soon to be in want, and his partner was looking over his shoulder. *Que voulez-vous?*

Alexander Wilson did not long survive his meeting with Audubon. On his trip through the South he contracted malaria and probably also dysentery. He died soon after, a pathetic and a noble figure of a poet who failed, and a scientist who did not live to see his success.

The specter of Alexander Wilson was to haunt Audubon for years. Often in this book we shall find Audubon assiduously seeking to correct his predecessor. Often he had, in accepting the praise that came to him, to share it with Wilson. When he was preparing to publish, in Edinburgh, Ord and Bonaparte issued a new European edition of Wilson just when Audubon was seeking hardest to find subscribers. One adventurer in publishing even tried to bring out an edition of Wilson with 'Audubonized' illustrations — that is, with the birds in action, surrounded by their natural scenes and foods. On the whole

Louisville in Kentucky

Audubon suffered all these comparisons and rivalries with sincere good patience. He quotes Wilson, reverently and affectionately, as his friend, acknowledges the pioneering nature of his work, corrects him respectfully. Only once did he seriously err with respect to his dead rival, when he asserts that Wilson, in Louisville, borrowed his (Audubon's) drawing of the small-headed flycatcher, copied it, and afterward published it as his own. A comparison of their drawings does not seem to bear this out, and the point is no longer important, since there is no such bird! Both authors apparently mistook the immature plumage of some sort of warbler for this fabulous species.

Louisville in Kentucky has always been a favorite place of mine. The beauty of its situation on the banks of *La Belle Rivière*, just at the commencement of the famed rapids, commonly called the Falls of the Ohio, had attracted my notice, and when I removed to it, immediately after my marriage, I found it more agreeable than ever. The prospect from the town is such that it would please even the eye of a Swiss. It extends along the river for seven or eight miles, and is bounded on the opposite side by a fine range of low mountains, known by the name of the Silver Hills. The rumbling sound of the waters as they tumble over the rock-paved bed of the rapids is at all times soothing to the ear. Fish and game are abundant. But, above all, the generous hospitality of the inhabitants, and the urbanity of their manners, had induced me to fix upon it as a place of residence; and I did so with the more pleasure when I found that my wife was as much gratified as myself by the kind attentions which were shown to us, utter strangers as we were, on our arrival.

No sooner had we landed, and made known our intention of remaining, than we were introduced to the principal inhabitants of the place and its vicinity, although we had not brought a single letter of introduction, and could not but see, from their unremitting kindness, that the Virginian spirit of hospitality displayed itself in all the words and actions of our newly formed friends. I wish here to name those persons who so unexpectedly came forward to render our stay among them agreeable, but feel at a loss with whom to begin, so equally deserving are they of our gratitude. The Croghans, the Clarks (our great traveller included), the Berthouds, the Galts, the Maupins, the Tarascons, the Beals, and the Booths, form but a small portion of the long list which I could give. The matrons acted like mothers to my wife, and daughters proved agreeable associates, and the husbands and sons were friends and companions to me. If I absented myself on business, or otherwise, for any length of time, my wife was removed to the hospitable abode of some friend in the neighborhood until my return, and then, kind reader, I was several times obliged to spend a week or more with these good people before they could be prevailed upon to let us return to our own residence. We lived for two years at Louisville, where we enjoyed many of the best pleasures which this life can afford; and whenever we have since chanced to pass that way, we have found the kindness of our former friends unimpaired.

During my residence at Louisville, much of my time was employed in my ever favorite pursuits. I drew and noted the habits of everything which I procured, and my collection was daily augmenting, as every individual who carried a gun always sent me such birds or quadrupeds as he thought might prove useful to me. My portfolios already contained upwards of two hundred drawings. Dr. W. C. Galt being a botanist, was often consulted by me, as well as his friend, Dr. Ferguson. Mr. Gilly drew beautifully, and was fond of my pursuits. So was my friend, and now relative, N. Berthoud. As I have already said, our time was spent in the most agreeable manner, through the hospitable friendship of our acquaintance.

One fair morning I was surprised by the sudden entrance into our counting-room of Mr. Alexander Wilson, the celebrated author of the 'American Ornithology,' of whose existence I had never until that moment been apprised. This happened in March, 1810. How well do I remember him, as he walked up to me! His long, rather hooked nose, the keenness of his eyes, and his prominent cheek bones, stamped his countenance with a peculiar character. His dress, too, was of a kind not usually seen in that part of the country — a short coat, trousers, and a waistcoat of gray cloth. His stature was not above the middle size. He had two volumes under his arm, and as he approached the table at which I was working, I thought I discovered something like astonishment in his countenance. He, however, immediately proceeded to disclose the object of his visit, which was to procure subscriptions for his work. He opened his books, explained the nature of his occupations, and requested my patronage.

Louisville in Kentucky

I felt surprised and gratified at the sight of his volumes, turned over a few of the plates, and had already taken a pen to write my name in his favor, when my partner, rather abruptly, said to me in French, 'My dear Audubon, what induces you to subscribe to this work? Your drawings are certainly far better, and again, you must know as much of the habits of American birds as this gentleman.' Whether Mr. Wilson understood French or not, or if the suddenness with which I paused disappointed him, I cannot tell; but I clearly perceived he was not pleased. Vanity and the encomiums of my friend prevented me from subscribing. Mr. Wilson asked me if I had many drawings of birds. I rose, took down a large portfolio, laid it on the table, and showed him, as I would show you, kind reader, or any other person fond of such subjects, the whole of the contents, with the same patience with which he had shown me his own engravings.

His surprise appeared great, as he told me he never had the most distant idea that any other individual than himself had been engaged in forming such a collection. He asked me if it was my intention to publish, and when I answered in the negative, his surprise seemed to increase. And, truly, such was not my intention; for until long after, when I met the Prince of Musignano in Philadelphia, I had not the least idea of presenting the fruits of my labors to the world. Mr. Wilson now examined my drawings with care, asked if I should have any objections to lending him a few during his stay, to which I replied that I had none; he then bade me good-morning, not, however, until I had made an arrangement to explore the woods in the vicinity with him, and had promised to procure for him some birds of which I had drawings in my collection, but which he had never seen.

It happened that he lodged in the same house with us, but his retired habits, I thought, exhibited either a strong feeling of discontent or a decided melancholy. The Scotch airs which he played sweetly on his flute made me melancholy too, and I felt for him. I presented him to my wife and friends, and seeing that he was all enthusiasm, exerted myself as much as was in my power to procure for him the specimens which he wanted. We hunted together, and obtained birds which he had never before seen; but, reader, I did not subscribe to his work, for, even at that time, my collection was greater than his. Thinking that perhaps he might be pleased to publish the results of my researches, I offered them to him, merely on condition that what I had drawn, or might afterwards draw and send to him, should be mentioned in his work as coming from my pencil. I, at the same time, offered to open a correspondence with him, which I thought might prove beneficial to us both. He made no reply to either proposal, and before many days had elapsed, left Louisville, on his way to New Orleans, little knowing how much his talents were appreciated in our little town, at least by myself and my friends.

Some time elapsed, during which I never heard of him, or of his work. At length, having occasion to go to Philadelphia, I, immediately after my arrival there, inquired for him, and paid him a visit. He was then drawing a White-headed Eagle. He received me with civility, and took me to the exhibition rooms of Rembrandt Peale, the artist, who had then portrayed Napoleon crossing the Alps. Mr. Wilson spoke not of birds nor drawings. Feeling, as I was forced to do, that my company was not agreeable, I parted from him; and after that I never saw him again. But judge of my astonishment sometime after, when, on reading the thirty-ninth page of the ninth volume of 'American Ornithology,' I found in it the following paragraph:

> *March* 23, 1810. I bade adieu to Louisville, to which place I had four letters of recommendation, and was taught to expect much of everything there; but neither received one act of civility from those to whom I was recommended, one subscriber nor one new bird; though I delivered my letters, ransacked the woods repeatedly, and visited all the characters likely to subscribe. Science or literature has not one friend in this place.

KENTUCKY SPORTS

(Audubon meets Daniel Boone)

INTRODUCTION

WHEN describing the life and manners, the sportsmanship and marksmanship of the pioneer Kentuckians, Audubon is completely in his element. It is doubtful if there is a better account, of equal length. And if it is touched with high enthusiasm, one sees that Audubon balances this with some strictures upon his neighbors.

No less a Kentuckian than Daniel Boone moves through these pages. The question has been raised, I think needlessly, whether Audubon ever really knew Boone, or has simply illuminated his text with the famous scout, hunter, and Indian fighter. Audubon is certainly mistaken in thinking that Boone was the first to explore or to settle the Kentucky wilderness, though doubtless that was what he was told, for the Boone legend grew fast in Boone's own day.

Born in 1735 in Bucks County, Pennsylvania, Daniel Boone passed his young manhood in North Carolina on the banks of the Yadkin, and did not enter Kentucky until 1769. Indeed he seems to have been fired to this adventure by the tales of John Finley, a trapper who had adventured beyond the Appalachians as early as 1752, and it was finally Finley who showed Boone the way across the mountains to the Kentucky wilderness. It was not till 1775 that Boone definitely settled in Kentucky, and by 1799, having lost all his Kentucky lands through defective title, Boone removed across the Father of Waters into what was then Spanish territory, now Missouri, and settled about forty-five miles west of St. Louis. He had thus left Kentucky eleven years before Audubon entered it.

However, research has shown that he returned to Kentucky in 1810, with money he had saved for many years, to pay his debts. It must have been at this time that Audubon knew him, probably in Frankfort and, as he says elsewhere, spent a night with him under the same roof after a hunting expedition. Boone went back to Missouri the next year with just fifty-one cents left, after his lifetime of work. He who had burned, as a boy, to cross the Appalachians to the dark and bloody ground of Kentucky, died at eighty-five, yearning to explore the Rockies. In his time he had guided hundreds of immigrants into Kentucky, had saved the lives of hundreds more; the prestige of his name and presence had done more than anything else to cause the very influx of the settlers Audubon describes. In 1783 and 1784, twelve thousand had crossed the mountains — trappers, hunters, lawyers, doctors, 'sang diggers, tobacco planters, land sharks and storekeepers, women and children. Boone located towns for them, surveyed their lands, scouted, guided; to no one else did Kentucky owe such a debt. And it turned him out, legally, coldly.

Elsewhere Audubon describes Boone thus:

> The stature and general appearance of this wanderer of the western forests approached the gigantic. His chest was broad and prominent; his muscular powers displayed themselves in every limb; his countenance gave indication of his great courage, enterprise, and perseverance.

But other observers differ; they report him as being only five feet ten inches in height, 'stout,' and in weight about a hundred and seventy-five pounds. Perhaps Audubon remembered best the man's moral stature and, years later, applied it to the body of the wilderness scout.

Iᴛ ᴍᴀʏ not be amiss, kind reader, before I attempt to give you some idea of the pleasures experienced by the sportsmen of Kentucky, to introduce the subject with a slight description of that State.

Kentucky was formerly attached to Virginia, but in those days the Indians looked upon that portion of the western wilds as their own, and abandoned the district only when forced to do so, moving with disconsolate hearts farther into the recesses of the unexplored forests. Doubtless the richness of its soil, and the beauty of its borders, situated as they are along one of the most beautiful rivers in the world, contributed as much to attract the Old Virginians as the desire, so generally experienced in America, of spreading over the uncultivated tracts, and bringing into cultivation lands that have for unknown ages teemed with the wild luxuriance of untamed nature. The conquest of Kentucky was not performed without many difficulties. The warfare that long existed between the intruders and the Redskins was sanguinary and protracted; but the former at length made good their footing, and the latter drew off their shattered bands, dismayed by the mental superiority and indomitable courage of the white men.

This region was probably discovered by a daring hunter, the renowned Daniel Boone. The richness of its soil, its magnificent forests, its numberless navigable streams, its salt springs and licks, its saltpetre caves, its coal strata, and the vast herds of Buffaloes and Deer that browsed on its hills and amidst its charming valleys, afforded ample inducements to the new settler, who pushed forward with a spirit far above that of the most undaunted tribes which for ages had been the sole possessors of the soil.

The Virginians thronged towards the Ohio. An axe, a couple of horses, and a heavy rifle, with store of ammunition, were all that were considered necessary for the equipments of the man, who, with his family, removed to the new State, assured that, in that land of exuberant fertility, he could not fail to provide amply for all his wants. To have witnessed the industry and perseverance of these emigrants must at once have proved the vigor of their minds. Regardless of the fatigue attending every movement which they made, they pushed through an unexplored region of dark and tangled forests, guiding themselves by the sun alone, and reposing at night on the bare ground. Numberless streams they had to cross on rafts, with their wives and children, their cattle and their luggage, often drifting to considerable distances before they could effect a landing on the opposite shores. Their cattle would often stray amid the rice pasturage of these shores, and occasion a delay of several days. To these troubles add the constantly impending danger of being murdered, while asleep in their encampments, by the prowling and ruthless Indians; while they had before them a distance of hundreds of miles to be traversed, before they could reach certain places of rendezvous called *Stations*. To encounter difficulties like these must have required energies of no ordinary kind; and the reward which these veteran settlers enjoy was doubtless well merited.

Some removed from the Atlantic shores to those of the Ohio in more comfort and security. They had their wagons, their negroes, and their families. Their way was cut through the woods by their own axemen, the day before their advance, and when night overtook them, the hunters attached to the party came to the place pitched upon for encamping, loaded with the dainties of which the forest yielded an abundant supply, the blazing light of a huge fire guiding their steps as they approached, and the sounds of merriment that saluted their ears assuring them that all was well. The flesh of the Buffalo, the Bear, and the Deer soon hung, in large and delicious steaks, in front of the embers; the cakes already prepared were deposited in their proper places, and under the rich drippings of the juicy roasts were quickly baked. The wagons contained the bedding, and whilst the horses which had drawn them were turned loose to feed on the luxuriant undergrowth of the woods — some perhaps hoppled, but the greater number merely with a light bell hung by their neck, to guide their owners in the morning to the spot where they might have rambled — the party were enjoying themselves after the fatigues of the day.

In anticipation all is pleasure; and these migrating bands feasted in joyous sociality, unapprehensive of any greater difficulties than those to be encountered in forcing their way through the pathless woods to the land of abundance; and although it took months to accomplish the journey, and a skirmish now and then took place between them and the Indians, who sometimes crept unperceived into their very camp, still did the Virginians cheerfully proceed towards the western horizon, until the various groups all reached the Ohio, when, struck with the beauty of that magnificent stream, they at once commenced the task of clearing land, for the purpose of establishing a permanent residence.

Others, perhaps encumbered with too much luggage, preferred descending the stream. They prepared *arks* pierced with port-holes, and glided on the gentle current, more annoyed, however, than those who marched by land by the attacks of the Indians who watched their motions. Many travellers have described these boats, formerly called *arks*, but now named *flatboats*. But have they told you, kind reader, that in those times a boat thirty or forty feet in length, by ten or twelve in breadth, was considered a stupendous fabric; that this boat contained men, women and children, huddled together, with horses, cattle, hogs and poultry for their companions, while the remaining portion was crammed with vegetables and packages of seeds? The roof or deck of the boat was not unlike a farmyard, being covered with hay, ploughs, carts, wagons, and various agricultural implements, together with numerous others, among which the spinning-wheels of the matrons were conspicuous. Even the sides of the floating-mass were loaded with the wheels of the different vehicles, which themselves lay on the roof. Have they told you that these boats contained the little all of each family of venturous emigrants, who, fearful of being discovered by the Indians under night moved in darkness, groping their way from one part to another of these floating habitations, denying themselves the comfort of fire or light, lest the foe that watched them from the shore should rush upon them and destroy them? Have they told you that this boat was used, after the tedious voyage was ended, as the first dwelling of these new settlers? No, kind reader, such things have not been related to you before. The travellers who have visited our country have had other objects in view.

I shall not describe the many massacres which took place among the different parties of white and red men, as the former moved down the Ohio; because I have never been very fond of battles, and indeed have always wished that the world were more peaceably inclined than it is; and shall merely add that, in one way or other, Kentucky was wrested from the original owners of the soil. Let us, therefore, turn our attention to the sports still enjoyed in that now happy portion of the United States.

We have individuals in Kentucky, kind reader, that even there are considered wonderful adepts in the management of the rifle. To *drive a nail* is a common feat, not more thought of by the Kentuckians than to cut off a Wild Turkey's head, at a distance of a hundred yards. Others will *bark* off Squirrels one after another, until satisfied with the number procured. Some, less intent on destroying game, may be seen under night *snuffing a candle* at the distance of fifty yards, off-hand, without extinguishing it. I have been told that some have proved so expert and cool as to make choice of the eye of a foe at a wonderful distance, boasting beforehand of the sureness of their piece, which has afterwards been fully proved when the enemy's head has been examined!

Having resided some years in Kentucky, and having more than once been witness of rifle sport, I shall present you with the results of my observation, leaving you to judge how far rifle-shooting is understood in that State.

Several individuals who conceive themselves expert in the management of the gun are often seen to meet for the purpose of displaying their skill, and betting a trifling sum, put up a target, in the centre of which a common-sized nail is hammered for about two-thirds of its length. The marksmen make choice of what they consider a proper distance, which may be forty paces. Each man cleans the interior of his tube, which is called *wiping* it, places a ball in the palm of his hand, pouring as much powder from his horn upon it as will cover it. This quantity is supposed to be sufficient for any distance within a hundred yards. A shot which comes very close to the nail is considered as that of an indifferent marksman; the bending of the nail is, of course, somewhat better; but nothing less than hitting it right on the head is satisfactory. Well, kind reader, one out of three shots generally hits the nail, and should the shooters amount to half a dozen, two nails are frequently needed before each can have a shot. Those who drive the nail have a further trial amongst themselves, and the two best shots out of these generally settle the affair, when all the sportsmen adjourn to some house, and spend an hour or two in friendly intercourse, appointing, before they part, a day for another trial. This is technically termed *driving the nail*.

Barking off Squirrels is delightful sport, and in my opinion requires a greater degree of accuracy than any other. I first witnessed this manner of procuring Squirrels whilst near the town of Frankfort. The performer was the celebrated Daniel Boone. We walked out together, and followed the rocky margins of the Kentucky River, until we reached a piece of flat land thickly covered with black walnuts, oaks, and hickories. As the general mast was a good one that year, Squirrels were seen gambolling on every tree around us. My companion, a stout, hale, and athletic man, dressed in a homespun hunting-shirt, bare-legged and moccasined, carried a long and heavy rifle, which, as he was loading it, he said had proved efficient in all his former undertakings, and which he hoped would not fail on this occasion, as he felt proud to show me his skill. The gun was wiped, the powder measured, the ball patched with six-hundred-thread linen, and the charge sent home with a hickory rod. We moved not a step from the place, for the Squirrels were so numerous that it was unnecessary to go after them. Boone pointed to one of these animals which had observed us, and was crouched on a branch about fifty paces distant, and bade me mark well the spot where the ball should hit. He raised his piece gradually, until the *bead* (that being the name given by the Kentuckians to the *sight*) of the barrel was brought to a line with the spot which he intended to hit. The whip-like report resounded through the woods and along the hills, in repeated echoes. Judge of my surprise when I perceived that the ball had hit the piece of the bark immediately beneath the Squirrel, and shivered it into splinters, the concussion produced by which had killed the animal, and sent it whirling through the air, as if it had been blown up by the explosion of a powder magazine. Boone kept up his firing, and, before many hours had elapsed, we had procured as many Squirrels as we wished; for you must know, kind reader, that to load a rifle requires only a moment, and that if it is wiped once after each shot, it will do duty for hours. Since that first interview with our veteran Boone I have seen many other individuals perform the same feat.

The *snuffing of a candle* with a ball, I first had an opportunity of seeing near the banks of Green River, not far from a large Pigeon-roost to which I had previously made a visit. I heard many reports of guns during the early part of a dark night, and knowing them to be those of rifles, I went towards the spot to ascertain the cause. On reaching the place, I was welcomed by a dozen of tall stout men, who told me they were exercising, for the purpose of enabling them to shoot under night at the reflected light from the eyes of a Deer or Wolf, by torch-light, of which I shall give you an account somewhere else. A fire was blazing near, the smoke of which rose curling among the thick foliage of the trees. At a distance which rendered it scarcely distinguishable, stood a burning candle, as if intended for an offering to the goddess of night, but which in reality was only fifty yards from the spot on which we all stood. One man was within a few yards of it, to watch the effects of the shots, as well as to light the candle should it chance to go out, or to replace it should the shot cut it across. Each marksman shot in his turn. Some never hit either the snuff or the candle, and were congratulated with a loud laugh; while others actually snuffed the candle without putting it out, and were recompensed for their dexterity by numerous hurrahs. One of them, who was particularly expert, was very fortunate, and snuffed the candle three times out of seven, whilst all the other shots either put out the candle or cut it immediately under the light.

Of the feats performed by the Kentuckians with the rifle, I could say more than might be expedient on the present occasion. In every thinly peopled portion of the State, it is rare to meet one without a gun of that description, as well as a tomahawk. By way of recreation, they often cut off a piece of the bark of a tree, make a target of it, using a little powder wetted with water or saliva, for the bull's-eye, and shoot into the mark all the balls they have about them, picking them out of the wood again.

After what I have said, you may easily imagine with what ease a Kentuckian procures game, or despatches an enemy, more especially when I tell you that every one in the State is accustomed to handle the rifle from the time when he is first able to shoulder it until near the close of his career. That murderous weapon is the means of procuring them subsistence during all their wild and extensive rambles, and is the source of their principal sports and pleasures.

THE ECCENTRIC NATURALIST

(Audubon meets Rafinesque)

INTRODUCTION

U NDER the pseudonym of 'Mr. de T.' there is limned in the following episode a character who was recognized instantly by Audubon's contemporaries as Professor Rafinesque, a genius of restless curiosity and a devouring appetite for scientific knowledge. Linguist, member of many learned societies, prolific writer, he was a man of the most fantastic self-conceit and an ambition to be nothing less than a Paracelsus, an Aristotle, a Linnaeus and a Humboldt in one. His untidiness, his mania for describing new species, his wandering life and absent-mindedness made him the caricatured and traditional type of the old-fashioned professor of natural history. And Audubon did not miss a detail of his visitor's eccentricities. Perhaps he has exaggerated them, or dressed his story a little, yet his testimony is in general borne out by others who knew Rafinesque. Evidently the subject himself enjoyed the sketch, for he gave the *Ornithological Biography,* in which this first appeared, an enthusiastic review in 1831.

But Rafinesque must be understood a little better than Audubon was then able to understand him. He was not modest, he was not balanced, he was certainly a strange-acting individual; but he was, emphatically, great. The difficulty of judging Rafinesque arises in part from the circumstance that his earlier and sounder work was obscured in his later life by the madness that came upon him. And further, he had an unhappy faculty of making enemies out of his friends. They blackened his reputation — Harlan the mammalogist, Featherstonhaugh the geologist, Barton the botanist and others.

The fact is that were strict priority and just credit applied, it would be found that many of Rafinesque's genuine new species would antedate the work of Say in conchology, of Harlan in mammalogy, and of various botanists, while some of the work of Rafinesque on the Indian mounds of the Middle West was probably utilized, without proper acknowledgment, by others. Asa Gray warned European botanists to pay no attention to Rafinesque's madcap species, but in making such a generality he did injustice and obscured truth. Many of Rafinesque's botanical species are now restored. We find, too, that he is properly accredited as the first to describe the beautiful cliff swallow, *Petrochelidon albifrons*, Rafinesque, as well as being the author of the fictitious 'red-headed swallow' which Audubon jokingly imposed on him. Audubon jests him about the discovery of new genera and species of bats, but Rafinesque did find two new genera, *Eptisicus*, of which the large brown bat is a member, and *Nycticeius*, now known as Rafinesque's bat, and the probabilities are that he turned them up right under the mocking eyes of the future author of *The Quadrupeds of North America*. His visit to Audubon in Henderson, Kentucky, occurred in 1818, and in the same year he published these new genera. Audubon thrust upon Rafinesque another wonder-tale of the 'devil-jack diamond-fish' which Rafinesque credulously accepted; yet he is the author of a large number of genuine new species of fishes, which David Starr Jordan was later to verify and restore to the name and the credit of their author. Great damage was done to Rafinesque's reputation as an ichthyologist by Cuvier, who, unable to see the iridescent colors in the Mediterranean fishes which he described when they reached him after long immersion in preserving fluid, declared the man an impostor.

Constantine Samuel Rafinesque-Schmaltz, to give him his full title, was born in Constantinople, in 1783, of French-German parentage and was brought up in Genoa where, as a child, he early mastered many languages and became fascinated with the flora and the fishes of the Riviera. In young manhood he lived in Sicily, where he had an exporting business in olive oil, and ran a distillery. Here he married a Sicilian woman and had two children, and here he determined to write a complete natural history of the violent and brilliant island, with its orchards and flowers, its volcanoes and ruins of Grecian, Carthaginian, and Roman occupation, and its marvelous marine life. William Swain-

GREAT–FOOTED HAWK

(DUCK HAWK)

'The French and Spaniards of Louisiana have designated all the species of the genus Falco[1] by the name of "*Mangeurs de Poulets*;" and the farmers in other portions of the Union have bestowed upon them, according to their size, the appellations of "Hen Hawk," "Chicken Hawk," "Pigeon Hawk," &c. This mode of naming these rapacious birds is doubtless natural enough, but it displays little knowledge of the characteristic manners of the species. No bird can better illustrate the frequent inaccuracy of the names bestowed by ignorant persons than the present, of which on referring to the plate, you will see a pair enjoying themselves over a brace of ducks of different species. Very likely, were tame ducks as plentiful on the plantations in our States, as wild ducks are on our rivers, lakes and estuaries, these hawks might have been named by some of our settlers "*Mangeurs de Canards*."

'Look at these two pirates eating their *déjeuné à la fourchette*, as it were, congratulating each other on the savouriness of the food in their grasp. One might think them real epicures, but they are in fact true gluttons. The male has obtained possession of a Green-winged Teal, while his mate has procured a Gadwal Duck. Their appetites are equal to their reckless daring, and they well deserve the name of "Pirates," which I have above bestowed upon them.' — *Ornithological Biography*, vol. 1, p. 85.

[1] Audubon included most of the hawks in this genus. (He did not mean to say that any of the true falcons were ever called hen hawks.)

Drawn from Nature and Published by John J. Audubon F.R.S.E. M.W.S.

Great Footed Hawk. Male

FALCO PEREGRINUS

Engraved, Printed & Coloured by R. Havell & Son, London

son, who was later to be of such assistance to Audubon, visited him in Sicily and together they used to roam the fish markets, picking up strange new species brought in the nets of the Sicilians. This was perhaps the happiest and most promising part of his life.

Fired with ambition to make a fortune and discover new species in the New World, Rafinesque came to America, but his ship was wrecked in Long Island Sound, and the cargo in which he had invested all was totally lost. Hearing of this mishap to her husband's fortunes, his wife ran away with a strolling performer, and left Rafinesque unfriended in the world. He sought access to the scientific group in Philadelphia, and was admitted to it, not without strong objection upon the part of some of the more conventional Philadelphians, but he failed repeatedly in seeking professorships and curatorships. Finally, however, a rich patron, then removing to Kentucky, took him along, to be employed as a full-time naturalist upon his benefactor's wilderness estates. But this man died soon after, and Rafinesque was once again disappointed.

Presently he found employment as a professor in the rising Transylvania University at Lexington, a shining light, for those times, of cultivation on the frontier. Here he did not escape the ridicule of the students and the faculty, but he was almost unconscious of them, in his rapture over the virgin territory in which he found himself — the Ohio with its beautiful shells, the rich forest flora, the hosts of birds, the Mammoth Cave, the Indian mounds. He published papers on everything and anything, amassed great quantities of specimens, and was sailing on in fine style when he quarreled with President Holley, and quit the institution. It was just before this mishap that Rafinesque visited Audubon.

From this point on, Rafinesque's mental equilibrium begins to spin and totter. He could secure no more positions, and made his money out of selling a patent herb medicine for the cure of tuberculosis. (It is probable he believed sincerely in its efficacy.) His penury became increasingly painful, and his health went into a dreadful decline. When he died in Philadelphia in 1840 of an agonizing cancer, he was quite alone. His landlord, claiming rent, proposed to sell his body to the medical college. Friends lowered it secretly out the window and gave it burial in potter's field. Half a century later it was discovered that Rafinesque had announced a theory of evolution. And this many years before Darwin!

At a later date, David Starr Jordan and others exhumed Rafinesque's remains and reverently interred them beneath a permanent monument, and Rafinesque's genius is constantly being exhumed by somebody, who discovers him all over again and announces him to the world, so that he is one of the best-publicized of the forgotten men of science. Audubon was the first to perceive what rich literary materials lay in this strange wanderer's character. His life has been several times since described, once in a long narrative poem, and will doubtless form the subject both of curious research and of romance in the years to come.

W HAT an odd-looking fellow!' said I to myself, as, while walking by the river, I observed a man landing from a boat, with what I thought a bundle of dried clover on his back; 'how the boatmen stare at him! sure he must be an original!' He ascended with a rapid step, and approaching me asked if I could point out the house in which Mr. Audubon resided. 'Why, I am the man,' said I, 'and will gladly lead you to my dwelling.'

The traveller rubbed his hands together with delight, and drawing a letter from his pocket handed it to me without any remark. I broke the seal and read as follows: 'My dear Audubon, I send you an odd fish, which you may prove to be undescribed, and hope you will do so in your next letter. Believe, me always your friend B.' With all the simplicity of a woodsman I asked the bearer where the odd fish was, when M. de T. (for, kind reader, the individual in my presence was none else than that renowned naturalist) smiled, rubbed his hands, and with the greatest good-humor said, 'I am that odd fish I presume, Mr. Audubon.' I felt confounded and blushed, but contrived to stammer an apology.

We soon reached the house, when I presented my learned guest to my family, and was ordering a servant to go to the boat for M. de T.'s luggage, when he told me he had none but what he brought on his back. He then loosened the pack of weeds which had first drawn my attention. The ladies were a little surprised, but I checked their critical glances for the moment. The naturalist pulled off his shoes, and while engaged in drawing his stockings, not up, but down, in order to cover the holes about the heels, told us in the gayest mood imaginable that he had walked a great distance, and had only taken a passage on board the *ark*, to be put on this shore, and that he was sorry his apparel had suffered so much from his late journey. Clean clothes were offered, but he would not accept them, and it was with evident reluctance that he performed the lavations usual on such occasions before he sat down to dinner.

At table, however, his agreeable conversation made us all forget his singular appearance; and, indeed, it was only as we strolled together in the garden that his attire struck me as exceedingly remarkable. A long loose coat of yellow nankeen, much the worse for the many rubs it had got in its time, and stained all over with the juice of plants, hung loosely about him like a sac. A waistcoat of the same, with enormous pockets, and buttoned up to his chin, reached below over a pair of tight pantaloons, the lower parts of which were buttoned down to the ankles. His beard was as long as I have known my own to be during some of my peregrinations, and his lank black hair hung loosely over his shoulders. His forehead was so broad and prominent that any tyro in phrenology would instantly have pronounced it the residence of a mind of strong powers. His words impressed an assurance of rigid truth, and as he directed the conversation to the study of the natural sciences, I listened to him with as much delight as Telemachus could have listened to Mentor. He had come to visit me, he said, expressly for the purpose of seeing my drawings, having been told that my representations of birds were accompanied with those of shrubs and plants, and he was desirous of knowing whether I might chance to have in my collection any with which he was unacquainted. I observed some degree of impatience in his request to be allowed at once to see what I had. We returned to the house, when I opened my portfolios and laid them before him.

He chanced to turn over the drawing of a plant quite new to him. After inspecting it closely, he shook his head, and told me no such plant existed in nature; for, kind reader, M. de T., although a highly scientific man, was suspicious to a fault, and believed such plants only to exist as he had himself seen, or such as, having been discovered of old, had, according to Father Malebranche's expression, acquired a 'venerable beard.' I told my guest that the plant was common in the immediate neighborhood, and that I should show it him on the morrow. 'And why to-morrow, Mr. Audubon? Let us go now.' We did so, and on reaching the bank of the river I pointed to the plant. M. de T., I thought, had gone mad. He plucked the plants one after another, danced, hugged me in his arms, and exultingly told me that he had got not merely a new species, but a new genus. When we returned home, the naturalist opened the bundle which he had brought on his back, and took out a journal rendered water-proof by means of a leather case, together with a small parcel of linen, examined the new plant, and wrote its description. The examination of my drawings then went on. You would be pleased, kind reader, to hear his criticisms, which were of the greatest advantage to me, for, being well acquainted with books as well as with nature, he was well fitted to give me advice.

It was summer, and the heat was so great that the windows were all open. The light of the candles attracted many insects, among which was observed a large species of Scarabaeus. I caught one, and, aware of his inclination to believe only what he should himself see, I showed him the insect, and assured him it was so strong that it would crawl on the table with the candlestick on its back. 'I should like to see the experiment made, Mr. Audubon,' he replied. It was accordingly made, and the insect moved about, dragging its burden so as to make the candlestick change its position as if by magic, until coming upon the edge of the table, it dropped on the floor, took to wing, and made its escape.

When it waxed late, I showed him to the apartment intended for him during his stay, and endeavored to render him comfortable, leaving him writing materials in abundance. I was indeed heartily glad to have a naturalist under my roof. We had all retired to rest. Every person I imagined was in deep slumber save myself, when of a sudden I heard a great uproar in the naturalist's room. I got up, reached the place in a few moments, and opened the door, when to my astonishment, I saw my guest running about the room naked, holding the handle of my favorite violin, the body of which he had battered to pieces against the walls in attempting to kill the bats which had entered by the open window, probably attracted by the insects flying around his candle. I stood amazed, but he continued jumping and running round and round, until he was fairly exhausted, when he begged me to procure one of the animals for him, as he felt convinced they belonged to 'a new species.' Although I was convinced of the contrary, I took up the bow of my demolished Cremona, and administered a smart tap to each of the bats as it came up, soon got specimens enough. The war ended, I again bade him good-night, but could not help observing the state of the room. It was strewed with plants, which it would seem he had arranged into groups, but which were now scattered about in confusion. 'Never mind, Mr. Audubon,' quoth the eccentric naturalist, 'never mind, I'll soon arrange them again. I have the bats, and that's enough.'

Some days passed, during which we followed our several occupations. M. de T. searched the woods for plants, and I for birds. He also followed the margins of the Ohio, and picked up many shells, which he greatly extolled. With us, I told him, they were gathered into heaps to be converted into lime. 'Lime! Mr. Audubon; why, they are worth a guinea apiece in any part of Europe.' One day, as I was returning from a hunt in a cane-brake, he observed that I was wet and spattered with mud, and desired me to show him the interior of one of these places, which he said he had never visited.

The cane, kind reader, formerly grew spontaneously over the greater portions of the State of Kentucky and other western districts of our Union, as well as in many farther south. Now, however, cultivation, and introduction of cattle and horses, and other circumstances connected with the progress of civilization, have greatly altered the face of the country, and reduced the cane within comparatively small limits. It attains a height of from twelve to thirty feet, and a diameter of from one to two inches, and grows in great patches resembling osier-holts, in which occur plants of all sizes. The plants frequently grow so close together, and in course of time become so tangled, as to present an almost impenetrable thicket. A portion of ground thus covered with canes is called a *cane-brake*.

If you picture to yourself one of these cane-brakes growing beneath the gigantic trees that form our western forests, interspersed with vines of many species, and numberless plants of every description, you may conceive how difficult it is for one to make his way through it, especially after a heavy shower of rain or a fall of sleet, when the traveller, in forcing his way through, shakes down upon himself such quantities of water as soon reduce him to a state of the utmost discomfort. The hunters often cut little paths through the thickets with their knives, but the usual mode of passing through them is by pushing one's self backward, and wedging a way between the stems. To follow a Bear or a Cougar pursued by dogs through these brakes is a task the accomplishment of which may be imagined, but of the difficulties and dangers accompanying which I cannot easily give an adequate representation.

The canes generally grow on the richest soil, and are particularly plentiful along the margins of the great western rivers. Many of our new settlers are fond of forming farms in their immediate vicinity, as the plant is much relished by all kinds of cattle and horses, which feed upon it at all seasons, and again because these brakes are plentifully stocked with game of various kinds. It sometimes happens that the farmer clears a portion of the brake. This is done by cutting the stems — which are fistular and knotted, like those of other grasses — with a large knife or cutlass. They are afterwards placed in heaps, and when partially dried set fire to. The moisture contained between the joints is converted into steam, which causes the cane to burst with a smart report, and when a whole mass is crackling, the sounds resemble discharges of musketry. Indeed, I have been told that travellers floating down the rivers, and unacquainted with these circumstances, have been induced to pull their oars with redoubled vigor, apprehending the attack of a host of savages, ready to scalp every one of the party.

A day being fixed, we left home after an early breakfast, crossed the Ohio, and entered the woods. I had determined that my companion should view a cane-brake in all its perfection, and after leading him several miles in a direct course, came upon as fine a sample as existed in that part of the country. We entered, and for some time proceeded without much difficulty, as I led the way, and cut down the canes which were most likely to incommode him. The difficulties gradually increased, so that we were presently obliged to turn our backs to the foe, and push ourselves on the best way we could. My companion stopped here and there to pick up a plant and examine it. After a while we chanced to come upon the top of a fallen tree, which so obstructed our passage that we were on the eve of going round, instead of thrusting ourselves through amongst the branches, when, from its bed in the centre of the tangled mass, forth rushed a Bear, with such force, and snuffing the air in so frightful a manner, that M. de T. became suddenly terror-struck, and, in his haste to escape, made a desperate attempt to run, but fell amongst the canes in such a way that he looked as if pinioned. Perceiving him jammed in between the stalks, and thoroughly frightened, I could not refrain from laughing at the ridiculous exhibition which he made. My gayety, however, was not very pleasing to the *savant*, who called out for aid, which was at once administered. Gladly would he have retraced his steps, but I was desirous that he should be able to describe a cane-brake, and enticed him to follow me

[56]

by telling him that our worst difficulties were nearly over. We proceeded, for by this time the Bear was out of hearing.

The way became more and more tangled. I saw with delight that a heavy cloud, portentous of a thunder gust, was approaching. In the mean time, I kept my companion in such constant difficulties that he now panted, perspired, and seemed almost overcome by fatigue. The thunder began to rumble, and soon after a dash of heavy rain drenched us in a few minutes. The withered particles of leaves and bark attached to the canes stuck to our clothes. We received many scratches from briers, and now and then a switch from a nettle. M. de T. seriously inquired if we should ever get alive out of the horrible situation in which we were. I spoke of courage and patience, and told him I hoped we should soon get to the margin of the brake, which, however, I knew to be two miles distant. I made him rest, and gave him a mouthful of brandy from my flask; after which, we proceeded on our slow and painful march. He threw away all his plants, emptied his pockets of the fungi, lichens, and mosses which he had thrust into them, and finding himself much lightened, went on for thirty or forty yards with a better grace. But, kind reader, enough — I led the naturalist first one way, then another, until I had nearly lost myself in the brake, although I was well acquainted with it, kept him tumbling and crawling on his hands and knees until long after mid-day, when we at length reached the edge of the river. I blew my horn, and soon showed my companion a boat coming to our rescue. We were ferried over, and on reaching the house, found more agreeable occupation in replenishing our empty coffers.

M. de T. remained with us for three weeks, and collected multitudes of plants, shells, bats, and fishes, but never again expressed a desire of visiting a cane-brake. We were perfectly reconciled to his oddities, and, finding him a most agreeable and intelligent companion, hoped that his sojourn might be of long duration. But, one evening when tea was prepared, and we expected him to join the family, he was nowhere to be found. His grasses and other valuables were all removed from his room. The night was spent in searching for him in the neighborhood. No eccentric naturalist could be discovered. Whether he had perished in a swamp, or had been devoured by a Bear or a Garfish, or had taken to his heels, were matters of conjecture; nor was it until some weeks after that a letter from him, thanking us for our attention, assured me of his safety.

HUNTERS' TALES

HUNTERS' TALES

INTRODUCTION

THE PIONEERS who settled Kentucky and the old Northwest Territory and the Western Reserve came from very similar country in Pennsylvania, Virginia, and North Carolina. The difference between their old homes and their new was chiefly this, that in the old the forests had been felled and burned and thinned, law and order had taken the place of free-roaming license, and the deer and bear and other game had been made scarce. These people had been weaned to 'possum meat, and had slept under bearskin, and went capped in coonskin, and hung their guns upon antlers. But as such times became half legendary, they followed the game across the mountains, into virgin hunting grounds. In the brief decades between their arrival (in force, about 1784–1800) and the disappearance of the wilderness (a matter of less than fifty years), they lived the life that has become famous in history and legend, and is lived again in heart by every American child.

It has been said that the forest pioneer lived for and by the black bear. Its flesh and its hide were food and blanket; its extermination was necessary to the safety of the settlers. But for all that, the pioneer loved the bear in much the way that Indians loved the animals they hunted — as a sort of enemy who was yet the darling of the hunter's eye. For the pioneer male imitated the Indian brave, whom he despised as a vermin and a wolf, in considering that the main business in life was the hunt and warfare. So far as possible all other work, including plowing, was left to woman, and the mere rumor of a bear in the next

[61]

county was excuse enough for the man to call up his dogs and his sons, take down his rifle and stay away on the chase as long as possible. In short, where the black bear went, the forest pioneer went. And when there were no more bears to kill, and the tide of settlement had reached the prairie, the old Fenimore Cooper and Daniel Boone period of American history was over. The bear hunter, like the deer slayer, had come to the end of his trail, a trail that was not to be picked up again until decades later, and a thousand miles away and more, in the Far West. The prairie called for another sort of pioneer; the old type was bewildered when the trees stopped and the last bear had rolled over. He couldn't think what to do with the grass plains, except to move into the scattered prairie groves and cut those down too. Baffled, he moped, squatted, moved, fought, drank, sank.

What was true of the forest pioneer and the black bear was true of him and the Virginia deer, though it is doubtful if the pioneer was ever quite the deer stalker that the Indian was. Deer and Indian were equally matched in forest subtlety, the canoe and the arrow against the frightened ear and the springing hoofs. The pioneer was better matched to the fierce but clumsy bear.

In a lesser degree, but in just the same style, the old pioneer, like the negro today, loved and hunted ceaselessly the raccoon and the opossum, two uniquely American forest animals who have held their own better than the bear. The greasy meat of the opossum, the coarse fur of the 'coon, were just to the taste of the Tom Lincolns of those times, and as business the hunt came before anything, unless it was a court session where they could whittle and chew and hear their neighbors argued out of their lands or saved from the noose.

The cougar or mountain lion or American panther — 'painter' of the frontiersman, or even 'tiger' — furnished the pioneer with what modern sportsmen would call something like pure sport. The beast was hunted down because he was the biggest predator in the fauna, sometimes dangerous to man and at all times dangerous to the settler's stock. Opinions differ upon this big cat's courage or cowardice, sagacity or stupidity, inclination to attack man unprovoked or only at bay. Probably individual animals differed in these ways amongst themselves. But the fact is that he was no match for dogs and guns. Cougars were probably never numerous — great beasts of prey are seldom so, for in the biological pyramid they are necessarily the small stone at the top that caps all the broader and lowly tiers that are

Hunters' Tales

obliged to support it. This beast's very size told against him; he vanished even more swiftly than the black bear.

We must in fact conceive of the whole culture or society or way of life that Audubon is describing in these hunters' tales, as very brief, half a century or less at any one point, and the thin frontier on which it existed moved swiftly westward from the Atlantic coast, and moved with increasing velocity. Audubon saw almost the last of it, in its phase in the eastern forest belt. This makes his documents precious.

His account of the black bear comes from *The Quadrupeds of North America*. Most of the text of that work was written by his collaborator John Bachman, but this narrative seems to be certainly Audubon's. The other four sketches are drawn from the 'Episodes' first included among the ornithological biographies.

A RACCOON HUNT IN KENTUCKY

THE RACCOON, which is a cunning and crafty animal, is found in all our woods, so that its name is familiar to every child in the Union. The propensity which it evinces to capture all kinds of birds accessible to it in its nightly prowlings, for the purpose of feasting on their flesh, induces me to endeavor to afford you some idea of the pleasure which our western hunters feel in procuring it. With your leave, then, reader, I will take you to a 'Coon Hunt.'

A few hours ago the sun went down far beyond the 'far west.' The woodland choristers have disappeared, the matron has cradled her babe, and betaken herself to the spinning-wheel; the woodsman, his sons, and 'the stranger,' are chatting before a blazing fire, making wise reflections on past events, and anticipating those that are to come. Autumn, sallow and sad, prepares to bow her head to the keen blast of approaching winter; the corn, though still on its stalk, has lost its blades; the woodpile is as large as the woodsman's cabin; the nights have become chill, and each new morn has effected a gradual change in the dews, which now crust the withered herbage with a coat of glittering white. The sky is still cloudless; a thousand twinkling stars reflect their light from the tranquil waters; all is silent and calm in the forest, save the nightly prowlers that roam in its recesses. In the cheerful cabin all is happiness; its inmates generously strive to contribute to the comfort of the stranger who has chanced to visit them; and, as Raccoons are abundant in the neighborhood, they propose a hunt. The offer is gladly accepted. The industrious woman leaves her wheel, for she has listened to her husband's talk; now she approaches the fire, takes up the board shovel, stirs the embers, produces a basket filled with sweet potatoes, arranges its contents side by side in front of the hearth, and covers them with hot ashes and glowing coals. All this she does because she 'guesses' that hungry stomachs will be calling for food when the sport is over. Ah! reader, what 'homely joys' there are in such scenes, and how you would enjoy them! The rich may produce a better, or a more sumptuous meal, but his feelings can never be like those of the poor woodsman. Poor, I ought not to call him, for nature and industry bountifully supply all his wants; the woods and rivers produce his chief dainties, and his toils are his pleasures.

Now mark him! the bold Kentuckian is on his feet; his sons and the stranger prepare for the march. Horns and rifles are in requisition. The good man opens the wooden-hinged door, and sends forth a blast loud enough to scare a Wolf The Raccoons scamper away from the corn-fields, break through the fences, and hie to the woods. The hunter has taken an axe from the wood-pile, and returning, assures us that the night is fine, and that we shall have rare sport. He blows through his rifle to ascertain that it is clear, examines his flint, and thrusts a feather into the touch-hole. To a leathern bag swung at his side is attached a powder-horn; his sheath-knife is there also; below hangs a narrow strip of homespun linen. He takes from his bag a bullet, pulls with his teeth the wooden stopper from his powder-horn, lays the ball on one hand, and with the other pours the powder upon it until it is just overtopped. Raising the horn to his mouth, he again closes it with the stopper, and restores it to its place. He introduces the powder into the tube; springs the box of his gun, greases the 'patch' over with some melted tallow, or damps it; then places it on the honey-combed muzzle of his piece. The bullet is placed on the patch over the bore, and pressed with the handle of the knife, which now trims the edge of the linen. The elastic hickory rod, held with both hands, smoothly pushes the ball to its bed; once, twice, thrice has it rebounded. The rifle leaps as it were into the hunter's arms, the feather is drawn from the touch-hole, the powder fills the pan, which is closed. 'Now I'm ready,' cries the woodsman. His companions say the same. Hardly more than a minute has elapsed. I wish, reader, you had seen this fine fellow — but hark! the dogs are barking.

All is now bustle within and without; a servant lights a torch, and off we march to the woods. 'Don't mind the boys, my dear sir,' says the woodsman, 'follow me close, for the ground is covered with logs, and the grapevines hang everywhere across. Toby, hold up the light, man, or we'll never see the gullies. Trail your gun, sir, as General Clark used to say — not so, but this way — that's it; now then, no danger, you see; no fear of snakes, poor things! They are stiff enough, I'll be bound. The dogs have treed one. Toby, you old fool, why don't you turn to the right? — not so much; there — go ahead, and give us light. What's that? Who's there? Ah, you young rascals! you've played us a trick, have you? It's all well enough, but now just keep behind, or I'll ——' And, in fact, the boys, with eyes good enough to see in the dark, although not quite so well as an Owl's, had cut directly across the dogs, which had surprised a Raccoon on the ground, and bayed it until the lads knocked it on the head. 'Seek him, boys!' cried the hunter. The dogs, putting their noses to the ground, pushed off at a good rate. 'Master, they're making for the creek,' says old Toby. On towards it therefore we push. What woods, to be sure! No gentleman's park this, I assure you, reader. We are now in a low flat; the soil thinly covers the hard clay; nothing but beech-trees hereabouts, unless now and then a maple. Hang the limbs! says I — hang the supple-jacks too — here I am, fast by the neck; cut it with your knife. My knee has had a tremendous rub against a log; now my foot is jammed between two roots; and here I stick. 'Toby, come back; don't you know the stranger is not up to the woods? Halloo, Toby, Toby!' There I stood perfectly shackled, the hunter laughing heartily, and the lads glad of an opportunity of slipping off. Toby arrived, and held the torch near the ground, on which the hunter, cutting one of the roots with his hatchet, set me free. 'Are you hurt, sir?' — 'No, not in the least.' Off we start again. The boys had got up with the dogs, which were baying a Raccoon in a small puddle. We soon joined them with the light. 'Now, stranger, watch and see!'

The Raccoon was all but swimming, and yet had hold of the bottom of the pool with his feet. The glare of the lighted torch was doubtless distressing to him; his coat was ruffled, and his rounded tail seemed thrice its ordinary size; his eyes shone like emeralds; with foaming jaws he watched the dogs, ready to seize each by the snout if it came within reach. They kept him busy for several minutes; the water became thick with mud; his coat now hung dripping, and his draggled tail lay floating on the surface. His guttural growlings, in place of intimidating his assailants excited them the more; and they very unceremoniously closed upon him, curs as they were, and without the breeding of gentle dogs. One seized him by the rump, and tugged, but was soon forced to let go; another stuck to his side, but soon taking a better directed bite of his muzzle than another dog had just done of his tail, Coon made him yelp; and pitiful were the cries of luckless Tyke. The Raccoon would not let go, but in the mean time the other dogs seized him fast, and worried him to death, yet to the last he held by his antagonist's snout. Knocked on the head by an axe, he lay gasping his last breath, and the heaving of his chest was painful to see. The hunters stood gazing at him in the pool, while all around was by the flare of the torch rendered trebly dark and dismal. It was a good scene for a skilful painter.

We had now two Coons, whose furs were worth two quarters of a dollar, and whose bodies, which I must not forget, as Toby informed us, were worth two more. 'What now?' I asked. 'What now?' quoth the father; 'why, go after more, to be sure.' So we did, the dogs ahead, and I far behind. In a short time the curs treed another, and when we came up, we found them seated on their haunches, looking upwards, and barking. The hunters now employed their axes, and sent the chips about at such a rate that one of them coming in contact with my cheek, marked it so that a week after several of my friends asked me where, in the name of wonder, I had got that black eye. At length the tree began to crack, and slowly leaning to one side, the heavy mass swung rustling through the air, and fell to the earth with a crash. It was not one Coon that was surprised here, but three — ay, three of them, one of which, more crafty than the rest, leaped fairly from the main top while the tree was staggering. The other two stuck to the hollow of a branch, from which they were soon driven by one of the dogs. Tyke and Lion, having nosed the cunning old one, scampered after him, not mouthing like the well-trained hounds of our southern Fox-hunters, but yelling like furies. The hunter's sons attacked those on the tree, while the woodsman and I, preceded by Toby, made after the other; and busy enough we all were. Our animal was of extraordinary size, and after some parley, a rifleball was sent through his brain. He reeled once only; next moment he lay dead. The rest were despatched by the axe and the club, for a shot in those days was too valuable to be spent when it could be saved. It could procure a Deer, and therefore was worth more than a Coon's skin.

Now, look at the moon! how full and clear has she risen on the Raccoon hunters! Now is the time for sport! Onward we go, one following the long shadow of his precursor. The twigs are no impediment, and we move at a brisker pace, as we return to the hills. What a hue and cry! here are the dogs. Overhead and all around, on the forks of each tree, the hunter's keen eye searches for something round, which is likely to prove a coiled-up Raccoon. There's one! Between me and the moon I spied the cunning thing crouched in silence. After taking aim, I raise my barrel ever so little, the trigger is pressed; down falls the Raccoon to the ground. Another and another are on the same tree. Off goes a bullet, then a second; and we secure the prey. 'Let us go home, stranger,' says the woodsman; and contented with our sport, towards his cabin we trudge. On arriving there, we find a cheerful fire. Toby stays without, prepares the game, stretches the skins on a frame of cane, and washes the bodies. The table is already set; the cake and the potatoes are all well done; four bowls of butter-milk are ranged in order, and now the hunters fall to.

The Raccoon is a cunning animal, and makes a pleasant pet. Monkey-like, it is quite dexterous in the use of its fore-feet, and it will amble after its master, in the manner of a Bear, and even follow him into the street. It is fond of eggs, but prefers them raw, and it matters not whether it be morning, noon, or night when it finds a dozen in the pheasant's nest, or one placed in your pocket to please him. He knows the habits of mussels better than most conchologists. Being an expert climber he ascends to the hole of the Woodpecker, and devours the young birds. He knows, too, how to watch the soft-shelled Turtle's crawl, and, better still, how to dig up her eggs. Now, by the edge of the pond, grimalkin-like, he lies seemingly asleep, until the Summer-Duck comes within reach. No negro knows better when the corn is juicy and pleasant to eat; and although Squirrels and Woodpeckers know this too, the Raccoon is found in the corn-field longer in the season than any of them, the havoc he commits there amounting to a tithe. His fur is good in winter, and many think his flesh good also; but for my part, I prefer a live Raccoon to a dead one; and should find more pleasure in hunting one than in eating him.

VIRGINIAN OPOSSUM

'Hunting the Opossum is a very favourite amusement among domestics and field labourers on our Southern plantations, of lads broke loose from school in the holidays, and even of gentlemen, who are sometimes more fond of this sport than of the less profitable and more dangerous and fatiguing one of hunting the gray fox by moonlight.' — *The Quadrupeds*, vol. 2, p. 113.

Drawn from Nature by J.J.Audubon.F.R.S.F.L.S.

DIDELPHIS VIRGI

VIRGINIAN OP

FEMALE & YOUNG MALE

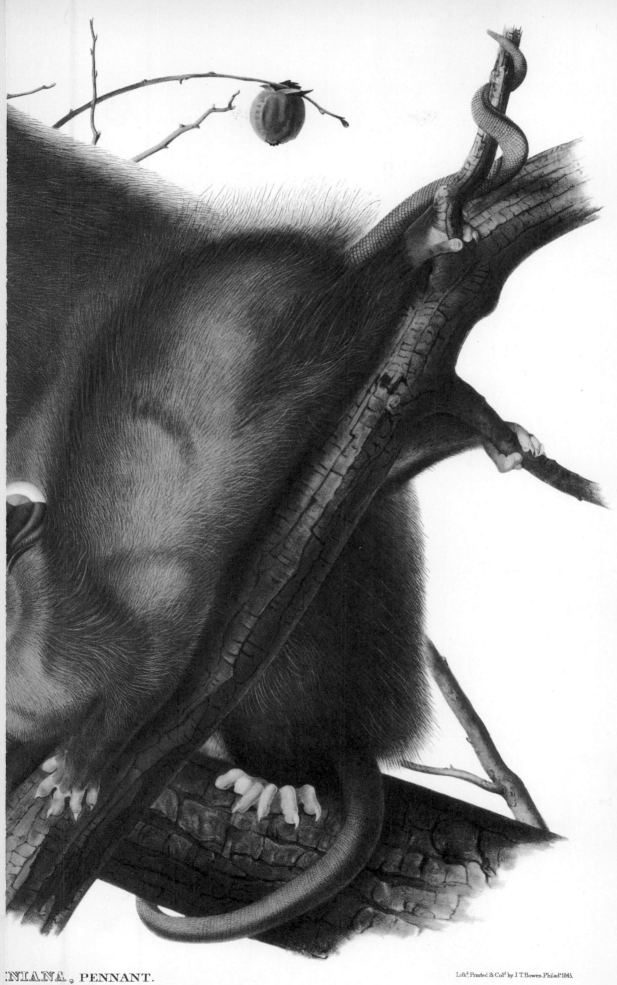

NIANA, PENNANT.

OSSUM.

, 7 MONTHS OLD.

Lith.d, Printed & Col.d by J.T.Bowen.Philad.a1845.

THE OPOSSUM

THIS singular animal is found more or less abundant in most parts of the Southern, Western, and Middle States of the Union. It is the *Didelphis virginiana* of Pennant, Harlan, and other authors who have given some accounts of its habits; but as none of them, so far as I know, have illustrated its propensity to dissimulate, and as I have had opportunities of observing its manners, I trust that a few particulars of its biography will prove amusing.

The Opossum is fond of secluding itself during the day, although it by no means confines its predatory rangings to the night. Like many other quadrupeds which feed principally on flesh, it is also both frugivorous and herbivorous, and, when very hard pressed by hunger, it seizes various kinds of insects and reptiles. Its gait, while travelling, and at a time when it supposes itself unobserved, is altogether ambling; in other words, it, like a young foal, moves the two legs of one side forward at once. The Newfoundland dog manifests a similar propensity. Having a constitution as hardy as that of the most northern animals, it stands the coldest weather, and does not hibernate, although its covering of fur and hair may be said to be comparatively scanty even during winter. The defect, however, seems to be compensated by a skin of considerable thickness, and a general subcutaneous layer of fat. Its movements are usually rather slow, and as it walks or ambles along, its curious prehensile tail is carried just above the ground, its rounded ears are directed forward, and at almost every step its pointed nose is applied to the objects beneath it, in order to discover what sort of creatures may have crossed its path.

Methinks I see one at this moment slowly and cautiously trudging over the melting snows by the side of an unfrequented pond, nosing as it goes for the fare its ravenous appetite prefers. Now it has come upon the fresh track of a Grouse or Hare, and it raises its snout and snuffs the keen air. At length it has decided on its course, and it speeds onward at the rate of a man's ordinary walk. It stops and seems at a loss in what direction to go, for the object of its pursuit has either taken a considerable leap or has cut backwards before the Opossum, entered its track. It raises itself up, stands for a while on its hind feet, looks around, snuffs the air again, and then proceeds; but now, at the foot of a noble tree, it comes to a full stand. It walks round the base of the huge trunk, over the snow-covered roots, and among them finds an aperture which it at once enters. Several minutes elapse, when it re-appears, dragging along a Squirrel already deprived of life, with which in its mouth it begins to ascend the tree. Slowly it climbs. The first fork does not seem to suit it, for perhaps it thinks it might there be too openly exposed to the view of some wily foe; and so it proceeds, until it gains a cluster of branches intertwined with grapevines, and there composing itself, it twists its tail round one of the twigs, and with its sharp teeth demolishes the unlucky Squirrel, which it holds all the while with its fore-paws.

The pleasant days of spring have arrived, and the trees vigorously shoot forth their buds; but the Opossum is almost bare, and seems nearly exhausted by hunger. It visits the margins of creeks, and is pleased to see the young frogs, which afford it a tolerable repast. Gradually the poke-berry and the nettle shoot up, and on their tender and juicy stems it gladly feeds. The matin calls of the Wild Turkey Cock delight the ear of the cunning creature, for it well knows that it will soon hear the female and trace her to her nest, when it will suck the eggs with delight. Travelling through the woods, perhaps on the ground, perhaps aloft, from tree to tree, it hears a cock crow, and its heart swells as it remembers the savory food on which it regaled itself last summer in the neighboring farm-yard. With great care, however, it advances, and at last conceals itself in the very hen-house.

Honest farmer! why did you kill so many Crows last winter? ay and Ravens too? Well, you have had your own way of it; but now hie to the village and procure a store of ammunition, clean your rusty gun, set your traps, and teach your lazy curs to watch the Opossum. There it comes. The sun is scarcely down, but the appetite of the prowler is keen; hear the screams of one of your best chickens that has been seized by him! The cunning beast is off with it, and nothing can now be done, unless you stand there to watch the Fox or the Owl, now exulting in the thought that you have killed their enemy and your own friend, the poor Crow. That precious hen under which you last week placed a dozen eggs or so is now deprived of them. The Opossum, notwithstanding her angry outcries and rufflings of feathers, has removed them one by one, and now look at the poor bird as she moves across your yard; if not mad, she is at least stupid, for she scratches here and there, calling to her chickens all the while. All this comes from your shooting Crows. Had you been more merciful or more prudent, the Opossum might have been kept within the woods, where it would have been satisfied with a Squirrel, a young Hare, the eggs of a Turkey, or the grapes that so profusely adorn the boughs of our forest trees. But I talk to you in vain.

There cannot be a better exemplification of maternal tenderness than the female Opossum. Just peep into that curious sack in which the young are concealed, each attached to a teat. The kind mother not only nourishes them with care, but preserves them from their enemies; she moves with them as the shark does with its progeny, and now, aloft on the tulip-tree, she hides among the thick foliage. By the end of two months they begin to shift for themselves; each has been taught its particular lesson, and must now practise it.

But suppose the farmer has surprised an Opossum in the act of killing one of his best fowls. His angry feelings urge him to kick the poor beast, which, conscious of its inability to resist, rolls off like a ball. The more the farmer rages, the more reluctant is the animal to manifest resentment; at last there it lies, not dead, but exhausted, its jaws open, its tongue extended, its eye dimmed; and there it would lie until the bottle-fly should come to deposit its eggs, did not its tormentor at length walk off. 'Surely,' says he to himself, 'the beast must be dead.' But no, reader, it is only ''possuming,' and no sooner has its enemy withdrawn than it gradually gets on its legs, and once more makes for the woods.

Once, while descending the Mississippi, in a sluggish flat-bottomed boat, expressly for the purpose of studying those objects of nature more nearly connected with my favorite pursuits, I chanced to meet with two well-grown Opossums, and brought them alive to the 'ark.' The poor things were placed on the roof or deck, and were immediately assailed by the crew, when, following their natural instinct, they lay as if quite dead. An experiment was suggested, and both were thrown overboard. On striking water, and for a few moments after, neither evinced the least disposition to move; but finding their situation desperate, they began to swim towards our uncouth rudder, which was formed of a long slender tree, extending from the middle of the boat thirty feet beyond its stern. They both got upon it, were taken up, and afterwards let loose in their native woods.

In the year 1829, I was in a portion of lower Louisiana, where the Opossum abounds at all seasons, and having been asked by the President and the Secretary of the Zoölogical Society of London, to forward live animals of this species to them, I offered a price a little above the common, and soon found myself plentifully supplied, twenty-five having been brought to me. I found them excessively voracious, and not less cowardly. They were put into a large box, with a great quantity of food, and conveyed to a steamer bound for New Orleans. Two days afterwards, I went to that city, to see about sending them off to Europe; but, to my surprise, I found that the old males had destroyed the younger ones, and eaten off their heads, and that only sixteen remained alive. A separate box was purchased for each, and some time after they reached my friends, the Rathbones of Liverpool, who, with their usual attention, sent them off to London, where, on my return, I saw a good number of them in the Zoölogical Gardens.

This animal is fond of grapes, of which a species now bears its name. Persimmons are greedily eaten by it, and in severe weather I have observed it eating lichens. Fowls of every kind, and quadrupeds less powerful than itself, are also its habitual prey.

The flesh of the Opossum resembles that of a young pig, and would perhaps be as highly prized, were it not for the prejudice generally entertained against it. Some 'very particular' persons, to my knowledge, have pronounced it excellent eating. After cleaning its body, suspend it for a whole week in the frosty air, for it is not eaten in summer; then place it on a heap of hot wood embers; sprinkle it when cooked with gunpowder; and now tell me, good reader, does it not equal the famed Canvas-back Duck? Should you visit any of our markets, you may see it there in company with the best game.

THE COUGAR

There is an extensive swamp in the section of the State of Mississippi which lies partly in the Choctaw territory. It commences at the borders of the Mississippi, at no great distance from a Chickasaw village situated near the mouth of a creek known by the name of Vanconnah, and partly inundated by the swellings of several large bayous, the principal of which, crossing the swamp in its whole extent, discharges its waters not far from the mouth of the Yazoo River. This famous bayou is called False River. The swamp of which I am speaking follows the windings of the Yazoo, until the latter branches off to the northeast, and at this point forms the stream named Cold Water River, below which the Yazoo receives the draining of another bayou inclining towards the northwest and intersecting that known by the name of False River at a short distance from the place where the latter receives the waters of the Mississippi. This tedious account of the situation of the swamp is given with the view of pointing it out to all students of nature who may happen to go that way, and whom I would earnestly urge to visit its interior, as it abounds in rare and interesting productions — birds, quadrupeds, and reptiles, as well as molluscous animals, many of which, I am persuaded, have never been described.

In the course of one of my rambles, I chanced to meet with a squatter's cabin on the banks of the Cold Water River. In the owner of this hut, like most of those adventurous settlers in the uncultivated tracts of our frontier districts, I found a person well versed in the chase, and acquainted with the habits of some of the larger species of quadrupeds and birds. As he who is desirous of instruction ought not to disdain listening to any one who has knowledge to communicate, however humble may be his lot, or however limited his talents, I entered the squatter's cabin, and immediately opened a conversation with him respecting the situation of the swamp, and its natural productions. He told me he thought it the very place I ought to visit, spoke of the game which it contained, and pointed to some Bear and Deer skins, adding that the individuals to which they had belonged formed but a small portion of the number of those animals which he had shot within it. My heart swelled with delight, and on asking if he would accompany me through the great morass, and allow me to become an inmate of his humble but hospitable mansion, I was gratified to find that he cordially assented to all my proposals. So I immediately unstrapped my drawing materials, laid up my gun, and sat down to partake of the homely but wholesome fare intended for the supper of the squatter, his wife, and his two sons.

The quietness of the evening seemed in perfect accordance with the gentle demeanor of the family. The wife and children, I more than once thought, seemed to look upon me as a strange sort of person, going about, as I told them I was, in search of birds and plants; and were I here to relate the many questions which they put to me in return for those I addressed to them, the catalogue would occupy several pages. The husband, a native of Connecticut, had heard of the existence of such men as myself, both in our own country and abroad, and seemed greatly pleased to have me under his roof. Supper over, I asked my kind host what had induced him to remove to this wild and solitary spot. 'The people are growing too numerous now to thrive in New England,' was his answer. I thought of the state of some parts of Europe, and calculating the denseness of their population compared with that of New England, exclaimed to myself, 'How much more difficult must it be for men to thrive in those populous countries!' The conversation then changed, and the squatter, his sons and myself, spoke of hunting and fishing until at length, tired, we laid ourselves down on pallets of Bear skins, and reposed in peace on the floor of the only apartment of which the hut consisted.

Day dawned, and the squatter's call to his hogs, which, being almost in a wild state, were suffered to seek the greater portion of their food in the woods, awakened me. Being ready dressed I was not long in joining him. The hogs and their young came grunting at the well-known call of their owner, who threw them a few ears of corn, and counted them, but told me that for some weeks their number had been greatly diminished by the ravages committed upon them by a large *Panther*, by which name the Cougar is designated in America, and that the ravenous animal did not content himself with the flesh of his pigs, but now and then carried off one of his calves, notwithstanding the many attempts he had made to shoot it. The *Painter*, as he sometimes called it, had on several occasions robbed him of a dead Deer; and to these exploits the squatter added several remarkable feats of audacity which it had performed, to give me an idea of the formidable character of the beast. Delighted by his description, I offered to assist him in destroying the enemy, at which he was highly pleased, but assured me that unless some of his neighbors should join us with their dogs and his own, the attempt would prove fruitless. Soon after, mounting a horse, he went off to his neighbors several of whom lived at a distance of some miles, and appointed a day of meeting.

The hunters, accordingly, made their appearance, one fine morning, at the door of the cabin, just as the sun was emerging from beneath the horizon. They were five in number, and fully equipped for the chase, being mounted on horses which in some parts of Europe might appear sorry nags, but which in strength, speed, and bottom, are better fitted for pursuing a Cougar or a Bear through woods and morasses than any in that country. A pack of large, ugly curs were already engaged in making acquaintance with those of the squatter. He and myself mounted his two best horses, whilst his sons were bestriding others of inferior quality.

Few words were uttered by the party until we had reached the edge of the swamp, where it was agreed that all should disperse and seek for the fresh track of the Painter, it being previously settled that the discoverer should blow his horn, and remain on the spot, until the rest should join him. In less than an hour, the sound of the horn was clearly heard, and, sticking close to the squatter, off we went through the thick woods, guided only by the now and then repeated call of the distant huntsmen. We soon reached the spot, and in a short time the rest of the party came up. The best dog was sent forward to track the Cougar, and in a few moments the whole pack were observed diligently trailing, and bearing in their course for the interior of the Swamp. The rifles were immediately put in trim, and the party followed the dogs, at separate distances, but in sight of each other, determined to shoot at no other game than the Panther.

The dogs soon began to mouth, and suddenly quickened their pace.

My companion concluded that the beast was on the ground, and putting our horses to a gentle gallop, we followed the curs, guided by their voices. The noise of the dogs increased, when, all of a sudden their mode of barking became altered, and the squatter, urging me to push on, told me that the beast was *treed*, by which he meant that it had got upon some low branch of a large tree to rest for a few minutes, and that should we not succeed in shooting him when thus situated, we might expect a long chase of it. As we approached the spot, we all by degrees united into a body, but on seeing the dogs at the foot of a large tree, separated again, and galloped off to surround it.

Each hunter now moved with caution, holding his gun ready, and allowing the bridle to dangle on the neck of his horse, as it advanced slowly towards the dogs. A shot from one of the party was heard, on which the Cougar was seen to leap to the ground, and bound off with such velocity as to show that he was very unwilling to stand our fire longer. The dogs set off in pursuit with great eagerness and a deafening cry. The hunter who had fired came up and said that his ball had hit the monster, and had probably broken one of his fore-legs near the shoulder, the only place at which he could aim. A slight trail of blood was discovered on the ground, but the curs proceeded at such a rate that we merely noticed this, and put spurs to our horses, which galloped on towards the centre of the Swamp. One bayou was crossed, then another still larger and more muddy; but the dogs were brushing forward, and as the horses began to pant at a furious rate, we judged it expedient to leave them and advance on foot. These determined hunters knew that the Cougar being wounded, would shortly ascend another tree, where in all probability he would remain for a considerable time, and that it would be easy to follow the track of the dogs. We dismounted, took off the saddles and bridles, set the bells attached to the horses' necks at liberty to jingle, hoppled the animals, and left them to shift for themselves.

Now, kind reader, follow the group marching through the swamp, crossing muddy pools, and making the best of their way over fallen trees and amongst the tangled rushes that now and then covered acres of ground. If you are a hunter yourself, all this will appear nothing to you; but if crowded assemblies of 'beauty and fashion,' or the quiet enjoyment of your 'pleasure grounds' alone delight you, I must mend my pen before I attempt to give you an idea of the pleasure felt on such an expedition.

The Cougar

After marching for a couple of hours, we again heard the dogs. Each of us pressed forward, elated at the thought of terminating the career of the Cougar. Some of the dogs were heard whining, although the greater number barked vehemently. We felt assured that the Cougar was treed, and that he would rest for some time to recover from his fatigue. As we came up to the dogs, we discovered the ferocious animal lying across a large branch, close to the trunk of a cottonwood tree. His broad breast lay towards us; his eyes were at one time bent on us and again on the dogs beneath and around him; one of his fore-legs hung loosely by his side, and he lay crouched, with his ears lowered close to his head, as if he thought he might remain undiscovered. Three balls were fired at him, at a given signal, on which he sprang a few feet from the branch, and tumbled headlong to the ground. Attacked on all sides by the enraged curs, the infuriated Cougar fought with desperate valor; but the squatter, advancing in front of the party, and almost in the midst of the dogs, shot him immediately behind and beneath the left shoulder. The Cougar writhed for a moment in agony, and in another lay dead.

The sun was now sinking in the west. Two of the hunters separated from the rest to procure venison, whilst the squatter's sons were ordered to make the best of their way home, to be ready to feed the hogs in the morning. The rest of the party agreed to camp on the spot. The Cougar was despoiled of its skin, and its carcass left to the hungry dogs. Whilst engaged in preparing our camp, we heard the report of a gun, and soon after one of our hunters returned with a small Deer. A fire was lighted, and each hunter displayed his *pone* of bread, along with a flask of whiskey. The deer was skinned in a trice, and slices placed on sticks before the fire. These materials afforded us an excellent meal, and as the night grew darker, stories and songs went round, until my companions, fatigued, laid themselves down, close under the smoke of the fire, and soon fell asleep.

I walked for some minutes round the camp, to contemplate the beauties of that nature from which I have certainly derived my greatest pleasures. I thought of the occurrences of the day, and glancing my eye around, remarked the singular effects produced by the phosphorescent qualities of the large decayed trunks which lay in all directions around me. How easy, I thought, would it be for the confused and agitated mind of a person bewildered in a swamp like this, to imagine in each of these luminous masses some wondrous and fearful being, the very sight of which might make the hair stand erect on his head. The thought of being myself placed in such a predicament burst over my mind, and I hastened to join my companions, beside whom I laid me down and slept, assured that no enemy could approach us without first rousing the dogs, which were growling in fierce dispute over the remains of the Cougar.

At daybreak we left our camp, the squatter bearing on his shoulder the skin of the late destroyer of his stock, and retraced our steps until we found our horses, which had not strayed far from the place where we had left them. These we soon saddled, and jogging along, in a direct course, guided by the sun, congratulating each other in the destruction of so formidable a neighbor as the Panther had been, we soon arrived at my host's cabin. The five neighbors partook of such refreshment as the house could afford, and dispersing, returned to their homes, leaving me to follow my favorite pursuits.

BLACK BEAR

THE BLACK BEAR, however clumsy in appearance, is active, vigilant, and persevering, possesses great strength, courage, and address, and undergoes with little injury the greatest fatigues and hardships in avoiding the pursuit of the hunter. Like the deer it changes its haunts with the seasons, and for the same reason, viz. the desire of obtaining suitable food, or of retiring to the more inaccessible parts, where it can pass the time in security, unobserved by man, the most dangerous of its enemies.

During the spring months it searches for food in the low rich alluvial lands that border the rivers, or by the margins of such inland lakes as, on account of their small size, are called by us ponds. There it procures abundance of succulent roots and tender juicy plants, upon which it chiefly feeds at that season. During the summer heat, it enters the gloomy swamps, passes much of its time in wallowing in the mud like a hog, and contents itself with crayfish, roots, and nettles, now and then seizing on a pig, or perhaps a sow, a calf, or even a full-grown cow. As soon as the different kinds of berries which grow on the mountains begin to ripen, the Bears betake themselves to the high grounds, followed by their cubs.

In retired parts of the country, where the plantations are large and the population sparse, it pays visits to the corn-fields, which it ravages for a while. After this, the various species of nuts, acorns, grapes, and other forest fruits, that form what in the western States is called *mast*, attract its attention. The Bear is then seen rambling singly through the woods to gather this harvest, not forgetting, meanwhile, to rob every *bee-tree* it meets with, Bears being expert at this operation.

The Black Bear is a capital climber, and now and then *houses* itself in the hollow trunk of some large tree for weeks together during the winter, when it is said to live by sucking its paws.

At one season, the Bear may be seen examining the lower part of the trunk of a tree for several minutes with much attention, at the same time looking around, and snuffing the air. It then rises on its hind-legs, approaches the trunk, embraces it with the fore-legs, and scratches the bark with its teeth and claws for several minutes in continuance. Its jaws clash against each other until a mass of foam runs down on both sides of the mouth. After this it continues its rambles.

The female Black Bear generally brings forth two cubs at a time, although, as we have heard, the number is sometimes three or four. The period of gestation is stated to be from six to seven weeks, but is mentioned as one hundred days by some authors. When born the young are exceedingly small, and if we may credit the accounts of hunters with whom we have conversed on the subject, are not larger than kittens. They are almost invariably brought forth in some well concealed den, or great hollow tree, and so cautious is the dam in selecting her place of accouchment, that it is extremely difficult to discover it, and consequently very rarely that either the female or her cubs are seen until the latter have obtained a much larger size than when born, are able to follow their dam, and can climb trees with facility.

Most writers on the habits of this animal have stated that the Black Bear does not eat animal food from choice, and never unless pressed by hunger. This we consider a great mistake, for in our experience we have found the reverse to be the case, and it is well known to our frontier farmers that this animal is a great destroyer of pigs, hogs, calves, and sheep, for the sake of which we have even known it to desert the pecan groves in Texas. At the same time, as will have been seen by our previous remarks, its principal food generally consists of berries, roots, and other vegetable substances. It is very fond also of fish, and during one of our expeditions to Maine and New Brunswick, we found the inhabitants residing near the coast unwilling to eat the flesh of the animal on account of its fishy taste. In our western forests, however, the Bear feeds on so many nuts and well tasted roots and berries, that its meat is considered a great delicacy, and in the city of New York we have generally found its market price three or four times more than the best beef per pound. The fore-paw of the Bear when cooked presents a striking resemblance to the hand of a child or young person, and we have known some individuals to be hoaxed by its being represented as such.

Perhaps the most acrid vegetable eaten by the Bear is the Indian turnip (*Arum triphyllum*), which is so pungent that we have seen people almost distracted by it, when they had inadvertently put a piece in their mouth.

As we were once standing at the foot of a large sycamore tree on the borders of a long and deep pond, on the edge of which, in our rear, there was a thick and extensive 'cane-brake,' we heard a rushing roaring noise, as if some heavy animal was bearing down and passing rapidly through the canes, directly towards us. We were not kept long in suspense, for in an instant or two, a large Bear dashed out of the dense cane, and plunging into the pond without having even seen us, made off with considerable speed through the water towards the other shore. Having only bird-shot in our gun we did not think it worth while to call his attention to us by firing at him, but turned to the cane-brake, expecting to hear either dogs or men approaching shortly. No further noise could be heard, however, and the surrounding woods were as still as before this adventure. We supposed the Bear had been started at some distance, and that his pursuers, not being able to follow him through the almost impenetrable canes, had given up the hunt.

Being one night sleeping in the house of a friend who was a Planter in the State of Louisiana, we were awakened by a servant bearing a light, who gave us a note, which he said his master had just received. We found it to be a communication from a neighbour, requesting our host and ourself to join him as soon as possible, and assist in killing some Bears at that moment engaged in destroying his corn. We were not long in dressing, and on entering the parlour, found our friend equipped. The overseer's horn was heard calling up the negroes. Some were already saddling our horses, whilst others were gathering all the cur-dogs of the plantation. All was bustle. Before half an hour had elapsed, four stout negro men, armed with axes and knives, and mounted on strong nags, were following us at a round gallop through the woods, as we made directly for the neighbour's plantation.

The night was none of the most favourable, a drizzling rain rendering the atmosphere thick and rather sultry; but as we were well acquainted with the course, we soon reached the house, where the owner was waiting our arrival. There were now three of us armed with guns, half a dozen servants, and a good pack of dogs of all kinds. We jogged on towards the detached field in which the Bears were at work. The owner told us that for some days several of these animals had visited his corn, and that a negro who was sent every afternoon to see at what part of the enclosure they entered, had assured him there were at least five in the field that night. A plan of attack was formed: the bars at the usual entrance of the field were to be put down without noise; the men and dogs were to divide, and afterwards proceed so as to surround the Bears, when, at the sounding of our horns, every one was to charge towards the centre of the field, and shout as loudly as possible, which it was judged would so intimidate the animals as to induce them to seek refuge upon the dead trees with which the field was still partially covered.

The plan succeeded: the horns sounded, the horses galloped forward, the men shouted, the dogs barked and howled. The shrieks of the negroes were enough to frighten a legion of bears, and by the time we reached the middle of the field we found that several had mounted the trees, and having lighted fires, we now saw them crouched at the junction of the larger branches with the trunks. Two were immediately shot down. They were cubs of no great size, and being already half dead, were quickly dispatched by the dogs.

We were anxious to procure as much sport as possible, and having observed one of the Bears, which from its size we conjectured to be the mother of the two cubs just killed, we ordered the negroes to cut down the tree on which it was perched, when it was intended the dogs should have a tug with it, while we should support them, and assist in preventing the Bear from escaping, by wounding it in one of the hind-legs. The surrounding woods now echoed to the blows of the axemen. The tree was large and tough, having been girded more than two years, and the operation of felling it seemed extremely tedious. However, at length it began to vibrate at each stroke; a few inches alone now supported it, and in a short time it came crashing to the ground.

The dogs rushed to the charge, and harassed the Bear on all sides, whilst we surrounded the poor animal. As its life depended upon its courage and strength, it exercised both in the most energetic manner. Now and then it seized a dog and killed him by a single stroke. At another time, a well administered blow of one of its fore-legs sent an assailant off, yelping so piteously that he might be looked upon as

Black Bear

hors du combat. A cur had daringly ventured to seize the Bear by the snout, and was seen hanging to it, covered with blood, whilst several others scrambled over its back. Now and then the infuriated animal was seen to cast a revengeful glance at some of the party, and we had already determined to dispatch it, when, to our astonishment, it suddenly shook off all the dogs, and before we could fire, charged upon one of the negroes, who was mounted on a pied horse. The Bear seized the steed with teeth and claws, and clung to its breast. The terrified horse snorted and plunged. The rider, an athletic young man and a capital horseman, kept his seat, although only saddled on a sheep-skin tightly girthed, and requested his master not to fire at the Bear. Notwithstanding his coolness and courage, our anxiety for his safety was raised to the highest pitch, especially when in a moment we saw rider and horse come to the ground together; but we were instantly relieved on witnessing the masterly manner in which Scipio dispatched his adversary, by laying open his skull with a single well directed blow of his axe, when a deep growl announced the death of the Bear.

In our country no animal, perhaps, has been more frequently the theme of adventure or anecdote than the Bear, and in some of our southwestern States it is not uncommon to while away the winter evenings with Bear stories that are not only interesting on account of the traits of the habits of the animal with which they are interspersed, but from the insight they afford the listener into the characteristics of the bold and hardy huntsmen of those parts.

In the State of Maine the lumbermen (wood-cutters) and the farmers set guns to kill this animal, which are arranged in this way: A funnel-shaped space about five feet long is formed by driving strong sticks into the ground in two converging lines, leaving both the ends open, the narrow end being wide enough to admit the muzzle of an old musket, and the other extremity so broad as to allow the head and shoulders of the Bear to enter. The gun is then loaded and fastened securely so as to deliver its charge facing the wide end of the enclosure. A round and smooth stick is now placed behind the stock of the gun, and a cord leading from the trigger passed around it, the other end of which, with a piece of meat or a bird tied to it (an owl is a favourite bait), is stretched in front of the gun, so far that the Bear can reach the bait with his paw. Upon his pulling the meat towards him, the string draws the trigger and the animal is instantly killed.

On the coast of Labrador we observed the Black Bear catching fish with great dexterity, and the food of these animals in that region consisted altogether of the fishes they seized in the edge of the water inside the surf. Like the Polar Bear, the present species swims with ease and rapidity, and it is a difficult matter to catch a full grown Bear with a skiff, and a dangerous adventure to attempt its capture in a canoe, which it could easily upset.

We were once enjoying a fine autumnal afternoon on the shores of the beautiful Ohio, with two acquaintances who had accompanied us in quest of some swallows that had built in a high sandy bank, when we observed three hunters about the middle of the river in a skiff, vigorously rowing, the steersman paddling too, with all his strength, in pursuit of a Bear which, about one hundred and fifty yards ahead of them, was cleaving the water and leaving a widening wake behind him on its unrippled surface as he made for the shore, directly opposite to us. We all rushed down to the water at this sight, and launching a skiff we then kept for fishing, hastily put off to intercept the animal, which we hoped to assist in capturing. Both boats were soon nearing the Bear, and we, standing in the bow of our skiff, commenced the attack by discharging a pistol at his head. At this he raised one paw, brushed it across his forehead, and then seemed to redouble his efforts. Repeated shots from both boats were now fired at him, and we ran alongside, thinking to haul his carcase triumphantly on board; but suddenly, to our dismay, he laid both paws on the gunwale of the skiff, and his great weight brought the side for an instant under water, so that we expected the boat would fill and sink. There was no time to be lost: we all threw our weight on to the other side, to counterpoise that of the animal, and commenced a pell-mell battery on him with the oars and a boat-hook; the men in the other boat also attacked him, and driving the bow of their skiff close to his head, one of them laid his skull open with an axe, which killed him instanter. We jointly hurraed, and tying a rope round his neck, towed him ashore behind our boats.

The Black Bear is very tenacious of life, and like its relative, the Grizzly Bear, is dangerous when irritated or wounded. It makes large beds of leaves and weeds or grasses, in the fissures of rocks, or sleeps in hollow logs, when no convenient den can be found in its neighbourhood; it also makes lairs in the thick cane-brakes and deep swamps, and covers itself with a heap of leaves and twigs, like a wild sow when about to litter.

[84]

Black Bear

The Black Bear is rather docile when in confinement, and a 'pet' Bear is occasionally seen in various parts of the country. In our large cities, however, where civilization (?) is thought to have made the greatest advances, this animal is used to amuse the gentlemen of the fancy, by putting its strength and 'pluck' to the test, in combat with bull-dogs or mastiffs. When the Bear has not been so closely imprisoned as to partially destroy his activity, these encounters generally end with the killing of one or more dogs; but occasionally the dogs overpower him, and he is rescued for the time by his friends, to 'fight (again) some other day.'

We are happy to say, however, that Bear-baiting and bull-baiting have not been as yet fully naturalized amongst us, and are only popular with those who, perhaps, in addition to the natural desire for excitement, have the hope and intention of winning money, to draw them to such cruel and useless conditions.

DEER HUNTING

THE different modes of Deer hunting are probably too well understood, and too successfully practised in the United States; for, notwithstanding the almost incredible abundance of these beautiful animals in our forests and prairies, such havoc is carried on amongst them that, in a few centuries, they will probably be as scarce in America as the Great Bustard now is in Britain.

We have three modes of hunting Deer, each varying in some slight degree in the different States and districts. The first is termed *still hunting*, and is by far the most destructive. The second is called *fire-light hunting*, and is next in its exterminating effects. The third, which may be looked upon as a mere amusement, is named *driving*. Although many Deer are destroyed by this latter method, it is not by any means so pernicious as the others. These methods I shall describe separately.

Still hunting is followed as a kind of trade by most of our frontier-men. To be practised with success it requires great activity, an expert management of the rifle, and a thorough knowledge of the forest, together with an intimate acquaintance with the habits of the Deer, not only at different seasons of the year, but also at every hour of the day, as the hunters must be aware of the situations which the game prefers, and in which it is most likely to be found at any particular time. I might here present you with a full account of the habits of our Deer, were it not my intention to lay before you, at some future period, in the form of a distinct work, the observations which I have made on the various quadrupeds of our extensive territories.

Illustrations of any kind require to be presented in the best possible light. We shall therefore suppose that we are now about to follow the

Deer Hunting

true hunter, as the 'still hunter' is also called, through the interior of the tangled woods, across morasses, ravines, and such places, where the game may prove more or less plentiful, even should none be found there in the first instance. We shall allow our hunter all the agility, patience, and care which his occupation requires, and will march in his rear, as if we were spies, watching all his motions.

His dress, you observe, consists of a leather hunting-shirt, and a pair of trousers of the same material. His feet are well moccasined; he wears a belt round his waist; his heavy rifle is resting on his brawny shoulder; on one side hangs his ball pouch, surmounted by the horn of an ancient Buffalo, once the terror of the herd, but now containing a pound of the best gunpowder; his butcher knife is scabbarded in the same strap; and behind is a tomahawk, the handle of which has been thrust through his girdle. He walks with so rapid a step that probably few men, beside ourselves, that is, myself and my kind reader, could follow him, unless for a short distance, in their anxiety to witness his ruthless deeds. He stops, looks to the flint of his gun, its priming, and the leather cover of the lock, then glances his eye towards the sky, to judge of the course most likely to lead him to the game.

The heavens are clear, the red glare of the morning sun gleams through the lower branches of the lofty trees, the dew hangs in pearly drops at the top of every leaf. Already has the emerald hue of the foliage been converted into the more glowing tints of our autumnal months. A slight frost appears on the fence-rails of his little corn-field. As he proceeds he looks to the dead foliage under his feet, in search of the well-known traces of a buck's hoof. Now he bends towards the ground, on which something has attracted his attention. See! he alters his course, increases his speed, and will soon reach the opposite hill. Now he moves with caution, stops at almost every tree, and peeps forward, as if already within shooting distance of the game. He advances again, but how very slowly! He has reached the declivity, upon which the sun shines in all its growing splendor; but mark him! he takes the gun from his shoulder, has already thrown aside the leathern cover of the lock, and is wiping the edge of the flint with his tongue. Now he stands like a monumental figure, perhaps measuring the distance that lies between him and the game which he has in view. His rifle is slowly raised, the report follows, and he runs. Let us run also. Shall I speak to him, and ask him the result of this first essay? Assuredly, reader, for I know him well.

'Pray, friend, what have you killed?' for to say, 'What have you shot at?' might imply the possibility of having missed, and so might hurt his feelings. 'Nothing but a buck.' 'And where is it?' 'Oh, it has taken a jump or so, but I settled it, and will soon be with it. My ball struck, and must have gone through his heart.' We arrive at the spot where the animal had laid itself down among the grass in a thicket of grape-vines, sumach, and spruce bushes, where it intended to repose during the middle of the day. The place is covered with blood, the hoofs of the Deer have left deep prints in the ground, as it bounced in the agonies produced by its wound; but the blood that has gushed from its side discloses the course which it has taken. We soon reach the spot. There lies the buck, its tongue out, its eye dim, its breath exhausted; it is dead. The hunter draws his knife, cuts the buck's throat almost asunder, and prepares to skin it. For this purpose he hangs it upon the branch of a tree. When the skin is removed, he cuts off the hams, and abandoning the rest of the carcass to the Wolves and Vultures, reloads his gun, flings the venison, enclosed by the skin, upon his back, secures it with a strap, and walks off in search of more game, well knowing that, in the immediate neighbourhood, another at least is to be found.

Had the weather been warmer, the hunter would have sought for the buck along the *shadowy* side of the hills. Had it been the spring season, he would have led us through some thick cane-brake, to the margin of some remote lake, where you would have seen the Deer immersed to his head in the water, to save his body from the tormenting attacks of mosquitoes. Had winter overspread the earth with a covering of snow, he would have searched the low, damp woods, where the mosses and lichens, on which at that period the Deer feeds, abound; the trees being generally crusted with them for several feet from the ground. At one time he might have marked the places where the Deer clears the velvet from his horns by rubbing them against the low stems of bushes, and where he frequently scrapes the earth with his fore-hoofs; at another he would have betaken himself to places where persimmons and crab-apples abound, as beneath these trees the Deer frequently stops to munch their fruits. During early spring our hunter would imitate the bleating of the doe, and thus frequently obtain both her and the fawn, or, like some tribes of Indians, he would prepare a Deer's head, placed on a stick, and creeping with it amongst the tall grass of the prairies, would decoy Deer in reach of his rifle. But, kind

COMMON or VIRGINIAN DEER

*An example of the work of Audubon's
younger son John Woodhouse Audubon.*

'John Woodhouse Audubon, like his brother, Victor, inherited
decided artistic abilities, and from a youth had been his father's
assistant, field companion and friend. . . . Under his father's tuition
John Audubon became an observant and self-reliant collector in the
field, and an animal painter and draughtsman of no mean powers.
At twenty-one, as we have seen, he accompanied his father's expedition to Labrador, was with him and Harris in Florida and Texas
in 1837, made successive visits to England, and traveled again in
Texas and in Mexico, all in the interests of his father's works. He
painted nearly one-half of the large plates of the *Quadrupeds.*' —
Audubon the Naturalist by Francis Hobart Herrick, D. Appleton and
Company, 1917, vol. 2, pp. 297 and 298.

CERVUS VIRGI

COMMON OR VIRG

OLD MALE &

NIANUS, PENNANT.

NIAN DEER.
FEMALE.

Lithᵈ Printed & Colᵈ by J. T. Bowen. Philadᵃ 1848.

Deer Hunting

reader, you have seen enough of the *still hunter*. Let it suffice for me to add that by the mode pursued by him thousands of Deer are annually killed, many individuals shooting these animals merely for the skin, not caring for even the most valuable portions of the flesh, unless hunger, or a near market, induce them to carry off the hams.

The mode of destroying deer by *fire-light*, or, as it is named in some parts of the country, *forest-light*, never fails to produce a very singular feeling in him who witnesses it for the first time. There is something in it which at times appears awfully grand. At other times a certain degree of fear creeps over the mind, and even affects the physical powers of him who follows the hunter through the thick undergrowth of our woods, having to leap his horse over hundreds of huge fallen trunks, at one time impeded by a straggling grape-vine crossing his path, at another squeezed between two stubborn saplings, whilst their twigs come smack in his face, as his companion has forced his way through them. Again, he now and then runs the risk of breaking his neck, by being suddenly pitched headlong on the ground, as his horse sinks into a hole covered over with moss. But I must proceed in a more regular manner, and leave you, kind reader, to judge whether such a mode of hunting would suit your taste or not.

The hunter has returned to his camp or his house, has rested and eaten of his game. He waits impatiently for the return of night. He has procured a quantity of pine knots filled with resinous matter, and has an old frying-pan, that, for aught I know to the contrary, may have been used by his great-grandmother, in which the pine-knots are to be placed when lighted. The horses stand saddled at the door. The hunter comes forth, his rifle slung on his shoulder, and springs upon one of them, while his son, or a servant, mounts the other with the frying-pan and the pine-knots. Thus accoutred, they proceed towards the interior of the forest. When they have arrived at the spot where the hunt is to begin, they strike fire with a flint and steel, and kindle the resinous wood. The person who carries the fire moves in the direction judged to be the best. The blaze illuminates the near objects, but the distant parts seem involved in deepest obscurity. The hunter who bears the gun keeps immediately in front, and after a while discovers before him two feeble lights, which are produced by the reflection of the pine-fire from the eyes of an animal of the Deer or Wolf kind. The animal stands quite still. To one unacquainted with this strange mode of hunting, the glare from its eyes might bring to his imagination some lost hobgoblin that has strayed from its usual haunts. The hunter, however, nowise intimidated, approaches the object, sometimes so near as to discern its form, when, raising the rifle to his shoulder, he fires and kills it on the spot. He then dismounts, secures the skin and such portions of the flesh as he may want, in the manner already described, and continues his search through the greater part of the night, sometimes until the dawn of day, shooting from five to ten Deer, should these animals be plentiful. This kind of hunting proves fatal, not to the Deer alone, but also sometimes to Wolves, and now and then to a horse or cow, which may have straggled far into the woods.

Now, kind reader, prepare to mount a generous, full-blood Virginian hunter. See that your gun is in complete order, for hark to the sound of the bugle and horn, and the mingled clamor of a pack of harriers! Your friends are waiting for you, under the shade of the wood, and we must together go *driving* the light-footed Deer. The distance over which one has to travel is seldom felt when pleasure is anticipated as the result; so galloping we go pell-mell through the woods, to some well-known place where many a fine buck has drooped its antlers under the ball of the hunter's rifle. The servants, who are called the drivers, have already begun their search. Their voices are heard exciting the hounds, and unless we put spurs to our steeds, we may be too late at our stand, and thus lose the first opportunity of shooting the fleeting game as it passes by. Hark again! The dogs are in chase, the horn sounds louder and more clearly. Hurry, hurry on, or we shall be sadly behind!

Here we are at last! Dismount, fasten your horse to this tree, place yourself by the side of that large yellow poplar, and mind you do not shoot me! The Deer is fast approaching; I will to my own stand, and he who shoots him dead wins the prize.

The Deer is heard coming. It has inadvertently cracked a dead stick with its hoof, and the dogs are now so near that it will pass in a moment. There it comes! How beautifully it bounds over the ground! What a splendid head of horns! How easy its attitudes, depending, as it seems to do, on its own swiftness for safety! All is in vain, however; a gun is fired, the animal plunges and doubles with incomparable speed. There he goes! He passes another stand, from which a second shot, better directed than the first, brings him to the ground. The dogs, the servants, the sportsmen are now rushing forward to the spot. The

Deer Hunting

hunter who has shot it is congratulated on his skill or good luck, and the chase begins again in some other part of the woods.

A few lines of explanation may be required to convey a clear idea of this mode of hunting. Deer are fond of following and retracing paths which they have formerly pursued, and continue to do so even after they have been shot at more than once. These tracks are discovered by persons on horseback in the woods, or a Deer is observed crossing a road, a field, or a small stream. When this has been noticed twice, the deer may be shot from the places called *stands* by the sportsman, who is stationed there, and waits for it, a line of stands being generally formed so as to cross the path which the game will follow. The person who ascertains the usual pass of the game, or discovers the parts where the animal feeds or lies down during the day, gives intimation to his friends, who then prepare for the chase. The servants start the Deer with the hounds, and by good management generally succeed in making it run the course that will soonest bring it to its death. But, should the Deer be cautious, and take another course, the hunters, mounted on swift horses, gallop through the woods to intercept it, guided by the sound of the horns and the cry of the dogs, and frequently succeed in shooting it. This sport is extremely agreeable, and proves successful on almost every occasion.

Hoping that this account will be sufficient to induce you, kind reader, to go *driving* in our western and southern woods, I now conclude my chapter on Deer Hunting by informing you that the species referred to above is the Virginia Deer, *Cervus virginianus*; and that, until I be able to present you with a full account of its habits and history, you may consult for information respecting it the excellent 'Fauna Americana' of my esteemed friend Dr. Harlan, of Philadelphia.

PIONEER TYPES

THE PRAIRIE

INTRODUCTION

THE close escape from death which Audubon relates in this incident occurred to him in 1812, for in that year he journeyed from Ste. Genevieve, in Missouri, to Henderson in Kentucky. It is impossible to say whether Audubon has in any way rounded out a good story here from an initial set of circumstances, or whether it all happened just as he relates. The essential facts were, however, quite probable. The frontier was then a lawless place, where men actually did murder in order to rob the lonely traveler of small valuables. Indeed Meriwether Lewis, the great explorer, met his death in just this way, when taking up a temporary shelter in a lonely cabin in eastern Tennessee. And similar atrocities are not unknown in our day.

ON MY RETURN from the Upper Mississippi I found myself obliged to cross one of the wide prairies which, in that portion of the United States, vary the appearance of the country. The weather was fine; all around me was as fresh and blooming as if it had just issued from the bosom of Nature. My knapsack, my gun, and my dog were all I had for baggage and company. But, although well moccasined, I moved slowly along, attracted by the brilliancy of the flowers, and the gambols of the fawns around their dams, to all appearance as thoughtless of danger as I felt myself.

My march was of long duration; I saw the sun sinking below the horizon long before I could perceive any appearance of woodland, and nothing in the shape of man had I met with that day. The track which I followed was only an old Indian trace, and as darkness overshadowed the prairie I felt some desire to reach at least a copse, in which I might lie down to rest. The Night Hawks were skimming over and around me, attracted by the buzzing wings of the beetles which form their food, and the distant howling of wolves gave me some hope that I should soon arrive at the skirts of some woodlands.

I did so, and almost at the same instant, a firelight attracting my eye, I moved towards it, full of confidence that it proceeded from the camp of some wandering Indians. I was mistaken: I discovered by its glare that it was from the hearth of a small log cabin, and that a tall figure passed and repassed between it and me, as if busily engaged in household arrangements.

I reached the spot, and presenting myself at the door, asked the tall figure, which proved to be a woman, if I might take shelter under her roof for the night. Her voice was gruff, and her attire negligently thrown about her. She answered in the affirmative. I walked in, took a wooden stool, and quietly seated myself by the fire. The next object that attracted my notice was a finely formed young Indian, resting his head between his hands, with his elbows on his knees. A long bow rested against the log wall near him, while a quantity of arrows and two or three Raccoon skins lay at his feet. He moved not; he apparently breathed not. Accustomed to the habits of Indians, and knowing that they pay little attention to the approach of civilized strangers (a circumstance which in some countries is considered as evincing the apathy of their character), I addressed him in French, a language not infrequently partially known to the people in that neighborhood. He raised his head, pointed to one of his eyes with his finger, and gave me a significant glance with the other. His face was covered with blood. The fact was that an hour before this, as he was in the act of discharging an arrow at a Raccoon in the top of a tree, the arrow had split upon the cord, and sprung back with such violence into his right eye as to destroy it forever.

Feeling hungry, I inquired what sort of fare I might expect. Such a thing as a bed was not to be seen, but many large untanned Bear and Buffalo hides lay piled in a corner. I drew a fine time-piece from my breast, and told the woman that it was late, and that I was fatigued.

[96]

The Prairie

She had espied my watch, the richness of which seemed to operate upon her feelings with electric quickness. She told me there was plenty of venison and jerked buffalo meat, and that on removing the ashes I should find a cake. But my watch had struck her fancy, and her curiosity had to be gratified by an immediate sight of it. I took off the gold chain that secured it, from around my neck, and presented it to her; she was all ecstasy, spoke of its beauty, asked me its value, and put the chain round her brawny neck, saying how happy the possession of such a watch would make her. Thoughtless, and as I fancied myself in so retired a spot secure, I paid little attention to her talk or her movements. I helped my dog to a good supper of venison, and was not long in satisfying the demands of my own appetite.

The Indian rose from his seat, as if in extreme suffering. He passed and repassed me several times, and once pinched me on the side so violently that the pain nearly brought forth an exclamation of anger. I looked at him. His eye met mine, but his look was so forbidding that it struck a chill into the more nervous part of my system. He again seated himself, drew his butcher-knife from its greasy scabbard, examined its edge, as I would do that of a razor suspected dull, replaced it, and again taking his tomahawk from his back, filled the pipe of it with tobacco, and sent me expressive glances, whenever our hostess chanced to have her back towards us.

Never until that moment had my senses been awakened to the danger which I now suspected to be about me. I returned glance for glance to my companion, and rested well assured that, whatever enemies I might have, he was not of their number.

I asked the woman for my watch, wound it up, and under pretence of wishing to see how the weather might probably be on the morrow, took up my gun, and walked out of the cabin. I slipped a ball into each barrel, scraped the edges of my flints, renewed the primings, and returning to the hut gave a favorable report of my observations. I took a few Bear skins, made a pallet of them, and calling my faithful dog to my side, lay down, with my gun close to my body, and in a few minutes was, to all appearance, fast asleep.

A short time had elapsed when some voices were heard, and from the corner of my eye I saw two athletic youths making their entrance, bearing a dead stag on a pole. They disposed of their burden, and asking for whiskey, helped themselves freely to it. Observing me and the wounded Indian, they asked who I was, and why the devil that

[97]

rascal (meaning the Indian, who, they knew, understood not a word of English) was in the house. The mother — for so she proved to be — bade them speak less loudly, made mention of my watch, and took them to a corner, where a conversation took place, the purport of which it required little shrewdness in me to guess. I tapped my dog gently. He moved his tail, and with indescribable pleasure I saw his fine eyes alternately fixed on me, and raised towards the trio in the corner. I felt that he perceived danger in my situation. The Indian exchanged a last glance with me.

The lads had eaten and drunk themselves into such a condition that I already looked upon them as *hors de combat*; and the frequent visits of the whiskey bottle to the ugly mouth of their dam, I hoped would soon reduce her to a like state. Judge of my astonishment, reader, when I saw this incarnate fiend take a large carving-knife, and go to the grindstone to whet its edge; I saw her pour the water on the turning machine, and watched her working away with the dangerous instrument, until the cold sweat covered every part of my body, in despite of my determination to defend myself to the last. Her task finished, she walked to her reeling sons, and said: 'There, that'll soon settle him! Boys, kill yon —— ——, and then for the watch.'

I turned, cocked my gun-locks silently, touched my faithful companion, and lay ready to start up and shoot the first who might attempt my life. The moment was fast approaching, and that night might have been my last in this world, had not Providence made preparations for my rescue. All was ready. The infernal hag was advancing slowly, probably contemplating the best way of despatching me, whilst her sons should be engaged with the Indian. I was several times on the eve of rising and shooting her on the spot; but she was not to be punished thus. The door was suddenly opened, and there entered two stout travellers, each with a long rifle on his shoulder. I bounced up on my feet, and making them most heartily welcome, told them how well it was for me that they should have arrived at that moment. The tale was told in a minute. The drunken sons were secured, and the woman, in spite of her defence and vociferations, shared the same fate. The Indian fairly danced with joy, and gave us to understand that, as he could not sleep for pain, he would watch over us. You may suppose we slept much less than we talked. The two strangers gave me an account of their once having been themselves in a somewhat similar situation. Day came, fair and rosy, and with it the punishment of our captives.

They were now quite sobered. Their feet were unbound, but their arms were still securely tied. We marched them into the woods off the road, and having used them as Regulators were wont to use such delinquents, we set fire to the cabin, gave all the skins and implements to the young Indian warrior, and proceeded, well pleased, towards the settlements.

During upwards of twenty-five years, when my wanderings extended to all parts of our country, this was the only time at which my life was in danger from my fellow-creatures. Indeed, so little risk do travellers run in the United States that no one born there ever dreams of any to be encountered on the road; and I can only account for this occurrence by supposing that the inhabitants of the cabin were not Americans.

Will you believe, good-natured reader, that not many miles from the place where this adventure happened, and where fifteen years ago, no habitation belonging to civilized man was expected, and very few ever seen, large roads are now laid out, cultivation has converted the woods into fertile fields, taverns have been erected, and much of what we Americans call comfort is to be met with? So fast does improvement proceed in our abundant and free country.

THE REGULATORS

INTRODUCTION

I<small>T IS</small> a characteristic of any frontier that there is often little law
upon it except force. And that the first to realize this fact is usually
the vicious element. The robber, the pirate, the gangster and murderer
understand no other answer; so that eventually the respectable portions of the community have to take justice into their own hands and,
by banding together, track down every wrongdoer and bring him to
punishment. The hardened criminal, contemptuous of gullible and
unarmed citizens, seems to have a great respect for the law when
administered by an infuriated community with weapons and with a
knowledge of the country equal to his own.

In Audubon's day, in the Ohio and Mississippi valleys, there oper-
ated a gang of thieves, raiders, river pirates, extortionists and murderers
whose rendezvous was Cave-in Rock, on the Illinois side of the Ohio.
Two of the leaders and most pitiless and desperate characters were
Samuel Mason and Micajah Harpe, and the terror of their names,
from about 1797 to 1803, spread consternation among the pioneers
and boatmen. To combat them and their followers, the honest settlers formed a band called the Regulators, and their justice was sum-
mary and gruesome. Audubon is recounting here the methods and the
history of the Regulators, as he knew it and had heard about it. In
particular he is relating the bad end of a bad man, the notorious Mason.
But Mason died in 1803, seven years before the ornithologist came to
Kentucky, and Audubon has confused the way in which he died with
the death of Micajah Harpe — or rather it is probably Audubon's

informants who confused the two. In later years Audubon would never have trusted hearsay, for he learned to confine himself to what he knew or had verified on high authority.

Samuel Mason, the subject of Audubon's memoir, was born about 1750 of, it is whispered, the distinguished Mason family of Virginia, but from childhood he seemed determined to go to the bad. Nevertheless he served with great courage and distinction in the Virginia militia during the Revolution. He married while still a boy, and seems to have supported his family by petty theft until driven out of Virginia to Tennessee. Here too he soon fell foul of the citizens, and disappeared permanently from respectable communities.

Mason now took to open outlawry around Russellville, Kentucky, and then moved his operations to the neighborhood of Henderson. The honest folk armed against him, and in 1797 he took to cover at Cave-in Rock. Suddenly he appeared upon the Natchez Trace, an immigrant trail, and also began to harass the lower Mississippi. In 1803 near New Madrid, Missouri, he and four sons and the wife and three children of one of the boys were all captured by the Spanish authorities on the west side of the river. The Spanish deeming, however, that his depredations had been committed east of the Mississippi, turned him over to the American authorities. But Mason overpowered his captors and the whole band escaped and scattered. The price on his head had now reached tempting heights, and in that same year his own son Setton, with 'Little' Harpe, Micajah's brother, waylaid him in Mississippi and shot him. Setton cut off his father's head and took it to the nearest town to claim the reward, but he and Harpe were recognized and arrested, and finally hanged at Greenville, Mississippi, in 1804.

Now although Audubon has not given the historical facts in the case of Mason, he has given the spirit of the times, the fear and hatred aroused by Mason, and the swift and awful vengeance of the Regulators. That he saw the methods of Regulators in action is borne out by his episode called 'The Prairie.' Audubon's document is historically valuable, in spite of its defects, for its insight into the operations of hand-made law on the old frontier. And when we consider some of the lamentable results of lawyers' law — the dispossessing of Daniel Boone from his lands by legal tricks, or the dismal coils of bankruptcy that entangled Audubon — we can feel much sympathy with the Regulators.

In fact if one will run an eye over American life and history from that day to the present, one finds that the case of the Regulators versus Mason and his gang is an early conflict in a long war in which the moral values have shifted from one side to the other, sometimes with little to choose between the two in bloodthirsty tendencies, but in which the same fundamental principle remains. This is a disposition of the 'respectable' citizenry to take the law into their own hands and to inflict a fearsome punishment lest the law may not punish the culprit enough, or may even let him escape. So we get the Vigilante committees of the disorderly days of California, the Ku Klux Klan of the Reconstruction, and less organized and nameless mobs that beat or hang anarchists, I.W.W. agitators, and communists.

On the other side we find lineal descendants of Mason in the guerillas of the Civil War, whose savage depredations are generally blamed upon the Northern armies, although a large part of the guerillas were Southerners in assumed uniforms, deserters or army evaders drawn from the worst elements in the South. The western underworld of the period 1850–1880 would seem to be Masons gone west, and the methods of combating them were similar to those of the Regulators. In modern times the closest parallel would be perhaps the kidnapers. It is doubtful if the city gangsters of the present, with their foreign make-up and their methodical foes, the 'G-men,' are closely analogous. Still, a rural Indiana community produced John Dillinger, and southern Illinois was not long ago terrorized by a gang that seems to echo the old pirates of Cave-in Rock.

THE POPULATION of many parts of America is derived from the refuse of every other country. I hope I shall elsewhere prove to you, kind reader, that even in this we have reason to feel a certain degree of pride, as we often see our worst denizens becoming gradually freed from error, and at length changing to useful and respectable citizens. The most depraved of these emigrants are forced to retreat farther and farther from the society of the virtuous, the restraints imposed by whom they find incompatible with their habits and the gratification of their unbridled passions. On the extreme verge of civilization, however, their evil propensities find more free scope, and the dread of punishments for their deeds, or the infliction of that punishment, are the only means that prove effectual in reforming them.

In those remote parts, no sooner is it discovered that an individual has conducted himself in a notoriously vicious manner, or has committed some outrage upon society, than a conclave of the honest citizens takes place, for the purpose of investigating the case, with a rigor without which no good result could be expected. These honest citizens, selected from among the most respectable persons in the district, and vested with power suited to the necessity of preserving order on the frontiers, are named Regulators. The accused person is arrested, his conduct laid open, and if he is found guilty of a first crime, he is warned to leave the country, and go farther from society, within an appointed time. Should the individual prove so callous as to disregard the sentence, and remain in the same neighborhood, to commit new crimes, then woe be to him; for the Regulators, after proving him guilty a second time, pass and execute a sentence which, if not enough to make him perish under the infliction, is at least forever impressed upon his memory. The punishment inflicted is usually a severe castigation, and the destruction by fire of his cabin. Sometimes, in cases of reiterated theft or murder, death is considered necessary; and, in some instances, delinquents of the worst species have been shot, after which their heads have been stuck on poles, to deter others from following their example. I shall give you an account of one of these desperadoes, as I received it from a person who had been instrumental in bringing him to punishment.

The name of Mason is still familiar to many of the navigators of the Lower Ohio and Mississippi. By dint of industry in bad deeds, he became a notorious horse-stealer, formed a line of worthless associates from the eastern part of Virginia (a State greatly celebrated for its fine breed of horses) to New Orleans, and had a settlement on Wolf Island, not far from the confluence of the Ohio and Mississippi, from which he issued to stop the flatboats, and rifle them of such provisions and other articles as he and his party needed. His depredations became the talk of the whole Western country; and to pass Wolf Island was not less to be dreaded than to anchor under the walls of Algiers. The horses, the negroes, and the cargoes, his gang carried off and sold. At last, a body of Regulators undertook, at great peril, and for the sake of the country, to bring the villain to punishment.

Mason was as cunning and watchful as he was active and daring.

Many of his haunts were successively found out and searched, but the numerous spies in his employ enabled him to escape in time. One day, however, as he was riding a beautiful horse in the woods he was met by one of the Regulators, who immediately recognized him, but passed him as if an utter stranger. Mason, not dreaming of danger, pursued his way leisurely, as if he had met no one. But he was dogged by the Regulator, and in such a manner as proved fatal to him. At dusk, Mason, having reached the lowest part of a ravine, no doubt well known to him, hoppled (tied together the fore-legs of) his stolen horse, to enable it to feed during the night without chance of straying far, and concealed himself in a hollow log to spend the night. The plan was good, but proved his ruin.

The Regulator, who knew every hill and hollow of the woods, marked the place and the log with the eye of an experienced hunter, and as he remarked that Mason was most efficiently armed, he galloped off to the nearest house where he knew he should find assistance. This was easily procured, and the party proceeded to the spot. Mason, on being attacked, defended himself with desperate valor; and as it proved impossible to secure him alive he was brought to the ground with a rifle ball. His head was cut off, and stuck on the end of a broken branch of a tree, by the nearest road to the place where the affray happened. The gang soon dispersed, in consequence of the loss of their leader, and this infliction of merited punishment proved beneficial in deterring others from following a similar predatory life.

The punishment by castigation is performed in the following manner. The individual convicted of an offence is led to some remote part of the woods, under the escort of some forty or fifty Regulators. When arrived at the chosen spot, the criminal is made fast to a tree, and a few of the Regulators remain with him, while the rest scour the forest to assure themselves that no strangers are within reach, after which they form an extensive ring, arranging themselves on their horses, well armed with rifles and pistols, at equal distances and in each other's sight. At a given signal that 'all's ready,' those about the culprit, having provided themselves with young twigs of hickory, administer the number of lashes prescribed by the sentence, untie the sufferer, and order him to leave the country immediately.

One of these castigations, which took place more within my personal knowledge, was performed on a fellow who was neither a thief nor a murderer, but who had misbehaved otherwise sufficiently to bring himself under the sentence with mitigation. He was taken to a place where nettles were known to grow in great luxuriance, completely stripped and so lashed with them that, although not materially hurt, he took it as a hint not to be neglected, left the country, and was never again heard of by any of the party concerned.

Probably at the moment when I am copying these notes respecting the early laws of our frontier people, few or no Regulating Parties exist, the terrible examples that were made having impressed upon the new settlers a salutary dread, which restrains them from the commission of flagrant crimes.

HOSPITALITY IN THE WOODS

INTRODUCTION

IN OCTOBER of 1823 Audubon and his son Victor, then fourteen years old and recently ill of yellow fever, came up the Mississippi on a steamboat from Louisiana as far as the mouth of the Ohio. Thence they were obliged to walk, the river being too low for navigation and no horses procurable, all the way to Louisville, Kentucky. Two companions accompanied them, a lazy drunk and a rather delicate gentleman, and together these four made their way through canebrakes and forests, sleeping and eating now well, now ill. The boy's strength was at first taxed to the limit; he often lay panting, or wept silently. Gradually, however, the child's youthful strength rallied itself, and at the end he was outdistancing everybody.

It was on this occasion that Audubon enjoyed what he considered (with some generosity of spirit) a case of typical frontier hospitality, and without having anything exciting or dramatic to tell, he makes a memorable idyll of it.

HOSPITALITY is a virtue the exercise of which, although always agreeable to the stranger, is not always duly appreciated. The traveller who has acquired celebrity is not unfrequently received with a species of hospitality which is much alloyed by the obvious attention of the host to his own interest; and the favor conferred upon the stranger

Hospitality in the Woods

must have less weight when it comes mingled with almost interminable questions as to his perilous adventures. Another receives hospitality at the hands of persons who, possessed of all the comforts of life, receive the way-worn wanderer with pomposity, lead him from one part of their spacious mansion to another, and bidding him good-night, leave him to amuse himself in his solitary apartment, because he is thought unfit to be presented to a party of friends. A third stumbles on a congenial spirit, who receives him with open arms, offers him servants, horses, perhaps even his purse, to enable him to pursue his journey, and parts from him with regret. In all these cases the traveller feels more or less under obligation, and is accordingly grateful. But, kind reader, the hospitality received from the inhabitant of the forest, who can offer only the shelter of his humble roof and the refreshment of his homely fare, remains more deeply impressed on the memory of the bewildered traveller than any other. This kind of hospitality I have myself frequently experienced in our woods, and now proceed to relate an instance of it.

I had walked several hundred miles, accompanied by my son, then a stripling, and, coming upon a clear stream, observed a house on the opposite shore. We crossed in a canoe, and finding that we had arrived at a tavern, determined upon spending the night there. As we were both greatly fatigued, I made an arrangement with our host to be conveyed in a light Jersey wagon a distance of a hundred miles, the period of our departure to be determined by the rising of the moon. Fair Cynthia, with her shorn beams, peeped over the forest about two hours before dawn, and our conductor, provided with a long twig of hickory, took his station in the fore-part of the wagon. Off we went at a round trot, dancing in the cart like peas in a sieve. The road, which was just wide enough to allow us to pass, was full of deep ruts, and covered here and there with trunks and stumps, over all which we were hurried. Our conductor, Mr. Flint, the landlord of the tavern, boasting of his perfect knowledge of the country, undertook to drive us by a short cut, and we willingly confided ourselves to his management. So we jogged along, now and then deviating to double the fallen timber. Day commenced with promise of fine weather, but several nights of white frost having occurred, a change was expected. To our sorrow, the change took place long before we got to the road again. The rain fell in torrents; the thunder bellowed; the lightning blazed. It was now evening, but the storm had brought perfect night, black and dismal. Our cart had no cover. Cold and wet, we sat silent and melancholy, with no better expectation than that of passing the night under the little shelter the cart could afford us.

To stop was considered worse than to proceed. So we gave the reins to the horses, with some faint hope that they would drag us out of our forlorn state. Of a sudden the steeds altered their course, and soon after we perceived the glimmer of faint light in the distance, and almost at the same moment heard the barking of dogs. Our horses stopped by a high fence and fell a-neighing, while I hallooed at such a rate that an answer was speedily obtained. The next moment a flaming pine torch crossed the gloom, and advanced to the spot where we stood. The negro boy who bore it, without waiting to question us, enjoined us to follow the fence, and said that Master had sent him to show the strangers to the house. We proceeded, much relieved, and soon reached the gate of a little yard, in which a small cabin was perceived.

A tall, fine-looking young man stood in the open door, and desired us get out of the cart and walk in. We did so, when the following conversation took place. 'A bad night this, strangers; how came you to be along the fence? You certainly must have lost your way, for there is no public road within twenty miles.' 'Ay,' answered Mr. Flint, 'sure enough we lost our way; but, thank God! we have got to a house; and thank *you* for your reception.' 'Reception!' replied the woodsman; 'no very great thing after all; you are all here safe, and that's enough. Eliza,' turning to his wife, 'see about some victuals for the strangers, and you, Jupiter,' addressing the negro lad, 'bring some wood and mend the fire. Eliza, call the boys up, and treat the strangers the best way you can. Come, gentlemen, pull off your wet clothes, and draw to the fire. Eliza, bring some socks and a shirt or two.'

For my part, kind reader, knowing my countrymen as I do, I was not much struck at all this; but my son, who had scarcely reached the age of thirteen, drew near to me, and observed how pleasant it was to have met with such good people. Mr. Flint bore a hand in getting his horses put under a shed. The young wife was already stirring with so much liveliness that to have doubted for a moment that all she did was a pleasure to her would have been impossible. Two negro lads made their appearance, looked at us for a moment, and going out, called the dogs. Soon after the cries of the poultry informed us that good cheer was at hand. Jupiter brought more wood, the blaze of which illumined the cottage. Mr. Flint and our host returned, and we

COMMON FLYING–SQUIRREL

'During the half hour before sunset nature seemed to be in a state of silence and repose. The birds had retired to the shelter of the forest. The night-hawk had already commenced his low evening flight, and here and there the common red bat was on the wing; still for some time not a Flying-Squirrel made its appearance. Suddenly, however, one emerged from its hole and ran up to the top of a tree; another soon followed, and ere long dozens came forth, and commenced their graceful flights from some upper branch to a lower bough. At times one would be seen darting from the topmost branches of a tall oak, and with wide-extended membranes and outspread tail gliding diagonally through the air, till it reached the foot of a tree about fifty yards off, when at the moment we expected to see it strike the earth, it suddenly turned upwards and alighted on the body of the tree. It would then run to the top and once more precipitate itself from the upper branches, and sail back again to the tree it had just left. Crowds of these little creatures joined in these sportive gambols; there could not have been less than two hundred. Scores of them would leave each tree at the same moment, and cross each other, gliding like spirits through the air, seeming to have no other object in view than to indulge a playful propensity. We watched and mused till the last shadows of day had disappeared, and darkness admonished us to leave the little triflers to their nocturnal enjoyments.' — *The Quadrupeds*, vol. 1, p. 218.

Drawn from Nature by J. Audubon, F.R.S.F.L.S.

Lith. Printed & Col⁴ by J. T. Bowen, Philad.ᵃ 1843.

PTEROMYS VOLUCELLA, GMEL.
COMMON FLYING SQUIRREL.
1.2 MALE. 3. 9. FEMALE. 4. YOUNG.

already began to feel the comforts of hospitality. The woodsman remarked that it was a pity we had not chanced to come that day three
weeks; 'for,' said he, 'it was our wedding-day, and father gave us a
good housewarming, and you might have fared better; but, however,
if you can eat bacon and eggs, and a broiled chicken, you shall have
that. I have no whiskey in the house, but father has some capital cider,
and I'll go over and bring a keg of it.' I asked how far off his father
lived. 'Only three miles, sir, and I'll be back before Eliza has cooked
your supper.' Off he went accordingly, and the next moment the
galloping of his horse was heard. The rain fell in torrents, and now I
also became struck with the kindness of our host.

To all appearance the united ages of the pair under whose roof
we had found shelter did not exceed two score. Their means seemed
barely sufficient to render them comfortable, but the generosity of
their young hearts had no limits. The cabin was new. The logs of
which it was formed were all of the tulip-tree, and were nicely pared.
Every part was beautifully clean. Even the coarse slabs of wood that
formed the floor looked as if newly washed and dried. Sundry gowns
and petticoats of substantial homespun hung from the logs that formed
one of the sides of the cabin, while the other was covered with articles
of male attire. A large spinning-wheel, with rolls of wool and cotton,
occupied one corner. In another was a small cupboard, containing
the little stock of new dishes, cups, plates, and tin pans. The table was
small also, but quite new, and as bright as polished walnut could be.
The only bed that I saw was of domestic manufacture, and the counter-
pane proved how expert the young wife was at spinning and weaving.
A fine rifle ornamented the chimney-piece. The fireplace was of such
dimensions that it looked as if it had been purposely constructed for
holding the numerous progeny expected to result from the happy union.

The black boy was engaged in grinding some coffee. Bread was prepared by the fair hands of the bride, and placed on a flat board in front
of the fire. The bacon and eggs already murmured and spluttered in
the frying-pan, and a pair of chickens puffed and swelled on a grid-
iron over the embers, in front of the hearth. The cloth was laid, and
everything arranged, when the clattering of hoofs announced the return
of the husband. In he came, bearing a two-gallon keg of cider. His
eyes sparkled with pleasure as he said, 'Only think, Eliza; father wanted
to rob us of the strangers, and was for coming here to ask them to his
own house, just as if we could not give them enough ourselves; but

here's the drink. Come, gentlemen, sit down and help yourselves.'
We did so, and I, to enjoy the repast, took a chair of the husband's
making, in preference to one of those called *Windsor*, of which there
were six in the cabin. This chair was bottomed with a piece of Deer's
skin tightly stretched, and afforded a very comfortable seat.

The wife now resumed her spinning, and the husband filled a jug
with the sparkling cider, and, seated by the blazing fire, was drying his
clothes. The happiness he enjoyed beamed from his eye, as at my
request he proceeded to give us an account of his affairs and prospects,
which he did in the following words: 'I shall be twenty-two next
Christmas-day,' said our host. 'My father came from Virginia when
young, and settled on the large tract of land where he yet lives, and
where with hard working he has done well. There were nine children
of us. Most of them are married and settled in the neighborhood. The
old man has divided his lands among some of us, and bought others
for the rest. The land where I am he gave me two years ago, and a
finer piece is not easily to be found. I have cleared a couple of fields,
and planted an orchard. Father gave me a stock of cattle, some hogs,
and four horses, with two negro boys. I camped here for most of the
time when clearing and planting; and when about to marry the young
woman you see at the wheel, father helped me in raising this hut.
My wife, as luck would have it, had a negro also, and we have begun
the world as well off as most folks, and, the Lord willing, may ——
But, gentlemen, you don't eat; do help yourselves. Eliza, maybe the
strangers would like some milk.' The wife stopped her work, and kindly
asked if we preferred sweet or sour milk; for you must know, reader,
that sour milk is by some of our farmers considered a treat. Both sorts
were produced, but, for my part, I chose to stick to the cider.

Supper over, we all neared the fire, and engaged in conversation.
At length our kind host addressed his wife as follows: 'Eliza, the gentlemen would like to lie down, I guess. What sort of bed can you fix for
them?' Eliza looked up with a smile, and said: 'Why, Willy, we will
divide the bedding, and arrange half on the floor, on which we can
sleep very well, and the gentlemen will have the best we can spare
them.' To this arrangement I immediately objected, and proposed
lying on a blanket by the fire; but neither Willy nor Eliza would listen.
So they arranged a part of their bedding on the floor, on which, after
some debate, we at length settled. The negroes were sent to their own
cabin, the young couple went to bed, and Mr. Flint lulled us all asleep

with a long story intended to show us how passing strange it was that he should have lost his way.

'Tired nature's sweet restorer, balmy sleep,' and so forth. But Aurora soon turned her off. Mr. Speed, our host, rose, went to the door, and returning assured us that the weather was too bad for us to attempt proceeding. I really believe he was heartily glad of it; but anxious to continue our journey, I desired Mr. Flint to see about his horses. Eliza by this time was up too, and I observed her whispering to her husband, when he immediately said aloud, 'To be sure, the gentlemen will eat breakfast before they go, and I will show them the way to the road.' Excuses were of no avail. Breakfast was prepared and eaten. The weather brightened a little, and by nine we were under way. Willy, on horseback, headed us. In a few hours our cart arrived at a road, by following which we at length got to the main one, and parted from our woodsman with the greater regret that he would accept nothing from any of us. On the contrary, telling Mr. Flint, with a smile, that he hoped he might some time again follow the longest track for a short cut, he bade us adieu, and trotted back to his fair Eliza and his happy home.

MEADVILLE

(*Audubon as Itinerant Artist*)

INTRODUCTION

As LITTLE as two years before Audubon's trip to Europe and success, we find him still unrecognized, a wanderer after birds, an itinerant artist, unknown both to the worlds of art and science, save at Philadelphia where he has just been received with unjust coldness. He has been touring up the Hudson and along the Mohawk, passing through Albany, Rochester, and Buffalo, and has now boarded a Lake Erie steamer. Here Audubon himself takes up the story.

Our hero's distinguished biographer, Mr. Herrick, has unearthed Meadville's own version of Audubon's stay. According to the facts dug out, the 'Hollander' whose portrait Audubon painted, and who procured him other sitters, was Mr. Augustus Colson, a merchant who lived at the tavern called the Torbett House. And among the sitters whom Colson secured was Miss Jennett Benedict, whose daughter, Mrs. Frederick A. Sterling of Cleveland, carefully preserved the portrait of her mother. It is signed 'J. J. Audubon — 1824,' and is reproduced in Mr. Herrick's book. When we consider that Audubon probably made this sketch in an hour or two, and that he received very likely not in excess of twenty-five dollars, and more probably five, we can only look with astonishment at so clear, so vigorous, so luminous a portrait. It may not be possible to judge of the likeness, and it may not be the work of a born portraitist, but it is the authentic touch of a great artist, albeit great in another kind of painting. Whether or not gaping

Meadville

Meadville recognized genius in the strange figure that this peripatetic artist cut, greatness passed that way, about September 1st, 1824, and long after, men were proud to say that they once had seen him to laugh at.

THE incidents that occur in the life of a student of nature are not all of the agreeable kind; in proof of which I shall present you, good reader, with an extract from one of my journals.

My money was one day stolen from me, by a person who perhaps imagined that to a naturalist it was of little importance. This happened on the shores of Upper Canada. The affair was as unexpected as it well could be, and as adroitly managed as if it had been planned and executed in Cheapside. To have repined when the thing could not be helped would certes not have been acting manfully. I therefore told my companion to keep a good heart, for I felt satisfied that Providence had some relief in store for us. The whole amount of cash left with two individuals fifteen hundred miles from home was just seven dollars and a half. Our passage across the lake had fortunately been paid for.

We embarked and soon got to the entrance of Presque Isle Harbor, but could not pass the bar, on account of a violent gale which came on as we approached it. The anchor was dropped, and we remained on board during the night, feeling at times very disagreeable, under the idea of having taken so little care of our money. How long we might have remained at anchor I cannot tell, had not that Providence on whom I have never ceased to rely come to our aid. Through some means to me quite unknown, Captain Judd, of the U.S. Navy, then probably commandant at Presque Isle, sent a gig with six men to our relief. It was on the 29th of August, 1824, and never shall I forget that morning. My drawings were put into the boat with the greatest care. We shifted into it, and seated ourselves according to directions politely given us. Our brave fellows pulled hard, and every moment brought us nearer to the American shore. I leaped upon it with elated heart. My drawings were safely landed, and for anything else I cared little at the moment. I searched in vain for the officer of our navy, to whom I still feel grateful, and gave one of our dollars to the sailors to drink the 'freedom of the waters'; after which we betook ourselves to a humble inn to procure bread and milk, and consider how we were to proceed.

Our plans were soon settled, for to proceed was decidedly the best. Our luggage was rather heavy, so we hired a cart to take it to Meadville, for which we offered five dollars. This sum was accepted, and we set off. The country through which we passed might have proved favorable to our pursuits, had it not rained nearly the whole day. At night we alighted and put up at a house belonging to our conductor's father. It was Sunday night. The good folks had not yet returned from a distant meeting-house, the grandmother of our driver being the only individual about the premises. We found her a cheerful dame, who bestirred herself as actively as age would permit, got up a blazing fire to dry our wet clothes, and put as much bread and milk on the table as might have sufficed for several besides ourselves.

Being fatigued by the jolting of the cart, we asked for a place in which to rest, and were shown into a room in which were several beds. We told the good woman that I should paint her portrait next morning for the sake of her children. My companion and myself were quickly in bed, and soon asleep, in which state we should probably have remained till morning, had we not been awakened by a light, which we found to be carried by three young damsels, who, having observed where we lay, blew it out, and got into a bed opposite to ours. As we had not spoken, it is probable the girls supposed us sound asleep, and we heard them say how delighted they would be to have their portraits taken, as well as that of their grandmother. My heart silently met their desire, and we fell asleep without further disturbance. In our backwoods it is frequently the case that one room suffices for all the members of a family.

Day dawned, and as we were dressing we discovered that we were alone in the apartment, the good country girls having dressed in silence, and left us before we had awakened. We joined the family and were kindly greeted. No sooner had I made known my intentions as to the portraits than the young folks disappeared, and soon after returned attired in their Sunday clothes. The black chalk was at work in a few minutes, to their great delight, and as the fumes of the breakfast that was meantime preparing reached my sensitive nose, I worked with redoubled ardor. The sketches were soon finished, and soon too was the breakfast over. I played a few airs on my flageolet, while our guide was putting the horses to the cart, and by ten o'clock we were once more under way towards Meadville. Never shall I forget Maxon Randell and his hospitable family. My companion was as pleased as myself, and as the weather was now beautiful we enjoyed our journey with all that happy thoughtlessness best suited to our character. The country now became covered with heavy timber, principally evergreens, the pines and the cucumber trees loaded with brilliant fruits, and the spruces throwing a shade over the land in good keeping for a mellow picture. The lateness of the crops was the only disagreeable circumstance that struck us; hay was yet standing, probably, however, a second crop; the peaches were quite small and green, and a few persons here and there, as we passed the different farms, were reaping oats. At length we came in sight of French Creek, and soon after reached Meadville. Here we paid the five dollars promised to our conductor, who instantly faced about, and applying the whip to his nags, bade us adieu, and set off.

We had now only one hundred and fifty cents. No time was to be lost. We put our baggage and ourselves under the roof of a tavern keeper known by the name of J. E. Smith, at the sign of the Traveller's Rest, and soon after took a walk to survey the little village that was to be laid under contribution for our further support. Its appearance was rather dull, but, thanks to God, I have never despaired while rambling thus for the sole purpose of admiring his grand and beautiful works. I had opened the case that contained my drawings, and putting my portfolio under my arm, and a few good credentials in my pocket, walked up Main Street, looking to the right and left, examining the different *heads* which occurred, until I fixed my eyes on a gentleman in a store who looked as if he might want a sketch. I begged him to allow me to sit down. This granted, I remained purposely silent until he very soon asked me what was '*in that portfolio.*' These three words sounded well, and without waiting another instant, I opened it to his view. This was a Hollander, who complimented me much on the execution of the drawings of birds and flowers in my portfolio. Showing him a sketch of the best friend I have in the world at present, I asked him if he would like one in the same style of himself. He not only answered in the affirmative, but assured me that he would exert himself in procuring as many more customers as he could. I thanked him, be assured, kind reader; and having fixed upon the next morning for drawing the sketch, I returned to the Traveller's Rest, with a hope that tomorrow might prove propitious. Supper was ready, and as in

America we generally have but one sort of *table d'hôte*, we sat down, when, every individual looking upon me as a missionary priest, on account of my hair, which in those days flowed loosely on my shoulders, I was asked to say grace, which I did with a fervent spirit.

Daylight returned. I visited the groves and woods around with my companion, returned, breakfasted, and went to the store, where, notwithstanding my ardent desire to begin my task, it was ten o'clock before the sitter was ready. But, reader, allow me to describe the *artist's room*. See me ascending a crazy flight of steps, from the back part of a store room into a large garret extending over the store and counting room, and mark me looking round to see how the light could be stopped from obtruding on me through no less than four windows facing each other at right angles. Then follow me scrutinizing the corners, and finding in one a cat nursing her young among a heap of rags intended for the paper mill. Two hogsheads filled with oats, a parcel of Dutch toys carelessly thrown on the floor, a large drum and a bassoon in another part, fur caps hanging along the wall, and the portable bed of the merchant's clerk swinging like a hammock near the centre, together with some rolls of sole leather, made up the picture. I saw all this at a glance, and closing the extra windows with blankets, I soon procured a *painter's light*.

A young gentleman sat to try my skill. I finished his phiz, which was approved of. The merchant then took the chair, and I had the good fortune to please him also. The room became crowded with the gentry of the village. Some laughed, while others expressed their wonder; but my work went on, notwithstanding the observations which were made. My sitter invited me to spend the evening with him, which I did, and joined him in some music on the flute and violin. I returned to my companion with great pleasure, and you may judge how much that pleasure was increased when I found that he also had made two sketches. Having written a page or two of our journals, we retired to rest.

The following day was spent much in the same manner. I felt highly gratified that from under my gray coat my talents had made their way, and I was pleased to discover that industry and moderate abilities prove at least as valuable as first-rate talents without the former of these qualities. We left Meadville on foot, having forwarded our baggage by wagon. Our hearts were light, our pockets replenished, and we walked in two days to Pittsburgh, as happy as circumstances permitted us to be.

THE RUNAWAY

INTRODUCTION

Every American knows, everyone in the English-speaking world has heard, of the agonizing plight of the negro slaves whose families were separated by sale. In many cases their owners were themselves deeply distressed, but, falling into debt and the legal maneuvers of creditors, they were frequently unable to prevent the heartless sale and separation of slave families. When Audubon wrote, slavery was still a flourishing institution and its evils were steadily increasing. Unwritten then were *Uncle Tom's Cabin*, *The Slave in the Dismal Swamp* and *Huckleberry Finn* with its touching picture of the runaway, 'Nigger Jim.' The incident Audubon relates here, which probably happened somewhere between 1821 and 1826, antedates them all.

A single defect marks this story, and that is the dignified and literary language used by the runaway slave. We do not know whether he spoke gumbo, that mixture of French, African, and English, which the Louisiana negroes commonly employed, or whether he merely spoke a negro dialect of American speech, but he almost certainly did not talk as Audubon makes him speak. This is due perhaps to Audubon's quite abandoning the attempt to render illiterate negro speech; more likely still it is due to the editing of his friend MacGillivray, who transposed all of Audubon's vivid and realistic colloquialisms into refined, early Victorian drawing-room conversation. To Englishmen, negro dialect is much more obscure than to Americans, and MacGillivray probably thought it necessary to transpose the whole diction in order to make the slave's meaning clear.

NEVER shall I forget the impression made on my mind by the *rencontre* which forms the subject of this article, and I even doubt if the relation of it will not excite in that of my reader emotions of varied character.

Late in the afternoon of one of those sultry days which render the atmosphere of the Louisiana swamps pregnant with baneful effluvia, I directed my course towards my distant home, laden with a pack, consisting of five or six Wood Ibises, and a heavy gun, the weight of which, even in those days, when my natural powers were unimpaired, prevented me from moving with much speed. Reaching the banks of a miry bayou, only a few yards in breadth, but of which I could not ascertain the depth, on account of the muddiness of its waters, I thought it might be dangerous to wade through it with my burden, for which reason, throwing to the opposite side each of my heavy birds in succession, together with my gun, powder-flask, and shot-bag, and drawing my hunting-knife from its scabbard, to defend myself, if need should be, against Alligators, I entered the water, followed by my faithful dog. As I advanced carefully, and slowly, 'Plato' swam around me, enjoying the refreshing influence of the liquid element that cooled his fatigued and heated frame. The water deepened, as did the mire of its bed; but with a stroke or two I gained the shore.

Scarcely had I stood erect on the opposite bank, when my dog ran to me, exhibiting marks of terror; his eyes seeming ready to burst from their sockets, and his mouth grinning with the expression of hatred, while his feelings found vent in a stifled growl. Thinking that all this was produced by the scent of a Wolf or Bear, I stooped to take up my gun, when a stentorian voice commanded me to 'stand still, or die!' Such a *qui vive* in these woods was as unexpected as it was rare. I instantly raised and cocked my gun; and although I did not yet perceive the individual who had thus issued so peremptory a mandate, I felt determined to combat with him for the free passage of the grounds. Presently a tall, firmly built negro emerged from the bushy underwood, where until that moment he must have been crouched, and in a louder voice repeated his injunction. Had I pressed a trigger, his life would have instantly terminated; but observing that the gun which he aimed at my breast, was a wretched, rusty piece, from which fire could not

The Runaway

readily be produced, I felt little fear, and therefore did not judge it necessary to proceed at once to extremities. I laid my gun at my side, tapped my dog quietly, and asked the man what he wanted.

My forbearance, and the stranger's long habit of submission, produced the most powerful effect on his mind. 'Master,' said he, 'I am a runaway; I might perhaps shoot you down; but God forbids it, for I feel just now as if I saw him ready to pass his judgment against me for such a foul deed, and I ask mercy at your hands. For God's sake, do not kill me, master!' 'And why,' answered I, 'have you left your quarters, where certainly you must have fared better than in these unwholesome swamps?' 'Master, my story is a short, but a sorrowful one. My camp is close by, and, as I know you cannot reach home this night, if you will follow me there, depend upon *my honor* you shall be safe until the morning, when I will carry your birds, if you choose, to the great road.'

The large, intelligent eyes of the negro, the complacency of his manners, and the tones of his voice, I thought invited me to venture; and as I felt that I was at least his equal, while moreover, I had my dog to second me, I answered that I would *follow him*. He observed the emphasis laid on the words, the meaning of which he seemed to understand so thoroughly that, turning to me, he said, 'There, master, take my butcher's knife, while I throw away the flint and priming from my gun!' Reader, I felt confounded: this was too much for me: I refused the knife, and told him to keep his piece ready, in case we might accidentally meet a Cougar or a Bear.

Generosity exists everywhere. The greatest monarch acknowledges its impulse, and all around him, from the lowliest menial to the proud nobles that encircle his throne, at times experience that overpowering sentiment. I offered to shake hands with the runaway. 'Master,' said he, 'I beg you thanks,' and with this he gave me a squeeze that alike impressed me with the goodness of his heart and his great physical strength. From that moment we proceeded through the woods together. My dog smelt at him several times, but as he heard me speak in my usual tone of voice, he soon left us and rambled around as long as my whistle was unused. As we proceeded, I observed that he was guiding me towards the setting of the sun, and quite contrary to my homeward course. I remarked this to him, when he with the greatest simplicity replied, 'Merely for our security.'

After trudging along for some distance, and crossing several bayous, at all of which he threw his gun and knife to the opposite bank, and stood still until I had got over, we came to the borders of an immense cane-brake, from which I had, on former occasions, driven and killed several Deer. We entered, as I had frequently done before, now erect, then on 'all fours.' He regularly led the way, divided here and there the tangled stalks, and, whenever we reached a fallen tree, assisted me in getting over it, with all possible care. I saw that he was a perfect Indian in his knowledge of the woods, for he kept a direct course as precisely as any 'Red-skin' I ever travelled with. All of a sudden he emitted a loud shriek, not unlike that of an Owl, which so surprised me, that I once more instantly levelled my gun. 'No harm, master, I only give notice to my wife and children I am coming.' A tremulous answer of the same nature gently echoed through the tree tops. The runaway's lips separated with an expression of gentleness and delight, when his beautiful set of ivory teeth seemed to smile through the dusk of evening that was thickening around us. 'Master,' said he, 'my wife, though black, is as beautiful to me as the President's wife is to him; she is my queen, and I look on our young ones as so many princes; but you shall see them all, for here they are, thank God.'

There, in the heart of the cane-brake, I found a regular camp. A small fire was lighted, and on its embers lay gridling some large slices of venison. A lad nine or ten years old was blowing the ashes from some fine sweet potatoes. Various articles of household furniture were carefully disposed around, and a large pallet of Bear and Deer skins, seemed to be the resting-place of the whole family. The wife raised not her eyes towards mine, and the little ones, three in number, retired into a corner, like so many discomfited Raccoons; but the Runaway, bold, and apparently happy, spoke to them in such cheering words, that at once one and all seemed to regard me as one sent by Providence to relieve them from all their troubles. My clothes were hung up by them to dry, and the negro asked if he might clean and grease my gun, which I permitted him to do, while the wife threw a large piece of Deer's flesh to my dog, which the children were already caressing.

Only think of my situation, reader! Here I was, ten miles at least from home, and four or five from the nearest plantation, in the camp of runaway slaves, and quite at their mercy. My eyes involuntarily followed their motions, but as I thought I perceived in them a strong desire to make me their confidant and friend, I gradually relinquished

AMERICAN CROSS FOX

'The specimen from which our drawing was made, was caught in a steel-trap by one of its fore-feet, not far from the falls of Niagara, and was purchased by J. W. Audubon of the proprietor of the "Museum" kept there to gratify the curiosity of the travellers who visit the great Cataract.' — *The Quadrupeds*, vol. 1, p. 51.

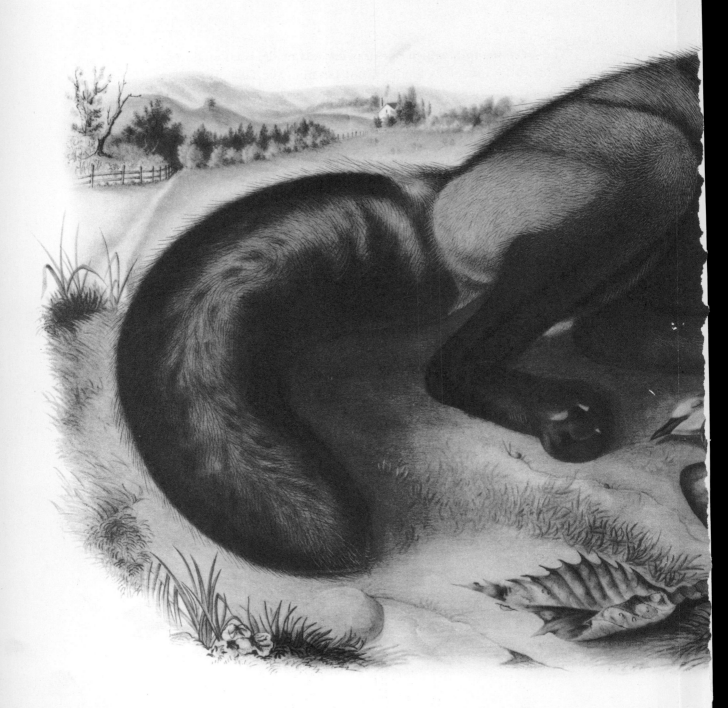

Drawn from Nature by J.J.Audubon, F.R.S.F.L.S.

CANIS (VULPES) F

VAR. DECU

AMERICAN CRO

MALE.

LVUS. DESMARET.

SATUS.

SS FOX.

Lith. Printed & Col.d by J.T.Bowen,Philad.a 1843.

The Runaway

all suspicions. The venison and potatoes looked quite tempting, and by this time I was in a condition to relish much less savory fare; so, on being humbly asked to divide the viands before us, I partook of as hearty a meal as I had ever done in my life.

Supper over, the fire was completely extinguished, and a small lighted pine-knot placed in a hollowed calabash. Seeing that both the husband and the wife were desirous of communicating something to me, I at once and fearlessly desired them to unburden their minds, when the Runaway told me a tale of which the following is the substance.

About eighteen months before, a planter, residing not very far off, having met with some losses, was obliged to expose his slaves at a public sale. The value of his negroes was well known, and on the appointed day the auctioneer laid them out in small lots, or offered them singly, in the manner which he judged most advantageous to their owner. The Runaway, who was well known as being the most valuable next to his wife, was put up by himself for sale, and brought an immoderate price. For his wife, who came next, and alone, eight hundred dollars were bidden and paid down. Then the children were exposed, and, on account of their breed, brought high prices. The rest of the slaves went off at rates corresponding to their qualifications.

The Runaway chanced to be bought by the overseer of the plantation; the wife was bought by an individual residing about a hundred miles off, and the children went to different places along the river. The heart of the husband and father failed him under this dire calamity. For a while he pined in sorrow under his new master; but having marked down in his memory the names of the different persons who had purchased each dear portion of his family, he feigned illness, if indeed, he whose affections had been so grievously blasted could be said to feign it, refrained from food for several days, and was little regarded by the overseer, who felt himself disappointed in what he had considered a bargain.

On a stormy night, when the elements raged with all the fury of a hurricane, the poor negro made his escape, and being well acquainted with all the neighboring swamps, at once made directly for the cane-brake in the centre of which I found his camp. A few nights afterwards he gained the abode of his wife, and the very next after their meeting, he led her away. The children, one after another, he succeeded in stealing, until at last the whole of the objects of his love were under his care.

To provide for five individuals was no easy task in those wilds, which after the first notice was given of the wonderful disappearance of this extraordinary family, were daily ransacked by armed planters. Necessity, it is said, will bring the Wolf from the forest. The Runaway seems to have well understood the maxim, for under the cover of night he approached his first master's plantation, where he had ever been treated with the greatest kindness. The house-servants knew him too well not to aid him to the best of their power, and at the approach of each morning he returned to his camp with an ample supply of provisions. One day, while in search of wild fruits, he found a Bear dead before the muzzle of a gun that had been set for the purpose. Both articles he carried to his home. His friends at the plantation managed to supply him with some ammunition, and on damp and cloudy days he first ventured to hunt around his camp. Possessed of courage and activity, he gradually became more careless, and rambled farther in search of game. It was on one of his excursions that I met him, and he assured me the noise which I made in passing the bayou had caused him to lose the chance of killing a fine Deer, 'although,' said he, 'my old musket misses fire sadly too often.'

The Runaways, after disclosing their secret to me, both rose from their seat, with eyes full of tears. 'Good master, for God's sake, do something for us and our children,' they sobbed forth with one accord. Their little ones lay sound asleep in the fearlessness of their innocence. Who could have heard such a tale without emotion? I promised them my most cordial assistance. They both sat up that night to watch my repose, and I slept close to their urchins, as if on a bed of the softest down.

Day broke so fair, so pure, and so gladdening that I told them such heavenly appearances were ominous of good, and that I scarcely doubted of obtaining their full pardon. I desired them to take their children with them, and promised to accompany them to the plantation of their first master. They gladly obeyed. My Ibises were hung round their camp, and, as a memento of my having been there, I notched several trees; after which I bade adieu, perhaps for the last time, to that cane-brake. We soon reached the plantation, the owner of which, with whom I was well acquainted, received me with all the generous kindness of a Louisiana planter. Ere an hour had elapsed, the Runaway and his family were looked upon as his own. He afterwards repurchased them from their owners, and treated them with his former kindness; so that they were rendered as happy as slaves generally are in that country, and continued to cherish that attachment to each other which had led to their adventures. Since this event happened, it has, I have been informed, become illegal to separate slave families without their consent.

THE SQUATTERS OF THE
MISSISSIPPI

INTRODUCTION

IF ANYBODY knew about the squatters of the Mississippi, it must have been Audubon. As he says, many foreigners or passing visitors have given their impressions, usually more or less unfavorable. Consult for instance *Martin Chuzzlewit* or Mrs. Trollope's *Domestic Manners of the Americans*. Consult indeed Audubon's own unflattering reflections upon the inhabitants of the Mississippi Valley, in many a passage of his journals of travel down the Ohio and the Mississippi. The second generation of the people he is here describing are to be found in *Huckleberry Finn*. So broad is the humor of these books that true though they may have been, in some ways, to the times, they are undoubtedly distorted pictures too.

In this sketch Audubon endeavors to do these people justice, and to write like a dispassionate historian. In that connection he does not fail to show that the agricultural settlers of Mississippi, Arkansas, Tennessee, and southern Missouri were on the whole not Creoles from Louisiana, or Ohio River settlers drifting south on the great tide, but Southerners from Virginia and points south, moving westward into virgin hunting grounds, onto richer, blacker soils, unexhausted by tobacco, cotton, rice and indigo. We hear so much of the westward course of New Englanders, New Yorkers, and Pennsylvanians into the Middle West and Northwest, that we are apt to forget that there was a corresponding movement from the Southeast into the Middle South and, finally, into the Southwest. It was slower, and there resulted, in the Middle South, no such phenomenally swift-sprung great cities; but it was sure and intensive. The culture that resulted was an agricultural one, not particularly urban. It gave rise to the small farm and the great plantation. And it was a civilization that arose under difficulties too often overlooked. Instead of winter pneumonia, there was autumnal malaria to dread (Audubon calls it ague), and instead of the drought of the prairies, there was the recurrent disaster of flood. In place of a bitter climate, the Mississippi settlers had an enervating one to contend with.

Audubon employs the word squatters, which is correct enough in the sense that these people often arrived and settled before the Government had defined the matter of ownership of public lands. But it is not to be assumed that he means shiftless and irresponsible nomads. These people had made the beginnings of a civilization when the Civil War burst upon them in its fury. No one, viewing its flowering, will deny that there were elements of beautiful cultivation in it, or that its manhood gave a stirring account of itself in battle.

ALTHOUGH every European traveller who has glided down the Mississippi, at the rate of ten miles an hour, has told his tale of the squatters, yet none has given any other account of them, than that they are 'a sallow, sickly looking sort of miserable beings,' living in swamps, and subsisting on pignuts, Indian-corn, and Bear's-flesh. It is obvious, however, that none but a person acquainted with their history, manners, and condition, can give any real information respecting them.

The individuals who become squatters, choose that sort of life of their own free will. They mostly remove from other parts of the United States, after finding that land has become too high in price, and they are persons who, having a family of strong and hardy children, are anxious to enable them to provide for themselves. They have heard from good authorities that the country extending along the great streams of the West, is of all parts of the Union, the richest in its soil, the growth of its timber, and the abundance of its game; that, besides, the Mississippi is the great road to and from all the markets in the world; and that every vessel borne by its waters affords to settlers some chance to selling their commodities, or of exchanging them for others. To these recommendations is added another, of even greater weight with persons of the above denomination, namely, the prospect of being able to settle on land, and perhaps to hold it for a number of years, without purchase, rent or tax of any kind. How many thousands of individuals in all parts of the globe would gladly try their fortune with such prospects, I leave to you, reader, to determine.

As I am not disposed too highly to color the picture which I am about to submit to your inspection, instead of pitching on individuals who have removed from our eastern boundaries, and of whom certainly there are a good number, I shall introduce to you the members of a family from Virginia, first giving you an idea of their condition in that country, previous to their migration to the west. The land which they and their ancestors have possessed for a hundred years, having been constantly forced to produce crops of one kind or another, is now completely worn out. It exhibits only a superficial layer of red clay, cut up by deep ravines, through which much of the soil has been conveyed to some more fortunate neighbor, residing in a yet rich and beautiful valley. Their strenuous efforts to render it productive have failed. They dispose of everything too cumbrous or expensive for them to remove, retaining only a few horses, a servant or two, and such implements of husbandry and other articles as may be necessary on their journey, or useful when they arrive at the spot of their choice.

I think I see them at this moment harnessing their horses, and attaching them to their wagons, which are already filled with bedding, provisions, and the younger children, while on their outside are fastened spinning-wheels and looms, and a bucket filled with tar and tallow swings between the hind wheels. Several axes are secured to the bolster, and the feeding-trough of the horses contains pots, kettles, and pans. The servant, now become a driver, rides the near saddled horse, the wife is mounted on another, the worthy husband shoulders his gun, and his sons, clad in plain substantial homespun, drive the cattle ahead, and lead the procession, followed by the hounds and other dogs. Their day's journey is short, and not agreeable; the cattle, stubborn or wild, frequently leave the road for the woods, giving the travellers much trouble; the harness of the horses here and there gives way, and needs immediate repair; a basket, which has accidentally dropped, must be gone after, for nothing that they have can be spared;

the roads are bad, and now and then all hands are called to push on the wagon, or prevent it from upsetting. Yet by sunset they have proceeded perhaps twenty miles. Rather fatigued, all assemble round the fire, which has been lighted, supper is prepared, and a camp being erected, there they pass the night.

Days and weeks, nay months, of unremitting toil, pass before they gain the end of their journey. They have crossed both the Carolinas, Georgia, and Alabama. They have been travelling from the beginning of May to that of September, and with heavy hearts they traverse the State of Mississippi. But now, arrived on the banks of the broad stream, they gaze in amazement on the dark deep woods around them. Boats of various kinds they see gliding downwards with the current, while others slowly ascend against it. A few inquiries are made at the nearest dwelling, and assisted by the inhabitants with their boats, and canoes, they at once cross the Mississippi, and select their place of habitation.

The exhalations arising from the swamps and morasses around them have a powerful effect on these new settlers, but all are intent on preparing for the winter. A small patch of ground is cleared by the axe and the fire, a temporary cabin is erected, to each of the cattle is attached a jingling bell before it is let loose into the neighboring cane-brake, and the horses remain about the house, where they find sufficient food at that season. The first trading-boat that stops at their landing, enables them to provide themselves with some flour, fish-hooks, and ammunition, as well as other commodities. The looms are mounted, the spinning-wheels soon furnish some yarn, and in a few weeks the family throw off their ragged clothes, and array themselves in suits adapted to the climate. The father and sons meanwhile have sown turnips and other vegetables; and from some Kentucky flatboat, a supply of live poultry has been procured.

October tinges the leaves of the forest, the morning dews are heavy, the days hot, the nights chill, and the unacclimated family in a few days are attacked with ague. The lingering disease almost prostrates their whole faculties, and one seeing them at such a period might well call them sallow and sickly. Fortunately the unhealthy season soon passes over, and the hoar-frosts make their appearance. Gradually each individual recovers strength. The largest ash-trees are felled; their trunks are cut, split, and corded in front of the building; a large fire is lighted at night on the edge of the waters, and soon a steamer calls to purchase the wood, and thus add to their comforts during the winter.

The first fruit of their industry imparts new courage to them; their exertions multiply, and when spring returns, the place has a cheerful look. Venison, Bear's-flesh, Wild Turkeys, Ducks and Geese, with now and then some fish, have served to keep up their strength, and now their enlarged field is planted with corn, potatoes, and pumpkins. Their stock of cattle, too, has augmented; the steamer, which now stops there as if by preference, buys a calf or a pig, together with the whole of their wood. Their store of provisions is renewed, and brighter rays of hope enliven their spirits.

Who is he of the settlers on the Mississippi that cannot realize some profit? Truly none who is industrious. When the autumnal months return, all are better prepared to encounter the ague which then prevails. Substantial food, suitable clothing, and abundant firing, repel its attacks; and before another twelvemonth has elapsed the family is naturalized. The sons have by this time discovered a swamp covered with excellent timber, and as they have seen many great rafts of saw logs, bound for the mills of New Orleans, floating past their dwelling, they resolve to try the success of a little enterprise. Their industry and prudence have already enhanced their credit. A few cross-saws are purchased, and some broad-wheeled 'carry-logs' are made by themselves. Log after log, is hauled to the bank of the river, and in a short time their first raft is made on the shore, and loaded with cord-wood. When the next freshet sets it afloat, it is secured by long grape-vines or cables, until the proper time being arrived, the husband and sons embark on it, and float down the mighty stream.

After encountering many difficulties, they arrive in safety at New Orleans, where they dispose of their stock, the money obtained for which may be said to be all profit, supply themselves with such articles as may add to their convenience or comfort, and with light hearts procure a passage on the upper deck of a steamer, at a very cheap rate, on account of the benefit of their labor in taking in wood or otherwise.

And now the vessel approaches their home. See the joyous mother and daughters as they stand on the bank! A store of vegetables lies around them, a large tub of fresh milk is at their feet, and in their hands are plates, filled with rolls of butter. As the steamer stops, three broad straw hats are waved from the upper deck, and soon husband and wife, brothers and sisters, are in each other's embrace. The boat carries off the provisions for which value has been left, and as the captain issues his orders for putting on the steam, the happy family enter their humble dwelling. The husband gives his bag of dollars to the wife, while the sons present some token of affection to the sisters. Surely, at such a moment, the squatters are richly repaid for all their labors.

Every successive year has increased their savings. They now possess a large stock of horses, cows, and hogs, with abundance of provisions, and domestic comfort of every kind. The daughters have been married to the sons of neighboring squatters, and have gained sisters to themselves by the marriage of their brothers. The government secures to the family the lands on which, twenty years before, they settled in poverty and sickness. Larger buildings are erected on piles, secure from the inundations; where a single cabin once stood, a neat village is now to be seen; warehouses, stores, and workshops increase the importance of the place. The squatters live respected, and in due time die regretted by all who knew them.

Thus are the vast frontiers of our country peopled, and thus does cultivation, year after year, extend over the western wilds. Time will no doubt be, when the great valley of the Mississippi, still covered with primeval forests interspersed with swamps, will smile with cornfields and orchards, while crowded cities will rise at intervals along its banks, and enlightened nations will rejoice in the bounties of Providence.

DEEP SOUTH

DOWN THE OHIO AND
MISSISSIPPI

INTRODUCTION

WE HAVE now reached the first of the regular day-to-day
journals which Audubon ever kept. It records his voyage down the
Ohio and Mississippi in 1821, in his own language, and in his own
whimsical spelling which is partly of a phonetic character, showing
us how Audubon spoke English ('feel' the air, for 'fill' the air). No
attempt has been made here, or in other cases where the original
manuscript was available, to improve or explain the vagaries of the
document just as it came from his pen. The italics accord with Audubon's unaccountable underscoring.

This journal, like the one that follows on his life in New Orleans, is
a remnant of what must have been extensive original documents.
Audubon's descendants, after editing and extracting all the materials
considered worth retaining or not too private to publish, destroyed
all in their possession. Fortunately a few escaped this lamentable
error in judgment, and were presented to Harvard College by Colonel
John E. Thayer in 1913. They were later (1929) printed in full by
the Club of Odd Volumes, Boston.

At the time, almost a hundred and twenty years ago, when Audubon
descended the Ohio and Mississippi, these two waterways were the
continuous highway of the America that lay west of the Appalachians.
Roads were poor and few, railroads non-existent. When any farmer,
hunter, or business man of Kentucky or Ohio, West Virginia or south-

ern Indiana or Illinois, wished to sell, he transported his wares upon the great river system. To embark for Europe, it was as practical to go to New Orleans then as to New York. The Ohio-Mississippi system was to the pioneers of what is now the Middle West and the Middle South, what the Nile was to the Egyptians. It was the cordon on which the towns were strung, the restorer of fertility to the lands, the abode of millions of waterfowl, the destroyer of levees and ravager of low-lying farms, and in its attendant marshes and ox-bow lakes bred the mosquitoes that brought malaria and yellow fever to the settlements strung out along it. As this shining flood was the guide of the hordes of migrating birds, so it was the path of the explorers, the lifeline of the settlers. It gave wealth and brought misery.

In Audubon's time, then, the rivers were crowded with crafts. The cheapest rafts lashed together, broadhorns, flatboats, keelboats, canoes, glittering swift steamboats — all these crowded the rivers. The floating world familiar to us from *Huckleberry Finn* and *Life on the Mississippi* was already in existence in Audubon's young days, decades earlier. In his time, the reader notes, there are still Indians abroad. This was that stirring and most passing moment in American history, when the African slave and the American savage just meet — the white of European origin lashing on the one, cheating and expelling the other. It was an era when deer still bounded in the flood plain woods, and children who slept on bearskin blankets and ate wild swans did not venture out at night for fear of cougars.

The purpose of Audubon's journey (and it was the first of the kind he made, after the momentous decision to portray all the birds of America) was to collect and draw ornithological specimens. He must let nothing escape him; his collections must not be merely ample; they must be complete. So we find him struggling over the identity of some birds which he cannot find in any book. He calls them 'black pelicans' and decides that they are somewhere near albatrosses; of course they are cormorants. He is eager to understand the perplexity of the two kinds of eagle; actually they are adult and young of the bald-headed eagle.

Two persons mentioned in this journal deserve comment. Nicholas Berthoud, whom he encounters in Natchez, is his brother-in-law, the husband of his wife's younger sister. The father of this Nicholas, the Marquis de Saint Pie, assumed the name Berthoud when he fled to America after the French Revolution; Madame Berthoud, when the

Down the Ohio and Mississippi

Marquise de Saint Pie, claimed to have been *dame d'honneur* to Marie Antoinette. The Berthouds had settled in Louisville, where Audubon and Lucy met them when they first came to that town. At all times, Nicholas was Audubon's staunch friend.

The other figure is Joseph Mason's, whom Audubon states to be eighteen years old, although subsequent research has shown that he was then only thirteen. (Born Cincinnati, 1807; died Brown County, Ohio, 1883.) Audubon had discovered him in Cincinnati and took him along as his assistant and companion, and the gifts, the industry, the obedience and loyalty of this boy are better than touching; they rise to genuine nobility. Jo shared his master's fortunes, and often literally starved with him, never forsaking him, never failing him. But most astonishing of all is the artistic gift of this lad. With his own hands he painted perhaps a hundred of the marvelous details of vegetation that illuminate the earlier *Birds of America*. In the technique of perspective and naturalism, Mason's flowers and fruits and leaves are just as bold and successful as Audubon's living birds. In coloration they are impeccably faithful. A botanist has no difficulty in identifying any of them at a glance, and with a wonderful feeling for wild life the boy has chosen in almost every case a native plant rather than the garden flowers and trees with which most artists are content.

I would call attention, for instance, to the pawpaws in Plate 2 (the yellow-billed cuckoos), with their dead-ripe fruits, the autumnal and tattered leaves flecked with a senescent fungus disease which can likewise be identified by anyone familiar with mycology. Hours and hours of labor did young Jo put into Plate 5, of the Canada warbler, with its magnolia in fruit, the scarlet seeds dangling from the cone by their extensile threads. See too the wonderful corn plant in Plate 7, being ravaged by grackles. Or the tulip tree in full flower in Plate 12 (Baltimore orioles), the Stewartia flowers in Plate 17 (mourning doves), where this child has equaled the work of Redouté, the prince of all rose painters. In my opinion no botanical illustration ever done in America has come up to Mason's.

Unfortunately in later years Audubon and Mason fell out, and I am afraid that Audubon was at least partly in the wrong. But no misunderstanding now mars their manly yet tender relationship, as they set off together upon the breast of '*la belle rivière*.'

Thursday — Ohio River Oct — 12th 1820   I left Cincinnati this afternoon at half past 4 o'clock, on Board of Mr. Jacob Aumack's flat Boat — bound to New Orleans — the feeling of a Husband and a Father, were My Lot when I kissed My Beloved Wife & Children with an expectation of being absent for Seven Months —

I took with me Joseph Mason a Young Man of about 18 years of age of good familly and naturally an aimiable Youth, he is intended to be a Companion, & a Friend; and if God will grant us a safe return to our famillies our Wishes will be congenial to our present feelings Leaving Home with a Determined Mind to fulfill our Object =

Without any Money My Talents are to be My Support and My enthusiasm my Guide in My Dificulties, the whole of which I am ready to exert to keep, and to surmount.

We only floated 14 Miles by the Break of the 13th of Octre the Day was fine, I prayed for the health of My family — prepared Our Guns and went on shore in Kentucky — Cap° Sam Cummings who left Cincinnati with an Intention of Noting the Channels of this River and the Mississipi accompanied us —

Sunday Oct. 15, 1820 — there was this morning as heavy a white frost as I Ever Saw, the Wind blew cold and heavy from the North Shott 2 *Tell Tale Godwits* — and chased a Deer in the River for some considerable time, but a Canoe with Two Indianna Men had the advantage of us and caught it as I rose to shoot it —

at 10 'oclock We were roused from sound sleep by the Boats having ran on Rocks — the hands had to go in the Watter to take them off, it was cold and Windy —

Tuesday Oct 17th 1820 The Turkeys extremely plenty and Crossing the River hourly from the North Side, great Number destroyed falling in the Stream from want of strength — the Partrige when Crossing also, and in fact, all the Game that Cannot propery be called Migratorius =

Thursday Oct.' — 19th 1820 Cap° Cummings Mr Aumack and Joseph after a Long Walk return to Dinner with only 7 Partridges and 1 Pheasant — Mr Shaw Shot 1 Pheasant — I finished my Drawing of the *Common Crow* and after Dinner Went a Shore with the Company — Killed 5 pheasants 14 Partridges 1 Squirel and 3 Turkeys, Shot *at once* by *Joseph* who was not a little proud when he heard 3 Chears given him from the Boats this was his first essay on Turkeys —

While absent the boats having put too to make Sweeps, a flock of Turkeys came among^t them and in tring to kill some with Aumack's pistols one was bustted and the other wounded Joseph's Scull pretty severely — saw an astonishing number of Gray Squirels — the Country being extremely hilly opposite *Wells Point* the hunting Was Laborious and fatiguing.

Wednesday Novemb' 1st 1820 Weather drizly and windy Landed a few hundred yards below *Evansville* in Indianna on a/c of M꞉ Aumack Who had some money to Collect — he brought on Board only a french Double Barrel Gun and a Gold Watch the man made for Sale —

Cap꞉ Cummings & Joseph parted in the Skiff for Henderson to Get *Dash* a slut I had Left in the Charge of M꞉ Brigs —

Thursday November 2nd, 1820 Cap꞉ Cummings Joseph & Dash arrived at one o'clock this morning having a severe rowing match of it We started about 5 and floated down slowly within 2 miles of Henderson when We experienced quite a *Gale* and Put to on the Indianna Shore opposite Henderson — The Wind Blew so violently that I could only make a very rough Drawing of that Place — I can scarcely Conceive that I staid there 8 Years and Passed them Comfortably for it undoubtedly is one the poorest Spots in the Western Country according to My present opinion =

So Warm to night that Bats are flying near the Boats — extremely anxious to be doing something in the Drawing Way —

Friday Novemb' 3rd, 1820 We left our harbour at day Break and passed Henderson about sun raise, I Looked on the Mill perhaps for the Last Time, and with thoughts that made my Blood almost Cold bid it an eternal farewell —

The *Indian Summer* that extraordinary Phenomenon of North America, is now in all its Splendor, the Blood Red Raising Sun — and the Constant *Smoky* atmosphere, is undoutedly not easily to be accounted for — it has been often supposed that the Indians, firing the Prairies of the West were the Cause, but since We have Left C. the Eastwardly Winds have prevailed without diminishing in any degree the Smoke — it is extremely bad to Most Eyes and particularly so to Mine —

Sunday November 5th, 1820 The Weather fair this morning, the Thermoter down at 30 — the sun rose beautifull and reflected through the Trees on the Placid Stream much like a Column of Lively fire — the frost was heavy on the decks and when the Sun Shun of it it Looked beautifull beyond expression —

We floated tolerably well the river being here contracted by Large Sand Barrs —

[137]

Gayly we were overtaken by a Skiff containing a Couple of Gentill Young Men, Bound to New Orleans they had Matrasses, Trunks, a Gun & Provisions —

Many Dears where Merely Gamboling on the Sand Barrs and excited us

as I promised You a Picture of the Caracters We have on Board of Both Boats I will attempt to Copy them. Could my Pen Act as a Black Chalk by the help of my fingers you might rely on the Exibition of the figures — Yet I undertake it with pleasure, knowing how sweet this May be to you & Myself some Years hence, while sitting together by the fireside Looking at Your Dear Mother reading to us —

being on Board of Boats Much in the situation of Passengers I am of Course Bound to give the preference to those who are termed Capitains and Mr Aumack is the First that I will bring to your attention —

You have seen him and of Course I have not much to say the acquaintance of Man When unconnected by Interest is *plain* easily *understood* & Seldom Deviates. —

he is a good Strong, Young Man, Generously Inclined rather Timorous on the River, Yet Brave and accustomed to hardships — he Commands the Boat where I am —

Mr Loveless is a good Natured, rough fellow brought up to Work without pride, rather anxious to Make Money — Playfull & fond of Jokes & Women —

Mr Shaw the owner of Most of the Cargo puts me in mind of some Jews, who are all Intent on their Interest & Wellfare; of a keen Visage & Manners; a Bostonian — Weak of Constitution but strong of Stomack — Would Live Well if at any one else' Expense. =

The Crew is Composed as follows

Ned Kelly a Wag of 21. Stout Well Made, handsome if Clean, possessed of Much Low Wit, produces Mirth to the Whole even in his Braggardism — Sings, dances and fiels always happy — he is Baltimorian —

2 Men from Pennsylvania although not brothers, are possessed of a great sameness of Caracters — these are *Anthony P. Bodley* & *Henry Sesler* — they Work Work Well, talk but little and are Carpenters by Trade.

The Last is Much Like the Last of every thing, the Worst Part — Joseph Seeg, Lazy, fond of Grog, says nothing because it cannot help himself, sleeps Sound, for he burns all his Cloths, while in the ashes

Cap^e Cummings Joseph & Myself form the Rear at Times and at

Down the Ohio and Mississippi

Times the Van — You have seen the Life and there Likeness could not give you a better Impression than that you have formed — We agree Well, and are Likely to agree Still —

Tuesday Novemb' 7th 1820 I felt very anxious during all the time of our stay to be off from this Place.

This Evening Ned Kelly & his Companion Joe Seeg having Drank rather freely of Grog, they had a Litle Scrape at the Expense of Mr Seeg's Eyes & Nose —

The People of Shawney Complaining of Sickness, the place improved but Litle

Thursday Novemb' 9th 1820 We Landed at Sun Set at the *Rockin Cave* [1] having Come only about 2 Miles —

The Tell Tales we eat to Day were very fat but very fishy — I eat the purple Grakle it tasted well —

Friday Novemb' 10th 1820 as soon as Day Light permitted me this morning — I Took Joseph on Shore and Lighted a good fire — took also My Drawing Book etc with a Skiff — the Morning pleasant and the Thermometer raised to 50° While I was taking My Sketch of the *Rockin Cave* Cap° Cummings took a Good Walk through the Woods — at 9 My Drawing was compleat — this Cave is one of the Curiosities that attract the attention of allmost every Traveler on the Ohio and thousands of Names & Dates ornament the sides & Cealing — there is a small upper room dificult of access imediatly above & through the Cealing of the Ground floord one, Large enough to Contain 4 or 5 persons when sitted on their hams — this place is said to have been for Many Years the *rendez Vous* of a noted Robber of the name of Mason [2] it is about 20 Miles below Shawaney town on the same side; had our Boats spent a Day there, I would have been pleased to take several Diferent Views of it — the Rocks are Blue Lime Stone containing in Many Parts Round Masses of a fine flinty appearance Darker than the Main Body —

Monday Novemb' 13th 1820 Saw a Bear on a Sand Barr, had a great run after it — to no purpose —

Joseph Made a *Faux Pas* this day — the Whole of our Folks not in the best humour — Killed 7 Partridges 1 G. Squirel & One Duck

Tuesday Novemb' 14th 1820 Drawing this Morning as soon as the Light would permit me — Started early —

We passed this Day *Fort Massacre* here the Ohio is Magnificent, the

---

[1] Audubon means to say Cave-in Rock.   [2] See "The Regulators."

river about one & ¼ mile Wide affords a view of 14 or 15 Miles, and this afternoon being Calm with one of those *Whimsical* sunsetts that only belong to America rendered the Scene extremely interesting.

Cap^e C. Brought an Oppossum, Dash after having broke I thought all its bones left it — it was thrown over Board as if dead, yet the moment he toucht the Watter he swam for the Boats — so tenacious of Life are these animals that it tooked a heavy blow of the Axe to finish him —

Thursday November 16th, 1820 We floated only about Two Miles & Landed at *America* — to sell some *Articles*; people very sickly, a miserable place altogether —

Friday November 17th 1820 We left early — I took the Skiff and Went to the Mouth of the Ohio, and round the point up the Misisipi —

Eleven Years ago on the 2 of January I ascended that Stream to St. Genevieve Ferdinand Rozier of *Nantes* my partner in a Large Keel Boat Loaded with Sundries to a Large Amount *our* property

The 10th of May 1819 I passed this place in an open Skiff Bound to New Orleans with two of My Slaves —

Now I enter it *poor* in fact *Destitute* of all things and reliing only on that providential Hope the Comforter of this Wearied Mind — in a flat Boat a Passenger —

The meeting of the Two Streams reminds me a little of the Gentle Youth who Comes in the World, spotles he presents himself, he is gradually drawn in to thousands of Dificulties that Makes him wish to keep apart, but at Last he is over done mixed, and lost in the Vortex —

The Beautifull & Transparent Watter of the Ohio when first entering the Misisipi is taken in small Drafts and Looks the More aquable to the Eye as it goes down surrounded by the Muddy Current, it keeps off as much as possible by running down on the Kentucky side for several miles but reduced to a narrow strip & is lost.

I saw here two Indians in a Canoe they spoke some French, had Bear traps, uncomonly clean kept, a few Venaison hams a gun and Looked so Independent, free & unconcerned with the World that I Gazed on them, admired their Spirits, & wished for their Condition = here the Traveller enters a New World, the current of the stream about 4 miles per hour, puts the steersman on the alert and awakes him to troubles and difficulties unknown on the Ohio, the Passenger feels a different atmosphere, a very diferent prospect — the Curling stream &

WHITE–HEADED EAGLE

(BALD EAGLE)

'*January 12 1821* Early this Morning I met an Italian painter at the Theatre. I . . . Shewed him the Drawing of the White Headed Eagle; he was much pleased, took me to his painting appartement at the Theatre, then to the Directors who very roughly offered me 100$ per Month to paint with Mons L'Italian.' — P. 162.

'The original of this admirable drawing had been shot at New Madrid, on the Ohio, on November 23, and Audubon, who immediately began to work on it, recorded his conviction that the White-headed or Bald Eagle and the "Brown Eagle," which he later called "The Bird of Washington," were two different species; he thought that the young of the former, which was also brown, was much smaller in size.' — *Audubon the Naturalist* by Francis Hobart Herrick, D. Appleton and Company, 1917, vol. 1, p. 310.

White-headed Eagle, Male

FALCO LEUCOCEPHALUS.

Fish Vulgo_Yellow mud Cat.

Engraved, Printed & Coloured by R. Havell & Son, London. _ 1828

its hue are the first objects — the caving in of the Banks and the Thick Set Growth of the Young Cotton Wood is the next = the Watter's dencity reduced the thermoter from 62 to 20 degrees = We Landed Very Early, Cap⁶ C & I Walked Through the Woods, and remark⁴ the Great Diference of Temperature so suddenly felt —

I bid my farewell to the Ohio at 2 o'clock P.M. and felt a fear gathering involuntarily, every moment draws me from all that is Dear to Me My Beloved Wife & Children —

The Boats separated on Entering the Mississipi, as being safer to navigate it singly — We felt the better for this and Hope good Cheer will revive again —

Sunday 19ᵗʰ November 1820 When We Left Cincinnati, we agreed to shave & Clean completely every Sunday = and often have been anxious to see the day come for certainly a shirt worn one week, hunting every day and sleeping in Buffalo robes at night soon becomes soiled and Desagreable.

Ivory Billed Wood Peckers are Now Plenty, Bears, Wolf, &c but the Country extremely Difficult of Access, the *caves* Extending in Many Places several Miles from the River —

On Sundays I look at My Drawings and particularly at that of My Beloved Wife — & like to spend about one hour in thoughts devoted to My family —

The Wild Geese here sits on the Banks Many feet above Watter and feed on the seeds of a small grape somewhat resembling *Fol Avoine* — but are extremely shy —

Monday 20ᵗʰ November 1820 The winds on this River are Contrary to our Wishes as that of an Ole Rich *Maid* to the wishes of a Lover of Wealth, We are anxious to Make progress on account of our Situation — but it is disposed off Diferently by a *Superior Power*

We Came but a few Miles and Landed about Noon in Such a Dreary place that Neither the Woods Nor the Stream would afford us any benefit — it rain⁴ in the evening —

Tuesday November 21ˢᵗ 1820 The Wind High all Day Landed at New Madrid at 3 o'clock P.M. —

This allmost deserted Village is one of the poorest that is seen on this River having a Name; the Country Back was represented to us as being good, but the Looks of the Inhabitants contradicted strongly their assertions — they are Clad in Bukskin pantaloons and a sort of Shirt of the same, this is seldom put aside unless so ragged or so

Blooded & Greased, that it will become disagreable even to the poor Wrecks that have it on —

The Indian is More decent, better off, and a thousand time more happy — here familly dicensions are at their Zenith, and to Kill a Neighbour is but More than a Kill Deer or a Racoon —

A M*rs* Maddis formerly the Lawfull Wife of M*r* Reignier of St. *Genevieve* resides and keeps a small store in Company with a French Gentleman. We where told that the Partnership was rendered agreable to both by a mutual wish of Nature — Went to this Lady's house who knew me first and exibited much of the french Manners

Felt dull, this evening for every object that brings *forward* the *Background* of My Life's Picture shew too often with poignancy the diference of situation —

All our Hands Playing Cards untill bed Tim about 9. oclock == The *Swamp Sparrows* and Snow Birds are plenty in the High Dry Grass that Lines the Banks of this River, but the Woods have Nothing in More than the *Pait Pait Pait* of the Monogamous — Wood Peckers —

Friday November 24th 1820 the Woods here are so Dreadfully tangled with *Bull rushes*, Green Briars and Canes that the Travelling through them is extremely Irksome ==

Immediately below us is a family of Three people in Two Skiffs a Woman & 2 men; they are Too Lazy to Make themselves Comfortable, and Lie on the Damp Earth, near the Edge of the Watter, have *Racoons* to Eat and Muddy Watter to help that food down, are from the Mouth of Cumberland and moving to a Worst Part of the Worst Without Doubt —

Sunday November 26th 1820 Drawed all day, floated 18 Miles — the family in the Skiffs came on Board this Morning. Nearly frozen, the Thermometer down at 22 — the ground very hard, and my being without a Shirt — Made Me feel rather unpleasant.

the Woman of the Skiffs Mending My Good Brown Breeches —

to Look on those people, and consider cooly their Condition, then; compare it to mine; they certainly are more Miserable to Common Eyes — but, it is all a Mistaken Idea, for poverty & Independance are the only friend that will travel together through this World.

Monday November 27th 1820 We are all unwell having eat too freely of the Buck.

While Looking at My Beloved Wife's Likeness this day I thought it was altered and Looked sorrowfull, it produced an Immediate sensation of Dread of her being in Want — yet I cannot hear from her for Weeks to Come — but Hope she and our Children are Well —

Tuesday November 28ᵗʰ 1820 We moved from our Landing of Last Night and only crossed the River for the rain Lowered the *Smoake* so Much that it was impossible to see, beyond 20 or 30 Yards; played great deal on the flutes, Looked at My Drawings, read as Much as I Could and yet found the day very Long and heavy for Although I am Naturally of light spirits and have often tried to Keep these good, when off from my Home, I have often dull Moments of Anguish — the rain abated for a few Minutes. Capᵉ C. Joseph & I took a Walk to a Sand Barr Where Joseph Killed a Large blue Crane, unfortunately a Young one —

Wednesday November 29ᵗʰ 1820 We are Landed at the foot of N° 35 a few miles above what the Navigators call the Devil's Raceground — but the whole of the Mississipi being so much of the same nature, it feels quite immatereal to follow the Devil's tracks any where along its Muddy Course —

Thursday Novembʳ 30ᵗʰ 1820 We found the race path of the Devil well cleared and beaten, and went through it with great Ease, Many places on this River are rendered More terrible in Idea by their Extraordinary Names than real dificulties —

We run a Race with Mʳ Lovelace's Boat of several miles that was well nigh terminating in a dispute — it reminded me of Gamblers that although playing for Nothing are allways grieved by Lossing —

We came 25 Miles and Landed a little below the Twelve Outlets, passed the third Chicasaw Bluffs, Some Men came on Board Mʳ L. Boat who said had Killed Three Bears a few days' before — saw a few Indians at a Small Encampment — this morning I remarked Two Flocks of *American Teals* flying up the River; the Parokeets Numerous in the Woods — a Large flock of Sand Hill Cranes Sailed over us for some time, sounding & Elevating themselves to a Considerable Hight took a southwardly course —

Friday December 1ˢᵗ 1820 Saw Early to day several Hundreds of Gull, playing over a Large Barr — When We attempted to Close on them, they rose high and off South — 4 White headed Eagles where at the same time regalling themselves on the Carcass of a Deer — The sworms of Grakles that are passing us is astonishing — the Purple Finches also very Numerous saw several hundreds in one flock — Where the Weather is Intensely Cold, scarcely a Fowl is to be seen

along the Banks, the ponds offering themselves at that time food &
Shelter Passed a Large Settlement of Wood Cutters —

We are Landed immediately at the foot of Old *Fort Pickering*. We
Walked up to it through a very narrow crooked path, and found in a
very decayed situation; the Position a Beautifull one the Land Rich
about it — and were told that the Spaniards own it it was an agreable
spot to Live at — about 2 Miles above this, the Mouth of Wolf river
came in from the East, and is the Landing place of a Town Called
Memphis = have runned 24 miles —

at the Watter Edge (then about midle Stage) there is a Bed of Coals
running Orisontally about 2 feet Deep above the surface — this and
the Eligeability of the Situation May become Valuable —

Sunday December 3ᵈ 1820 Three Keel Boats passed us about 2 o'clock
P.M. — they had left the Falls of Ohio 3 weeks ago — Left our Harbour
and floated about 4 Miles to the foot of Buck Island — here I saw with
the setting sun hundreds of Malards travelling *South* and the *Finest*
rainbow I ever beheld, the Clouds were also beautifull apposite it =
Looked at my Beloved Wife's Likeness Shaved and Cleaned One of the
few enjoyments Flat Boats Can afford — the Goose we eat at Dinner
extremely fishy.

Joseph who now is obliged to officiate as Cook does not appear to
relish the thing — the more I see Capᵉ C the more I Like him = Wish
that we could say the same of all the World —

Monday December 4th 1820 We had a dreadfull night of Wind, the
hands obliged to move the boats. I did not sleep, the Knocking of the
Boats against the Sand Barr very desagreable — This Morning the
Wind still blowing hard.

Tuesday December 5th 1820 Saw Several hundred of those Black Birds
yet unknown to me that I denominate *Black Pelicans* flying South forming a very obtuse Angle, without uttering any Noise — have some
Hopes therefore to see some of them on the Watters of Red River or
Washita — Sand Hill Cranes were also fling and We saw More Geese
than usual — Joseph Killed 4 American Teals — those fly up stream —
saw 3 Swans — While Geese are flying in a Travelling order the Young
or Smallest are about the center of the *Lines* and the Larger Gander
Lead the Van, the Oldest Goose Drives the Rear — the Weather
beautifull but cold, and No Doubt that the Frogs that Wistled so
merily Yesterday are well buried in the Mud this Morning —

Thursday December 7th 1820 At Day Break the Wind stiff a head, a

Couple of Light Showers Lulled it, and we put off — Mr Aumack Winged a *White headed Eagle,* brought it a live on board, the Noble Fellow Looked at his Ennemies with a Contemptible Eye. I tied a String on one of its Legs this Made him Jump over Board. My Surprise at Seeing it Swim well Was very great, it used its Wings with great Effect and Would have Made the Shore distant there about 200 *yds* Dragging a Pole Weighing at Least 15*lbs* — Joseph went after it with a Skiff, the Eagle Defended itself — I am glad to find that its Eyes were Coresponding with My Drawing — this Specimen rather less than the one I draw — the femelle hovered over us and shrieked for some time, exibiting the *true sorrow* of the *Constant Mate* — Prepared a Bed for My Slut *Dash* expecting her to be delivered from her Burthen every Day —

Our Eagle Eat of Fish freely about one hour after we had him, by fixing a piece on a stick and puting it to its Mouth — however while I was friendly Indian toward it it Lanced one of its feet and caught hold of My right thum, made it feel very sore —

Sunday 10th December 1820 We floated down to the *Caledonian point* or Petite Landing about 4 Mile above the *real* mouth of *White River*

here it was Concluded that Mr Aumack should *walk* to the old *Post of Arkansas* of course I & Joseph prepared and having made Enquiries concerning the road we determined to go by Watter to the mouth of the *Cut off* and then walk the remainder; Anthony joined us, and the Skiff doubled oared was taken; We left at 10 o'clock with Light hearts, Small Bottle of Whiskey a few Biscuits, and the determination of Reaching the Post that Night —

At the Entrance of White River we discovered that that stream Was full and Run Violently, the Watter a Dull Red Clay Color; We soon found ourselves forced to Land to Make a Natural Cordel of several *Grape Vines* and pull up by it — the distance to the Cutt off is Seven Miles that appeared at Least 10 to us: here We Met 2 Canoes of Indians from the *Osage Nation,* Landed our Skiff on the opposite side of White River Which we here found a *beautifull Clear Stream* and Backed by the Watters of Arkansas running through the Cut off; We Walked through a *Narrow Path* often so thickly beset with green Briars that We Would be forced to give back and go round — this followed through *Cypress Swamps* and round *Pounds* and Cane Breaks untill We reached the first Settlement owned by a Frenchman Called Monsr Duval. this friendly Man about going to bed offered us his assitance put on shoes

& clothing and Lead us 7 Miles through Mud & Watter to the Post; and at 9 o'clock P. M. We Entered the Only Tavern in the Country — *Wearied*, Muddy, Wet & hungry — the Supper Was soon calld for, and soon served, and to see 4 Wolfs taring an old Carcass would not give you a bad Idea of our Manners while helping *Ourselves* the *Bright Staring Eyes* of the Land Ladies Notwithstanding

however I found Mrs Montgomery a handsome Woman of good Manners and rather superior to those in her rank of Life — to Bed and to sleep sound was the next Wish for 32 Miles in such a Country May be Calculated as a full dose for any *Pedestrian per day* — Led into a Large Building that formerly perhaps saw the great *Concils of Spanish Dons* we saw 3 Beds containing 5 men, Yet, all was arrangd in a few moments and as the Breaches were Coming off our Legs, Mr Aumack & Anthony slided by into one and Joseph & myself into Another, to force Acquaintance with the strangers being of course necessary a Conversation ensued that Lulled Me a Sleep, and Nothing but the Want of *Blankets* Kept Me. from Resting Well, for I soon found a Place between the *Tugs* that Supported about 10 lbs of Wild Turkey Feathers to save (?), My roundest Parts from the Sharp Edges of An Homespun Bedstead —

The Morning broke and with it, Mirth *all about us*, the *Cardinals*, the Iowa Buntings, the Meadow Larks and Many Spcies of Sparrows, chearing the approach of a Benevolent sun Shining day — dressed and about to take a View of *all things* in this Place, Met a Mr *Thomas* known formerly when in the Paragon Steam Boat — he introduced Me generally to the Medley Circle, around, and from thence took Me to a Keel Boat to receive the Information I Wanted about the Upper Countries through Which this Noble Stream Meanders — think of My Surprise at seeing here a Man who 13 years ago gave me Letters of Introduction at Pittsburgh (Penn) for Men in Kentucky — this Was Mr. *Barbour* the former Partner of Cromwell — he Met Me with great Cordiality, told me of the absence of the *Governor*, the Indian agent and also that the Osage Missionaries had proceeded about 150 miles up to a Place called the Rocky Point.

disapointed to the utmost in Not Meeting those who I supposed Would of Course give me the best Information I requested of Mr Thomas to give the Governor My Letters and beg of him to Write Me a few Lines at New Orleans to the Care of Governor Robertson — Mr Barbour told Me that he had for Several years past gone up to the

Down the Ohio and Mississippi

Osage Nation about 900 Miles and that his Last Voyage he fell in with *Nutall* the *Botanist* and had him on board for 4 Months — that Many species of *Birds* were in that Country unknown in this and that the Navigation Was an agreable One, at the same time that it was rendered profitable by the enormous profits derived from the Trade with the Indians, whom he represented as friendly and Honoruble in all there dealings — that he would be extremely Happy of My Company and that of My Companions and that if I did not go with him at present that he Hoped I would Meet him when coming down the Arkansas Next Spring or Summer for he is about 6 Months employd each Voyage —

The Post of Arkansas is Now a poor, Nearly deserted Village, it flourished in the time that the Spaniards & French kept it, and One 100 years passed it could have been called and agreable Small Town — at present, the decripid Visages of the Worn out Indian Traders and a few American famillies are all that gives it Life, the Natural situation is a handsome One, on a high Bank formerly the Edge of a *Prairie*, but rendered extremely sickly by the Back Neighborhood of Many Overflowing Lakes & Swamps. —

I was assured that only Two frosts had been felt here this Season and that the Ice in the River never Stopped the Navigation —

the Town now Prospering at *Point Rock* is high healthy and in the Center of a Rich tract of Wood & Prairie Lands — and probably may flourish — the *Arkansas River* flows a Thick Current of red Clay & Sand, and if not for its coloring would have much of the appearance of the Mississippi — Cotton is raised here With some advantage — Corn grows Well, game & Fish are plenty —

I here feel Inclined to tell you that an oportunit of Good; Fresh Flour Whiskey, Candles, Cheese, Apples, Porter, Cider, Butter Onions, Tow Linen and Blankets would meet with advantageous Sales during Winter, accompanied by *Powder Lead*, *Flint*, Butchers Knives, Rifles, and *blue Shrouds* for the Indians.

After Breakfast We Left the Post of Arkansas with a Wish to see the Country above, and so *Strong* is My Anthusiasm to Enlarge the Ornithological Knowledge of My Country that I felt as if I wish Myself *Rich again* and thereby able to Leave My familly for a Couple of Years — We travelled fast — reached the Cutt off and Landd our Skiff. The Indians still at their Canoes, We Hailed, and gave them a Drachem of Whiskey, and as they could not speak either french or English, I

Drew a *Deer* with a stroke across its hind parts, and thereby Made them Know our Wants of Venaison hams —

they brought 2 We gave them 50^{cts} and a Couple Loads of Gun Powder to each, brought our smiles, and a Cordial Shaking of Hands — a Squaw with them a *Handsome Woman* waded to us as Well as the Men and drank freely — Whenever I meet *Indians* I feel the greatness of our Creator in all its Splendor, for there I see the Man Naked from his Hand and yet free from Acquired Sorrow =

before I leave the Trip to the *Arkansas Post* I think I will give you More of it — We saw there a *Velocipede* Judge how fast the Arts & Sciences Improved in this Southwestern Country.

Wednesday Decemb^r 13th 1820 A Beautifull day, Walked up the Arkansas in Search of a Lake but the Cane so thick that we give it up —

about One Mile below the Mouth of Arkansas in a Thick patch of *Cane* are Two *Women* the remainder of a party of Wandering Vagarounds that about 2 years ago Left some part of the Eastern State to proceed to the *Promised Land* — these Two Wretches, Never Wash Comb or Scarcely clad themselves, and subsist from the Scant generosity of the Neighbours — Now and then doing a little Sawing and Washing —

Thursday Decemb^r 14th 1820 After Long consideration, our Gentlemen determined to do *Nothing*, and We *Cutt Loose* about 10 this Morning, the Weather quite Warm, Distant frequent Clapps of Thunder announcing a change — it soon begain to Rain, the Fog raised and We Landed again about 2 o'clock — saw here 5 Ivory Bill Wood Peckers feeding on the Berries of Some Creeper they were gentle — Keeping a Constant Cry of *Pet Pet Pet* —

Sunday December 17th 1820 Landed at *Pointe Chico* a few Miles before this the *Spanish Beard* is seen — Pointe Chico is a handsome spot on this river that never overflows — and answers well for the Growth of Cotton Corn &^{c} — Peach & Aple Trees flourish well here, but Sugar will not grow —

Wednesday Decemb^r 20th 1820 Cap^e Cummings Shot at an *Ivory Billed Wood Pecker Picus Principallis* broke his Wing and When he Went to take it up it Jump up and claimed a tree, as fast as a Squirel to the Very Top, he gave it up having but a few Loads of Shot — Joseph Came and saw it — Shot at it and brought him down —

We Boiled 10 Parokeets to night for Dash who has had 10 Welps — purposely to try the effect of the Poisoning effect of their hearts on animals. Yesterday We Were told that 7 Cats had been Killed Last

Down the Ohio and Mississippi

Summer by Eating as Many Parokeets — Killed Two Geese — Several Boats Landed along us to night

Friday December 22ᵈ 1820 Started at 5 o'clock this Morning, and certainly deserves Noting — after breakfast Joseph & I push off as usual in the Skiff in which we remained untill near Sun Down — Saw *Three Black Hawks*, Shot at this Twice, but these Birds are So Shy that I dared not advance nearer than Rifle Shot and Missed them — Went to a house, to Warm our fingers, the wind blowing rather Sharp this morning — found a Handsome familly of Young Brats who as well as their Mamma Looked Clean and healthy — here We saw the *Pameta Plants* along the Fences —

in the afternoon the sun Shown Warm, the Geese where in Thousands on the Willow Bar, fighting and Mating.

a little before Sun down a Steam Boat Called the *Mars* passed us, a poor running Machine — apparently an Old Barge —

Saturday Decembᵉ 23ᵈ 1820 the Moon shining beautifully Clear, the Weather, calm a heavy White frost — started at 3 o'clock —

as soon as the fog disapeared, J. & I putt off for the Mouth of the *Yazoo River*, seeing some Geese Made for them and Killed One — in the Mouth of that River I perceived a Large flock of My unknown *Blackbirds* that I suppose Brown Pelicans — Landed below them, and after crawling on My belly for about 300 yards I arrived within about 45 yards I fired at 3 that were perched Close together on a dead Stick about 7 feet above the Watter, at my shot they all fell as so many stones. I expected them to be all dead but to My surprise, those and about 20 swimming under them had dove, they soon rose and took Wing after running on the Watter about 50 Yᵈˢ at the exception of the One I had taken aim on — it would not raise, the Skiff brought up We rowed after it, diving below us up the Yazoo Nearly one Mile, Yet I could not give it up, it became Warier, & remained Less under Watter and Nearer We approach when at Last Joseph Shot at its *head* & Neck (the only part in view Looking much Like a Snake) and Keeled it over — I took it up with great pleasure and anxiety — but I could Not ascertain its Genus — for I could not Make it an *Albatros* the only Bird I can discover any relation to —

We had to exert ourselves to reach our Boats — this done, I began Drawing — We passed to day the *Walnut Hills* a handsome situation on the Mississipi covered with Cotton plantations —

The *Yazoo River* flowed a Beautifull Stream of transparent Watter,

Covered with 1000^{ds} of Geese & Ducks and filled With Fish — the Entrance Low Willows & Cotton Trees — We run to day 49 Miles — the Weather rather too Warm —

Monday December 25th 1820 Christmas day We are Now Landed about 15 Miles above Natchez, and if No head Wind takes place Must reach that City To morrow

I Hope that My Familly wishes me as good a Christmas as I do them — Could I have spent it with My Beloved Wife & Children, the exchange of situation would have been most Agreable — I hope to have some tidings of them Tomorrow = the Shores are now Lined with Green Willows the Weather much Like May — at *Henderson* — The Thermometer is allmost every day from 60 to 65 —

Tuesday Decemb^r 26th 1820 Beautifull Morning, Light frost — I began my drawing as soon as I could see — drawing all day —

We saw to day probably *Millions* of those *Irish Geese* or Cormorants, flying Southwest — they flew in Single Lines for several Hours extremely high —

At half Past 11 o'clock The Boats Landed at the Natchez Bluffs amongst about 100 More, several S.B.^{ts} were also at this place = the Carrion Crows first attracted my Attention, hundreds of them flying constantly Low over the Shores and alighting on the Houses —

So Busy I have been all day drawing, that I did not even go to the Shore — a Little before Dusk I saw from our Boat Roof the Magnolia & Pines that ornement the Hills above this Place —

As we approach Natchez I remarked in several places — Saw Mills, placed over ditches cut from the River and running to the Swamps which in time of floods afford a Good Current — these ditches also serve to furnish the Mills with timbers floated through them from the Interior =

We have also seen very Large Rafts of Long Logs Intended for Mr Livingston's Warf at New Orleans — a Rafter assured us of having rec^d 6000$ for the Last Parcel he stole from the Government's Land —

Wednesday Decemb^r 27th 1820 As soon as my drawing was finished, I cleaned and Went to Natchez properly speaking — there to my uttmost surprise I met Nicholas Berthoud, who accosted Me Kindly, and ask^d me to go to New Orleans in his Boat — I accepted his offer —

from the River opposite Natchez, that place presents a Most Romantick scenery, the Shore Lined by Steam vessels Barges & flat Boats,

[150]

seconded by the Lower town, consisting of Ware Houses, Grogg, Chops, Decayed Boats proper for the uses of Washer Women, and the sidling Road raising along the Caving Hills on an oblique of a quarter of a Mile and about 200 feet High covered with Goats feeding peaceally on its declivities, while hundreds of Carts, Horses and foot travellers are constantly, meeting and Crossing each Other reduced to Miniature by the distance renders the whole really picturesque; on the Top of this the Traveller comes in sight of the town as he enters avenues of regularly planted Trees Leading to the diferent Streets running at right Angles towards the River; on the left the *Theater* a poor framed Building and a New and Elegant Mansion the property of Mr Postlewait attract the Anxious eye — on the right the rollings of the hearth thinly diversified by poor habitations soon close the prospect — advancing, he is Led into Main Street; this as well as the generality of the place too Narrow to be Handsome, is rendered Less Interesting by the poorness & Iregularity of the Houses, few of which are Bricks — and at this season very much encumbered by Bales of Cotton — the Jail, Court House are New and tolerable in their form the Lower part of the former a Boarding House of some Note. there are Two Miserable Looking Churches; I dare not say unattended but think so —

the Natchez's Hotel is a good House built on the Spanish plan, i.e. with Large Piazas and Many Doors and Windows — Well Kept by Mr John Garnier and is the rendez vous of all Gentile Travellers and Boarders — Several Large tavern which I did not Visit furnish Amply the Wants of the Strangers that at all times abound from different parts of the Union — this place now Contain about 2000 — inhabitants and Houses, has a Bank in good Credit — a Post Office receiving the Diferent Mails Thrice per Week, a Public reading Room and 2 printing offices —

the Naturalist will immediatly remark the general Mildness of the temperature on seeing at this season the premature Growth of Lettuces, Radishes and other vegetables that in our Eastern Latitudes are Carefully nursed in April and sometimes in May —

The Numberless prostrated Carrion Crows in the less frequented Streets prove to him the unhalhiness of the atmosphere — those certainly may be considered as necessary Evils, for no Birds are more disagreable at the same time that few are More Valuable in Climates Like this —

the Country back of Natchez was represented as Good and fitted by rich planters who once raised a Large quantity of Cotton the principal article of Export — Opposite this the Lands are extremely Low and overflow to a great Extent and Depth the Mail in Times of flood goes by Watter through the Woods nearly 40 Miles Toward Natchitoches on Red River.

Indians are Daily seen here with diferent sorts of Game — for which they receive high Prices, I saw Small Wild Turkey sold by them for One Dollar each, Malards at 50^{cts}

Although the Weather is Comparatively Mild, the Orange trees will not bear the Winters in open air = and sometimes the frosts for a day or two are severely felt — the remains of an Ancient Spanish fort are perceivable, the Center is now Honored by the Gallows and the Ditch serves as buriing ground for Slaves — the Cemetiere Lies at the extremity of the Town — about 2 Years ago a Large part of the Hill gave Way, Sunk probably 150 feet and Carried Many Houses into the River — this was occasioned by the quick Sand Running Springs that flows into the Strata of Clay and pebles of Which the Hill is Composed —

this sunken part is Now used as the depot of Dead Carcasses, and often times during the Summer emits such Exalaisons as attract hundreds, Nay I was told Thousands of Carrion Crows = an Engine is now Nearly in Operation Intended to raise the Watter of one of the springs or *ecoulement* or drains to suply the City — This indeed is much wanted, Watter hauled from the River is sold at 50^{cts} p^r Barrel taken out of the Eddy very impure = I found few Men Interested towards Ornithology except those who had heard or pleased to Invent Wonderfull Stories respecting a few Species —

Having Not one Cent when I Landed here I imediately Looked for something to do in the Likeness Way for our Support (unfortunately Naturalists are Obliged to eat and have some sort of Garb) I entered the room of a Portrait Painter Naming himself *Cook* but I assure you he was scarcely fit for a Scullion, Yet the *Gentleman* had some politeness and procured me the drawing of two Sketches for 5$ each, this was fine sauce to our empty stomacks

One was imediately paid for, the other a very excellent resemblance of Mr *Mathewson* probably never will be, for that Gentleman absented the same Evening and never Left orders to any body to pay — I merely put this down to give you the Best advice a Father Can present you with. Never to Sell or Buy without imediately paying for the same —

NATCHEZ, MISSISSIPPI, in 1822

This painting in oils is one of the few known landscapes by John James Audubon. It now hangs in Melrose, the home of Mrs. George M. D. Kelly in Natchez, and is reproduced through the courtesy of the owner.

a constant adherence of this Maxim will Keep your Mind and person all times free, & Happy

Mr Cook much pleased with My Drawings and quickness of performance, desired to travel with us if suitable Mutual arrangements could be Made. I Asked him to pay me Two Dollars per day Monthly in advance and furnish besides, One Third of the Whole Expenses, providing himself with Whatever Materials might be necessary —

He spoke of Joining us in a Couple of Weeks; I thought it very uncertain — the awkwardness I felt when I sat to Dinner at the Hotel was really justified to me; having not used a fork and Scarcely even a Plate since I left Louisville, I involuntarily took Meet and Vegetables with My fingers several times; on Board the flat Boats We seldom eat together and very often the hungry Cooked, this I perform^d when in need by Plucking & Cleaning a Duck, or a Partridge and throwing it on the Hot embers; few Men have eat a Teal with better appetite than I have dressed in this manner —

Others prefering Bacon would Cut a Slice from the *Side* that hung by the Chimney and Chew that raw with a hard Biscuit — Such Life is well intended to drill men Gradually to hardships to go to Sleep with Wet Muddy Clothing on a Buffalo skin stretch on a Board — to hunt through Woods filled with fallen trees, Entengled with Vines, Briars, Canes, high Rushes and at the same time giving under foot; produces heavy sweats strong Appetite, & Keeps the Imagination free from Worldly thoughts, I Would advise Many *Citisens* particularly our Eastern *Dandys* to try the experiment — leaving their high heeled Boots, but not their *Corsets*, for, this would no doubt be Serviceable whenever food giving way, they might wish to depress their stomacks for the occasion —

Thursday December 28th 1820 Weather sultry. Saw some Mocking Birds and was assured that they remained during the Winter here —

Nicholas having invited me to stay at his Lodgings I Breakfasted at the Hotel of Mr Garnier a French Gentleman of Agreable Manners who kindly procured me Willson's Ornithology from Mr James Wilkins to whom I was introduced to by Nicholas.

Friday December 29th 1820 The weather this Morning had taken a remarquable Change, the Thermometer had fallen from 72 to 36 — it snowed and blew hard from the Northwest — Last night the Musquitoes, were quite troublesome

I made Two Sketches to day for 5$ each; after Many Inquiries for the 9ᵗʰ Volume of Willson I was disapointed in my wish of examining it none of the subscribers had recᵈ it —

Joseph and Capᵉ Cummings still remained on Board of Mʳ Aumack's Boat — I had the satisfaction of ransacking the *Fables* of Lafontaine, with Engravings

Saturday Decembʳ 30ᵗʰ 1820 Mʳ Aumack Left this Morning in our Boat taking with him Capᵉ Cummings — I felt Sorry at parting With that really agreable Compagnion

Sunday Decembʳ 31ᵗʰ 1820 I drew this afternoon — and here I have to tell a sad Misfortune that took place this Morning — having Carried under My Arm My Smallest Port Folio and Some other articles I Laid the Whole on the Ground and ordered Mʳ Berthow's Servant to take them on Board

I unfortunately Went off to Natchez again to breakfast the Servant forgot My Folio on the Shore and Now I am Without, any Silver paper, to preserve my Drawings, have Lost some very Valuable Drawings, and My Beloved Wife's Likeness = the greatest Exercions I now Must Make to try to find it again, but so dull do I feel about it that I am nearly Made Sick

I Wrote to Mʳ John Garnier, requesting him to advertise and procure some one to try to find My Port Folio but no Hopes can I have of ever seeing it when Lost amongst 150 or 160 flat Boats and Houses filled with the Lowest of Caracters — No doubt My Drawings will serve to ornement their Parlours or will be Nailed on Some of The Steering Oars —

Monday January 1ˢᵗ 1821 This day 21 Years since I was at *Rochefort* in France. I spent most of that day at Copying Letters of My Father to the Minister of the Navy —

What I have seen, and felt since, would fill a Large Volume — the Whole of Which Would end at *this Day January 1ˢᵗ 1821. I am on Board a Keel Boat going down to New Orleans the poorest Man on it* — & What I have seen and felt has brought some very dearly purchased Experience, and Yet Yesterday I forgot that No servant could do for Me What I might do Myself; had I acted accordingly; My Port Folio Would now have been safe in my possession —

The Lands are flatening fast — the Orange trees are now and then seen near the Rich Planter's habitation — and the Verdure along all the shore is very Luxuriant and agreeable. At half past 6 o'clock P.M. we came opposite *Baton Rouge* but the Steam Boat had left and of Course we proceeded on our Way floating — this Last place is a Thrifty

Down the Ohio and Mississippi

Villege on the New Orleans State — from some distance above *Levees* have made their appearance — I saw a Negro Man fishing by deeping a Scoup Net every moment in the Watter immediately at a point Where the current ran swift forming an eddy below, he had taken several tolerably Large Cat Fishes —

Tuesday January 2ᵈ 1821 We floated all night without accidents, the river since Natchez is much deeper, and free of Sawers and Snaggs — at day Breake found ourselves about 50 Miles below Baton Rouge; the day Cloudy, raw, and some Wind a head —

the Plantations increase in number, and the Shores have Much the Appearance of those on Some of the Large rivers of France, their Lowness Excepted, the points are quite diferent to those on the River above, One May see the River below them by Looking across in Many places — and from the Boat we can only have a View of the upper windows, Roofs and Tops of the Trees about them. the Whole is backed by a dark Curtain of Thickly Moss covered Cypresses — flat Boats are Landed at nearly every Plantation, this being a Sure method of disposing of their produce to a better profit, travellers on horse Back or Gigg go by us full Gallop as if their Life depended on the accelerity of their movements —

our Situation in this Boat is quite Comfortable — We have a good Servant to wait on us, are served with regular Meals, Clean and in Plates — Move much faster than With Messʳˢ Aumack & Lovelace, having here 8 Roaers who dare not contradict orders —

— I drew the Likeness of Mʳ Dickerson the Master of the Boat — he paid me in Gold — took the Outlines of Both *the Warblers by Candle Light to afford Me time to morow to finish both* —

—— *3ᵈ* —— Raining & Blowing hard all Night the weather cooled Considerably. much Like some of our April day at Henderson — took a Walk Early, while waiting for the Light to Increase and enable Me to Work — passed through a Large Cotton Plantation yet unpicked Looked Like if a Heavy Snow had fell and frose on every Pod —

the great regularity with which this is sowed and raised attracts the Eye imediately; it Lays in rows I believe allways runing at right Angle to the River, about 6 feet distant from each other and the plants about 3 and so straight that your Eye is Carried to the farthest extremity of the field without the Lease obstruction — even at this time that the Cotton has Ceased to be attended for Many weeks, it is quite free from Weeds of any sort —

the Woods here have a new and very romantic appearance — the Plant Called Pamitta raises promiscuously through them the Moss on every tree darkens the under growth and affords to the melancholy Mind a retreat thooted [suited?] by the Chirpings of hundreds of Beautifully Plumed Inhabitants —

the flocks of *Blackbirds* taking the Species En Masse, feel the air, they pass Southwest constantly; forming a Line Like disbanded Soldiers all anxious to reach the point of destination each hurring to pass the companion before him —

I drew both My Birds, the first on a plant in full bloom that I plucked Near the Boat —

We were Visited by several *french Creoles* this is a Breed of animals that Neither speak French English nor Spanish correctly but have a Jargon composed of the Impure parts of these three —

they Stared at My Drawing, and when a litle Composed Gazed and Complimented Me very Highly — on asking them the names of about a dozen diferent Birds then lying on the Table they Made at once and without hesitating a Solid Mass of *Yellow Birds* of the Whole — One of them a young Man told Me that he could procure 3 or 4 dozen of them every Night by hunting the Orange trees with a Lantern — I can said he 'see the Rascalls White belies and Knok them down with a Stick very handy' — few of these good Natured Souls could answer any valuable account of the Country —

Thursday January 4ᵗʰ 1821   at 4 o'clock this morning the wind was so high, that it forced us to Come to a litle above *Bonne Care's* Church — the weather was rather cold, as soon as day broke walkᵈ over to the Swamp

I paid my Respects to the Pastor, to make some Inquiries respecting Mʳ *Lecorgne, George Crogham*, and the country; but I found only a tall thin dirty Creole who could not say much besides the prayer for the prosperity of the Brick Church now erecting — from this pennsionary of Bigots I went to a School House; there I had the pleasure of meeting an Old, Polite, and well Instructed French Gentleman in charge of about a dozen of Pupils of Both Sexes — he told me that *George Crogham* resided about 3 Miles from this Place across the Mississipi, that he was not acquainted with Lecorgne's name — that this Country was a fine field for my Wishes; walked to the Boats, examined attentively My Drawings and told Me that having Left Europe and the World of Talents for so many Years such a Sight was very gratifying

[156]

Down the Ohio and Mississippi

The country is here richly adorned by handsome dwelling Houses, Many Sugar and Cotton Plantations running about One Mile and half to the Swamp, free from Old trees and Stumps — every house a *L'Espagnole* — orange trees, now hanging with their golden fruits forming avenues and Edges — the fields Well fenced in and dreaned by ditches running to the Swamps —

the Mocking Birds are so Gentle that I followed one along a fence this morning for nearly one Mile Keeping only one panel between us the whole of the distance — I have Not heard one sing yet; but imitating Many Birds —

about 5 o'clock we again ventured off and again the Wind drove us in Shore and now we are Landed on a point where our Boat rolls merily — raining hard — thermometer to day at 52 — this morning the french Gentlemen Wrap^d up in their Cloaks Kept their Handkerchiefs to their Noses — What would become of them on the Rocky Mountains at this Season — our Captain Exchanged some Apples for Oranges receiving 2 for 1 —

Friday January 5th 1821   Paid a Visit to a Cottager a French Creole, handsome Children who were all afraid of me — the Lady *remarkably handsome* their Little Garden was adorned with a few orange Trees some fine Lettuces filled the Borders; Gren Peas nearly in bloom, Artichaux, reminding me of the Happy days spent in France — bought some delightfull radishes, and Enquired of Birds of Course; One League distant is a fine Lake, now the rendez vous of Ducks, Geese, &^c but could not obtain Valuable remarks — the transient Cool Weather as rendered the Mocking Birds so gentle that they Scarcely would move out of the Way —

Saturday January 6th 1821   We were blowed a Shore opposite *Monsieur St Armand's* Sugar Plantation —

Out on Shore with Guns imediately — the Swamps about 3 Miles back we gave up going to them fearing the departure of our boat while absent that far — here Was the finest Plantations we have seen Mr S. A^d own 70 Negroes and Makes about 400 Hogshead of Sugar — besides raising, Corn Hay, Rice &^c — this Gentleman, apparently Young was Shooting Red Winged Starlings, on the Wing for his amusement, had a richly ornemented Doubled Barelled Gun of which he Made excellent use — the Slaves employed at Cutting the Sugar Cane — this they perform with Large heavy Knifes not unlike those used by Butchers to Chop — some cutting the Head of the plants and others the Cane itself — tying the Last in small fagots with the Tops. Carts with Entire Wooden Wheels drawn by 4 oxen haul it to the House where it is, bruised, pressed Boiled & Made into Sugar — the Miserable Wretches at Work begged a Winter Falcon We had Killed, saying *it Was a great treat for them*; the Overseer a Good Looking Black Man, told us of his being in the same Employ for 8 Years and had obtain so much of his Master's Confidence, as to have the Entire Care of the Plantation — he Spoke roughly to his under servants but had a good indulgent Eye, and no doubt does what he Can to Accomodate, Master and All — those Immense Sugar Plantations Looked Like Prairies early in Summer for Scarce a Tree is to be seen, and particularly here where the Horizon was bounded by Cleared Land —

We saw Many Catle, Horses, and Sheep, but all poor and Slack, the Latters have but Litle Wool and that only on the back the Rams wear a Long Kind of hairy beard Like Goats —

the Gardens were beautifull. Roses in full bloom revive the Eye of the Traveller — who for lengthy Days has been Confined to the Smoky inside of a Dark flat Bottomed Boat — the Wind entirely Lulled away at Sun Set — the Moon's Disk assured us of a fine Night and We Left our Station to drop within a few Miles of the City — Tomorow perhaps May take us there, yet so uncertain is this World that I should not be Surprised if I never Was to reach it — the further removed, the Stronger My anxiety to see My familly again presses on My Mind — and Nothing but the astonishing desire I have of Compleating my work Keeps My Spirits at par —

NEW ORLEANS IN 1821

INTRODUCTION

THE Creole capital which Audubon entered penniless early in January of 1821 was then in a stage of transition. It had been less than a score of years in American possession, but already it was filling up with Yankee business men, southern men of wealth (much of it sudden), who formed a plutocracy eager to become an aristocracy, while Kentucky woodsmen, Indiana corn farmers, Illinois rail-splitters came downstream to mingle on its docks with salt-water sailors from the Gulf — Norwegians, Russians, Portuguese, and Cubans. Abraham Lincoln, in a broadhorn, followed Audubon to New Orleans only five years later, there to see chained slaves sold in the open market. For always, of course, there were the black people, strong of back, endlessly fertile, resistant to malaria, on whose strength rested in a light elegance the Creole aristocracy.

The Creoles were predominantly French in blood, and their language a patois French; the *mores*, however, sound rather more Spanish than French — entailing a certain Mediterranean way of life: Sundays a little gayer than other days, feast days and holidays crowding the calendar, emphasis on the duello and the duenna, and a tendency to call tomorrow as good as today. (One reason, perhaps, why Audubon had such trouble in collecting payments due him.) New Orleans was a seaport, in touch with Havana, New York, Liverpool, Cadiz, and Bordeaux. Yet it was, practically, out of touch with both its Spanish and its French origins. Into this closed colonial society, little new blood had flowed for some time. Its life, though colorful and gay enough within its small wealthy circles, was indeed a life traveling around in circles, content to repeat old experiences, more or less locked against new ideas.

Audubon, alas, was one of these. Ornithology was unappreciated in New Orleans then, except as sport. It was not primarily an intellectual society but rather a social one, where the opera was the best supported of the arts, with family portraiture a second. Here lay Audubon's chief resource, but of course the field was not uncontested. We find that the most fashionable clientèle was that of John Vanderlyn, and Audubon cannot get anywhere without this rival's approbation. Vanderlyn had been one of David's pupils. His most famous subjects were historical; though grandiose and often hollow, they were then the vogue. 'Marius in the Ruins of Carthage' received a Paris gold medal in 1808, and is still the picture by which he is oftenest remembered, though his painting of Aaron Burr and his daughter is his finest portrait. He turned to the painting of vast panoramas of Paris, Athens, Mexico City and Versailles. In later years Audubon met him again in New York, where Vanderlyn was doing General Jackson's portrait. The head was from the life, but the soldier had refused to sit longer. So that Audubon was asked to don the general's uniform, which he did, with the result that the picture of the hero is Audubon from the shoulders down.

Vanderlyn died in 1852 in utter destitution, a year after Audubon, who died amid all the honors the world could bestow. But at the moment we find him rich and proud, and Audubon penniless, cap in hand before him.

This journal, like the one immediately preceding it, was one of those saved from the destruction wrought by the Audubon descendants, and given by Colonel Thayer to Harvard College, and finally published by the Club of Odd Volumes in 1929. It is given verbatim, without attempts to improve upon the vagaries of Audubon's spelling or punctuation. Only so, it is believed, can the precious first impressions of our author be preserved.

Sunday January 7ᵗʰ 1821   at New Orleans at Last — We arrived here about 8 o'clock this Morning. I saw Mʳ Prentice, who directed me to the House of Messʳˢ *Gordon* & *Grant* where he told me N. Berthound Was; I saw him and was Introduced to Mʳ Gordon of whom I shall have opportunity of speaking probably frequently hereafter and the *British Consul* Mr Davisson I heard that my familly Was Well, and saw a Note from My Wife to N. Berthound, that accompanied a p^re of Gloves made by her for him —

We walked out, Met Col^l George Croghan, our former acquaintance saw Many of the Louisville Gentry too tedious to mention names —

Arrived at the House of Mr Arnauld an old friend of N. B^ds father. we were invited to take dinner, and although we had engaged previously to Mr Gordon we staid, We had a good dinner and great deal of Mirth that I call *french Gayety* that really sickened me. I thought Myself in Bedlam, every body talk^d Loud at once and the topics dry Jokes — Yet every one appeared good, well disposed, Gentlemen, and were very polite to us — a Monkey amused the Company a good deal by his Gambols and pranks — formerly I would have been able as well as anxious to go to the Theatre but now I can only partake of the Last, and after having paid a Short Visit to Mr Gordon I retired to the Keel Boat; with a bad head Hake occasioned by drinking some Wine — and very sorry that I probably Could not have Letters from the Post Office untill Tuesday, Tomorow being a grand French Fete the aniversary of the Memorable Batle of Orleans

Joseph had spent his day visiting the Town and was not prepossessed in its favor —

Monday January 8th 1821 at Day breake, went to Market having received information that Much and great variety of game was brought to it — We found Vast Many Malards, some teals, some American widgeons, Canada Geese Snow Geese, Mergansers, Robins; Blue Birds; Red wing Starlings — Tell Tale Godwits — every thing selling extremely high $1.25 for one pa^re of Ducks, 1.50 for a Goose &^c Much surprised and diverted on finding a *Barred Owl* Clean^d and Exposed for sale Value 25^cts — some fine Fish; Indiferent Meat — some Vegetables both of this Country and West Indies = these Latters are put up in Small parcels on the ground opposite the owner, who has fixed prices for each Lot — I went to the review and will remember it and the 8th of January forever — My Pocket was rifled of my pocket Book taken in this Morning with an intention of going to the Governor with the Letters I had received for him, and to Mr Wheeler's brother in Law — when I mention^d My Loss to N. Berthoud he called me a *Green Horn*, I do not Know the Color of My Horns but well, *those* of some Neighbours of Mine —

Not blaming fortune as is generally the Case I peaceably pack the whole of Myself and will try to grow Wiser if possible — I think the Knave who took it is now good deal disapointed and probably wishes I had it — the Parade was only tolerable I had a view of the Governor that is now no doubt all I May expect, he Looked about 60 a french face at good Countenance — We Walked to Bayou St John absolutly to Kill the time, the whole City taken with the festivals of the day — Joseph rec^d a Letter from his Parents —

this evening one of our Men Called *Smith* fell over board drunk and Would have drowned if Providence had not interfered a Women heard the Noise and the Yawl of the S. B^t U. States saw him —

—— *9th* —— My Spirits very Low — Weather Cloudy & Sultry. Wished I had remained at Natchez — having found No Work to do remained on Board the Keel Boat opposite the Market, the Dirtiest place in all the Cities of the United States —

Wednesday Jany 10th 1821 Raining hard all day wrote My Brother G. L. Dupuy Gaudeau and to My Mother — in the afternoon Cap^n Cummings arrived and dined with us — his appearance much Worst — the Weather so bad that I had no opportunity of doing any thing toward procuring Work — Strong thoughts of returning to Natchez Saw Cap^n Penniston who rec^d me very Politely

—— *11* —— Spent the Day Walking about trying to find some work Shewed My Drawings to Mr Gordon & the British Consul Mr Davisson — spoke good of the Publication — the former raised My Expectations of their value —

Remarked in Market, Blue Cranes, great Many Coots Caldwall Ducks, some Geese, Keeldeers — 1 White Crane — or Herons and one Sand Hill Crane —

Was sometime with Mr Prentice who gave me a letter to Doctor Hunter, whom I wished to see, to procure the Information I so much Need about the Red River, What life &^{c} — Joseph Employed in Making Enquiries about the Lost Port Folio from every Boat Landing from Natchez — No Work yet — rain, Warm, the Frogs all piping —

—— *12th* —— Early this Morning I Met an Italian, painter at the Theatre. I took him to N. B^d Room and Shewed me the Drawing of the White Headed Eagle, he was much pleased, took me to his painting appartement at the Theatre, then to the Directors who very roughly offered me 100$ per Month to paint with Mons L'Italian.

I believe really now that my talents must be poor or the Country —

Dined with Mr Gordon, conversation Birds & Drawings, Must exibit some again and again as New Guests came in —

I Rec^d to day a Letter from My Beloved Wife Dated Novr 28th 1820 — gave My Letter from Mr Garnier to the Columbus — No work yet — paid a Visit to Monsieur *Pamar* but Audubon was poor to day and he Knew it when I made my bow —

Wrote this Evening to Henry Clay Es^{qr} for another Letter of Recommandation —

Saturday 13th January 1821 I rose early tormented by many disagreable thoughts, nearly again without a cent, in a Busling City where no one cares a fig for a Man in my situation — I walked to *Jarvis* the Painter and shewed him some of my Drawings — he overlooked them, said nothing then Leaned down and examined them minutely but never said they Were good or bad — Merely that when he drew an Eagle for Instance, he made it resemble a Lyon, and covered it with Yellow hair and not Feathers — some fools who entered the room, were so pleased at seeing my Eagle that they prised it, and Jarvis wistled — I called him aside, While Joseph Rolled up our Papers and asked him if he needed assistance to finish his Portraits i.e. the Clothing and Grounds — he stared, I repeated my question and told him I would not turn my Back to any one for Such employment and that I had received good Lessons from good Masters — he then asked me to come the following day and Would think about it —

in following N. B. through the street while nothing better could be done, We entered the Warehouse of Mr Pamar and at once was surprised to hear *him* ask what I Charged for my Drawings of Faces; 25$; — but said he I have 3 Children and you May put them all on one piece; then I must have 100$ —

N. B^d requested me to make a Sketch of the Litle Girl then present; a sheet of Paper was procured, My Pencil Sharped and Sitting on a Crate was soon at Work and soon finished; the Likeness was Striking; the Father Smiled, the Clerks stared me emased and the servant was dispatched to shew My Success (as it Was Called) to Mistress — Monsieur Pamar *Civilly* told me that I Must do my Best for him and Left it to Myself as to the Price — I would have Liked to earn the half of the Money that day, but the Eldest Daughter could not be ready perhaps for several Days — Yet here is found Hopes — how I Calculated on 100 Dollars; What relief to My Dear Wife and Children for Said I if I get this, I may send it her and no doubt I will soon procure some more Work —

I spent the remainder of this day in better Spirits took a Long Walk With Joseph toward the Lake — Saw an Aligator —

Wrote this Evening to Doct^r D^l Drake — and read some Interesting tales, borrowed from Mr Prentice —

Sunday 14th January 1821 Dressed I Went to Jarvis — he took me imediately in his painting room, and asked me many questions, until *I thought* that he *feared* my assistance he very Simply told me he could not believe that I might help him in the Least — I rose, bowed, and Walk^d out without one Word, and No doubt he Looked on Me as I did on him as an Original, and a Craked Man —

The Levee early was Crowded by people of all sorts as well as Colors, the Market, very aboundant the Church Bell ringing the Billiard Balls Knocking, the Guns heard all around. What a Display this is for a Steady Quaker of Philad^a or Cincinnati — the day was beautifull and the crowd Increased considerably — I saw however no handsome Woman and the Citron hue of allmost all is very disgusting to one who Likes the rosy Yankee or English Cheeks —

At Dark took a Walk to Mr Gordon, from there on to Mr *Laville* where We saw some *White Ladies* and Good Looking ones — returning on Board the Quartroom Ball attracted My View but as it cost 1$ Entrance I Merely Listened a Short time to the Noise and came Home as We are pleased to Call it —

Yesterday I Made My Long Acquaintance's Likeness John B. Gilly purposely to expose it to the Public — it is considered by every one who Knows him to be perfect — and to shew it this Morning (for I made it in a few hours) to Pamar procured Me the Making of that of his heldest Daughter; by the time We receive the pay for it, We will be penny Less —

to day I rec^d a letter from My Beloved Wife who rufled My Spirits Sadly it Was dated Cincinnati Decr 31. 1820 I answered it.

Saw in Market — 2 White Herons — one New Species of Snipe, but could not Draw any of them, being partly pluck^d — Joseph Who hunted all day Yesterday, Killed Nothing New — saw Many Warblers —

		British Consul's Likeness	$25.00
19	Friday —	Euphraim Pamar's Likeness	25.00
20	Saturday —	Another Sister "	25.00
21	Sunday		
22	Monday	Mrs Pamar	25.00
23	Tuesday	Little Daughter of D	25.00

24	Wednesday	Mr Forestall D°	$25.00
25	Thursday	Young Lucin D°	25.00
26	Friday	Mrs Lucin D°	20.00
27	Saturday	Mr Carabie D°	25.00
			$220.00

28 Sunday Drawing a Brown Pelican — fatigued, Wearied of Body but in good Spirits having plenty to do at good Prices, and my Work much admired — only sorry that the Sun Sets —

Monday January 29ᵗʰ 1821 Drawing all day the Brown Pelican, Collected My Earnings purchased a Crate of queens Ware for My Beloved Wife, Wrote to her, Wᵐ Bakewell and Charles Briggs forwarding her by Letter and Parcel care of Mr Buckamain of Louisville 270 Dollars — the Crate Cost 36: 33$ —

Tuesday 30th Mr Duchamp's Likeness 25$

Thursday — February 1st 1821 — Began a Likeness of Mr Louallier and Drew a Common Gull —

Friday 2d Mr Smith began hunting for Meat 25 $ per Month stopped Thursday Morning — and the Girl *Began Cooking for us at 10$ per Month with washing*

Monday February 5th 1821 Running about pretty much all day trying to procure some More Work and also Enquiring about Willson's Ornithology, but in Vain — the high Value set on that work now particularly Lately as rendered it extremely rare, and the few who possess it will not Lend it — the Weather extremely sultry and Damp heavy Rains and thunder —

February 15th 1821 Wrote to My Beloved Wife this Day per N. Berthoud List of Drawings Sent My Beloved Wife February 17th by Nicholas Berthoud of Shipping port Esqʳᵉ

    1   Common gallinule — Not Described by Willson
    2   D° — Gull —   Do   Do   Do
    3   Marsh Hawk
    4   Boat Tailed Grakles Male & femelle — Not Described
          by Willson
    5   Common Crow
    6   Fish Crow
    7   Rail or Sora
    8   Marsh Tern —
    9   Snipe Not Described by Willson
   10   Hermit Thrush

11   Yellow Red Pole Warbler
12   Savannah Finch
13   Bath Ground Warbler Not Described by Willson
14   Brown Pelican Not Described by Willson
15   Great footed Hawk
16   Turkey Hen — Not Described by Willson
17   Cormorant — Do   Do   Do
18   Carrion Crow or Black Vulture
19   Imber Diver
20   White Headed or Bald Eagle

May I have the Satisfaction of Looking at these and Many More in good Order on My return the fruits of a Long Journey —

Monday 19th February 1821   the Weather beautifull, Clear & Warm, the Wind having blown hard from the Southwest for 2 days & nights —

Saw this Morning Three Immense flocks of *Bank Swallows* that past over Me with the Rapidity of a Storm, going Northeast, their Cry was heard distinctly, and I knew them first by the Noise they made in the air coming from behind Me; the falling of their Dung resembled a heavy but thinly falling Snow; No appearance of any feeding While in our Sight — Which Lasted but a few Minutes —

I was much pleased to see these arbingers of Spring but Where could they be moving so rapidly at this early Season I am quite at a Loss to think & yet their Passage here was about as long after the purple Martins that Went By on the 9th Instant as is their arrival in Kentucky a Month hence — perhaps Were they forced by the last Winds and now Enticed to proceed by the Mildness of the Weather the Thermometer being at 68 —

how far More south Must I go Next January & February to see these Millions of Swallows Spending their Winter as Thousands of Warblers, fly Catchers, Thrushes and Myriads of Ducks, Geese, Snipes &c Do here?

the Market is regularly furnished with the *English Snipe* Which the french Call *Cache Cache*. Robins Blue Wingd Teals, Common Teals, Spoon Bill Ducks, Malards, Snow Geese, Canada Geese, Many Cormorants.   Coots, Watter Hens, Tell Tale (Godwits, calld here *Clou Clou*) Yellow Shank Snipes, Some Sand Hill Cranes, Strings of Bleu Warblers, Cardinal Grosbeaks, Common Turtle Doves, Golden Wingd Wood Peckers &ᶜ

Wednesday 21st February 1821   I Met this morning with one of those slight discouraging Incidents connected with the life of the artists; I had a Likeness Spoken of in very rude terms by the fair Lady it was Made for, and perhaps will Loose My time and the reward expected for My Labour, — Mrs *Andre* I here mention the Name as I May Speak More of the Likeness as the occasion Will require —

Thursday New Orleans February 22d 1821 We at Last have the Keel Boat off and have moved on the hearth again — Our present situation is quite a Curious one to Me, the room we are in and for which We pay $10 per Month is situated in Barraks Street near the Corner of that & Royal Street — between Two Shops of Grocers and divided from them and our Yellow Landlady by Mere Board Partitions, receiving at once all the new Matter that Issues from the thundering Mouths of all these groupes — the *Honest Woman* spoke much of honesty in Strangers and required one Month paid in Advance, this however I could not do, and satisfied her with one half Not taking a Receipt although She appeared very urgent —

I walked a good deal about the City in search of Work & Willson's Ornithology but was not favored with any success — extremely anxious to receive some news from My familly — am very much fatigued of New Orleans Where I cannot *Shoot Two Birds with one Stone* I retired to our Lodgings at Dusk —

Sunday March 11th 1821 Walkd out this Morning with Joseph to try my Souvenir Gun and found it an excellent One.

Near our House a Mocking Bird regularly resorts to the South Angle of a Chimney top and salutes us with Sweetest Notes from the rising of the Moon untill about Midnight, and every Morning from about 8 o'clock untill 11, when it flys to the Convent Garden to feed — I have remarked that Bird allways in the Same Spot and Same Position, and have been particularly pleased at hearing him Imitate the Watchman's Cry of *All's Well* that Issues from the fort about 3 Squares Distant, and so well, has he sometimes performed that I Would have been mistaken if he had not repeated too often in the Space of a 10 minutes

March 16th Friday 1821 I had the pleasure of receiving a Letter this Morning from Mr. A. P. Bodley dated Natchez 8th Inst Informing me of my Port Folio having been found and Deposited at the office of the *Mississippi Republican* and that I could have it by writing —

I Acknowledge with a very sensible pleasure the Kindness of Mr. P. who worked his Passage down in Mr Aumack Boats — and at the same time cannot Conceive how the Book had escaped the researches of Mr Garnier — Mr Gordon had the goodness to write to a friend to have it forwarded imediately and pay whatever charges there might be, the Politeness of that Gentleman is remarkable to a Man who is no more than a Stranger to him, but No doubt it would be impossible for a Good heart to act otherwise —

I took a Walk with my Gun this afternoon to see the Passage of Millions of *Golden Plovers* Coming from the North Est and going Nearly South — the distruction of these innocent fugitives from a Winter Storm above us was really astonishing — the Sportsmen are here more numerous and at the same time more expert at shooting on the Wing than any where in the U. States on the first sight of these birds Early this Morning assembled in Parties of from 20 to 100 at Diferent places where they Knew by experience they told me the birds pass and arranged themselves at equal distances squatted on their hams, as a flock Came Near every man Called in a Masterly astonishing Manner, the Birds Imediately Lowered and Wheeled and coming about 40 or 50 yards run the Gantlet every Gun goes off in Rotation, and so well aimed that I saw several times a flock of 100 or More Plovers destroyed at the exception of 5 or 6 — the Dogs after each Voleys While the Shooters charged their Pieces brought the Same to each Individuals — this continued all day, When I Left One of those Lines of Sharp Shooters then the Sun Setting, they appeared as Intent on Killing More as when I arrived at the Spot at 4 o'clock —

a Man Near where I was seated had Killed 63 dozens — from the firing before & behind us I would suppose that 400 Gunners where out. Supposing each Man to have Killed 30 Dozen that day 144,000 must have been destroyed —

On Enquiring if these Passages where frequent I was told that Six Years ago there was about such an Instance, imediately after 2 or 3 days of Very Warm Weather a blow from the Northeast brought them, Which Was Nearly the Same to day — some few Were fat but the Greatest Number Lean, and all that I opened showed no food — the femelles Eggs extremely small.

Sunday March 18th 1821 Walking along the Levee to Mr Pamar Where I had an Appointment for a Likeness. I Was Invited to breakfast by Mr A. Liautaud — I Walked in and Met a Large Party, Well engaged round an old Gentleman at Pleasing him by the most extravagant round of praises — I understood the Caracter was rather Moony, and very gay When well managed, productive of Much Mirth to his hearers — During the Breakfast that Certainly Was a good one & on Which One

Prince Guest touchd heavily, We were several times struck by unexpected Voleys of Verses, composed for the Occasion, and that could not Indeed have had a better Effect that that produced — Every One enjoyed himself Very Much, particularly the Compositors who were highly Clapped, sometimes to be sure to put an end to his Loquacity.

Breakfast over I was told to remain and see the best part. Mr Liautaud the Learned Guest Was about being recd a *Mason* and My being a Brother entitled me at once to a seat — this was conducted in the most Ludicrous Manner any one can conceive, and I really pitied the Newly Initiated When all Ceremonies Were over the Man Was Burned in several parts, baptised in a Large Bucket of Watter, Tossed in a Blanket, and Make to Crawl Over about 50 Casks of Wine, on his belly and Knees, and When at Last given up for want of Invention, the Poor Devils Who had being praying for Mercy during all this was Left in the Necessary —

To this Man this Might be done perhaps again, but few could bear such treatment and I expected several times that his Cries or a Change of sensation from Cowardice to Courage would shew a very diferent scene but all however was Ended as Intended and the poor fellow took it for Granted that he really Was a Mason —

Wednesday March 21st 1821 In reading the Papers this morning at Mr Pamar, I saw the Treaty between Spain and our Country.

the 4th Article Speaking of an expedition to run the Line of Division formed by both Parties and to leave Natchitoches during the Course of this Year; I imediately went to Mr Gordon to know from him What steps Would be necessary to procure an Appointment as Draftsman for this So Long Wished for Journey — he advised me to see Mr Hawkins Who would introduce me to Governor Robinson —

I saw Mr Hawkins who very politely promised to See the Governor and Mention to him my Wishes and to Call at his office on the 23d

to Join in Such an enterprise and to leave all I am attachd to, perhaps for ever, produced Many diferent sensations & thought, but all are Counterbalanced When persuaded as I am that My Labours are all for their use & benefit.

I did not wait late on the 23d but My Spirits were sadly dampened when Mr Hawkins told Me that it was the Governor's opinion that nothing more would be done than to run the Line in question and that none but the surveyors would be Necessary;

Disapointed but not less anxious to try further I Calld on Mr Gordon, he Joined me in the Idea of My Adressing the President Directly and that he could Not think that a Journey so Interesting Would be performd only to say that Men had gone & Come back — in leaving this truly Kind Gentleman, I Met Mr Grayson of Louisville spoke to him to my thoughts and Wishes.

I Can render a Service I believe Mr A and I Will do it. I will give you some Letters to diferent Members of Congress With whom I am Well acquainted and that will be glad to Meet Your Views, but Write to the President —

This sounded better to my Ears —

full of My plans I went home & Wrote to N Berthoud to request his Imediate Assistance — Walkd out in the afternoon seeing Nothing but hundreds of New Birds, in Imagination and supposed Myself often on the Journey —

on the 24th I called again on Mr Hawkins. Mr Gordon had spoke of me to him and the former again to the Governor, I spoke of adressing the President, he acquiestd and promissed to give a Letter for the same and procure one from the Governor —

going through the Street Not unlike I dare say a Wild Man thinking too much to think at all My Eyes Were attracted by a handsome faced Man. I Knew him it was My Old Acquaintance & friend George Croghan. We Met freely and I was eased. he Knew what I was going to say having dined the day previous at the Governor's with Mr Hawkins. He said he had spoke of Me but Would do more and promissed to find Some Letters to Mr Hawkins for my use, and Invited Me with such forcible Kindness to go and spend Some time at his Plantation that I Accepted his offer — see me again Walking fast and Looking Wild, but recollecting the high price of time I hunted Mr D^d Prentice, and asked him if he would form a letter for Me — he answered Yes but told Me that I would do better by writing Myself and that he would freely give his advice and help if Needed — I Was then reduced to My poor thoughts to Express My Wishes — Anxious, and Determined to leave no power of Mine untried, I sat to the Paper & Wrote in as Great a Hurry as I am Now doing, a Letter, that Mr Prentice to My utmost astonishment pronounced *all suficient* — he spoke much about the Journey and anticipated he said the pleasure of reading My Journal on My return — feeling a great Weight off My Shoulders I returned to My Room, took Gun Ammunition & Joseph & to the Woods Went in Search of New Species —

New Orleans in 1821

My Life has been strewed with Many thorns but could I see Myself & the fruits of my Labour safe, with My Beloved familly *all Well* on a return from Such an expedition, how gratefull Would I feel to My Country and full of the Greatness of My Author —

Saturday March 31ˢᵗ 1821 I spent my time these 3 Last Days More at thinking than any thing else — and often indeed have I thought My Head very heavy —

This Morning I Waited on Mʳ Gordon with a Wish to receive from him an amendment to my Letter to the President, for all in my head is the Pacific Expedition he Wrote, I read it, but was Not altogether Satisfied — I Called on Mʳ Vanderlyn the Historical Painter With my Port Folio — to shew him some of my Birds with a View to Ask him for a few Lines of recommandation — he examined them attentively and *Called* them *handsomely* done, but being *far* from possessing any Knowledge of Ornithology or Natural History, I was quite satisfied *he* Was No Judge but of their being better or Worst *Shaded* Yet he spoke of the beautifull Coloring and Good positions and told Me that he would With pleasure give me a Certificate of his having *Inspected* them — Are all Men of Talents fools and Rude purposely or Naturally? I cannot assert, but have often thought that they were one or the other.

When I arrived at Mʳ V's Room, he spoke to me as if I had been an abject slave, and told Me in Walking Away to Lay my Drawings down *there the Dirty* that he would return *presently* and Look them over. — I felt so vexed that My first Intention Was to *Pack* off, but the Expedition Was in View, I thought how Long Kempbell the Actor Waitted Once at the theatre in England, and stood patiently *although* not Laying My Drawing *Down there*

About 30 Minutes Elapsed, he returned with an officer and with an air More becoming a Man Who *Once Was Much* in My situation ask me in his private room. Yet I could plainly see in his Eye that selfish Confidence that allways destroy in some degree the Greatest Man's Worth.

the Swet ran down My face as I hastily openᵈ My Drawings and Laid them on the floor; I Lookᵈ up to him. he Was Looking at them, the Officer's *By God* that's handsome, struck my eyars Vanderlyn took up a Bird Lookᵈ at it closely put it down and said they Were *handsomely done.*

I breathed, Not because I thought him a Man of the Most Superior Talents, for to come to such a pitch one Must have no faults, and I

With My Eyes *half Closed* (as you know the pretended Juges of our Day Look at Painting) saw a great Deffect in One of his figures of Women (the deffect that had being Corrected by the Lady I drew Lately.) but because this Gentleman had *some Talents*, that he Was Look^d on as a Very Excellent Judge and that I had been Told that a few Words from him Might be serviceable — of My Likeness he spoke very diferently, the one I had Was fair, hard, and Without Effect, although he Acknowledged it Must have been a Strong one —

he sat, he Wrote, and I, thinking More of Journeying to the Pacific Ocean, than of Likenesses, Cared not a *Pecayon* about these Later observations —

as I Was Walking away from his house corner of St Louis and Royal Streets — the *Corner of Events* the officer who had followed me, ask^d me, the price of My *Black Chalk* Likeness and where I resided — all answered; I thought how Strange it was that a poor Devil Like me Could Steal the Custom of the Great Vanderlein — but fortunate if not *blind* certainly Most have his Lunatic Moments — the officer said he would Call on Me Liking My Style Very Much —

Mr Hawkings saw this afternoon some of My Drawings and I gave him My Letter to the President. He was apparently Much pleased With both — and told me he Would do all in his Power for Me —

I Put My Letters to My Beloved Wife — N. Berthoud & Judge Fowles in the Mail that Leaves every Sunday at 8 o'clock, and return^d to our Lodging with a compound of Ideas Not Easily to be described —

The Politeness of Mr Vanderlyn Will be remembered — a long time by me; and When ever I Look over these Scrawls it will do me good to have a Litle of the same feelings — the following is the Copy of the Lines he handed me —

Mr John J. Audubon has shewed me several Specimens of his Drawings in Natural History — such as Birds, with their Natural Colors, & other Drawings in plain Black & White Which Appear to be done With great truth & Accuracy of representation as much so as any I have seen in our Country — the Above Gentleman wishes Me to give this as My Opinion in Writting believing it may Serve as a Recommendation to his being employed as a Draftsman in any Expedition to the interiors of our Country.

J. Vanderlyn

New Orleans 20th March 1821

New Orleans in 1821

April 5ᵗʰ 1821 I have just now recovered My Lost Port Folio Mᵣ Garnier sent it me a fortnight ago to the Care of his son the trouble this gave me I will mention hereafter — I have to thank Mᵣ Garnier but More *he* that found it on the River Bank and took Such very remarkable good Care of it — for on opening it I found the Contents in as good order as the day it Was Lost and *Only* One Plate Missing —

Blue Yellow Back Warblers
Orchard Orioles
Cardinal Grosbeaks
Yellow Eyed Cuckoos
Large Crested Fly Catchers
White Eyed — " — "
Night Hawks at Dawn of Day Plenty
Turkey Buzards
Carrion Crows
Common Gulls
Carolina Wrens by Vast Number
Partridges a few Very Shy

to see these in hunt of others I Was out since half past 2 o'clock this Morning untill 4 this afternoon Wading often to our Midles through the Swamps and then Walking through the Thickest Woods I believe I had yet seen —

April Sunday 22ᵈ 1821 Dined at Mᵣ Pamar as I usually do on Sundays. My Pupils all religiously inclined did not give them Lessons — the great Ease and of Course Comfort that I find in the Company of Mʳˢ Pamar's familly renders my visits at that house quite what I wish and often need for a relief of exersions — Finished to day a Drawing of a *Snowy Heron Ardea Candidissima* a beautifull Male — Joseph Drawing Flowers all day —

Tuesday April 24ᵈ 1821 Much in want of Cash Walked to the Columbus Steam Boat and Made *Baxter Town's* Portrait for 25$ — gave My Likeness and Drew the *Black Poll* Warbler Male — *Sylvia Striata*, pleased with my days Work, recᵈ a letter from My Son Victor. — Much pleased also at his improved hand write —

Wednesday 25 — Went again on board Columbus recᵈ My Pay from Towns — Made Mᵣ Hall's *Portrait* one of the best I believe I ever have taken — Met Gwathway & Thompson from Louisville — Dined at Mᵣ Pamar had a great Wish to see General Jackson but no time to spare yet — Paid our Board Rent & Washing to day — 15$ for the 2 first Items and 5 for the Latter — raining hard —

I am forced here to Complain of the bad figure that My friend Willson has given of the Warbler I drew yesterday, in the Bill only the length exceed that of Nature ⅛ of an Inch — an enormous diference — and he has runned a broad White line round over the Eye that does not exist —

April Friday 27ᵗʰ 1821 General Jackson Left the City about Twelve I saw him *thrice* found Vanderlyn's Likeness the Only good One I have seen, *Tully's* Plate *Miserable* — John De Hart's Likeness being Intended for Mʳˢ Hall took it there. Spent a few Hours with her extremely agreably —

Monday April 30ᵗʰ 1821 Steam Boat Paragon arrived No Letter for me — Mʳ Gordon had one from Mʳ Berthoud — sadly disapointed almost sicken, could not do any thing —

May 1ˢᵗ Tuesday 1821 Walked some, Wrote to My Wife but the boat I Intended for, not going — extremely uneasy about My Wife's health or her Children — done Nothing —

Thursday 3ᵈ Bought 15 yᵈˢ Nankeen for Summer Clothes — found Mʳˢ H more aimiable if Possible than usual, talked freely to Me — became acquainted With an other Sister — Workᵈ at Mʳˢ Hechburgers Portrait — Weather fine Monday Morning Very disagreably Hot — Thermoter, at 88–89 — and to day at 3 o'clock in the Shade at 90 —
Cases of Yellow fever in the City I was told —

May Sunday 1821 Recᵈ a Letter by the Cincinnati from My Wife. Not Very agreable to My feelings, surprised at having Nothing from N. Berthoud — appraised *Joseph* of his Father's Death. Bore it well — Saw Mʳ Jesse Embrie of the Cincinnati Museum = Spent all day very Dull dined at *Hetchberger*

Wednesday 8ᵗʰ finished My Letter to My Lucy and Wrote a Short one to N. Berthoud — put them on Board the Fayette, the Rose, the one I expected to Leave first Not being ready — *thought* to day that a Certain Gentleman to Whom I go to dayly felt *uncomfortable* While I was present, seldom before My coming to New Orleans did I think that I was Looked on so favorably by the *fair* sex as I have *Discovered* Lately —
Saw Hoyteura at Mʳ Hawkins in a High State of Spirits I dare not Call it Intoxication — he sailed this Evening for Liverpool — paid a Visit to the Amiable Vanderlyn, this Gentleman Like all substantial Men gained on acquaintance saw his Portrait of My Fair Pupil Mʳˢ H — the Likeness good but roughly painted — he complimented me on My Drawings I thought too Much to be true — saw Gilly about

settling for our Passage to Missingsat should I determine on going there —

Wrote to My Wife, N. Berthoud, Henry Clay, D^l Drake, on the 16th forwarded all by S. B.^{t} Paragon —

Dined at Governor Robertson, Polite reception, promessed Me a recommendatory letter to Mr Monroe

No news from Mr Berthoud yet. —

17th May 1821 begun lessons with Young Mr Bollin @ $1.50 per Lesson

begun lessons with Miss Perry $2.00 per Lesson

begun lessons with Miss Dimitry $2.00 per Lesson

New Orleans May 20th 1821 Sent a few lines to My Wife by the S. B.^{t} Tamerlane — Last Week I Rec^d a letter from Mr J. Hawkins and one from Mr Robertson the Governor for the President of the U. States — favors from Men of High Stations are favors indeed —

The Governor a Man of Strong Information extremely Polite —

Since So long without any news from my familly, My Spirits have failed me, and it is With Dificulty that I sit to Write at all — My Journal Suffers through the same Cause that affects me — attention —

June 16th New Orleans — 1821 Left this City at about ½ past 12 o'clock — in the Steam Boat Columbus Cap^e John de Hart — bound to Shippingport Kentucky —

pressed by much work on hand within some weeks passed, during every day, and too much incommodated by Musquitoes at evenings My poor Journal as been put a side events and a wish not to discontinue to put down incidents that are of some Note and agreable to My Mind I come again to it —

a personnage who had some week ago boasted of his Interest towards me, and who on one occasion carried his attention quite too far and awkwardly must first take my attention — and here I will give you a Lesson, should you ever be Employed as a Teacher to any ostantatious oppolent person —*flatter*, Keep flattering and end in flattery or else expect No pay —

My Misfortunes often occur through a want of attention to that Maxim in similar Cases after having with assiduity attended on a Gentleman's Lady (Whose Name I will not at present Mention) for forty Days, I received the rudest of dismisal and My pride would not admit me to the House — to even ask any compensation — how agreable the first Lessons were I shall allways remember. *She thought* herself endowed with superior talents, and her Looking glass pleasing her

Vanity I dare say made her believe She was a Star dropped from the heavens to ornament this Hearth — but dificulties augmented and of Course drawing seased to please, I could not well find time to finish every piece that I had began for her, and Constancy the Lady said was never to be found the Companion of Genius — toward the Last she Would be unwell when I walk^d in, Yawn^d and postponed to the morrow — I believe the Husband saw her Weakness, but the good Man Like *one* or *Two* More of My Acquaintances Was Weaker still —

I Knew well that My conduct had been correct and I felt a great pleasure in Leaving them, and, the One hundred Dollars I had hearned *with them*

The *Dimitry* familly on Whose's Daughters I had the pleasure of *attending* as a Drawing Master — had become peculiarly agreable and I left them with anxiety for their wellfare and the pleasure that anticipation produces, having some Hopes of seeing them Next Winter, — Young Dimitry I never will forget a Youth of More genuine Natural Ability I never have Met — his sarcastism had much the turn of Dr Walcot's I Rec^d from the Young Ladies Miss Aimee & Euphrosine Two handsome Plants for My Beloved Lucy that I forward^d under the Care of Cap^e De Hart —

My True friend R. Pamar and his most amiable and Kind Wife I have to thank for all that I can Call the pleasures I met with at New Orleans — I Eat there whenever I could find time, and I was so Loved by the Children that I felt as if I parted from Mine when I left them — I had found^d a very slight acquaintance with Mr P. some years ago as he descended the Ohio on his way home — I had been Polite to him when he called at My Poor Log House at Henderson and he said often that Kindness had not been profuted to him that he was Well able to remember the Instances and that if I did Not please to Make free with his house he Would be Sorry for it —

I Rec^d Many attentions from Mr Laville and Lady — Mr Hollander the Partner of My old but too rich Acquaintance Vincent Nolte I had the pleasure of seing — he I believe saw that I had No wish to disgrace the Handsome Rich furniture of the Wealthy with My Intrusions when reduced to My Grey Breeches, and taking Me by both Hands One day as I was trying to Make Way from him, he said My Dear Mr Audubon Come and see me. I promise you I shall Not have any one at table and I will try to Raise your Spirits. I have some fine Paintings, and please bring Your Birds that I am Anxious to see — then You see that although I lived extremely retired and general show^d those that I thought I Would Incomodate I now & then stumbled on an Less Indiferent Member of this Life toward his fellows Who like Me have been rich and poor alternatly —

I had attended a Miss Perrie to Enhance her Natural tallen for Drawing, for some days When her Mother Whom I intend Noticing in due time, asked Me to Think about My Spending the summer and fall at their farm Near Bayou Sarah; I Was glad of such an overture, but would have greatly prefered her Living in the Floridas — We Concluded the Bargain promissing Me 60 Dollars per Month for One half of My time to teach Miss Eliza all I could in Drawing Music Dancing &^{c} &^{c} furnishing us with a Room &^{c} for Joseph & Myself — so that after the One hundred Diferent Plans I had form^d as Opposite as Could be to this, I found Myself bound for several Months on a Farm in Louisiana.

We left our abode in Quartier Street and Old Miss Louise without the Least regret, the filthiness of her Manners, did not agree with our feeling; and by this time We had fully discovered that a Clean Sweet HouseKeeper is quite Necessary to a Naturalist —

THE FLORIDA KEYS

INTRODUCTION

IN THE middle of April, 1832, Lieutenant Robert Day, of the United States Revenue Cutter *Marion*, called upon Audubon to inform him that his ship was now ready to make the tour of the east coast and keys of Florida, the trip so long desired by the ornithologist. The cruise of the *Marion* lasted six weeks, and extended from Saint Augustine to Key West as well as the Tortugas. Audubon was able to add only two new species to systematic ornithology as a result of this portion of his trip — the Florida cormorant and the great white heron — and regarded all his Florida forays as 'rather unprofitable expeditions.' Yet he did just about all that could have been done, ornithologically, in those times, and he came back with over a thousand specimens and many new drawings and new life histories.

As assistants Audubon had with him Henry Ward, a young taxidermist, and George Lehman, a Swiss landscape painter whom he had first fallen in with in Pittsburgh in the autumn of 1824. Lehman, I believe, contributed these charming backgrounds to *The Birds of America*: the miniature panorama of Charleston in the picture of the long-billed curlew, Plate 231; the plantation houses in Plate 242 of the snowy egret; and Plate 243 of Wilson's snipe; the typical Florida inlet in Plate 252 of the double-crested cormorant; the old Spanish fort at Saint Augustine in Plate 269 of the green-shanks; the palm-topped key in the picture of white-rumped sandpipers, Plate 268; and the view of Key West behind the great white heron, Plate 281.

In this sketch Audubon experiences a storm which he calls a hurricane, but it was obviously nothing more than a violent squall, since it lasted only an hour or two and had no destructive effects sufficiently worth Audubon's while to describe; a genuine tropical hurricane (which would scarcely have struck Florida in spring in any event) would have raged forty-eight hours at a minimum, have wrecked or beached the *Marion*, piled from six to ten feet of tidewaters over the keys, and probably cost the life of the naturalist.   Among the other 'Episodes' Audubon elsewhere describes a 'hurricane' in the Middle West, but plainly what he saw was a tornado.   Audubon never developed an absolutely accurate ear for English words describing superlative, vast, phenomenal, or disastrous matters, and employed them too freely.

Audubon lived in an age when birds were so plentiful everywhere that he hardly stops to tell us of the incredible congregation of water birds on the Florida Keys.   One can learn more, of course, of his impressions and experiences by hunting up his life histories of the great white heron, the snowy egret, the green-shanks, the limpkin, the flamingo, and the roseate spoonbill.   This, indeed, is exactly what I hope the reader will feel moved to do.

The Florida Keys and the Cape Sable region, or extreme southern tip of the Florida mainland, were in Audubon's time inhabited chiefly by Wreckers, or people who preyed upon ships which came to grief on the coral reefs or in the storms, and by Eggers and Turtlers, all of them leading predatory and more or less furtive lives.   The present sketch, however, is valuable chiefly for the glimpse that it gives into the life of a busy field naturalist who has just entered a territory absolutely new to him, where he must, as it were, collect with one hand and draw with the other.   The time at his disposal is very limited, for he cannot detain the United States revenue cutter long.   So all these impressions are first impressions; it may be charged against them that they are consequently superficial.   But how unhampered they are by fatigue, discouragement, debt, and self-defense!   Not a dozen years separates this account from the one that just precedes it in these pages, when Audubon is tramping the streets of New Orleans trying to find work and buying his specimens out of the markets to draw because he cannot get to the woods to see them himself.   Here he is surrounded with every form of assistance, a man with a clearly marked job in the world to do and the strength to do it.   Let us watch him at his task.

I

As THE *Marion* neared the Inlet called 'Indian Key,' which is situated on the eastern coast of the peninsula of Florida, my heart swelled with uncontrollable delight. Our vessel once over the coral reef that everywhere stretches along the shore like a great wall reared by an army of giants, we found ourselves in safe anchoring grounds, within a few furlongs of the land. The next moment saw the oars of a boat propelling us towards the shore, and in brief time we stood on the desired beach. With what delightful feelings did we gaze on the objects around us! — the gorgeous flowers, the singular and beautiful plants, the luxuriant trees. The balmy air which we breathed filled us with animation, so pure and salubrious did it seem to be. The birds which we saw were almost all new to us; their lovely forms appeared to be arrayed in more brilliant apparel than I had ever seen before, and as they fluttered in happy playfulness among the bushes, or glided over the light green waters, we longed to form a more intimate acquaintance with them.

Students of nature spend little time in introductions, especially when they present themselves to persons who feel an interest in their pursuits. This was the case with Mr. Thruston, the deputy collector of the island, who shook us all heartily by the hand, and in a trice had a boat manned, and at our service. Accompanied by him, his pilot and fishermen, off we went, and after a short pull landed on a large key. Few minutes had elapsed when shot after shot might be heard, and down came whirling through the air the objects of our desire. One thrust himself into the tangled groves that covered all but the beautiful coral beach that in a continued line bordered the island, while others gazed on the glowing and diversified hues of the curious inhabitants of the deep. I saw one of my party rush into the limpid element to seize on a crab, that, with claws extended upward, awaited his approach, as if determined not to give way. A loud voice called him back to the land, for sharks are as abundant along these shores as pebbles, and the hungry prowlers could not have found a more savory dinner.

The pilot, besides being a first-rate shot, possessed a most intimate acquaintance with the country. He had been a 'conch diver,' and no matter what number of fathoms measured the distance between the

AMERICAN SNIPE

(WILSON'S SNIPE)

'The Market is regularly furnished with the *English Snipe*[1] Which the French Call *Cache Cache*.' — P. 166.

The background, a South Carolina plantation near Charleston, is probably by George Lehman, the Swiss landscape painter. (See p. 178.)

[1] 'English snipe' is the old gunners' name for our American Wilson's Snipe.

Drawn from Nature, by J.J. Audubon. F.R.S. F.L.S.

American

SCOLOPAX V

South Carolina Plant

Snipe. Male 1. Female 2,3.

WILSONII,

...tion near Charleston.

Engraved, Printed, & Coloured. by R. Havell. London. 1835.

surface of the water and its craggy bottom, to seek for curious shells in their retreat seemed to him more pastime than toil. Not a Cormorant or Pelican, a Flamingo, an Ibis, or Heron had ever in his days formed its nest without his having marked the spot; and as to the Keys to which the Doves are wont to resort, he was better acquainted with them than many fops are with the contents of their pockets. In a word, he positively knew every channel that led to these islands, and every cranny along their shores. For years his employment had been to hunt those singular animals called Sea-cows or Manatees, and he had conquered hundreds of them, 'merely,' as he said, because the flesh and hide bring 'a fair price' at Havana. He never went anywhere to land without 'Long Tom,' which proved indeed to be a wonderful gun, and which made smart havoc when charged with 'groceries' a term by which he designated the large shot he used. In like manner, he never paddled his light canoe without having by his side the trusty javelin with which he unerringly transfixed such fishes as he thought fit either for market or for his own use. In attacking Turtles, netting, or overturning them, I doubt if his equal ever lived on the Florida coast. No sooner was he made acquainted with my errand, than he freely offered his best services, and from that moment until I left Key West he was seldom out of my hearing.

While the young gentlemen who accompanied us were engaged in procuring plants, shells, and small birds, he tapped me on the shoulder, and with a smile said to me, 'Come along, I'll show you something better worth your while.' To the boat we betook ourselves, with the captain and only a pair of tars, for more he said would not answer. The yawl for a while was urged at a great rate, but as we approached a point, the oars were taken in, and the pilot alone sculling desired us to make ready, for in a few minutes we should have 'rare sport.' As we advanced, the more slowly did we move, and the most profound silence was maintained, until suddenly coming almost in contact with a thick shrubbery of mangroves, we beheld, right before us, a multitude of Pelicans. A discharge of artillery seldom produced more effect; the dead, the dying, and the wounded, fell from the trees upon the water, while those unscathed flew screaming through the air in terror and dismay. 'There,' said he, 'did not I tell you so; is it not rare sport?' The birds, one after another, were lodged under the gunwales, when the pilot desired the captain to order the lads to pull away. Within about half a mile we reached the extremity of the Key. 'Pull away,'

[181]

cried the pilot, 'never mind them on the wing, for those black rascals don't mind a little firing — now, boys, lay her close under the nests.' And there we were with four hundred Cormorant's nests over our heads. The birds were sitting, and when we fired, the number that dropped as if dead, and plunged into the water was such, that I thought by some unaccountable means or other we had killed the whole colony. You would have smiled at the loud laugh and curious gestures of the pilot. 'Gentlemen,' said he, 'almost a blank shot!' And so it was, for, on following the birds as one after another peeped up from the water, we found only a few unable to take to wing. 'Now,' said the pilot, 'had you waited until *I had spoken* to the black villains, you might have killed a score or more of them.' On inspection, we found that our shots had lodged in the tough dry twigs of which these birds form their nests, and that we had lost the more favorable opportunity of hitting them, by not waiting until they rose. 'Never mind,' said the pilot, 'if you wish it, you may load *The Lady of the Green Mantle* with them in less than a week. Stand still, my lads; and now, gentlemen, in ten minutes you and I will bring down a score of them.' And so we did. As we rounded the island, a beautiful bird of the species called Peale's Egret came up, and was shot. We now landed, took in the rest of our party, and turned to Indian Key, where we arrived three hours before sunset.

The sailors and other individuals to whom my name and pursuits had become known, carried our birds to the pilot's house. His good wife had a room ready for me to draw in, and my assistant might have been seen busily engaged in skinning, while George Lehman was making a sketch of the lovely isle.

Time is ever precious to the student of nature. I placed several birds in their natural attitudes, and began to outline them. A dance had been prepared also, and no sooner was the sun lost to our eye, than males and females, including our captain and others from the vessel, were seen advancing gayly towards the house in full apparel. The birds were skinned, the sketch was on paper, and I told my young men to amuse themselves. As to myself, I could not join in the merriment, for, full of the remembrance of you, reader, and of the patrons of my work both in America and in Europe, I went on 'grinding' — not on an organ, like the Lady of Bras d'Or, but on paper, to the finishing not merely of my outlines, but of my notes respecting the objects seen this day.

The Florida Keys

The room adjoining that in which I worked was soon filled. Two miserable fiddlers screwed their screeching, silken strings — not an inch of catgut graced their instruments — and the bouncing of brave lads and fair lasses shook the premises to the foundation. One with a slip came down heavily on the floor, and the burst of laughter that followed echoed over the isle. Diluted claret was handed round to cool the ladies, while a beverage of more potent energies warmed their partners. After supper our captain returned to the *Marion*, and I, with my young men, slept in light swinging hammocks under the eaves of the piazza.

It was the end of April, when the nights were short, and the days therefore long. Anxious to turn every moment to account, we were on board Mr. Thruston's boat at three next morning. Pursuing our way through the deep and tortuous channels that everywhere traverse the immense muddy soap-like flats that stretch from the outward Keys to the Main, we proceeded on our voyage of discovery. Here and there we met with great beds of floating seaweeds, which showed us that Turtles were abundant there, these masses being the refuse of their feeding. On talking to Mr. Thruston of the nature of these muddy flats, he mentioned that he had once been lost amongst their narrow channels for several days and nights, when in pursuit of some smugglers' boat, the owners of which were better acquainted with the place than the men who were along with him. Although in full sight of several of the Keys, as well as of the main land, he was unable to reach either until a heavy gale raised the water, when he sailed directly over the flats, and returned home almost exhausted with fatigue and hunger. His present pilot often alluded to the circumstance afterwards, ending with a great laugh, and asserting that had he 'been there, the rascals would not have escaped.'

Coming under a Key on which multitudes of Frigate Pelicans had begun to form their nests, we shot a good number of them, and observed their habits. The boastings of our pilot were here confirmed by the exploits which he performed with his long gun, and on several occasions he brought down a bird from a height of fully a hundred yards. The poor bird, unaware of the range of our artillery, sailed calmly along, so that it was not difficult for 'Long Tom,' or rather for his owner, to furnish us with as many as we required. The day was spent in this manner, and towards night we returned, laden with booty, to the hospitable home of the pilot.

[183]

The next morning was delightful. The gentle seabreeze glided over the flowery isle, the horizon was clear, and all was silent, save the long breakers that rushed over the distant reefs. As we were proceeding towards some Keys seldom visited by men, the sun rose from the bosom of the waters with a burst of glory that flashed on my soul the idea of that power which called into existence so magnificent an object. The moon, thin and pale, as if ashamed to show her feeble light, concealed herself in the dim west. The surface of the waters shone in its tremulous smoothness, and the deep blue of the clear heavens was pure as the world that lies beyond them. The Heron heavily flew towards the land, like a glutton retiring at daybreak, with well lined paunch, from the house of some wealthy patron of good cheer. The Night Heron and the Owl, fearful of day, with hurried flight sought safety in the recesses of the deepest swamps; while the Gulls and Terns, ever cheerful, gambolled over the water, exulting in the prospect of abundance. I also exulted in hope, my whole frame seemed to expand; and our sturdy crew showed by their merry faces that nature had charms for them too. How much of beauty and joy is lost to them who never view the rising sun, and of whose waking existence, the best half is nocturnal.

Twenty miles our men had to row before we reached 'Sandy Island,' and as on its level shores we all leaped, we plainly saw the southernmost cape of the Floridas. The flocks of birds that covered the shelly beaches, and those hovering overhead, so astonished us that we could for a while scarcely believe our eyes. The first volley procured a supply of food sufficient for two days' consumption. Such tales, you have already been told, are well enough at a distance from the place to which they refer; but you will doubtless be still more surprised when I tell you that our first fire among a crowd of the Great Godwits laid prostrate sixty-five of these birds. Rose-colored Curlews stalked gracefully beneath the mangroves. Purple Herons rose at almost every step we took, and each cactus supported the nest of a White Ibis. The air was darkened by whistling wings, while, on the waters, floated Gallinules and other interesting birds. We formed a kind of shed with sticks and grass, the sailor cook commenced his labors, and ere long we supplied the deficiencies of our fatigued frames. The business of the day over, we secured ourselves from insects by means of mosquito-nets, and were lulled to rest by the cacklings of the beautiful Purple Gallinules!

When we laid ourselves down in the sand to sleep, the waters almost

The Florida Keys

bathed our feet; when we opened our eyes in the morning, they were at an immense distance. Our boat lay on her side, looking not unlike a whale reposing on a mud bank. The birds in myriads were probing their exposed pasture-ground. There great flocks of Ibises fed apart from equally large collections of Godwits, and thousands of Herons gracefully paced along, ever and anon thrusting their javelin bills into the body of some unfortunate fish confined in a small pool of water. Of Fish-Crows, I could not estimate the number, but from the havoc they made among the crabs, I conjecture that these animals must have been scarce by the time of next ebb. Frigate Pelicans chased the Jager, which himself had just robbed a poor Gull of its prize, and all the Gallinules, ran with spread wings from the mud-banks to the thickets of the island, so timorous had they become when they perceived us.

Surrounded as we were by so many objects that allured us, not one could we yet attain, so dangerous would it have been to venture on the mud; and our pilot, having assured us that nothing could be lost by waiting, spoke of our eating, and on this hint told us that he would take us to a part of the island where 'our breakfast would be abundant although uncooked.' Off we went, some of the sailors carrying baskets, others large tin pans and wooden vessels, such as they use for eating their meals in. Entering a thicket of about an acre in extent, we found on every bush several nests of the Ibis, each containing three large and beautiful eggs, and all hands fell to gathering. The birds gave way to us, and ere long we had a heap of eggs that promised delicious food. Nor did we stand long in expectation, for, kindling a fire, we soon prepared in one way or other enough to satisfy the cravings of our hungry maws. Breakfast ended, the pilot, looking at the gorgeous sunrise, said: 'Gentlemen, prepare yourselves for fun; the tide is coming.'

Over these enormous mud-flats, a foot or two of water is quite sufficient to drive all the birds ashore, even the tallest Heron or Flamingo, and the tide seems to flow at once over the whole expanse. Each of us, provided with a gun, posted himself behind a bush, and no sooner had the water forced the winged creatures to approach the shore than the work of destruction commenced. When it at length ceased, the collected mass of birds of different kinds looked not unlike a small haycock. Who could not with a little industry have helped himself to a few of their skins? Why, reader, surely no one as fond of these things as I am.

[185]

Every one assisted in this, and even the sailors themselves tried their hand at the work.

Our pilot, good man, told us he was no hand at such occupations and would go after something else. So taking 'Long Tom' and his fishing-tackle, he marched off quietly along the shores. About an hour afterwards we saw him returning, when he looked quite exhausted, and on our inquiring the cause said, 'There is a dewfish yonder, and a few balacoudas, but I am not able to bring them, or even to haul them here; please send the sailors after them.' The fishes were accordingly brought, and as I had never seen a dewfish, I examined it closely, and took an outline of its form, which some days hence you may perhaps see. It exceeded a hundred pounds in weight, and afforded excellent eating. The balacouda is also a good fish, but at times a dangerous one, for, according to the pilot, on more than one occasion 'some of these gentry' had followed him when waist-deep in the water, in pursuit of a more valuable prize, until in self-defence, he had to spear them, fearing that 'the gentlemen' might at one dart cut off his legs, or some other nice bit, with which he was unwilling to part.

Having filled our cask from a fine well, long since dug in the sand of Cape Sable, either by Seminole Indians or pirates, no matter which, we left Sandy Isle about full tide, and proceeded homeward, giving a call here and there at different Keys, with the view of procuring rare birds, and also their nests and eggs. We had twenty miles to go, 'as the birds fly,' but the tortuosity of the channels rendered our course fully a third longer. The sun was descending fast, when a black cloud suddenly obscured the majestic orb. Our sails swelled by a breeze that was scarcely felt by us; and the pilot, requesting us to sit on the weather gunwale, told us that we were 'going to get it.' One sail was hauled in and secured, and the other was reefed, although the wind had not increased. A low murmuring noise was heard, and across the cloud that now rolled along in tumultuous masses shot vivid flashes of lightning. Our experienced guide steered directly across a flat towards the nearest land. The sailors passed their quids from one cheek to the other, and our pilot having covered himself with his oil jacket, we followed his example. 'Blow, sweet breeze,' cried he at the tiller, and 'we'll reach the land before the blast overtakes us, for, gentlemen, it is a furious cloud yon.'

A furious cloud indeed was the one which now, like an eagle on outstretched wings, approached so swiftly that one might have deemed it in haste to destroy us. We were not more than a cable's length from the shore, when, with an imperative voice, the pilot calmly said to us, 'Sit quite still, gentlemen, for I should not like to lose you overboard just now; the boat can't upset, my word for that, if you will but sit still —— Here we have it!'

Reader, persons who have never witnessed a hurricane, such as not unfrequently desolates the sultry climates of the South, can scarcely form an idea of their terrific grandeur. One would think that, not content with laying waste all on land, it must needs swamp the waters of the shallows quite dry, to quench its thirst. No respite for an instant does it afford to the objects within the reach of its furious current. Like the scythe of the destroying angel, it cuts everything by the roots, as it were, with the careless ease of the experienced mower. Each of its revolving sweeps collects a heap that might be likened to the full-sheaf which the husbandman flings by his side. On it goes with a wildness and fury that are indescribable, and when at last its frightful blasts have ceased, Nature, weeping and disconsolate, is left bereaved of her beauteous offspring. In some instances, even a full century is required before, with all her powerful energies, she can repair her loss. The planter has not only lost his mansion, his crops, and his flocks, but he has to clear his lands anew, covered and entangled as they are with the trunks and branches of trees that are everywhere strewn. The bark, overtaken by the storm, is cast on the lee-shore, and if any are left to witness the fatal results, they are the 'wreckers' alone, who, with inward delight, gaze upon the melancholy spectacle.

Our light bark shivered like a leaf the instant the blast reached her sides. We thought she had gone over; but the next instant she was on the shore. And now in contemplation of the sublime and awful storm, I gazed around me. The waters drifted like snow; the tough mangroves hid their tops amid their roots, and the loud roaring of the waves driven among them blended with the howl of the tempest. It was not rain that fell; the masses of water flew in a horizontal direction, and where a part of my body was exposed I felt as if a smart blow had been given me on it. But enough — in half an hour it was over. The pure blue sky once more embellished the heavens, and although it was now quite night, we considered our situation a good one.

The crew and some of the party spent the night in the boat. The pilot, myself, and one of my assistants took to the heart of the mangroves, and having found high land, we made a fire as well as we could, spread a tarpauling, and fixing our insect bars over us, soon forgot in sleep the horrors that had surrounded us.

Next day the *Marion* proceeded on her cruise, and in a few more days, having anchored in another safe harbor, we visited other Keys, of which I will, with your leave, give you a short account.

The deputy-collector of Indian Isle gave me the use of his pilot for a few weeks, and I was the more gratified by this, that besides knowing him to be a good man, and a perfect sailor, I was now convinced that he possessed a great knowledge of the habits of birds, and could without loss of time lead me to their haunts. We were a hundred miles or so farther to the south. Gay May, like a playful babe, gambolled on the bosom of his mother Nature, and everything was replete with life and joy. The pilot had spoken to me of some birds which I was very desirous of obtaining. One morning, therefore, we went in two boats to some distant isle, where they were said to breed. Our difficulties in reaching that Key might to some seem more imaginary than real, were I faithfully to describe them. Suffice it for me to tell you that after hauling our boats and pushing them with our hands, for upwards of nine miles, over the flats, we at last reached the deep channel that usually surrounds each of the mangrove islands. We were much exhausted by the labor and excessive heat, but we were now floating on deep water, and by resting a short while under the shade of some mangroves, we were soon refreshed by the breeze that gently blew from the Gulf. We further repaired our strength by taking some food; and I may as well tell you here that, during all the time I spent in that part of the Floridas, my party restricted themselves to fish and soaked biscuit, while our only and constant beverage was molasses and water. I found that in these warm latitudes, exposed as we constantly were to alternate heat and moisture, ardent spirits and more substantial food would prove dangerous to us. The officers, and those persons who from time to time kindly accompanied us, adopted the same regimen, and not an individual of us had ever to complain of so much as a headache.

But we were under the mangroves; at a great distance on one of the flats, the Heron which I have named *Ardea occidentalis* was seen moving majestically in great numbers. The tide rose and drove them away, and as they came towards us, to alight and rest for a time on the tallest trees, we shot as many as I wished. I also took under my charge several of their young alive.

[188]

The Florida Keys

At another time we visited the 'Mule Keys.' There the prospect was in many respects dismal in the extreme. As I followed their shores, I saw bales of cotton floating in all the coves, while spars of every description lay on the beach, and far off on the reefs I could see the last remains of a lost ship, her dismantled hulk. Several schooners were around her; they were wreckers. I turned me from the sight with a heavy heart. Indeed, as I slowly proceeded, I dreaded to meet the floating or cast-ashore bodies of some of the unfortunate crew. Our visit to the Mule Keys was in no way profitable, for besides meeting with but a few birds, in two or three instances I was, whilst swimming in a deep channel of a mangrove isle, much nearer a large shark than I wish ever to be again.

'The service' requiring all the attention, prudence, and activity of Captain Day and his gallant officers, another cruise took place, of which you will find some account in the sequel; and while I rest a little on the deck of the *Lady of the Green Mantle*, let me offer my humble thanks to the Being who has allowed me the pleasure of thus relating to you, kind reader, a small part of my adventures.

FOUR PROUD FOWL

WILD TURKEY

INTRODUCTION

Among Audubon's strictly ornithological writings, there are nearly five hundred life histories from which to choose. None of Audubon's writings are better known, and about nothing else did he write so profusely. Indeed, it has seemed to the present editor wisest not to permit the bird biographies to overflow the limits of this book, when so much that is less well known in his writings awaits fuller recognition.

But no one would think of passing by the bird biographies wholly; and so there have been chosen here four life histories of impressive and famous birds peculiarly American, heroic-sized birds of an heroic age, who began to leave us from the moment we began to come to them.

The subject of Plate 1 in Audubon's great work is, appropriately enough, the wild turkey. The history of this bird's disappearance over vast tracts of territory is the history of the advance of intensive settlement, and we may say, in a figure of speech, that when the farms were so close together that one chanticleer could hear another salute the dawn, the wild turkey had not room to strut, and must depart.

> The early explorers and colonists [writes John T. Zimmer in a Zoölogical Leaflet of Field Museum, Chicago] were unanimous in speaking of the tremendous numbers of this magnificent species. When Francisco Fernandez reached the northern coast of Yucatan in 1517, he found great numbers of turkeys domesticated by the natives, as did Grijalva farther west in 1518, and Cortez a little later. The colonists in New England found

a bountiful supply of these birds in the forests, and the use to which they put them is well exemplified by the prominent part the turkey plays in our Thanksgiving festivals today, a role which has come down to us from the first Thanksgiving of those early times. The French 'voyageurs,' in penetrating the western wilds, discovered the Wild Turkey in great numbers and recorded their gratefulness for the welcome food supply thus furnished. The accounts of Capt. John Smith, Roger Williams, Father Marquette and La Salle, among many others, show clearly that the Wild Turkey must have existed in countless numbers.

As early as 1760, a change began to appear in these accounts, especially in those relating to the northeastern portions of the country. In this year there was written an article relating to southern Canada in which the writer remarks that turkeys were to be found 'except in the neighborhood of plantations.' In 1765, a writer in Maryland stated that Wild Turkeys, formerly abundant, were then rarely seen. In 1770 the species was reported as very scarce in Pennsylvania. By 1792, in Connecticut, the turkey had retired to the inland mountainous region, while in 1812 there was given what appears to be the last record of its occurrence for the entire state. In 1842 an author reports the species as 'exceedingly rare in all parts of New England.'

In the western states, the turkey held its own for a longer time, owing to the slower development of the region, and in 1846 great numbers were still reported from the bottom lands of the upper Mississippi. In 1892, however, it had almost totally disappeared from Minnesota. In 1892 it was given as rare, if at all present, in Michigan. In 1897 the same was true of Indiana. In 1903 it was all but extinct in Ohio; in 1907, practically extinct in Iowa; in 1915, extinct in Nebraska; in 1920 extinct in South Dakota. The exact date of disappearance in these states is uncertain. In Illinois it was thought by Ridgway to be extinct in 1913, but more recently it has been found to occur sparingly in extreme southern portions of the state. In Pennsylvania there is no doubt that the species still occurs in some numbers, locally, for as late as 1913 the game warden of that state reported 733 Wild Turkeys as having been killed by sportsmen during one season. Farther south and west there are numerous localities in which the birds are still common, and records are given more or less regularly from southern Missouri, Mississippi, Arkansas, Oklahoma, Colorado, Texas, North and South Carolina, Louisiana, Florida and some other adjoining states. Even in these, however, the distribution is purely local, and the turkeys are confined to suitable localities in restricted areas.

Now while the wild turkey was continually losing ground before the advance of European settlement, the domestic turkey was brought right along with all the settlers except the very earliest. Oddly enough this American bird, like that American tuber, the potato, was carried from Europe to America! The explanation of this lies in the fact

Wild Turkey

that the bird introduced into Europe and domesticated there before being brought to what is now the United States was the Mexican form, a creature with white tips on its tail. By this means ornithologists can always distinguish the native turkey from the Mexican-domesticated bird, for our wild turkey has rich chestnut tail-bands. So we get the curious and irrational spectacle of a bird differing chiefly in having white tail-bands, being assiduously protected against its enemies, and its *Lebensraum* widened from an originally rather restricted range in Central America to include a large part of the North American continent, while a bird with chestnut tail-bands is driven from its great range by the plough and the dog and the gun, until it occupies only remote and inaccessible coverts, and even here is pursued like an enemy.

Attempts have been made to introduce the native species into areas from which it has been exterminated or where it was not formerly found (California, for instance). But in vain; like the buffalo and the passenger pigeon, the wild turkey seems to require a great temperate wilderness in order to flourish, and only fragments of wilderness remain.

ABOUT the beginning of October, when scarcely any of the seeds and fruits have yet fallen from the trees, these birds assemble in flocks, and gradually move towards the rich bottom lands of the Ohio and Mississippi. The males, or, as they are more commonly called, the *gobblers*, associate in parties of from ten to a hundred, and search for food apart from the females; while the latter are seen either advancing singly, each with its brood of young, then about two-thirds grown, or in connexion with other families, forming parties often amounting to seventy or eighty individuals, all intent on shunning the old cocks, which, even when the young birds have attained this size, will fight with, and often destroy them by repeated blows on the head. Old and young, however, all move in the same course, and on foot, unless their progress be interrupted by a river, or the hunter's dog force them to take wing. When they come upon a river, they betake themselves to the highest eminences, and there often remain a whole day, or sometimes two, as if for the purpose of consultation. During this time, the males are heard *gobbling*, calling, and making much ado, and are

[195]

seen strutting about, as if to raise their courage to a pitch befitting the emergency. Even the females and young assume something of the same pompous demeanour, spread out their tails, and run around each other, *purring* loudly, and performing extravagant leaps. At length, when the weather appears settled, and all around is quiet, the whole party mounts to the tops of the highest trees, whence, at a signal, consisting of a single *cluck*, given by a leader, the flock takes flight for the opposite shore. The old and fat birds easily get over, even should the river be a mile in breadth; but the younger and less robust frequently fall into the water — not to be drowned, however, as might be imagined. They bring their wings close to their body, spread out their tail as a support, stretch forward their neck, and, striking out their legs with great vigour, proceed rapidly towards the shore; on approaching which, should they find it too steep for landing, they cease their exertions for a few moments, float down the stream until they come to an accessible part, and by a violent effort generally extricate themselves from the water. It is remarkable, that immediately after thus crossing a large stream, they ramble about for some time, as if bewildered. In this state, they fall an easy prey to the hunter.

As early as the middle of February, they begin to experience the impulse of propagation. The females separate, and fly from the males. The latter strenuously pursue, and begin to gobble or to utter the notes of exultation. The sexes roost apart, but at no great distance from each other. When a female utters a call-note, all the gobblers within hearing return the sound, rolling note after note with as much rapidity as if they intended to emit the last and the first together, not with spread tail, as when fluttering round the females on the ground, or practising on the branches of the trees on which they have roosted for the night, but much in the manner of the domestic Turkey, when an unusual or unexpected noise elicits its singular hubbub. If the call of the female comes from the ground, all the males immediately fly towards the spot, and the moment they reach it, whether the hen be in sight or not, spread out and erect their tail, draw the head back on the shoulders, depress their wings with a quivering motion, and strut pompously about, emitting at the same time a succession of puffs from the lungs, and stopping now and then to listen and look. But whether they spy the female or not, they continue to puff and strut, moving with as much celerity as their ideas of ceremony seem to admit. While thus occupied, the males often encounter each other, in which case desperate battles take place, ending in bloodshed, and often in the loss of many lives, the weaker falling under the repeated blows inflicted upon their head by the stronger.

I have often been much diverted, while watching two males in fierce conflict, by seeing them move alternately backwards and forwards, as either had obtained a better hold, their wings drooping, their tails partly raised, their body-feathers ruffled, and their heads covered with blood. If, as they thus struggle, and gasp for breath, one of them should lose his hold, his chance is over, for the other, still holding fast, hits him violently with spurs and wings, and in a few minutes brings him to the ground. The moment he is dead, the conqueror treads him under foot, but, what is strange, not with hatred, but with all the motions which he employs in caressing the female.

When the male has discovered and made up to the female (whether such a combat has previously taken place or not), if she be more than one year old, she also struts and gobbles, turns round him as he continues strutting, suddenly opens her wings, throws herself towards him, as if to put a stop to his idle delay, lays herself down, and receives his dilatory caresses. If the cock meet a young hen, he alters his mode of procedure. He struts in a different manner, less pompously and more energetically, moves with rapidity, sometimes rises from the ground, taking a short flight around the hen, as is the manner of some Pigeons, the Red-breasted Thrush, and many other birds, and on alighting, runs with all his might, at the same time rubbing his tail and wings along the ground, for the space of perhaps ten yards. He then draws near the timorous female, allays her fears by purring, and when she at length assents, caresses her.

When a male and a female have thus come together, I believe the connexion continues for that season, although the former by no means confines his attentions to one female, as I have seen a cock caress several hens, when he happened to fall in with them in the same place, for the first time. After this the hens follow their favourite cock, roosting in his immediate neighbourhood, if not on the same tree, until they begin to lay, when they separate themselves, in order to save their eggs from the male, who would break them all, for the purpose of protracting his sexual enjoyments. The females then carefully avoid him, except during a short period each day. After this the males become clumsy and slovenly, if one may say so, cease to fight with each other, give up gobbling or calling so frequently, and assume so careless a habit, that the hens are obliged to make all the advances themselves. They *yelp* loudly and almost continually for the cocks, run up to them, caress them, and employ various means to rekindle their expiring ardour.

Turkey-cocks when at roost sometimes strut and gobble, but I have more generally seen them spread out and raise their tail, and emit the pulmonic puff, lowering their tail and other feathers immediately after. During clear nights, or when there is moonshine, they perform this action at intervals of a few minutes, for hours together, without moving from the same spot, and indeed sometimes without rising on their legs, especially towards the end of the love-season. The males now become greatly emaciated, and cease to gobble, their *breast-sponge* becoming flat. They then separate from the hens, and one might suppose that they had entirely deserted their neighbourhood. At such seasons I have found them lying by the side of a log, in some retired part of the dense woods and cane thickets, and often permitting one to approach within a few feet. They are then unable to fly, but run swiftly, and to a great distance. A slow turkey-hound has led me miles before I could flush the same bird. Chases of this kind I did not undertake for the purpose of killing the bird, it being then unfit for eating, and covered with ticks, but with the view of rendering myself acquainted with its habits. They thus retire to recover flesh and strength, by purging with particular species of grass, and using less exercise. As soon as their condition is improved, the cocks come together again, and recommence their rambles. Let us now return to the females.

After the middle of April, when the season is dry, the hens begin to look out for a place in which to deposit their eggs. This place requires to be as much as possible concealed from the eye of the Crow, as that bird often watches the Turkey when going to her nest, and, waiting in the neighbourhood until she has left it, removes and eats the eggs. The nest, which consists of a few withered leaves, is placed on the ground, in a hollow scooped out, by the side of a log, or in the fallen top of a dry leafy tree, under a thicket of sumach or briars, or a few feet within the edge of a cane-brake, but always in a dry place. The eggs, which are of a dull cream colour, sprinkled with red dots, sometimes amount to twenty, although the more usual number is from ten to fifteen. When depositing her eggs, the female always approaches the nest with extreme caution, scarcely ever taking the same course twice; and when about to leave them, covers them carefully with leaves, so that it is

HEN TURKEY AND YOUNG

A STUDY IN MINIATURE OF PLATE 6 OF THE ELEPHANT FOLIO
REPRODUCED FROM THE ORIGINAL DRAWING THROUGH THE COURTESY
OF DR. THOMAS BARBOUR, DIRECTOR OF THE MUSEUM OF COMPARATIVE ZOÖLOGY
HARVARD UNIVERSITY

Wild Turkey

very difficult for a person who may have seen the bird to discover the nest.

Several hens sometimes associate together, I believe for their mutual safety, deposit their eggs in the same nest, and rear their broods together. I once found three sitting on forty-two eggs. In such cases, the common nest is always watched by one of the females, so that no Crow, Raven, or perhaps even Pole-cat, dares approach it.

The mother will not leave her eggs, when near hatching, under any circumstances, while life remains. She will even allow an enclosure to be made around her, and thus suffer imprisonment, rather than abandon them. I once witnessed the hatching of a brood of Turkeys, which I watched for the purpose of securing them together with the parent. I concealed myself on the ground within a very few feet, and saw her raise herself half the length of her legs, look anxiously upon the eggs, cluck with a sound peculiar to the mother on such occasions, carefully remove each half-empty shell, and with her bill caress and dry the young birds, that already stood tottering and attempting to make their way out of the nest. Yes, I have seen this, and have left mother and young to better care than mine could have proved — to the care of their Creator and mine. I have seen them all emerge from the shell, and, in a few moments after, tumble, roll, and push each other forward, with astonishing and inscrutable instinct.

Before leaving the nest with her young brood, the mother shakes herself in a violent manner, picks and adjusts the feathers about her belly, and assumes quite a different aspect. She alternately inclines her eyes obliquely upwards and sideways, stretching out her neck, to discover hawks or other enemies, spreads her wings a little as she walks, and softly clucks to keep her innocent offspring close to her. They move slowly along, and as the hatching generally takes place in the afternoon, they frequently return to the nest to spend the first night there. After this, they remove to some distance, keeping on the highest undulated grounds, the mother dreading rainy weather, which is extremely dangerous to the young, in this tender state, when they are only covered by a kind of soft hairy down, of surprising delicacy.

The young Turkeys now advance rapidly in growth, and in the month of August are able to secure themselves from unexpected attacks of Wolves, Foxes, Lynxes, and even Cougars, by rising quickly from the ground, by the help of their powerful legs, and reaching with ease the highest branches of the tallest trees. The young cocks shew the tufts on the breast about this time, and begin to gobble and strut, while the young hens pur and leap, in the manner which I have already described.

The old cocks have also assembled by this time, and it is probable that all the Turkeys now leave the extreme northwestern districts, to remove to the Wabash, Illinois, Black river, and the neighbourhood of Lake Erie.

The Wild Turkeys cannot be said to confine themselves to any particular kind of food, although they seem to prefer the pecan-nut and winter-grape to any other, and, where these fruits abound, are found in the greatest numbers. They eat grass and herbs of various kinds, corn, berries, and fruit of all descriptions. I have even found beetles, tadpoles, and small lizards in their crops.

Turkeys are now generally extremely shy, and the moment they observe a man, whether of the red or white race, instinctively move from him. Their usual mode of progression is what is termed walking, during which they frequently open each wing partially and successively, replacing them again by folding them over each other, as if their weight were too great. Then, as if to amuse themselves, they will run a few steps, open both wings and fan their sides, in the manner of the common fowl, and often take two or three leaps in the air and shake themselves.

When, after a heavy fall of snow, the weather becomes frosty, so as to form a hard crust on the surface, the Turkeys remain on their roosts for three or four days, sometimes much longer, which proves their capability of continued abstinence. When near farms, however, they leave the roosts, and go into the very stables and about the stacks of corn, to procure food. During melting snow-falls, they will travel to an extraordinary distance, and are then followed in vain, it being impossible for hunters of any description to keep up with them. They have then a dangling and straggling way of running, which, awkward as it may seem, enables them to outstrip any other animal. I have often, when on a good horse, been obliged to abandon the attempt to put them up, after following them for several hours. This habit of continued running, in rainy or very damp weather of any kind, is not peculiar to the Wild Turkey, but is common to all gallinaceous birds. In America, the different species of Grouse exhibit the same tendency.

When a Turkey is merely winged by a shot, it falls quickly to the ground in a slanting direction. Then, instead of losing time by tumbling and rolling over, as other birds often do when wounded, it runs off at such a rate, that unless the hunter be provided with a swift dog, he may bid farewell to it. I recollect coming on one shot in this manner, more than a mile from the tree where it had been perched, my dog having traced it to this distance, through one of those thick cane-brakes that cover many portions of our rich alluvial lands near the banks of our western rivers. Turkeys are easily killed if shot in the head, the neck, or the upper part of the breast; but if hit in the hind parts only, they often fly so far as to be lost to the hunter. During winter many of our *real* hunters shoot them by moonlight, on the roosts, where these birds will frequently stand a repetition of the reports of a rifle, although they would fly from the attack of an Owl, or even perhaps from his presence. Thus sometimes nearly a whole flock is secured by men capable of using these guns in such circumstances. They are often destroyed in great numbers when most worthless, that is, early in the fall or autumn, when many are killed in their attempt to cross the rivers, or immediately after they reach the shore.

Whilst speaking of the shooting of Turkeys, I feel no hesitation in relating the following occurrence, which happened to myself. While in search of game, one afternoon late in autumn, when the males go together, and the females are by themselves also, I heard the clucking of one of the latter, and immediately finding her perched on a fence, made towards her. Advancing slowly and cautiously, I heard the yelping notes of some gobblers, when I stopped and listened in order to ascertain the direction in which they came. I then ran to meet the birds, hid myself by the side of a large fallen tree, cocked my gun, and waited with impatience for a good opportunity. The gobblers continued yelping in answer to the female, which all this while remained on the fence. I looked over the log and saw about thirty fine cocks advancing rather cautiously towards the very spot where I lay concealed. They came so near that the light in their eyes could easily be perceived, when I fired one barrel, and killed three. The rest, instead of flying off, fell a strutting around their dead companions, and had I not looked on shooting again as murder without necessity, I might have secured at least another. So I showed myself, and marching to the place where the dead birds were, drove away the survivors. I may also mention, that a friend of mine shot a fine hen, from his horse, with a pistol, as the poor thing was probably returning to her nest to lay.

During spring, Turkeys are *called*, as it is termed, by drawing the air in a particular way through one of the second joint bones of a wing of that bird, which produces a sound resembling the voice of the female, on hearing which the male comes up, and is shot. In managing this, however, no fault must be committed, for Turkeys are quick in distinguishing counterfeit sounds, and when *half civilized* are very wary and cunning. I have known many to answer to this kind of call, without moving a step, and thus entirely defeat the scheme of the hunter, who dared not move from his hiding-place, lest a single glance of the gobbler's eye should frustrate all further attempts to decoy him. Many are shot when at roost, in this season, by answering with a rolling gobble to a sound in imitation of the cry of the Barred Owl.

But the most common method of procuring Wild Turkeys, is by means of *pens*. These are placed in parts of the woods where Turkeys have been frequently observed to roost, and are constructed in the following manner. Young trees of four or five inches diameter are cut down, and divided into pieces of the length of twelve or fourteen feet. Two of these are laid on the ground parallel to each other, at a distance of ten or twelve feet. Two other pieces are laid across the ends of these, at right angles to them; and in this manner successive layers are added, until the fabric is raised to the height of about four feet. It is then covered with similar pieces of wood, placed three or four inches apart, and loaded with one or two heavy logs to render the whole firm. This done, a trench about eighteen inches in depth and width is cut under one side of the cage, into which it opens slantingly and rather abruptly. It is continued on its outside to some distance, so as gradually to attain the level of the surrounding ground. Over the part of this trench within the pen, and close to the wall, some sticks are placed so as to form a kind of bridge about a foot in breadth. The trap being now finished, the owner places a quantity of Indian corn in its centre, as well as in the trench, and as he walks off drops here and there a few grains in the woods, sometimes to the distance of a mile. This is repeated at every visit to the trap, after the Turkeys have found it. Sometimes two trenches are cut, in which case the trenches enter on opposite sides of the trap, and are both strewn with corn. No sooner has a Turkey discovered the train of corn, than it communicates the circumstance to the flock by a cluck, when all of them come up, and searching for the grains scattered about, at length come upon the trench, which they follow, squeezing themselves one after another through the passage under the bridge. In this manner the whole flock sometimes enters, but more commonly six or seven only, as they are alarmed by the least noise, even the cracking of a tree in frosty weather. Those within, having gorged themselves, raise their heads, and try to force their way through the top or sides of the pen, passing and repassing on the bridge, but never for a moment looking down, or attempting to escape through the passage by which they entered. Thus they remain until the owner of the trap arriving, closes the trench, and secures his captives. I have heard of eighteen Turkeys having been caught in this manner at a single visit to the trap. I have had many of these pens myself, but never found more than seven in them at a time. One winter I kept an account of the produce of a pen which I visited daily, and found that seventy-six had been caught in it, in about two months. When these birds are abundant, the owners of the pens sometimes become satiated with their flesh, and neglect to visit the pens for several days, in some cases for weeks. The poor captives thus perish for want of food; for, strange as it may seem, they scarcely ever regain their liberty, by descending into the trench, and retracing their steps. I have, more than once, found four or five, and even ten, dead in a pen, through inattention. Where Wolves or Lynxes are numerous, they are apt to secure the prize before the owner of the trap arrives. One morning, I had the pleasure of securing in one of my pens, a fine Black Wolf, which, on seeing me, squatted, supposing me to be passing in another direction.

Wild Turkeys often approach and associate with tame ones, or fight with them, and drive them off from their food. The cocks sometimes pay their address to the domesticated females, and are generally received by them with great pleasure, as well as by their owners, who are well aware of the advantages resulting from such intrusions, the half-breed being much more hardy than the tame, and, consequently, more easily reared.

While at Henderson, on the Ohio, I had, among many other wild birds, a fine male Turkey, which had been reared from its earliest youth under my care, it having been caught by me when probably not more than two or three days old. It became so tame that it would follow any person who called it, and was the favourite of the little village. Yet it would never roost with the tame Turkeys, but regularly betook itself at night to the roof of the house, where it remained until dawn. When two years old, it began to fly to the woods, where it remained for a considerable part of the day, to return to the enclosure as night approached. It continued this practice until the following spring, when I saw it several times fly from its roosting place to the top of a high cotton-tree, on the bank of the Ohio, from which, after resting a little, it would sail to the opposite shore, the river being there nearly half a mile wide, and return towards night. One morning I saw it fly off, at a very early hour, to the woods, in another direction, and took no particular notice of the circumstance. Several days elapsed, but the bird did not return. I was going towards some lakes near Green river to shoot, when, having walked about five miles, I saw a fine large gobbler cross the path before me, moving leisurely along. Turkeys being then in prime condition for the table, I ordered my dog to chase it, and put it up. The animal went off with great rapidity, and as it approached the Turkey, I saw, with great surprise, that the latter paid little attention. Juno was on the point of seizing it, when she suddenly stopped, and turned her head towards me. I hastened to them, but you may easily conceive my surprise when I saw my own favourite bird, and discovered that it had recognised the dog, and would not fly from it; although the sight of a strange dog would have caused it to run off at once. A friend of mine happening to be in search of a wounded deer, took the bird on his saddle before him, and carried it home for me. The following spring it was accidentally shot, having been taken for a wild bird, and brought to me on being recognised by the red ribbon which it had around its neck. Pray, reader, by what word will you designate the recognition made by my favourite Turkey of a dog which had been long associated with it in the yard and grounds? Was it the result of instinct, or of reason — an unconsciously revived impression, or the act of an intelligent mind?

WHOOPING CRANE

INTRODUCTION

THE most imposing and stentorian of all North American fowl, a creature out of some world to which belong great auks and dodoes and ostriches, the whooping crane was the marvel of the pioneers. It once ranged over the whole United States, though it was always rare on the Atlantic seaboard and most abundant in the Mississippi Valley, and extended its migrations into the central Canadian provinces and Mexico. As the wild turkey was a creature characteristic of the virgin woods of America, so this crane was the voice and symbol of the virgin prairies, enjoying the freedom of a great empire of grass and lakes and rivers that extended from Texas to Saskatchewan.

But as fast as the prairies were settled, the whooping crane vanished. A wide and shining mark for the gunner, this proud and stately animal is by instinct extremely wary and shy. The mere presence of settlement within a broad radius seems enough to send it away. At the present time it has all but given up the struggle, though it has not begun to suffer the persecutions meted out to birds like bobwhites, which still manage to hold their own. One would say that it is doomed by its very grandeur, like an aristocrat in a social revolution.

The crane at the present time is known to breed only on the south-central prairies of Canada, where its haunts lie directly athwart that swift advance of an intensive agricultural civilization which is rapidly displacing all marshes and ranges in favor of wheat. Formerly the migrant birds went as far south as Florida, but the remnants of the great race are said by Arthur Bent, their latest historian, to spend the inclement season 'in the great wild fowl sanctuaries of the Louisiana coast or on the open coastal prairies of Texas or in Mexico. It is a very rare bird even here and is restricted to a few favored localities where it is not disturbed.' There is some indication of the increase of cranes in Texas, but in order to insure their preservation, the reservation of large tracts of wild country in Canada for their breeding ground would be necessary. An unpenetrated wilderness of many miles in extent — to the rim of the prairie horizon, indeed — is scarce enough, it would seem, to give the breeding birds the sense of lonely possession that is their security.

THE variegated foliage of the woods indicates that the latter days of October have arrived; gloomy clouds spread over the heavens; the fierce blasts of the north, as if glad to escape from the dreary regions of their nativity, sport in dreadful revelry among the forests and glades. Showers of sleet and snow descend at intervals, and the careful husbandman gathers his flocks, to drive them to a place of shelter. The traveller gladly accepts the welcome of the forester, and as he seats himself by the blazing fire, looks with pleasure on the spinning-wheels of the industrious inmates. The lumberer prepares to set out on his long voyage, the trapper seeks the retreats of the industrious beaver, and the red Indian is making arrangements for his winter hunts. The Ducks and Geese have already reached the waters of the western ponds; here a Swan or two is seen following in their train, and as the observer of nature stands watching the appearances and events of this season of change, he hears from on high the notes of the swiftly travelling but unseen Whooping Crane. Suddenly the turbid atmosphere clears, and now he can perceive the passing birds. Gradually they descend, dress their extended lines, and prepare to alight on the earth. With necks outstretched, and long bony legs extended behind, they proceed, supported by wings white as the snow but tipped with jet, until arriving over the great savannah they wheel their circling flight, and slowly approach the ground, on which with half-closed wings, and outstretched feet they alight, running along for a few steps to break the force of their descent.

Reader, see the majestic bird shake its feathers, and again arrange

Whooping Crane

them in order. Proud of its beautiful form, and prouder still of its power of flight, it stalks over the withering grasses with all the majesty of a gallant chief. With long and measured steps he moves along, his head erect, his eye glistening with delight. His great journey is accomplished, and being well acquainted with a country which has often been visited by him, he at once commences his winter avocations.

The Whooping Crane reaches the Western Country about the middle of October, or the beginning of November, in flocks of twenty or thirty individuals, sometimes of twice or thrice that number; the young by themselves, but closely followed by their parents. They spread from Illinois over Kentucky, and all the intermediate States, until they reach the Carolinas on the southern coast, the Floridas, Louisiana, and the countries bordering on Mexico, in all of which they spend the winter, seldom returning northward until about the middle of April, or towards the beginning of May. They are seen on the edges of large ponds supplied with rank herbage, on fields or savannahs, now in swampy woods, and again on extensive marshes. The interior of the country, and the neighbourhood of the sea shores, suit them equally well, so long as the temperature is sufficiently high. In the Middle States, it is very seldom indeed that they are seen; and to the eastward of these countries they are unknown; for all their migrations are performed far inland, and thus they leave and return to the northern retreats where, it is said, they breed and spend the summer. While migrating they appear to travel both by night and by day, and I have frequently heard them at the former, and seen them at the latter time, as they were proceeding toward their destination. Whether the weather be calm or tempestuous, it makes no difference to them, their power of flight being such as to render them regardless of the winds. Nay, I have observed them urging their way during very heavy gales, shifting from high to low in the air with remarkable dexterity. The members of a flock sometimes arrange themselves in the form of an acute-angled triangle; sometimes they move in a long line; again they mingle together without order, or form an extended front; but in whatever manner they advance, each bird sounds his loud note in succession, and on all occasions of alarm these birds manifest the same habit.

I had, in 1810, the gratification of taking Alexander Wilson to some ponds within a few miles of Louisville, and of showing him many birds of this species, of which he had not previously seen any other than stuffed specimens. I told him that the white birds were the adults, and that the grey ones were the young. Wilson, in his article on the Whooping Crane, has alluded to this, but, as on other occasions, has not informed his readers whence the information came.

The wariness of this species is so remarkable, that it takes all the cunning and care of an Indian hunter to approach it at times, especially in the case of an old bird. The acuteness of their sight and hearing is quite wonderful. If they perceive a man approaching, even at the distance of a quarter of a mile, they are sure to take to wing. Should you accidentally tread on a stick and break it, or suddenly cock your gun, all the birds in the flock raise their heads and emit a cry. Shut the gate of a field after you, and from that moment they all watch your motions. To attempt to crawl towards them, even among long grass, after such an intimation, would be useless; and unless you lie in wait for them, and be careful to maintain a perfect silence, or may have the cover of some large trees, heaps of brushwood, or fallen logs, you may as well stay at home. They generally see you long before you perceive them, and so long as they are aware that you have not observed them, they remain silent; but the moment that, by some inadvertency, you disclose to them your sense of their presence, some of them sound an alarm. For my part, reader, I would as soon undertake to catch a deer by fair running, as to shoot a Sand-hill Crane that had observed me. Sometimes, indeed, towards the approach of spring, when they are ready to depart for their breeding grounds, the voice of one will startle and urge to flight all within a mile of the spot. When this happens, all the birds around join into a great flock, gradually rise in a spiral manner, ascend to a vast height, and sail off in a straight course.

When wounded, these birds cannot be approached without caution, as their powerful bill is capable of inflicting a severe wound. Knowing this as I do, I would counsel any sportsman not to leave his gun behind, while pursuing a wounded Crane.

While in the Floridas, I saw only a few of these birds alive, but many which had been shot by the Spaniards and Indians, for the sake of their flesh and beautiful feathers, of which latter they make fans and fly-brushes.

According to circumstances, this species roosts either on the ground or on high trees. In the latter case, they leave their feeding-ground about an hour before sun-set, and going off in silence, proceed towards the interior of high land forests, where they alight on the largest

Whooping Crane

branches of lofty trees, six or seven settling on the same branch. For half an hour or so, they usually dress their plumage, standing erect: but afterwards they crouch in the manner of Wild Turkeys. In this situation they are sometimes shot by moonlight. Those which resort to plantations, situated in the vicinity of large marshes, covered with tall grasses, cat's tails, and other plants, spend the night on some hillock, standing on one leg, the other being drawn under the body, whilst the head is thrust beneath the broad feathers of the shoulder. In returning towards the feeding grounds, they all emit their usual note, but in a very low undertone, leaving their roost at an earlier or later hour, according to the state of the weather. When it is cold and clear, they start very early; but when warm and rainy, not until late in the morning. Their motions toward night are determined by the same circumstances. They rise easily from the ground after running a few steps, fly low for thirty or forty yards, then rise in circles, crossing each other in their windings, like Vultures, Ibises, and some other birds. If startled or shot at, they utter loud and piercing cries. These cries, which I cannot compare to the sounds of any instrument known to me, I have heard at the distance of three miles, at the approach of spring, when the males were paying their addresses to the females, or fighting among themselves. They may be in some degree represented by the syllables *kewrr, kewrr, kewrooh*; and strange and uncouth as they are, they have always sounded delightful in my ear.

IVORY-BILLED WOODPECKER

INTRODUCTION

THE commercialized destruction of the ivory-billed woodpecker began before Columbus discovered America, for according to Mark Catesby it was an old habit of the Indians to slaughter the birds for the kingly trophy of their bills, and to sell the bills to tribes who never saw the bird. Among Indians, as among other men, rare and showy objects brought from a distance commanded special prices, and the Indians of the Rockies drove a fine trade with the Plains Indians in grizzly bear claws, while those of Minnesota sold pipestone to distant tribes.

> The bills of these birds [explains Catesby, writing in 1731] are much valued by the Canada Indians, who made Coronets of 'em for their princes and great warriors, by fixing them round a Wreath, with their points outward. The Northern Indians having none of these Birds in their cold country, purchase them of the *Southern People* at the price of two, and sometimes three, Buck-skins a Bill.

In those days the range of the species extended throughout the Gulf States and as far north as North Carolina, southern Ohio and Illinois, without including the Appalachians. Today it is only found in a few isolated localities in Louisiana, Florida, South Carolina and possibly Georgia, where it hides in moss-hung southern swamps of mature and overmature great timber trees. Years go by in which no ornithologist in those regions reports a single bird of this magnificent species, the greatest of all our American woodpeckers and probably the finest in the world. This can only mean that it is gaining no ground at all, and cannot ever do so without special efforts in its behalf.

The disappearance of the ivory-bills after the arrival of the white man is due not to any particular traffic in their carcasses, nor to any value as game, for they possess none except to that low order of sports-man who has to shoot at any moving target. Rather the advance of agriculture in the South and the south-central Middle West has closed in upon this woodpecker's habitats and constricted or obliterated them. Wide, deep, and heavily forested swamps are not particularly easy to eradicate, but with gradual lowering of the water table, by manage-ment of streams, the conditions for swamp timber can become impov-erished, whereupon fire, borers, and fungi complete the deterioration; finally the ditcher, the axe and saw and tractor come in, in the name of sanitation and profit — and another habitat is lost to these kingly birds.

There exist two other splendid accounts of the ivory-bills when they were yet in their glory. Alexander Wilson's amusing and alarming experience with them is quoted at length in the present editor's *A Gathering of Birds*, and Nuttall's first-hand narrative is available in modern editions of his *Manual of Ornithology*.

I HAVE always imagined, that in the plumage of the beautiful Ivory-billed Woodpecker, there is something very closely allied to the style of colouring of the great Vandyke. The broad extent of its dark glossy body and tail, the large and well-defined white markings of its wings, neck, and bill, relieved by the rich carmine of the pendent crest of the male, and the brilliant yellow of its eye, have never failed to remind me of some of the boldest and noblest productions of that inimitable artist's pencil. So strongly indeed have these thoughts become in-grafted in my mind, as I gradually obtained a more intimate acquaint-ance with the Ivory-billed Woodpecker, that whenever I have ob-served one of these birds flying from one tree to another, I have men-tally exclaimed, 'There goes a Vandyke!' This notion may seem strange, perhaps ludicrous, to you, good reader, but I relate it as a fact, and whether or not it may be found in accordance with your own ideas, after you have inspected the plate in which is represented this splendid species of the Woodpecker tribe, is perhaps a little consequence.

The Ivory-billed Woodpecker confines its rambles to a comparatively very small portion of the United States, it never having been observed in the Middle States [1] within the memory of any person now living there. In fact, in no portion of these districts does the nature of the woods appear suitable to its remarkable habits.

Descending the Ohio, we meet with this splendid bird for the first time near the confluence of that beautiful river and the Mississippi; after which, following the windings of the latter, either downwards toward the sea, or upwards in the direction of the Missouri, we frequently observe it. On the Atlantic coast, North Carolina may be taken as the limit of its distribution, although now and then an individual of the species may be accidentally seen in Maryland. To the westward of the Mississippi, it is found in all the dense forests bordering the streams which empty their waters into that majestic river, from the very declivities of the Rocky Mountains. The lower parts of the Carolinas, Georgia, Alabama, Louisiana, and Mississippi, are, however, the most favourite resorts of this bird, and in those States it constantly resides, breeds, and passes a life of peaceful enjoyment, finding a profusion of food in all the deep, dark, and gloomy swamps dispersed throughout them.

I wish, kind reader, it were in my power to present to your mind's eye the favourite resort of the Ivory-billed Woodpecker. Would that I could describe the extent of those deep morasses, overshadowed by millions of gigantic dark cypresses, spreading their sturdy moss-covered branches, as if to admonish intruding man to pause and reflect on the many difficulties which he must encounter, should he persist in venturing farther into their almost inaccessible recesses, extending for miles before him, where he should be interrupted by huge projecting branches, here and there the massy trunk of a fallen and decaying tree, and thousands of creeping and twining plants of numberless species! Would that I could represent to you the dangerous nature of the ground, its oozing, spongy, and miry disposition, although covered with a beautiful but treacherous carpeting, composed of the richest mosses, flags, and water-lilies, no sooner receiving the pressure of the foot than it yields and endangers the very life of the adventurer, whilst here and there, as he approaches an opening, that proves merely a lake of

[1] He means Middle Atlantic States.

black muddy water, his ear is assailed by the dismal croaking of in‧ numerable frogs, the hissing of serpents, or the bellowing of alligators! Would that I could give you an idea of the sultry pestiferous atmosphere that nearly suffocates the intruder during the meridian heat of our dogdays, in those gloomy and horrible swamps! But the attempt to picture these scenes would be vain. Nothing short of ocular demonstration can impress any adequate idea of them.

How often, kind reader, have I thought of the difference of the tasks imposed on different minds, when, travelling in countries far distant from those where birds of this species and others as difficult to be procured are now and then offered for sale in the form of dried skins, I have heard the amateur or closet-naturalist express his astonishment that half-a-crown was asked by the person who had perhaps followed the bird when alive over miles of such swamps, and after procuring it, had prepared its skin in the best manner, and carried it to a market thousands of miles distant from the spot where he had obtained it. I must say, that it has at least grieved me as much as when I have heard some idle fop complain of the poverty of the Gallery of the Louvre, where he had paid nothing, or when I have listened to the same infatuated idler lamenting the loss of his shilling, as he sauntered through the Exhibition Rooms of the Royal Academy of London, or any equally valuable repository of art. But, let us return to the biography of the famed Ivory-billed Woodpecker.

The flight of this bird is graceful in the extreme, although seldom prolonged to more than a few hundred yards at a time, unless when it has to cross a large river, which it does in deep undulations, opening its wings at first to their full extent, and nearly closing them to renew the propelling impulse. The transit from one tree to another, even should the distance be as much as a hundred yards, is performed by a single sweep, and the bird appears as if merely swinging itself from the top of the one tree to that of the other, forming an elegantly curved line. At this moment all the beauty of the plumage is exhibited, and strikes the beholder with pleasure. It never utters any sound whilst on wing, unless during the love-season; but at all other times, no sooner has this bird alighted than its remarkable voice is heard, at almost every leap which it makes, whilst ascending against the upper parts of the trunk of a tree, or its highest branches. Its notes are clear, loud, and yet rather plaintive. They are heard at a considerable distance, perhaps half a mile, and resemble the false high note of a clarionet.

They are usually repeated three times in succession, and may be represented by the monosyllable *pait, pait, pait.* These are heard so frequently as to induce me to say that the bird spends few minutes of the day without uttering them, and this circumstance leads to its destruction, which is aimed at, not because (as is supposed by some) this species is a destroyer of trees, but more because it is a beautiful bird, and its rich scalp attached to the upper mandible forms an ornament for the war-dress of most of our Indians, or for the shot-pouch of our squatters and hunters, by all of whom the bird is shot merely for that purpose.

Travellers of all nations are also fond of possessing the upper part of the head and the bill of the male, and I have frequently remarked, that on a steamboat's reaching what we call a *wooding-place*, the *strangers* were very apt to pay a quarter of a dollar for two or three heads of this Woodpecker. I have seen entire belts of Indian chiefs closely ornamented with the tufts and bills of this species, and have observed that a great value is frequently put upon them.

The Ivory-billed Woodpecker nestles earlier in spring than any other species of its tribe. I have observed it boring a hole for that purpose in the beginning of March. The hole is, I believe, always made in the trunk of a live tree, generally an ash or a hagberry, and is at a great height. The birds pay great regard to the particular situation of the tree, and the inclination of its trunk; first, because they prefer retirement, and again, because they are anxious to secure the aperture against the access of water during beating rains. To prevent such a calamity, the hole is generally dug immediately under the junction of a large branch with the trunk. It is first bored horizontally for a few inches, then directly downwards, and not in a spiral manner, as some people have imagined. According to circumstances, this cavity is more or less deep, being sometimes not more than ten inches, whilst at other times it reaches nearly three feet downwards into the core of the tree. I have been led to think that these differences result from the more or less immediate necessity under which the female may be of depositing her eggs, and again have thought that the older the Woodpecker is, the deeper does it make its holes. The average diameter of the different nests which I have examined was about seven inches within, although the entrance, which is perfectly round, is only just large enough to admit the bird.

Both birds work most assiduously at this excavation, one waiting outside to encourage the other, whilst it is engaged in digging, and when the latter is fatigued, taking its place. I have approached trees whilst these Woodpeckers were thus busily employed in forming their nest, and by resting my head against the bark, could easily distinguish every blow given by the bird. I observed that in two instances, when the Woodpeckers saw me thus at the foot of the tree in which they were digging their nest, they abandoned it for ever. For the first brood there are generally six eggs. They are deposited on a few chips at the bottom of the hole, and are of a pure white colour. The young are seen creeping out of the hole about a fortnight before they venture to fly to any other tree. The second brood makes its appearance about the 15th of August.

In Kentucky and Indiana, the Ivory-bills seldom raise more than one brood in the season. The young are at first of the colour of the female, only that they want the crest, which, however, grows rapidly, and towards autumn, particularly in birds of the first breed, is nearly equal to that of the mother. The males have then a slight line of red on the head, and do not attain their richness of plumage until spring, or their full size until the second year. Indeed, even then, a difference is easily observed between them and individuals which are much older.

The food of this species consists principally of beetles, larvae, and large grubs. No sooner, however, are the grapes of our forests ripe than they are eaten by the Ivory-billed Woodpecker with great avidity. I have seen this bird hang by its claws to the vines, in the position so often assumed by a Titmouse, and, reaching downwards, help itself to a bunch of grapes with much apparent pleasure. Persimmons are also sought for by them, as soon as the fruit becomes quite mellow, as are hagberries.

The Ivory-bill is never seen attacking the corn, or the fruit of the orchards, although it is sometimes observed working upon and chipping off the bark from the belted trees of the newly-cleared plantations. It seldom comes near the ground, but prefers at all times the tops of the tallest trees. Should it, however, discover the half-standing broken shaft of a large dead and rotten tree, it attacks it in such a manner as nearly to demolish it in the course of a few days. I have seen the remains of some of these ancient monarchs of our forests so excavated, and that so singularly, that the tottering fragments of the trunk appeared to be merely supported by the great pile of chips by which its base was surrounded. The strength of this Woodpecker is such, that I have seen it detach pieces of bark seven or eight inches in length at a single blow of its powerful bill, and by beginning at the top branch of a dead tree, tear off the bark, to an extent of twenty or thirty feet, in the course of a few hours, leaping downwards with its body in an upward position, tossing its head to the right and left, or leaning it against the bark to ascertain the precise spot where the grubs were concealed, and immediately after renewing its blows with fresh vigour, all the while sounding its loud notes, as if highly delighted.

This species generally moves in pairs, after the young have left their parents. The female is always the most clamorous and the least shy. Their mutual attachment is, I believe, continued through life. Excepting when digging a hole for the reception of their eggs, these birds seldom, if ever, attack living trees, for any other purpose than that of procuring food, in doing which they destroy the insects that would otherwise prove injurious to the trees.

I have frequently observed the male and female retire to rest for the night, into the same hole in which they had long before reared their young. This generally happens a short time after sunset.

When wounded and brought to the ground, the Ivory-bill immediately makes for the nearest tree, and ascends it with great rapidity and perseverance, until it reaches the top branches, when it squats and hides, generally with great effect. Whilst ascending, it moves spirally round the tree, utters its loud *pait, pait, pait,* at almost every hop, but becomes silent the moment it reaches a place where it conceives itself secure. They sometimes cling to the bark with their claws so firmly, as to remain cramped to the spot for several hours after death. When taken by the hand, which is rather a hazardous undertaking, they strike with great violence, and inflict very severe wounds with their bill as well as claws, which are extremely sharp and strong. On such occasions, this bird utters a mournful and very piteous cry.

CAROLINA PARROT

INTRODUCTION

SOLE North American representative of the great parrot tribe, the Carolina paroquet or parakeet once ranged from Florida north to the southern shores of the Great Lakes, and west to Nebraska, Kansas, Colorado and the Indian Territory. It seems almost impossible to imagine that this tropical creature ever screeched and clawed in our northern woods, ever ate the seeds of our common field growth, or nested in trees of the temperate zone. Audubon's magnificent picture, on which, as he justifiably boasts, he has lavished his workmanship and zest, does not strengthen our belief, but only makes it more difficult. The bird thus brought before our eyes is even more gorgeous and more improbable than words can make it.

Yet here is Audubon's testimony for its abundant presence in Kentucky in pioneer times, and Wilson tells how a tame one rode on his shoulder as he entered Louisville, Kentucky, in 1810. No reader will want to miss Wilson's parallel account of the parakeet, a quotation from which will be found in the present editor's *A Gathering of Birds*.

The extermination of the parakeet was hastened by the merciless activities of professional bird catchers and even more by plume hunters. It was also a favorite with sportsmen who could not bring down so successfully the more wary and intelligent birds (the parakeet was rather a stupid and sluggish species). But in any case it was probably doomed to disappear, for unfortunately it was, and would be if we could restore it to its old haunts, a most destructive pest on farms and in orchards. The farmer, planting his first fruits on virgin soil, found that he and his sons had often to defend it by gunfire against the wild parrots. No matter how many times they were driven up by the discharge, all survivors immediately returned, with a callous determination, to devouring the crop. Under these circumstances the farmer had no choice but to kill till all were dead.

Doctor Frank Chapman believes that he saw the last parakeets near Taylor Creek, northeast of Lake Okeechobee, in 1904. In his own words: 'I saw thirteen and shot four.'

DOUBTLESS, kind reader, you will say, while looking at the figures of Parakeets represented in the plate, that I spared not my labour. I never do, so anxious am I to promote your pleasure.

These birds are represented feeding on the plant commonly called the *Cockle-bur*. It is found much too plentifully in every State west of the Alleghanies, and in still greater profusion as you advance towards the Southern Districts. It grows in every field where the soil is good. The low alluvial lands along the Ohio and Mississippi are all supplied with it. Its growth is so measured that it ripens after the crops of grain are usually secured, and in some rich old fields it grows so exceedingly close, that to make one's way through the patches of it, at this late period, is no pleasant task. The burs stick so thickly to the clothes, as to prevent a person from walking with any kind of ease. The wool of sheep is also much injured by them; the tails and manes of horses are converted into such tangled masses, that the hair has to be cut close off, by which the natural beauty of these valuable animals is impaired. To this day, no useful property has been discovered in the cockle-bur, although in time it may prove so valuable either in medicine or chemistry as many other plants that had long been considered of no importance.

Well, reader, you have before you one of these plants, on the seeds of which the Parrot feeds. It alights upon it, plucks the bur from the stem with its bill, takes it from the latter with one foot, in which it turns it over until the joint is properly placed to meet the attacks of the bill, when it bursts it open, takes out the fruit, and allows the shell to drop. In this manner, a flock of these birds, having discovered a field ever so well filled with these plants, will eat or pluck off all their

CAROLINA PARROT

(CAROLINA PAROQUET)

'Doubtless, kind reader, you will say, while looking at the figures of Parakeets represented in the plate, that I spared not my labour. I never do, so anxious am I to promote your pleasure.' — P. 218.

Carolina Parrot Males 1. F. 2. Young 3.

PSITACUS CAROLINENSIS.

Plant Vulgo. Cuckle Burr.

Drawn from Nature & Published by John J. Audubon. F.R.S.E. F.L.S. M.W.S.

Engraved Printed & Coloured by R Havell & Son.London.

Carolina Parrot

seeds, returning to the place day after day until hardly any are left. The plant might thus be extirpated, but it so happens that it is reproduced from the ground, being perennial, and our farmers have too much to do in securing their crops, to attend to the pulling up of the cockle-burs by the roots, the only effectual way of getting rid of them.

The Parrot does not satisfy himself with cockle-burs, but eats or destroys almost every kind of fruit indiscriminately, and on this account is always an unwelcome visitor to the planter, the farmer, or the gardener. The stacks of grain put up in the field are resorted to by flocks of these birds, which frequently cover them so entirely, that they present to the eye the same effect as if a brilliantly coloured carpet had been thrown over them. They cling around the whole stack, pull out the straws, and destroy twice as much of the grain as would suffice to satisfy their hunger. They assail the pear and apple-trees, when the fruit is yet very small and far from being ripe, and this merely for the sake of the seeds. As on the stalks of corn, they alight on the apple-trees of our orchards, or the pear-trees in the gardens, in great numbers; and, as if through mere mischief, pluck off the fruits, open them up to the core, and, disappointed at the sight of the seeds, which are yet soft and of a milky consistence, drop the apple or pear, and pluck another, passing from branch to branch, until the trees which were before so promising, are left completely stripped, like the ship water-logged and abandoned by its crew, floating on the yet agitated waves, after the tempest has ceased. They visit the mulberries, pecan-nuts, grapes, and even the seeds of the dog-wood, before they are ripe, and on all commit similar depredations. The maize alone never attracts their notice.

Do not imagine, reader, that all these outrages are borne without severe retaliation on the part of the planters. So far from this, the Parakeets are destroyed in great numbers, for whilst busily engaged in plucking off the fruits or tearing the grain from the stacks, the husbandman approaches them with perfect ease, and commits great slaughter among them. All the survivors rise, shriek, fly round about for a few minutes, and again alight on the very place of most imminent danger. The gun is kept at work; eight or ten, or even twenty, are killed at every discharge. The living birds, as if conscious of the death of their companions, sweep over their bodies, screaming as loud as ever, but still return to the stack to be shot at, until so few remain alive, that the farmer does not consider it worth his while to spend more of his ammunition. I have seen several hundreds destroyed in this manner in the course of a few hours, and have procured a basketful of these birds at a few shots, in order to make choice of good specimens for drawing the figures by which this species is represented in the plate now under your consideration.

The flight of the Parakeet is rapid, straight, and continued through the forests, or over fields and rivers, and is accompanied by inclinations of the body which enable the observer to see alternately their upper and under parts. They deviate from a direct course only when impediments occur, such as the trunks of trees or houses, in which case they glance aside in a very graceful manner, merely as much as may be necessary. A general cry is kept up by the party, and it is seldom that one of these birds is on wing for ever so short a space without uttering its cry. On reaching a spot which affords a supply of food, instead of alighting at once, as many other birds do, the Parakeets take a good survey of the neighbourhood, passing over it in circles of great extent, first above the trees, and then gradually lowering until they almost touch the ground, when suddenly re-ascending they all settle on the tree that bears the fruit of which they are in quest, or on one close to the field in which they expect to regale themselves.

They are quite at ease on trees or any kind of plant, moving sidewise, climbing or hanging in every imaginable posture, assisting themselves very dexterously in all their motions with their bills. They usually alight extremely close together. I have seen branches of trees as completely covered by them as they could possibly be. If approached before they begin their plundering, they appear shy and distrustful, and often at a single cry from one of them, the whole take wing, and probably may not return to the same place that day. Should a person shoot at them, as they go, and wound an individual, its cries are sufficient to bring back the whole flock, when the sportsman may kill as many as he pleases. If the bird falls dead, they make a short round, and then fly off.

On the ground these birds walk slowly and awkwardly, as if their tail incommodated them. They do not even attempt to run off when approached by the sportsman, should he come upon them unawares; but when he is seen at a distance, they lose no time in trying to hide, or in scrambling up the trunk of the nearest tree, in doing which they are greatly aided by their bill.

Their roosting-place is in hollow trees, and the holes excavated by the larger species of Woodpeckers, as far as these can be filled by them. At dusk, a flock of Parakeets may be seen alighting against the trunk cf a large sycamore or any other tree, when a considerable excavation exists within it. Immediately below the entrance the birds all cling to the bark, and crawl into the hole to pass the night. When such a hole coes not prove sufficient to hold the whole flock, those around the entrance hook themselves on by their claws, and the tip of the upper mandible, and look as if hanging by the bill. I have frequently seen them in such positions by means of a glass, and am satisfied that the bill is not the only support used in such cases.

When wounded and laid hold of, the Parakeet opens its bill, turns its head to seize and bite, and, if it succeed, is capable of inflicting a severe wound. It is easily tamed by being frequently immersed in water, and eats as soon as it is placed in confinement. Nature seems to have implanted in these birds a propensity to destroy, in consequence of which they cut to atoms pieces of wood, books, and, in short, every thing that comes in their way. They are incapable of articulating words, however much care and attention may be bestowed upon their education; and their screams are so disagreeable as to render them at best very indifferent companions. The woods are the habitation best fitted for them, and there the richness of their plumage, their beautiful mode of flight, and even their screams, afford welcome intimation that our darkest forests and most sequestered swamps are not destitute of charms.

They are fond of sand in a surprising degree, and on that account are frequently seen to alight in flocks along the gravelly banks about the creeks and rivers, or in the ravines of old fields in the plantations, when they scratch with bill and claws, flutter and roll themselves in the sand, and pick up and swallow a certain quantity of it. For the same purpose, they also enter the holes dug by our Kingfisher. They are fond of saline earth, for which they visit the different *licks* interspersed in our woods.

Our Parakeets are very rapidly diminishing in number; and in some districts, where twenty-five years ago they were plentiful, scarcely any are now to be seen. At that period, they could be procured as far up the tributary waters of the Ohio as the Great Kenhawa, the Scioto, the heads of Miami, the mouth of the Manimee at its junction with Lake Erie, on the Illinois river, and sometimes as far north-east as Lake Ontario, and along the eastern districts as far as the boundary line between Virginia and Maryland. At the present day, very few are to be found higher than Cincinnati, nor is it until you reach the mouth of the Ohio that Parakeets are met with in considerable numbers. I should think that along the Mississippi there is not now half the number that existed fifteen years ago.

Their flesh is tolerable food, when they are young, on which account many of them are shot. The skin of their body is usually much covered with the mealy substances detached from the roots of the feathers. The head especially is infested by numerous minute insects, all of which shift from the skin to the surface of the plumage, immediately after the bird's death. Their nest, or the place in which they deposit their eggs, is simply the bottom of such cavities in trees as those to which they usually retire at night. Many females deposit their eggs together. I am of opinion that the number of eggs which each individual lays is two, although I have not been able absolutely to assure myself of this. They are nearly round, and of a light greenish-white. The young are at first covered with soft down, such as is seen on young Owls. During the first season, the whole plumage is green; but towards autumn a frontlet of carmine appears. Two years, however, are passed before the male or female are in full plumage. The only material differences which the sexes present externally are, that the male is rather larger, with more brilliant plumage.

DOWN EAST FOR BIRDS AND SUBSCRIBERS

AUDUBON'S FARTHEST NORTH

INTRODUCTION

IT HAD long been Audubon's dream to visit the Gulf of St. Lawrence and the Labrador coast, in search of its marvelous bird life, unique upon the American shores of the Atlantic. Indeed, by 1833 it had become a pressing necessity so to do, if *The Birds of America* was to be complete, for Audubon's experience of our avifauna had been all in the South and the Mississippi Valley. True, many of the shore birds and oceanic species he had seen in Florida and elsewhere, but in winter plumage; their courtships, their bridal songs, their nestings, he did not know, nor was science familiar with the habits of many of these birds in the north.

At Eastport, Maine, Audubon chartered and provisioned a ship, the *Ripley* — and what a happiness it was to him, at last, to have the funds, the authority, to organize his expedition just as he wished! And this time he was assisted by five strong and eager young men, his son John, Joseph Coolidge, William Ingalls, Thomas Lincoln, and George Shattuck, later a doctor and, like his father, a philanthropist. They all worked like demons to assist the master, then at the height of his powers, and never did Audubon spare himself so little. It was in the painting of these northern birds' portraits that young John Audubon made his début as an artist, doing the landscapes for his father's birds. See particularly Plate 213, the marvelous scene of nesting puffins, Plate 214 of the razor-billed auks, Plate 219, the guillemots, and the spruce grouse which form Plate 176.

In this journal, which was edited by Elliott Coues, Audubon re-

[225]

peatedly addresses his Lucy, for in some measure the journals were letters, too; but then, he had his beloved wife ever in mind, and all beautiful things reminded him of her. It is unique among the Audubon journals for portraying a subarctic landscape, and the beauty and terror of these wild coasts, the storms, the sudden crystal days, the tender beauty and profusion of the flora, the sweet, brief, wild court-ship of the birds, who sang songs perhaps never before heard by an ornithologist, and lined their nests, some of them, with ermine and sable — all the spell of the northern wilderness is in these pages, which seem perpetually wind-swept and rain-drenched and sun-dried.

We find Audubon, too, much more a scientific ornithologist than in any previous journals. He knows what he is seeing, even when it is new; a deep background of the years gives him perspective on every nuance of bird behavior or nidification or plumage. At the same time he has never been a more polished stylist. Note, too, the growth here of Audubon's sensitivity to the destruction of bird life. It is apparently just at this point that he becomes a bird protectionist, after having been an ardent sportsman and an almost phlegmatic collector. He brought back what was a small number of specimens — only two hundred skins. But twenty-three large drawings were the immortal results of this arduous voyage.

Thursday, June 6 [1833]. We left the wharf of Eastport about one o'clock P.M. Every one of the male population came to see the show, just as if no schooner the size of the 'Ripley' had ever gone from this mighty port to Labrador. Our numerous friends came with the throng, and we all shook hands as if never to meet again. The batteries of the garrison, and the cannon of the revenue cutter, saluted us, each firing four loud, oft-echoing reports.

June 8: The wind was from the northeast, blowing fresh, and we were dancing on the waters, all shockingly sea-sick, crossing that worst of all dreadful bays, the Bay of Fundy. We passed between the Seal Islands and the Mud Islands; in the latter *Procellaria wilsonii*, the Stormy Petrel, breeds abundantly; their nests are dug out of the sand in an oblique direction to the depth of two, or two and a half feet. At the bottom of these holes, and on the sand, the birds deposit their pure white eggs. The holes are perforated, not in the banks like the Bank Swallow, but are like rat holes over the whole of the islands.

[226]

Audubon's Farthest North

June 10, we found ourselves not more than thirty miles from Cape Canseau, ordinarily called Cape Cancer. The wind was so fair for proceeding directly to Labrador that our captain spoke of doing so, provided it suited my views; but, anxious as I am not to suffer any opportunity to escape of doing all I can to fulfil my engagements, I desired that we should pass through what is called 'The Gut of Canseau,' and we came into the harbor of that name at three of the afternoon. Here we found twenty vessels, all bound to Labrador, and, of course, all fishermen. We had been in view of the southeastern coast of Nova Scotia all day, a dreary, poor, and inhospitable-looking country. As we dropped our anchor we had a snowfall, and the sky had an appearance such as I never before recollect having seen. Going on shore we found not a tree in blossom, though the low plants near the ground were all in bloom; I saw azaleas, white and blue violets, etc., and in some situations the grass really looked well. The Robins were in full song; one nest of that bird was found; the White-throated Sparrow and Savannah Finch were also in full song. About a dozen houses form this settlement; there was no Custom House officer, and not an individual who could give an answer of any value to our many questions.

June 11. After sailing for twenty-one miles, and passing one after another every vessel of the fleet, we entered the Gut of Canseau, so named by the Spanish on account of the innumerable Wild Geese which, in years long past and forgotten, resorted to this famed passage. The land rises on each side in the form of an amphitheatre, and on the Nova Scotia side, to a considerable height. Many *appearances* of dwellings exist, but the country is too poor for comfort; the timber is small, and the land, very stony. Here and there a small patch of ploughed land, planted, or to be planted, with potatoes, was all we could see evincing cultivation. Near one house we saw a few apple-trees, yet without leaves. The general appearance of this passage reminded me of some parts of the Hudson River, and accompanied as we were by thirty smaller vessels, the time passed agreeably. Saw some Indians in a bark canoe, passed Cape Porcupine, a high, rounding hill, and Cape George, after which we entered the Gulf of St. Lawrence. From this place, on the 20th of May last year, the sea was a complete sheet of ice as far as a spy-glass could inform. As we advanced, running parallel with the western coast of Cape Breton Island, the country looked well, at the distance we were from it; the large, undulating hills

were scattered with many hamlets, and here and there a bit of cultivated land was seen.

Magdalene Island, June 13. This day week we were at Eastport, and I
am sure not one of our party thought of being here this day. At four
this morning we were seated at breakfast around our great drawing-
table; the thermometer was at 44°; we blew our fingers and drank our
coffee, feeling as if in the very heart of winter, and when we landed
I felt so chilled that it would have been quite out of the question to use
my hands for any delicate work. We landed between two great bluffs,
that looked down upon us with apparent anger, the resort of many a
Black Guillemot and noble Raven, then following a tortuous path, suddenly came plump upon one of God's best finished jewels, a woman.
She saw us first, for women are always keenest in sight and sympathy,
in perseverance and patience, in fortitude, and love, and sorrow, and
faith, and, for aught I know, much more. At the instant that my
eyes espied her, she was in full run towards her cottage, holding to her
bosom a fine babe, simply covered with a very short shirt, the very
appearance of which set me shivering. The woman was dressed in
coarse French homespun, a close white cotton cap which entirely surrounded her face tied under her chin, and I thought her the wildest-
looking woman, both in form and face, I had seen for many a day.
At a venture, I addressed her in French, and it answered well, for she
responded in a wonderful jargon, about one third of which I understood, and abandoned the rest to a better linguist, should one ever
come to the island. She was a plain, good woman, I doubt not, and
the wife of an industrious fisherman.

We walked through the woods, and followed the *road* to the church.
Who would have thought that on these wild islands, among these impoverished people, we should have found a church; that we should
have been suddenly confronted with a handsome, youthful, vigorous,
black-haired, black-bearded fellow, in a soutane as black as the
Raven's wedding-dress, and with a heart as light as a bird on the wing?
Yet we met with both church and priest, and our ears were saluted
by the sound of a bell which measures one foot by nine and a half
inches in diameter, and weighs thirty pounds; and this bell may be
heard a full quarter of a mile. It is a festival day, *La Petite Fête de Dieu*.
The chapel was illuminated at six o'clock, and the inhabitants, even
from a distance, passed in; among them were many old women, who,
staff in hand, had trudged along the country road. Their backs were

bent by age and toil, their eyes dimmed by time; they crossed their hands upon their breasts, and knelt before the sacred images in the church with so much simplicity and apparent truth of heart that I could not help exclaiming, 'This is indeed religion!'

The priest, Père Brunet, is originally from Quebec. These islands belong, or are attached, to Lower Canada; he, however, is under the orders of the Bishop of Halifax. He is a shrewd-looking fellow, and, if I mistake not, has a dash of the devil in him. He told me there were no reptiles on the island, but this was an error; for, while rambling about, Tom Lincoln, Ingalls, and John saw a snake, and I heard Frogs a-piping. He also told me that Black and Red Foxes, and the changeable Hare, with Rats lately imported, were the only quadrupeds to be found, except cows, horses, and mules, of which some had been brought over many years ago, and which had multiplied, but to no great extent. The land, he assured us, was poor in every respect — soil, woods, game; that the Seal fisheries had been less productive these last years than formerly. On these islands, about a dozen in number, live one hundred and sixty families, all of whom make their livelihood by the Cod, Herring, and Mackerel fisheries. One or two vessels from Quebec come yearly to collect this produce of the ocean. Not a bird to be found larger than a Robin, but certainly thousands of those. Père Brunet said he lived the life of a recluse, and invited us to accompany him to the house where he boarded, and take a glass of good French wine.

June 14, off the Gannett Rocks. Our anchor was raised, and we bid adieu to the Magdalenes. Our pilot, a Mr. Godwin from Nova Scotia, put the vessel towards what he called 'The Bird Rocks,' where he told us that Gannets (*Sula bassana*) bred in great numbers. For several days past we have met with an increased number of Gannets, and as we sailed this morning we observed long and numerous files, all flying in the direction of the rocks. Their flight now was low above the water, forming easy undulations, flapping thirty or forty times, and sailing about the same distance; these were all returning from fishing, and were gorged with food for their mates or young. About ten a speck rose on the horizon, which I was told was the Rock; we sailed well, the breeze increased fast, and we neared this object apace. At eleven I could distinguish its top plainly from the deck, and thought it covered with snow to the depth of several feet; this appearance existed on every portion of the flat, projecting shelves. Godwin said, with the coolness of a man who had visited this Rock for ten successive seasons, that what we saw was not snow — but Gannets!

I rubbed my eyes, took my spy-glass, and in an instant the strangest picture stood before me. They were birds we saw — a mass of birds of such a size as I never before cast my eyes on. The whole of my party stood astounded and amazed, and all came to the conclusion that such a sight was of itself sufficient to invite any one to come across the Gulf to view it at this season. The nearer we approached, the greater our surprise at the enormous number of these birds, all calmly seated on their eggs or newly hatched brood, their heads all turned to windward, and towards us. The air above for a hundred yards, and for some distance around the whole rock, was filled with Gannets on the wing, which from our position made it appear as if a heavy fall of snow was directly above us.

Our pilot told us the wind was too high to permit us to land, and I felt sadly grieved at this unwelcome news. Anxious as we all were, we decided to make the attempt; our whale-boat was overboard, the pilot, two sailors, Tom Lincoln, and John pushed off with guns and clubs. Our vessel was brought to, but at that instant the wind increased, and heavy rain began to fall. Our boat neared the rock, and went to the lee of it, and was absent nearly an hour, but could not land. The air was filled with Gannets, but no difference could we perceive on the surface of the rock. The birds, which we now could distinctly see, sat almost touching each other and in regular lines, seated on their nests quite unconcerned. The discharge of the guns had no effect on those that were not touched by the shot, for the noise of the Gulls, Guillemots, etc., deadened the sound of the gun; but where the shot took effect, the birds scrambled and flew off in such multitudes, and in such confusion, that whilst some eight or ten were falling into the water either dead or wounded, others pushed off their eggs, and these fell into the sea by hundreds in all directions. The sea now becoming very rough, the boat was obliged to return, with some birds and some eggs; but the crew had not climbed the rock, a great disappointment to me.

Godwin tells me the top of the rock is about a quarter of a mile wide, north and south, and a little narrower east and west; its elevation above the sea between three and four hundred feet. The sea beats round it with great violence, except after long calms, and it is extremely difficult to land upon it, and much more so to climb to the top of it, which is a platform; it is only on the southeast shore that a landing can be made, and the moment a boat touches, it must be hauled up on the rocks. The whole surface is perfectly covered with nests, placed about two feet apart, in such regular order that you may look through the lines as you would look through those of a planted patch of sweet potatoes or cabbages. The fishermen who kill these birds, to get their flesh for codfish bait, ascend in parties of six or eight, armed with clubs; sometimes, indeed, the party comprises the crews of several vessels. As they reach the top, the birds, alarmed, rise with a noise like thunder, and fly off in such hurried, fearful confusion as to throw each other down, often falling on each other till there is a bank of them many feet high. The men strike them down and kill them until fatigued or satisfied. Five hundred and forty have been thus murdered in one hour by six men. The birds are skinned with little care, and the flesh cut off in chunks; it will keep fresh about a fortnight.

The nests are made by scratching down a few inches, and the edges surrounded with sea-weeds. The eggs are pure white, and as large as those of a Goose. By the 20th of May the rock is already covered with birds and eggs; about the 20th of June they begin to hatch. So great is the destruction of these birds annually that their flesh supplies the bait for upwards of forty fishing-boats, which lie close to the Byron Island each season. When the young are hatched they are black, and for a fortnight or more the skin looks like that of the dog-fish. They become gradually downy and white, and when two months old look much like young lambs. Even while shooting at these birds, hundreds passed us carrying great masses of weeds to their nests. The birds were thick above our heads, and I shot at one to judge of the effect of the report of the gun; it had none.

A great number of Kittiwake Gulls breed on this rock, with thousands of Foolish Guillemots. The Kittiwake makes its nest of eel-weeds, several inches in thickness, and in places too small for a Gannet or a Guillemot to place itself; in some instances these nests projected some inches over the edge of the rock. We could not see any of their eggs. The breeze was now so stiff that the waves ran high; so much so that the boat was perched on the comb of the wave one minute, the next in the trough. John steered, and he told me afterwards he was nearly exhausted. The boat was very cleverly hauled on deck by a single effort. The stench from the rock is insufferable, as it is covered with the remains of putrid fish, rotten eggs, and dead birds, old and young.

No man who has not seen what we have this day can form the least idea of the impression the sight made on our minds.

By dark it blew a gale and we are now most of us rather shaky; rain is falling in torrents, and the sailors are reefing. I forgot to say that when a man walks towards the Gannets, they will now and then stand still, merely opening and shutting their bills; the Gulls remained on their nests with more confidence than the Guillemots, all of which flew as we approached. The feathering of the Gannet is curious, differing from that of most other birds, inasmuch as each feather is concave, and divided in its contour from the next. Under the roof of the mouth and attached to the upper mandible, are two fleshy appendages like two small wattles.

June 17. I was on deck at three this morning; the sun, although not above the horizon, indicated to the mariner at the helm one of those doubtful days the result of which seldom can be truly ascertained until sunset. The sea was literally covered with Foolish Guillemots, playing in the very spray of the bow of our vessel, plunging under it, as if in fun, and rising like spirits close under our rudder. The breeze was favorable, although we were hauled to the wind within a point or so. The helmsman said he saw land from aloft, but the captain pronounced his assertion must be a mistake, by true calculation. We breakfasted on the best of fresh codfish, and I never relished a breakfast more. I looked on our landing on the coast of Labrador as a matter of great importance. My thoughts were filled, not with airy castles, but with expectations of the new knowledge of birds and quadrupeds which I hoped to acquire. The 'Ripley' ploughed the deep, and proceeded swiftly on her way; she always sails well, but I thought that now as the land was expected to appear every moment, she fairly skipped over the waves.

At five o'clock the cry of land rang in our ears, and my heart bounded with joy; so much for anticipation. We sailed on, and in less than an hour the land was in full sight from the deck. We approached, and saw, as we supposed, many sails, and felt delighted at having hit the point in view so very closely; but, after all, the sails proved to be large snow-banks. We proceeded, however, the wind being so very favorable that we could either luff or bear away. The air was now filled with Velvet Ducks; *millions* of these birds were flying from the northwest towards the southeast. The Foolish Guillemots and the *Alca torda* [1]

[1] Razor-billed Auk.

were in immense numbers, flying in long files a few yards above the water, with rather undulating motions, and passing within good gun-shot of the vessel, and now and then rounding to us, as if about to alight on the very deck.

We now saw a schooner at anchor, and the country looked well at this distance, and as we neared the shore the thermometer, which had been standing at 44°, now rose up to nearly 60°; yet the appearance of the great snow-drifts was forbidding. The shores appeared to be margined with a broad and handsome sand-beach; our imagination now saw Bears, Wolves, and Devils of all sorts scampering away on the rugged shore. When we reached the schooner we saw beyond some thirty fishing-boats, fishing for cod, and to our great pleasure found Captain Billings of Eastport standing in the bow of his vessel; he bid us welcome, and we saw the codfish thrown on his deck by thousands.

We were now opposite to the mouth of the Natasquan River, where the Hudson's Bay Company have a fishing establishment, but where no American vessels are allowed to come in. The shore was lined with bark-covered huts, and some vessels were within the bight, or long point of land which pushes out from the extreme eastern side of the entrance of the river. We went on to an American Harbor, four or five miles distant to the westward, and after a while came to anchor in a small bay, perfectly secure from any winds. And now we are positively on the Labrador coast, latitude 50° and a little more — farther north than I ever was before.

But what a country! When we landed and passed the beach, we sank nearly up to our knees in mosses of various sorts, producing as we moved through them a curious sensation. These mosses, which at a distance look like hard rocks, are, under foot, like a velvet cushion. We scrambled about, and with anxiety stretched our necks and looked over the country far and near, but not a square foot of *earth* could we see. A poor, rugged, miserable country; the trees like so many mops of wiry composition, and where the soil is not rocky it is boggy up to a man's waist. We searched and searched; but, after all, only shot an adult Pigeon-Hawk, a summer-plumage Tell-tale Godwit, and an *Alca torda*.

We visited all the islands about the harbor; they were all rocky, nothing but rocks. The *Larus marinus* was sailing magnificently all about us. The Great Tern was plunging after shrimps in every pool, and we found four eggs of the *Totanus macularius*;¹ the nest was situated under a rock in the grass, and made of a quantity of dried grass, forming a very decided nest, at least much more so than in our Middle States, where the species breed so very abundantly. Tom Lincoln and John heard a Ptarmigan. Toads were abundant. We saw some rare plants, which we preserved, and butterflies and small bees were among the flowers which we gathered. We found a dead Basking Shark, six and a half feet long; this fish had been wounded by a harpoon and ran ashore, or was washed there by the waves.

June 20. Calm and beautiful. I have drawn seventeen and a half hours this day, and my poor head aches badly enough. The Eider Ducks are seen leaving the islands on which they breed, at daybreak every fair morning, in congregated flocks of males or females separately, and proceed to certain fishing grounds where the water is only a few fathoms deep, and remain till towards evening, when the females sit on their eggs for the night, and the males group on the rocks by themselves. This valuable bird is extremely abundant here; we find their nests without any effort every time we go out. So sonorous is the song of the Fox-colored Sparrow that I can hear it for hours, most distinctly, from the cabin where I am drawing, and yet it is distant more than a quarter of a mile.

June 21. I drew all day at an adult Gannet which we brought from the great rock of which I have spoken; it was still in good order. Many eggs of the Arctic Tern were collected today, two or three in a nest; these birds are as shy here as all others, and the moment John and Coolidge landed, or indeed approached the islands on which they breed, they all rose in the air, passed high overhead, screaming and scolding all the time the young men were on the land. When one is shot the rest plunge towards it, and can then be easily shot. Sometimes when wounded in the body, they sail off to extraordinary distances, and are lost.

When our captain returned he brought about a dozen female Eider Ducks, a great number of their eggs, and a bag of down; also a fine Wild Goose, but nothing new for the pencil. In one nest of the Eider ten eggs were found; this is the most we have seen as yet in any one nest. The female draws the down from her abdomen as far towards her breast as her bill will allow her to do, but the *feathers* are not pulled, and on examination of several specimens I found these well and regu-

¹ Spotted Sandpiper, now *Actitis macularia.*

larly planted, and cleaned from their original down, as a forest of trees is cleared of its undergrowth. In this state the female is still well clothed, and little or no difference can be seen in the plumage unless examined. These birds have now nearly all hatched in this latitude, but we are told that we shall over-reach them in that, and meet with nests and eggs as we go northeast until August. So abundant were the nests of these birds on the islands of Partridge Bay, about forty miles west of this place, that a boat load of their eggs might have been collected if they had been fresh; they are then excellent eating.

Our captain called on a half-breed Indian in the employ of the Northeast Fur and Fish Co., living with his squaw and two daughters. A potato patch of about an acre was planted in *sand*, for not a foot of *soil* is there to be found hereabouts. The man told him his potatoes grew well and were good, ripening in a few weeks, which he called the summer. The mosquitoes and black gnats are bad enough on shore. I heard a Wood Pewee. The Wild Goose is an excellent diver, and when with its young uses many beautiful stratagems to save its brood, and elude the hunter. They will dive and lead their young under the surface of the water, and always in a contrary direction to the one expected; thus if you row a boat after one it will dive under it, and now and then remain under it several minutes, when the hunter with outstretched neck, is looking, all in vain, in the distance for the *stupid Goose!* Every time I read or hear of a stupid animal in a wild state, I cannot help wishing that the stupid animal who speaks thus, was half as wise as the brute he despises, so that he might be able to thank his Maker for what knowledge he may possess. I found many small flowers open this day, where none appeared last evening. All vegetable life here is of the pygmy order, and so ephemeral that it shoots out of the tangled mass of ages, blooms, fructifies, and dies, in a few weeks.

June 22. It was very rainy, and thermometer 54°. After breakfast dressed in my oilskins and went with the captain in the whale-boat to the settlement at the entrance of the true Natasquan, five miles east. On our way we saw numerous Seals; these rise to the surface of the water, erect the head to the full length of the neck, snuff the air, and you also, and sink back to avoid any further acquaintance with man. On entering the river we saw several nets set across a portion of the stream for the purpose of catching salmon; these seines were fastened in the stream about sixty yards from either shore, supported by buoys;

the net is fastened to the shore by stakes that hold it perpendicular to the water; the fish enter these, and entangle themselves until removed by the fishermen.

On going to a house on the shore, we found it a tolerably good cabin, floored, containing a good stove, a chimney, and an oven at the bottom of this, like the ovens of the French peasants, three beds, and a table whereon the breakfast of the family was served. This consisted of coffee in large bowls, good bread, and fried salmon. Three Labrador dogs came and sniffed about us, and then returned under the table whence they had issued, with no appearance of anger. Two men, two women, and a babe formed the group, which I addressed in French. They were French Canadians and had been here several years, winter and summer, and are agents for the Fur and Fish Co., who give them food, clothes, and about $80 per annum. They have a cow and an ox, about an acre of potatoes planted in sand, seven feet of snow in winter, and two-thirds less salmon than was caught here ten years since. Then three hundred barrels was a fair season; now one hundred is the maximum; this is because they will catch the fish both ascending and descending the river.

During winter the men hunt Foxes, Martens, and Sables, and kill some Bear of the black kind, but neither Deer nor other game is to be found without going a great distance in the interior, where Reindeer are now and then procured. One species of Grouse and one of Ptarmigan, the latter white at all seasons; the former I suppose to be the Willow Grouse. The men would neither sell nor give us a single salmon, saying that so strict were their orders that, should they sell *one*, the place might be taken from them. If this should prove the case everywhere, I shall not purchase many for my friends. The furs which they collect are sent off to Quebec at the first opening of the waters in spring, and not a skin of any sort was here for us to look at.

We met here two large boats containing about twenty Montagnais Indians, old and young, men and women. They carried canoes lashed to the sides, like whale-ships, for the Seal fishery. The men were stout and good-looking, spoke tolerable French, and skin redder than any Indians I have ever seen, and more *clear*; the women appeared cleaner than usual, their hair braided and hanging down, jet black, but short. All were dressed in European costume except the feet, on which coarse moccasins of sealskin took the place of shoes. I made a bargain with them for some Grouse, and three young men were despatched at once.

Audubon's Farthest North

On leaving the harbor this morning we saw a black man-of-war-like looking vessel entering it with the French flag; she anchored near us, and on our return we were told it was the Quebec cutter. I wrote a note to the officer commanding, enclosing my card, and requesting an interview. The commander replied he would receive me in two hours. His name was Captain Bayfield, the vessel the 'Gulnare.' The sailor who had taken my note was asked if I had procured many birds, and how far I intended to proceed. After dinner, which consisted of hashed Eider Ducks, which were very good, the females always being fat when sitting, I cut off my three weeks' beard, put on clean linen, and with my credentials in my pocket went to the 'Gulnare.' I was received politely, and after talking on deck for a while, was invited into the cabin, and was introduced to the doctor, who appeared to be a man of talents, a student of botany and conchology. Thus men of the same tastes meet everywhere, yet surely I did not expect to meet a naturalist on the Labrador coast. The vessel is on a surveying cruise, and we are likely to be in company the whole summer. The first lieutenant studies ornithology and collects. After a while I gave my letter from the Duke of Sussex to the captain, who read and returned it without comment.

June 23. This evening we have been visiting the Montagnais Indians' camp, half a mile from us, and found them skinning Seals, and preparing the flesh for us. Saw a robe the size of a good blanket made of seal-skins tanned so soft and beautiful, with the hair on, that it was as pliant as a kid glove; they would not sell it. The chief of the party proves to be well informed, and speaks French so as to be understood. He is a fine-looking fellow of about forty; has a good-looking wife and fine babe. His brother is also married, and has several sons from fourteen to twenty years old. When we landed the men came to us, and after the first salutations, to my astonishment offered us some excellent rum. The women were all seated apart outside of the camp, engaged in closing up sundry packages of provisions and accoutrements. We entered a tent, and seated ourselves round a cheerful fire, the smoke of which escaped through the summit of the apartment, and over the fire two kettles boiled. I put many questions to the chief and his brother, and gained this information.

The country from here to the first settlement of the Hudson's Bay Co. is as barren and rocky as that about us. Very large lakes of great depth are met with about two hundred miles from this seashore; these lakes abound in very large trout, carp, and white fish, and many mussels, unfit to eat, which they describe as black outside and purple within, and are no doubt unios. Not a bush is to be met with, and the Indians who now and then go across are obliged to carry their tent poles with them, as well as their canoes; they burn moss for fuel. So tedious is the travelling said to be that not more than ten miles on an average per day can be made, and when the journey is made in two months it is considered a good one. Wolves and Black Bear are frequent, no Deer, and not many Caribous; not a bird of any kind except Wild Geese and Brent about the lakes, where they breed in perfect peace. When the journey is undertaken in the winter, which is very seldom the case, it is performed on snow-shoes, and no canoes are taken. Fur animals are scarce, yet some few Beavers and Otters are caught, a few Martens and Sables, and some Foxes and Lynx, but every year diminishes their numbers. The Fur Company may be called the exterminating medium of these wild and almost uninhabitable climes, where cupidity and the love of gold can alone induce man to reside for a while. Where can I go now, and visit nature undisturbed?

June 25. The waters of all the streams which we have seen are of a rusty color, probably on account of the decomposed mosses, which appear to be quite of a peaty nature. The rivers appear to be formed by the drainage of swamps, fed apparently by rain and the melting snows, and in time of freshets the sand is sifted out, and carried to the mouth of every stream, where sand-bars are consequently met with. Below the mouth of each stream proves to be the best station for cod-fishing, as there the fish accumulate to feed on the fry which runs into the river to deposit spawn, and which they follow to sea after this, as soon as the fry make off from the rivers to deep water. It is to be remarked that so shy of strangers are the agents of the Fur and Fish Company that they will evade all questions respecting the interior of the country, and indeed will willingly tell you such untruths as at once disgust and shock you. All this through the fear that strangers should attempt to settle here, and divide with them the profits which they enjoy.

June 27. We shot a Ruby-crowned Wren; no person who has not heard it would believe that the song of this bird is louder, stronger, and far more melodious than that of the Canary bird. It sang for a long time ere it was shot, and perched on the tops of the tallest fir-trees removing from one to another as we approached. So strange, so beautiful was that song that I pronounced the musician, ere it was shot, a

CANADA LYNX

'The Canada Lynx is more retired in its habits than our common wild cat, keeping chiefly far from the habitations of even the settlers who first penetrate into the depths of the wilderness ... The specimen from which we drew the figure of this animal was sent to us from Halifax, Nova Scotia. It had been taken in a wolf-trap, after having (as we supposed) destroyed several sheep. We kept it alive for a few weeks, feeding it on fresh raw meat. When a dog approached the cage in which it was confined, it drew back to the farthest part of it, and with open jaws spit forth like a cat at the intruder. We often admired the brilliancy of its large eyes, when it glared at us from a corner of its prison.' — *The Quadrupeds*, vol. 1, p. 139.

CANADA LYNX

'The Canada Lynx is more retired in its habits than our common wild cat, keeping chiefly far from the habitations of even the settlers who first penetrate into the depths of the wilderness . . . The specimen from which we drew the figure of this animal was sent to us from Halifax, Nova Scotia. It had been taken in a wolf-trap, after having (as we supposed) destroyed several sheep. We kept it alive for a few weeks, feeding it on fresh raw meat. When a dog approached the cage in which it was confined, it drew back to the farthest part of it, and with open jaws spit forth like a cat at the intruder. We often admired the brilliancy of its large eyes, when it glared at us from a corner of its prison.' — *The Quadrupeds*, vol. 1, p. 139.

Lynx Canadi

CANADA

MALE

ENSIS, GEOFF.

LYNX.

Lith. Printed & Colᵈ by J.T.Bowen, Philadᵃ.

new species of Warbler. John shot it; it fell to the ground, and though the six of us looked for it we could not find it, and went elsewhere; in the course of the afternoon we passed by the spot again, and John found it and gave it to me.

June 29. At three this morning we were off the land about fifteen miles, and about fifty from American Harbor. Wind favorable, but light; at about ten it freshened. We neared the shore, but as before our would-be pilot could not recognize the land, and our captain had to search for the harbor where we now are, himself. We passed near an island covered with Foolish Guillemots. From this island we went to another, and there found the *Mormon arcticus*[1] breeding in great numbers. We caught many in their burrows, killed some, and collected some of the eggs. On this island their burrows were dug in the light black loam formed of decayed moss, three to six feet deep, yet not more than about a foot under the surface. The burrows ran in all directions, and in some instances connected; the end of the burrow is rounded, and there is the pure white egg. Those caught at the holes bit most furiously and scratched shockingly with the inner claw, making a mournful noise all the time. The whole island was perforated with their burrows.

July 2. A beautiful day for Labrador. Went on shore, and was most pleased with what I saw. The country, so wild and grand, is of itself enough to interest any one in its wonderful dreariness. Its mossy, gray-clothed rocks, heaped and thrown together as if by chance, in the most fantastical groups imaginable, huge masses hanging on minor ones as if about to roll themselves down from their doubtful-looking situations, into the depths of the sea beneath. Bays without end, sprinkled with rocky islands of all shapes and sizes, where in every fissure a Guillemot, a Cormorant, or some other wild bird retreats to secure its egg, and raise its young, or save itself from the hunter's pursuit. The peculiar cast of the sky, which never seems to be certain, butterflies flitting over snow-banks, probing beautiful dwarf flowerets of many hues pushing their tender stems from the thick bed of moss which everywhere covers the granite rocks.

Then the morasses, wherein you plunge up to your knees, or the walking over the stubborn, dwarfish shrubbery, making one think that as he goes he treads down the *forests* of Labrador. The unexpected Bunting, or perhaps Sylvia, which perchance, and indeed as if by

[1] The Common Puffin, now called *Fratercula arctica*.

chance alone, you now and then see flying before you, or hear singing from the creeping plants on the ground. The beautiful fresh-water lakes, on the rugged crests of greatly elevated islands, wherein the Red and Black-necked Divers swim as proudly as swans do in other latitudes, and where the fish appear to have been cast as strayed beings from the surplus food of the ocean. All — all is wonderfully grand, wild — aye, and terrific.

And yet how beautiful it is now, when one sees the wild bee, moving from one flower to another in search of food, which doubtless is as sweet to it, as the essence of the magnolia is to those of favored Louisiana. The little Ring Plover rearing its delicate and tender young, the Eider Duck swimming man-of-war-like amid her floating brood, like the guardship of a most valuable convoy; the White-crowned Bunting's sonorous note reaching the ear ever and anon; the crowds of sea-birds in search of places wherein to repose or to feed — how beautiful is all this wonderful rocky desert at this season, the beginning of July, compared with the horrid blasts of winter which here predominate by the will of God.

I watched the Ring Plover for some time; the parents were so intent on saving their young that they both lay on the rocks as if shot, quivering their wings and dragging their bodies as if quite disabled. We left them and their young to the care of the Creator. I would not have shot one of the old ones, or taken one of the young for any consideration, and I was glad my young men were as forbearing.

July 3. We had a regular stiff gale from the eastward the whole day, accompanied with rain and cold weather, and the water so rough that I could not go ashore to get plants to draw. This afternoon, however, the wind and waves abated, and we landed for a short time. The view from the topmost rock overlooking the agitated sea was grand; the small islets were covered with the angry foam. Thank God! we were not at sea. I had the pleasure of coming immediately upon a Cormorant's nest, that lay in a declivity not more than four or five yards below me; the mother bird was on her nest with three young; I was unobserved by her for some minutes, and was delighted to see how kindly attentive she was to her dear brood; suddenly her keen eye saw me, and she flew off as if to dive in the sea.

July 5. John and Lincoln returned at sunset with a Red-necked Diver, and one egg of that bird. They saw several Loons and *tolled* them by running towards them hallooing and waving a handkerchief, at which sight and cry the Loon immediately swam towards them, until within twenty yards. This 'tolling' is curious and wonderful. Many other species of water-fowl are deceived by these manoeuvres, but none so completely as the Loon.

I drew from four o'clock this morning till three this afternoon. Feeling the want of exercise, went off with the captain a few miles, to a large rough island. To tread over the spongy moss of Labrador is a task beyond conception until tried; at every step the foot sinks in a deep, soft cushion which closes over it, and it requires a good deal of exertion to pull it up again. Where this moss happens to be over a marsh, then you sink a couple of feet deep every step you take; to reach a bare rock is delightful, and quite a relief. This afternoon I thought the country looked more terrifyingly wild than ever; the dark clouds, casting their shadows on the stupendous masses of rugged rock, lead the imagination into regions impossible to describe.

July 9. The wind east, of course disagreeable; wet and foggy besides. The most wonderful climate in the world. Cold as it is, mosquitoes in profusion, plants blooming by millions, and at every step you tread on such as would be looked upon with pleasure in more temperate climes. I wish I were a better botanist, that I might describe them as I do birds. Dr. Wm. Kelly has given me the list of such plants as he has observed on the coast as far as Macatine Island.

July 10. Could I describe one of these dismal gales which blow ever and anon over this desolate country, it would in all probability be of interest to one unacquainted with the inclemency of the climate. Nowhere else is the power of the northeast gale, which blows every week on the coast of Labrador, so keenly felt as here. I cannot describe it; all I can say is that whilst we are in as fine and safe a harbor as could be wished for, and completely land-locked all round, so strong does the wind blow, and so great its influence on our vessel, that her motion will not allow me to draw, and indeed once this day forced me to my berth, as well as some others of our party. One would imagine all the powers of Boreas had been put to work to give us a true idea of what his energies can produce, even in so snug a harbor. What is felt outside I cannot imagine, but greatly fear that few vessels could ride safely before these horrid blasts, that now and then seem strong enough to rend the very rocks asunder.

The rain is driven in sheets which seem scarcely to fall on sea or land; I can hardly call it rain, it is rather a mass of water, so thick that all objects at any distance from us are lost to sight every three or four minutes, and the waters comb up and beat about us in our rock-bound harbor as a newly caged bird does against its imprisoning walls. The Great Black-backed Gull alone is seen floating through the storm, screaming loudly and mournfully as it seeks its prey; not another bird is to be seen abroad; the Cormorants are all settled in the rocks close to us, the Guillemots are deep in the fissures, every Eider Duck lays under the lee of some point, her brood snugly beneath her opened wings, the Loon and the Diver have crawled among the rankest weeds, and are patiently waiting for a return of fair weather, the Grouse is quite hid under the creeping willow, the Great Gray Owl is perched on the southern declivity of some stupendous rock, and the gale continues as if it would never stop.

July 14. Our harbor is the very representation of the bottom of a large bowl, in the centre of which our vessel is now safely at anchor, surrounded by rocks fully a thousand feet high, and the wildest-looking place I ever was in. After supper we all went ashore; some scampered up the steepest hills next to us, but John, Shattuck, and myself went up the harbor, and after climbing to the top of a mountain (for I cannot call it a hill) went down a steep incline, up another hill, and so on till we reached the crest of the island, and surveyed all beneath us. Nothing but rocks — barren rocks — wild as the wildest of the Apennines everywhere; the moss only a few inches deep, and the soil or decomposed matter beneath it so moist that, wherever there was an incline, the whole slipped from under our feet like an avalanche, and down we slid for feet or yards. The labor was excessive; at the bottom of each dividing ravine the scrub bushes intercepted our way for twenty or thirty paces, over which we had to scramble with great exertion, and on our return we slid down fifty feet or more into an unknown pit of moss and mire, more or less deep.

July 18. We all, with the exception of the cook, left the 'Ripley' in three boats immediately after our early breakfast, and went to the main land, distant some five miles. The fog was thick enough, but the wind promised fair weather, and we have had it. As soon as we landed the captain and I went off over a large extent of marsh ground, the first we have yet met with in this country; the earth was wet, our feet sank far in the soil, and walking was extremely irksome.

In crossing what is here called a wood, we found a nest of *Parus hudsonicus* containing four young, able to fly; we procured the parents also, and I shall have the pleasure of drawing them tomorrow; this bird has never been figured that I know.[1] Their *manners* resemble those of the Black-headed Titmouse, or Chickadee, and their notes are fully as strong, and clamorous, and constant as those of either of our own species. Few birds do I know that possess more active powers. The nest was dug by the bird out of a dead and rotten stump, about five feet from the ground; the aperture, one and a quarter inches in diameter, was as round as if made by a small Woodpecker, or a Flying-squirrel. The hole inside was four by six inches; at the bottom a bed of chips was found, but the nest itself resembled a purse formed of the most beautiful and softest hair imaginable — of Sables, Ermines, Martens, Hares, etc.; a warmer and snugger apartment no bird could desire, even in this cold country.

I heard the delightful song of the Ruby-crowned Wren again and again; what would I give to find the nest of this *northern Humming-bird?*[2]

July 19. So cold, rainy, and foggy has this day been that no one went out shooting, and only a ramble on shore was taken by way of escaping the motion of the vessel, which pitched very disagreeably, the wind blowing almost directly in our harbor; and I would not recommend this anchorage to a *painter naturalist*, as Charles Bonaparte calls me. I have drawn two *Parus hudsonicus*, and this evening went on shore with the captain for exercise, and enough have I had. We climbed the rocks and followed from one to another, crossing fissures, holding to the moss hand and foot and with difficulty, for about a mile, when suddenly we came upon the deserted mansion of a Labrador sealer. It looked snug outside, and we entered it.

It was formed of short slabs, all very well greased with seal oil; an oven without a pipe, a salt-box hung on a wooden peg, a three-legged stool, and a wooden box of a bedstead, with a flour-barrel containing some hundreds of seine-floats, and an old Seal seine, completed the list of goods and chattels. Three small windows, with four panes of glass each, were still in pretty good order, and so was the low door, which moved on wooden hinges, for which the maker has received no patent, I'll be bound. This cabin made of hewn logs, brought from

[1] Acadian Chickadee.

[2] Audubon means of course the Ruby-crowned Kinglet, a common migrant and winter bird of the United States; the voice and nest of this northern species (one of the nearest relatives of the European warblers, including the nightingale, which we have in America) were then just as unknown to science and Audubon as they are today to the average American.

[243]

the main, was well put together, about twelve feet square, well roofed with bark of birch and spruce, thatched with moss, and every aperture rendered airtight with oakum. But it was deserted and abandoned; the Seals are all caught, and the sealers have nought to do here now-a-days. We found a pile of good hard wood close to this abode, which we will have removed on board our vessel tomorrow. I discovered that this cabin had been the abode of two French Canadians; first, because their almanac, written with chalk on one of the logs, was in French; and next, the writing was in two very different styles.

July 21. I write now from a harbor which has no name, for we have mistaken it for the right one, which lies two miles east of this; but it matters little, for the coast of Labrador is all alike comfortless, cold and foggy, yet grand. We left Little Macatine at five this morning, with a stiff southwest breeze, and by ten our anchor was dropped here. We passed Captain Bayfield and his two boats engaged in the survey of the coast. We have been on shore; no birds but about a hundred Eider Ducks and Red-breasted Mergansers in the inner bay, with their broods all affrighted as our boats approached. Returning on board, found Captain Bayfield and his lieutenants, who remained to dine with us. They were short of provisions, and we gave them a barrel of ship-bread, and seventy pounds of beef. I presented the captain with a ham, with which he went off to their camp on some rocks not far distant.

This evening we paid him a visit; he and his men are encamped in great comfort. The tea-things were yet arranged on the iron-bound bed, the trunks served as seats, and the sail-cloth clothes-bags as pillows. The moss was covered with a large tarred cloth, and neither wind nor damp was admitted. I gazed on the camp with much pleasure, and it was a great enjoyment to be with men of education and refined manners, such as are these officers of the Royal Navy; it was indeed a treat. We talked of the country where we were, of the beings best fitted to live and prosper here, not only of our species, but of all species, and also of the enormous destruction of everything here, except the rocks; the aborigines themselves melting away before the encroachments of the white man, who looks without pity upon the decrease of the devoted Indian, from whom he rifles home, food, clothing, and life.

For as the Deer, the Caribou, and all other game is killed for the dollar which its skin brings in, the Indian must search in vain over the devastated country for that on which he is accustomed to feed, till, worn out by sorrow, despair, and want, he either goes far from his early haunts to others, which in time will be similarly invaded, or he lies on the rocky seashore and dies. We are often told rum kills the Indian; I think not; it is oftener the want of food, the loss of hope as he loses sight of all that was once abundant, before the white man intruded on his land and killed off the wild quadrupeds and birds with which he has fed and clothed himself since his creation. Nature herself seems perishing. Labrador must shortly be depeopled, not only of aboriginal man, but of all else having life, owing to man's cupidity. When no more fish, no more game, no more birds exist on her hills, along her coasts, and in her rivers, then she will be abandoned and deserted like a worn-out field.

July 22. At six this morning, Captain Bayfield and Lieutenant Bowen came alongside in their respective boats to bid us farewell, being bound westward to the 'Gulnare.' We embarked in three boats and proceeded to examine a small harbor about a mile east, where we found a whaling schooner of fifty-five tons from Cape Gaspé in New Brunswick. When we reached it we found the men employed at boiling blubber in what, to me, resembled sugar boilers. The blubber lay heaped on the shore in chunks of six to twenty pounds, and looked filthy enough. The captain, or owner, of the vessel appeared to be a good, sensible man of that class, and cut off for me some strips of the skin of the whale from under the throat, with large and curious barnacles attached to it. They had struck four whales, of which three had sunk and were lost; this, I was told, was a very rare occurrence.

We found at this place a French Canadian, a Seal-catcher, who gave me the following information. This portion of Labrador is free to any one to settle on, and he and another man had erected a small cabin, have Seal-nets, and traps to catch Foxes, and guns to shoot Bears and Wolves. They carry their quarry to Quebec, receive fifty cents per gallon for Seal oil, and from three to five guineas for Black and Silver-Fox skins, and other furs in proportion. From November till spring they kill Seals in great numbers. Two thousand five hundred were killed by seventeen men in three days; this great feat was done with short sticks, each Seal being killed with a single blow on the snout, while resting on the edges of the field ice. The Seals are carried to the camp on sledges drawn by Esquimaux dogs, that are so well trained that on reaching home they push the Seals off the sledge with their noses, and return to the hunters with despatch. (Remember, my Lucy, this is hearsay.) At other times the Seals are driven into nets one after another, until the poor animals become so hampered and confined that, the gun being used, they are easily and quickly despatched.

He showed me a spot within a few yards of his cabin where, last winter, he caught six Silver-gray Foxes; these had gone to Quebec with his partner, who was daily expected. Bears and Caribous abound during winter, as well as Wolves, Hares, and Porcupines. The Hare (I suppose the Northern one) is brown at this season, and white in winter; the Wolves are mostly of a dun color, very ferocious and daring. A pack of about thirty followed a man to his cabin, and have more than once killed his dogs at his very door. I was the more surprised at this, as the dogs he had were as large as any Wolves I have ever seen. These dogs are extremely tractable; so much so that, when harnessed to a sledge, the leader starts at the word of command, and the whole pack gallops off swiftly enough to convey a man sixty miles in the course of seven or eight hours. They howl like Wolves, and are not at all like our common dogs. They were extremely gentle, came to us, jumped on us, and caressed us, as if we were old acquaintances. They do not take to the water, and are only fitted for drawing sledges and chasing Caribou. They are the only dogs which at all equal the Caribou in speed.

As soon as winter's storms and thick ice close the harbors and the spaces between the mainland and the islands, the Caribous are seen moving in great gangs, first to the islands, where, the snow being more likely to be drifted, the animal finds places where the snow has blown away, and he can more easily reach the moss, which at this season is its only food. As the season increases in severity, the Caribous follow a due northwestern direction, and gradually reach a comparatively milder climate; but nevertheless, on their return in March and April, which return is as regular as the migration of birds, they are so poor and emaciated that the white man himself takes pity on them, and does not kill them. (Merciful beings, who spare life when the flesh is off the bones, and no market for the bones is at hand.) The Otter is tolerably abundant; these are principally trapped at the foot of the waterfalls to which they resort, these places being the latest to freeze, and the first to thaw. The Marten and the Sable are caught, but are by no means abundant, and every winter makes a deep impression on beast as well as on man.

These Frenchmen receive their supplies from Quebec, where they send their furs and oil. At this time, which the man here calls 'the idle time,' he lolls about his cabin, lies in the sunshine like a Seal, eats, drinks, and sleeps his life away, careless of all the world, and the world, no doubt, careless of him. His dogs are his only companions until his partner's return, who, for all I know, is not himself better company than a dog. They have placed their very small cabin in a delightful situation, under the protection of an island, on the southwestern side of the main shore, where I was surprised to find the atmosphere quite warm, and the vegetation actually rank; for I saw plants with leaves fully a foot in breadth, and grasses three feet high. The birds had observed the natural advantages of this little paradise, for here we found the musical Winter Wren in full song, the first time in Labrador, the White-crowned Sparrow, or Bunting, singing melodiously from every bush, the Fox-tail Sparrow, the Black-cap Warbler, the Shore Lark nesting, but too cunning for us; the White-throated Sparrow and a Peregrine Falcon, besides about half a dozen of Lincoln's Finch.

July 23. We visited today the Seal establishment of a Scotchman, Samuel Robertson, situated on what he calls Sparr Point, about six miles east of our anchorage. He received us politely, addressed me by name, and told me that he had received intimation of my being on a vessel bound to this country, through the English and Canadian newspapers. This man has resided here twenty years, married a Labrador lady, daughter of a Monsieur Chevalier of Bras d'Or, a good-looking woman, and has six children. His house is comfortable, and in a little garden he raises a few potatoes, turnips, and other vegetables. He appears to be lord of these parts and quite contented with his lot. He told me his profits last year amounted to £600. He will not trade with the Indians, of whom we saw about twenty, of the Montagnais tribes, and employs only white serving-men. His Seal-oil tubs were full, and he was then engaged in loading two schooners for Quebec with that article. I bought from him the skin of a Cross Fox for three dollars.

He complained of the American fishermen very much, told us they often acted as badly as pirates towards the Indians, the white settlers, and the eggers, all of whom have been more than once obliged to retaliate, when bloody encounters have been the result. He assured me he had seen a fisherman's crew kill thousands of Guillemots in the course of a day, pluck the feathers from the breasts, and throw the bodies into the sea. He also told me that during mild winters his little harbor is covered with pure white Gulls (the Silvery), but that all leave at the first appearance of spring. The traveling here is effected altogether on the snow-covered ice, by means of sledges and Esquimaux dogs, of which Mr. Robertson keeps a famous pack. With them, at the rate of about six miles an hour, he proceeds to Bras d'Or seventy-five miles, with his wife and six children, in one sledge drawn by ten dogs.

Mr. R.'s newspapers tell of the ravages of cholera in the south and west, of the indisposition of General Jackson at the Tremont House, Boston, etc.; thus even here the news circulates now and then.

July 26. At daylight we found ourselves at the mouth of Bras d'Or harbor, where we are snugly moored. Our Pilot not knowing a foot of the ground, we hoisted our ensign, and Captain Billings came to us in his Hampton boat and piloted us in. Bras d'Or is the grand rendezvous of almost all the fishermen that resort to this coast for codfish. We found here a flotilla of about one hundred and fifty sail, principally fore-and-aft schooners, a few pickaxes, etc., mostly from Halifax and the eastern portions of the United States. There was a life and stir about this harbor which surprised us after so many weeks of wilderness and loneliness — the boats moving to and fro, going after fish, and returning loaded to the gunwales, others with seines, others with capelings for bait. A hundred or more were anchored out about a mile from us, hauling the poor codfish by thousands; hundreds of men engaged at cleaning and salting, their low jokes and songs resembling those of the Billingsgate gentry.

July 29. 'The Curlews are coming'; this is as much of a saying here as that about the Wild Pigeons in Kentucky. What species of Curlew, I know not yet, for none have been killed, but one of our men, who started with John and party, broke down, and was sent back; he assured me that he had seen some with bills about four inches long, and the body the size of a Wild Pigeon. The accounts given of these Curlews border on the miraculous, and I shall say nothing about them till I have tested the fishermen's stories.

August 1. At noon we were visited by an iceberg, which has been drifting within three miles of us, and is now grounded at the entrance of the bay; it looks like a large man-of-war dressed in light green muslin, instead of canvas, and when the sun strikes it, it glitters with intense brilliancy. When these transient monuments of the sea happen to tumble or roll over, the fall is tremendous, and the sound produced resembles that of loud, distant thunder; these icebergs are common here all summer, being wafted south with every gale that blows; as the winds are usually easterly, the coast of Newfoundland is more free [from] them than that of Labrador. I have determined to make a last thorough search of the mountain tops, plains and ponds, and if no success ensues, to raise anchor and sail towards the United States once more; and blessed will the day be when I land on those dear shores, where all I long for in the world exists and lives, I hope.

August 3. This afternoon we all went ashore, through a high and frightful sea which drenched us to the skin, and went to the table-lands; there we found the true Esquimau Curlew, *Numenius borealis*,[1] so carelessly described in Bonaparte's Synopsis. This species here takes the place of the Migratory Pigeon; it has now arrived; I have seen many hundreds this afternoon, and shot seven. They fly in compact bodies, with beautiful evolutions, overlooking a great extent of country ere they make choice of a spot on which to alight; this is done wherever a certain berry, called here 'curlew berry,' proves to be abundant. Here they balance themselves, call, whistle, and of common accord come to the ground, as the top of the country here must be called. They devour every berry, and if pursued squat in the manner of Partridges. A single shot starts the whole flock; off they fly, ramble overhead for a great distance ere they again alight. This rambling is caused by the scarcity of berries. The iceberg has been broken into thousands of pieces by the gale.

August 4. Still raining as steadily as ever; the morning was calm, and on shore the mosquitoes were shockingly bad, though the thermometer indicates only 49°. I have been drawing at the *Numenius borealis*; I find them difficult birds to represent. This species of Curlew, the smallest I ever saw, feeds on the berries it procures, with a rapidity equalled only by that of the Passenger Pigeon; in an instant all the ripe berries on the plant are plucked and swallowed, and the whole country is cleared of these berries as our Western woods are of the mast. In their evolutions they resemble Pigeons also, sweeping over the ground, cutting backward and forward in the most interesting manner, and now and then poising in the air like a Hawk in sight of quarry. There is scarcely any difference in the appearance of the adult and the young.

The *Alauda alpestris*[2] of this season has now made such progress in its growth that the first moulting is so forward that the small wing-

[1] Now extinct.

[2] The shore lark, the closest American representative of the European skylark.

coverts and secondaries are already come, and have assumed the beautiful rosy tints of the adults in patches at these parts; a most interesting state of their plumage, probably never seen by any naturalist before. It is quite surprising to see how quickly the growth is attained of every living thing in this country, either animal or vegetable. In six weeks I have seen the eggs laid, the birds hatched, their first moult half over, their association in flocks, and preparations begun for their leaving the country. That the Creator should have commanded millions of delicate, diminutive, tender creatures to cross immense spaces of country to all appearance a thousand times more congenial to them than this, to cause them to people, as it were, this desolate land for a time, to enliven it by the songs of the sweet feathered musicians for two months at most, and by the same command induce them to abandon it almost suddenly, is as wonderful as it is beautiful.

The fruits are now ripe, yet six weeks ago the whole country was a sheet of snow, the bays locked in ice, the air a constant storm. Now the grass is rich in growth, at every step flowers are met with, insects fill the air, the snow-banks are melting; now and then an appearance as of summer does exist, but in thirty days all is over; the dark northern clouds will enwrap the mountain summits; the rivulets, the ponds, the rivers, the bays themselves will begin to freeze; heavy snowfalls will cover all these shores, and nature will resume her sleeping state, nay, more than that, one of desolation and death. Wonderful! Wonderful!

August 10. I now sit down to post my poor book, while a heavy gale is raging furiously around our vessel. My reason for not writing at night is that I have been drawing so constantly, often seventeen hours a day, that the weariness of my body at night has been unprecedented, by such work at least. At times I felt as if my physical powers would abandon me; my neck, my shoulders, and, more than all, my fingers, were almost useless through actual fatigue at drawing. When at the return of dawn my spirits called me out of my berth, my body seemed to beg my mind to suffer it to rest a while longer; and as dark forced me to lay aside my brushes I immediately went to rest as if I had walked sixty-five miles that day, as I have done *a few times* in my stronger days. The young men think my fatigue is added to by the fact that I often work in wet clothes, but I have done that all my life with no ill effects. No! no! it is that I am no longer young.

August 15. Harbor of St. George, St. George's Bay, Newfoundland. We have had a beautiful day; this morning some Indians came alongside;

they had half a Reindeer or Caribou, and a Hare which I had never seen before. We took the forty-four pounds of fresh meat and gave in exchange twenty-one of pork and thirty-three of ship-biscuit, and paid a quarter of a dollar for the Hare, which plainly shows that these Indians know full well the value of the game which they procure. I spent a portion of the day in adding a plant to my drawing of the Red-necked Diver, after which we all went on shore to the Indians' camp across the bay.

We found them, as I expected, all lying down pellmell in their wig-wams. A strong mixture of blood was apparent in their skins, shape, and deportment; some indeed were nearly white, and sorry I am to say that the nearer to our own noble selves, the filthier and lazier they are; the women and children were particularly disgusting. Some of the former, from whom I purchased some rough baskets, were frightfully so. Other women had been out collecting the fruit called here 'baked apple' [*Rubus chamaemorus*]. When a little roasted it tasted exactly like baked apple. The children were engaged in catching lobsters and eels, of which there are numbers in all the bays here; at Labrador, lobsters are rare. The young Indians simply wade out up to their knees, turned the eel grass over, and secured their prey. After much parley, we engaged two hunters to go as guides into the interior to procure Caribou and Hares, for which they were to receive a dollar a day each. Our men caught ninety-nine lobsters, all of good size; the shores truly abound in this valuable shell-fish. The Indians roast them in a fire of brushwood, and devour them without salt or any other *et ceteras*.

The Caribous are now 'in velvet,' and their skins light gray, the flesh tender, but the animal poor. The average weight when in good condition, four hundred pounds. In the early part of March the Caribou leave the hills and come to the sea-shore to feed on kelp and sea-grasses cut off by the ice and cast on the shore. Groups of many hundreds may be seen thus feeding. The flesh here is held in low estimation; it tastes like poor venison.

August 22. After in vain attempting to reach Pictou, we concluded, after dinner, that myself and party should be put ashore anywhere, and the 'Ripley' should sail back towards the Straits of Canseau, the wind and tide being favorable. We drank a glass of wine to our wives and our friends, and our excellent little captain took us to the shore, while the vessel stood still, with all sails up, awaiting his return. We happened to land on an island called Ruy's Island, where, fortunately for us, we found some men making hay. Two of these we engaged to carry our trunks and two of the party to this place, Pictou, for two dollars — truly cheap. Our effects, or rather those we needed, were soon put up, we all shook hands most heartily with the captain — to whom we now feel really attached — said farewell to the crew, and parted, giving three hearty cheers.

We were now, thanks to God, positively on the mainland of our native country, and after four days' confinement in our berths, and sick of sea-sickness, the sea and all its appurtenances, we felt so refreshed that the thought of walking nine miles seemed like nothing more than dancing a quadrille. The air felt deliciously warm, the country, compared with those we have so lately left, appeared perfectly beautiful, and the smell of the new-mown grass was the sweetest that ever existed. Even the music of the crickets was delightful to mine ears, for no such insect does either Labrador or Newfoundland afford. The voice of a Blue Jay was melody to me, and the sight of a Humming-bird quite filled my heart with delight. The roads were good, or seemed to be so; the woods were all of tall timber, and the air that circulated freely was filled with perfume. Almost every plant we saw brought to mind some portion of the United States; in a word, all of us felt quite happy. Now and then, as we crossed a hill and looked back over the sea, we saw our beautiful vessel sailing freely before the wind, and as she gradually neared the horizon, she looked like a white speck, or an Eagle high in air. We wished our captain a most safe voyage to Quoddy.

We arrived opposite Pictou in two hours and a half, and lay down on the grass to await the arrival of the boat, enjoying the scenery around us. A number of American vessels were in the harbor, loading with coal; the village, placed at the upper end of a fine bay, looked well, though small. Three churches rose above the rest of the buildings, all of which are of wood, and several vessels were on the stocks. The whole country appeared in a high state of cultivation, and looked well; the population is about two thousand. Our boat came, we crossed the bay, and put up at the 'Royal Oak,' the best house, and have had what seemed to be, after our recent fare, a most excellent supper. The very treading on a carpeted floor was quite wonderful.

THE EGGERS OF LABRADOR

INTRODUCTION

Tʜᴇ traffic in sea birds' eggs has gone on in all parts of the world where the colonies of nesting oceanic fowl have been dense enough to make it worth men's while. Some of the human inhabitants of the islands off the northwest coast of Scotland used formerly to depend almost entirely for food upon the eggs of sea birds, and in consequence of their easy but narrow mode of gaining a subsistence, they long remained among the most backward of Scottish clans, while certain physical disorders attendant upon such a restricted diet became chronic among them. During the great influx of the gold-rush days in California, when it was almost impossible to supply the immigrants with food, the Farallon Islands, off San Francisco, were first visited by eggers, who sold their loot for an extravagant price, and subsequently for fifty years these islands were raided for their eggs. Only government protection finally puts a stop to such depredations, and even so the protection has sometimes come too late for certain species.

Of all the gathering places for seafowl on the American side of the North Atlantic, the bird rocks of the Gulf of St. Lawrence are the most renowned, where the auks and guillemots and gannets used to breed in countless thousands. And here the ugly traffic was already an old established thing when Audubon passed that way. He was himself an ardent sportsman, in the lavish style that wilderness conditions then made no crime. When he needed specimens of birds for study, he might shoot a hundred of any kind in a day, in order to secure a valuable series for comparison and description. But commercialized destruction made his gorge rise. It is good to think that, in our times, the destruction is over, and the birds are protected by law.

T HE distinctive appellation of Eggers is given to certain persons who follow, principally or exclusively, the avocation of procuring the eggs of wild birds, with the view of disposing of them at some distant port. Their great object is to plunder every nest, whenever they can find it, no matter where, or at whatever risk. They are the pest of the feathered tribes, and their brutal propensity to destroy the poor creatures after they have robbed them, is abundantly gratified whenever an opportunity presents itself.

Much has been said to me respecting these destructive pirates before I visited the coast of Labrador, but I could not entirely credit all their cruelties until I had actually witnessed their proceedings, which were such as to inspire no small degree of horror. But you shall judge for yourself.

See yon shallop shyly sailing along; — she sneaks like a thief, wishing as it were to shun the very light of heaven. Under the lee of every rocky isle some one at the tiller steers her course. Were his trade an honest one, he would not think of hiding his back behind the terrific rocks that seem to have been placed there as a resort to the myriads of birds that annually visit this desolate region of the earth, for the purpose of rearing their young, at a distance from all disturbers of their peace. How unlike the open, the bold, the honest mariner, whose face needs no mask, who scorns to skulk under any circumstances! The vessel herself is a shabby thing: — her sails are patched with stolen pieces of better canvas, the owners of which have probably been stranded on some inhospitable coast, and have been plundered, perhaps murdered, by the wretches before us. Look at her again! — Her sides are neither painted, nor even pitched; no — they are daubed over, plastered and patched with strips of sealskins, laid along the seams. Her deck has never been washed or sanded, her hold — for no cabin has she — though at present empty sends forth an odour pestilential as that of a charnel-house. The crew, eight in number, lie sleeping at the foot of their tottering mast, regardless of the repairs needed in every part of her rigging. But see! she scuds along, and as I suspect her crew to be bent on the commission of some evil deed, let us follow her to the first harbour.

There rides the filthy thing! The afternoon is half over. Her crew have thrown their boat overboard; they enter and seat themselves, each with a rusty gun. One of them sculls the skiff towards an island for a century past the breeding place of myriads of Guillemots, which are now to be laid under contribution. At the approach of the vile thieves, clouds of birds rise from the rock and fill the air around, wheeling and screaming over their enemies. Yet thousands remain in an erect posture, each covering its single egg, the hope of both parents. The reports of several muskets loaded with heavy shot are now heard while several dead and wounded birds fall heavily on the rock or into the water. Instantly all the sitting birds rise and fly off affrighted to their companions above, and hover in dismay over their assassins who walk forward exulting, and with their shouts mingling oaths and exe-crations. Look at them! See how they crush the chick within its shell, how they trample on every egg in their way with their huge and clumsy boots. Onward they go, and when they leave the isle, not an egg that they can find is left entire. The dead birds they collect and carry to their boat. Now they have regained their filthy shallop; they strip the birds by a single jerk of their feathery apparel, while the flesh is yet warm, and throw them on some coals, where in a short time they are broiled. The rum is produced when the guillemots are fit for eating, and after stuffing themselves with this oily fare, and enjoying the pleas-ure of beastly intoxication, over they tumble on the deck of their crazed craft, where they pass the short hours of night in turbid slumber.

The sun now rises above the snow-clad summit of the eastern mount. 'Sweet is the breath of morn' even in this desolate land. The gay Bunting erects his white crest, and gives utterances to the joy he feels in the presence of his brooding mate. The Willow Grouse on the rock crows his challenge aloud. Each floweret, chilled by the night air, expands its pure petals; the gentle breeze shakes from the blades of grass and heavy dewdrops. On the Guillemot Isle the birds have again settled, and now renew their loves. Startled by the light of day, one of the Eggers springs on his feet and rouses his companions, who stare around them for a while, endeavouring to recollect their senses. Mark them, as with clumsy fingers they clear their drowsy eyes! Slowly they rise on their feet. See how the filthy lubbers stretch out their arms and yawn; you shrink back, for verily 'that throat might frighten a shark.'

But the master, soon recollecting that so many eggs are worth a dollar or a crown, casts his eye toward the rock, marks the day in his memory, and gives orders to depart. The light breeze enables them to reach another harbour a few miles distant, one which, like the last, lies concealed from the ocean by some other rock isle. Arrived there, they re-act the scene of yesterday, crushing every egg they can find. For a week each night is passed in drunkenness and brawls, until, having reached the last breeding place on the coast, they return, touch at every isle in succession, shoot as many birds as they need, collect the fresh eggs, and lay in a cargo. At every step each ruffian picks up an egg so beautiful that any man with a feeling heart would pause to consider the motive which would induce him to carry it off. But nothing of this sort occurs to the Egger, who gathers and gathers, until he has swept the rock bare. The dollars alone chink in his sordid mind, and he assiduously plies the trade which no man would ply who had the talents and industry to procure subsistence by honourable means.

With a bark nearly half filled with fresh eggs they proceed to the principal rock, that on which they first landed. But what is their surprise when they find others there helping themselves as industriously as they can! In boiling rage they charge their guns, and ply their oars. Landing on the rock, they run up to the Eggers, who, like themselves, are desperadoes. The first question is a discharge of musketry, the answer another. Now, man to man, they fight like tigers. One is carried to his boat with a fractured skull, another limps with a shot in his leg, and a third feels how many of his teeth have been driven through the hole in his cheek. At last, however, the quarrel is settled; the booty is to be equally divided; and now see them all drinking together. Oaths and curses and filthy jokes are all that you hear; but see, stuffed with food, and reeling with drink down they drop one by one; groans and execrations from the wounded mingle with the snorings of the heavy sleepers. There let the brutes lie.

Again it is dawn, but no one stirs. The sun is high; one by one they open their heavy eyes, stretch their limbs, yawn, and raise themselves from the deck. But see, here comes a goodly company. A hundred honest fishermen, who for months past have fed on salt meat, have felt a desire to procure some eggs. Gallantly their boats advance, impelled by the regular pull of their long oars. Each buoyant bark displays the flag of its nation. No weapons do they bring, nor any thing that can be used as such save their oars and fists. Cleanly clad in Sunday attire, they arrive at the desired spot, and at once prepare to ascend the rock.

The Eggers of Labrador

The Eggers, now numbering a dozen, all armed with guns and bludgeons, bid defiance to the fishermen. A few angry words pass between the parties. One of the Eggers, still under the influence of drink, pulls his trigger, and an unfortunate sailor is seen to reel in agony. Three loud cheers fill the air. All at once rush on the malefactors; a horrid fight ensues, the result of which is, that every Egger is left on the rock beaten and bruised. Too frequently the fishermen man their boats, row to the shallops, and break every egg in the hold.

The Eggers of Labrador not only rob the birds in this cruel manner, but also the fishermen, whenever they can find an opportunity; and the quarrels they excite are numberless. While we were on the coast, none of our party ever ventured on any of the islands which these wretches call their own, without being well provided with means of defense. On one occasion, when I was present, we found two Eggers at their work of destruction. I spoke to them respecting my visit, and offered them premiums for rare birds and some of their eggs; but although they made fair promises, not one of the gang ever came near the 'Ripley.'

These people gather all the eider-down they can find; yet so inconsiderate are they, that they kill every bird that comes in their way. The eggs of Gulls, Guillemots, and Ducks are searched for with care; and the Puffins and some other birds they massacre in vast numbers for the sake of their feathers. So constant and persevering are their depredations, that these species, which, according to the accounts of the few settlers I saw in the country, were exceedingly abundant twenty years ago, have abandoned their ancient breeding places, and removed much farther north in search of peaceful security. Scarcely, in fact, could I procure a young Guillemot before the Eggers had left the coast, nor was it until late in July that I succeeded, after the birds had laid three or four eggs each, instead of one, and when nature having been exhausted, and the season nearly spent, thousands of these birds left the country without having accomplished the purpose for which they had visited it. This war of extermination cannot last many years more. The Eggers themselves will be the first to repent the entire disappearance of the myriads of birds that made the coast of Labrador their summer residence, and unless they follow the persecuted tribes to the northward, they must renounce their trade.

BUSINESS IN NEW ENGLAND

INTRODUCTION

WE THINK of Audubon as a man whose life was spent in the woods, on the great rivers, the prairies. We are apt to forget that a large proportion of it was devoted to business affairs. He had to secure subscriptions to all three of his voluminous works, and to do this he must personally canvass the centers of wealth and cultivation on two continents. Engaged for months at a time, and, cumulatively, for many years in this task, he eventually met an astounding number of famous and influential people in the United States of his time. His day-to-day journals (which were intended for the eyes of his family and are therefore in part like personal but unmailed letters) record these contacts, with all the flair of his original genius. Audubon was acutely sensitive to every sort of personality, was decisive in his judgments and usually very swift about making up his mind. In no part of the country did Audubon make a more thorough search for subscribers than in New England. Nowhere else did he meet so many notables. His New England journals, in which we find his expense accounts quaintly interpolated, are the richer in human details for the very reason that Audubon did little field work as a naturalist there. The birds of New England had been rather thoroughly collected before his time and with a few exceptions could boast no species not as advantageously studied elsewhere. So that Audubon in New England devoted himself to cities and men.

When he toured this region in 1840, he had still twelve years of life before him and six of highly active work. His powers were in their ascendancy; his fame preceded him everywhere. No one but had heard of him, or was honored to entertain him. Unconnected with any institution, he was the first naturalist in America who had ever supported himself on the proceeds from the sale of his works, and these all published at his own expense. At this time Audubon was still securing subscribers for the double elephant folio edition of *The Birds of America,* but he was also selling, and very successfully, the much more popularly priced quarto edition in which the pictures were reduced, the species arranged by families, and the text of the *Ornithological Biography* combined with the plates to make a highly valuable work. This sold for $100 a set, contrasted with $1000 for the original edition of the plates alone. In addition, Audubon was actively pushing the project of *The Quadrupeds of America.* And, finally, he was quite as busy in collecting for these sales as in getting the initial subscription, for the returns came in to him, as a rule, in installments.

Audubon in New England was always an outsider, a stranger, a foreigner. Pennsylvania, Kentucky, Louisiana, were home to him; in Charleston, his family connection with the influential Doctor Bachman made him a familiar. But he views New England with calm detachment, neither carried away with enthusiasm nor completely out of sorts with everyone and everything he saw, as in Florida. New England treated him well, and he acknowledges it gratefully. But his New England journals are that rather rare thing in Audubon's reflections, a balanced and dispassionate judgment. I mean to say that it is balanced and dispassionate — for Audubon.

The New England journals, then, may not be colored with Indians and bisons, river roustabouts or dandified Creoles; they may even have a certain Monday morning pedestrianism; but they are none the less real for that. It is interesting even to learn what it then cost to ride on the railways or to stay at the hotels of the time. The social life of the day with its dinners, the business life of the times with its banks, show us the beginnings of the modern New England that we know — early Beacon Hill, early Milk Street. It was an era, we learn, when the railroads already took the traveler everywhere, yet wild pigeons were plentiful around Plymouth. Industrialism has already come to New England, and indeed factory reform, for we find Audubon mentioning the 'model' mills at Lowell. It should be remarked that at the time they were so considered; it was only much later that labor troubles gathered there.

[259]

Audubon's America

Among all the prominent New Englanders Audubon met, two very interesting personalities may just possibly pass unnoticed under his casual reference. One is his friend and benefactor Doctor George Parkman who was murdered in 1849 by his colleague Professor Webster, his body being consumed in the chemical laboratory in Harvard Yard. Elihu Burritt, 'the learned blacksmith,' was a philanthropist, international pacifist, and linguist, born in New Britain, Connecticut; having at first followed the trade of the smith, he had already (he was only twenty-nine when Audubon met him) earned his picturesque title. His real fame was to come six years later when he made his study of the sufferings of the Irish peasantry in the great famine.

Daniel Webster also walks through these pages, and characteristically he is in pecuniary straits — this time in debt to Audubon. At this moment in his career the great orator has successfully crushed Senator Hayne of South Carolina in the nullification debate; he has dared to oppose President Jackson on the charter of the United States Bank, and only four years earlier carried Massachusetts in his attempt to reach the presidency. At the moment there are no greater statesmen in America than Jackson, Clay, and Webster, and the prestige of Webster's subscription, whether paid for or not, means much to Audubon.

Like the other journals and letters printed by the Club of Odd Volumes of Boston, the New England journals are among the few that did not fall to Audubon's descendants, who ultimately destroyed all original documents on which they could lay hands.

Plymouth. Sunday August 16th, 1840. Fine morning, walked out at 5 and went several miles out of town, and again to the different wharves before breakfast, afterwards went Botanizing with Messrs Gilbert and Russell. — Then to the old Unitarian Church. No Organ and vile fidlers! dined on Wild Pigeons now plentiful hereabouts. — Took a Walk of about 7 miles with 4 Gentlemen, to several ponds, but saw very few birds. brought some new plants to me and eat as many huckleberries as I could wish. — The country very hilly, stony sandy and poor! The harbour at Low Water a naked extensive mud flat. one Whaler at the Wharf, and Another in the stock. Procured one subscriber. Messrs Stoddard & called to see me this evening, and I gave each of them a copy of the work to look over at

LOON

'The Loon, as this interesting species of Diver is generally called in the United States, is a strong, active, and vigilant bird. When it has acquired its perfect plumage, which is not altered in colour at any successive moult, it is really a beautiful creature; and the student of Nature who has opportunities of observing its habits, cannot fail to derive much pleasure from watching it as it pursues its avocations. View it as it buoyantly swims over the heaving billows of the Atlantic, or as it glides along deeply immersed, when apprehensive of danger, on the placid lake, on the grassy islet of which its nest is placed; calculate, if you can, the speed of its flight, as it shoots across the sky; mark the many plunges it performs in quest of its finny food, or in eluding its enemies; list to the loud and plaintive notes which it issues, either to announce its safety to its mate, or to invite some traveller of its race to alight, and find repose and food; follow the anxious and careful mother-bird, as she leads about her precious charge; and you will not count your labour lost, for you will have watched the ways of one of the wondrous creations of unlimited Power and unerring Wisdom. You will find pleasure too in admiring the glossy tints of its head and neck, and the singular regularity of the unnumbered spots by which its dusky back and wings are checkered.' — *Ornithological Biography*, vol. 4, p. 43.

Drawn from Nature by J.J. Audubon, F.R.S. F.L.S.

Diver or Loon.

GLACIALIS. *L.*

Engraved, Printed & Coloured by R. Havell 1836.

home. Oh, I visited the burying ground, and saw the tomb stone of the last dead Pilgrims. — and Now Good night dearest friends all! — I left 2 setts N^{os} I @ 14 in the hands of Andrew Russel Es$^{qr.}$ of Plymouth Mass^{tts} because he expects to place them very soon. —

Plymouth. Mass. August 17th Monday 1840. Rec^d 3 names this day. M^r. Andrew Russell had the goodness to introduce me to all we met & to take me to peoples houses. — I was highly pleased with the Revd R. Hall. This afternoon he took me to Kingston 4½ miles distant, and we visited Several persons there also. — The evening has been delightful, we took Tea at Mr John Sever who has an interesting familly. — after we had returned to Plymouth Mr Gilbert (Lawyer) took me to Doc^r Thatcher a person more than 70 of age, who gave me a genuine piece of the Rock upon which our Great grand fathers first landed! I visited this evening, the Hall in which I saw many valuable relics of the famed Pilgrims, and a good painting representing them in the act of landing, received by the Indian Chief. —

18th Duxbury, Masstts. After my breakfast this morning, and after I had bid adieu to my friends of Plymouth, I hired a Wagon and was driven by Mr Gilbert to this place; and soon introduced to the Revd Josiah Moore, to whom I presented a letter from Andrew Russell of Plymouth. — I was received with extreme kindness; asked to make his house my home etc. his Lady and Young babe were to me most interesting. — Mr Gilbert returned to Plymouth almost immediately. I dined at Mr Moore, and afterwards he took me in his chaise to see what contributions the Village might afford; but alas! after all his troubles and good speaking, I procured only one name besides his own. I was introduced to the wife of a Phisician whom I found both handsome and aimiable, She is well acquainted with Dr Webster, where she has seen *my* great work several times, but she not knowing Mr W. as well as I do called the Volumes there *his* Copy??? When paid for! tomorrow I proceed to Ingham without calling at the house of Mr Webster although *his residence?* is only 3 Miles from this. I am now at the Tavern of Mr W. W. Winslow, w'l enough in all Conscience. Good Night Love and God bless you all.

Hingham, Masstts Augst 19th 1840. I was up at 4 this morning; the weather was beautiful and cool, my breakfast was ready at ½ past five and at 6 I was in a very coach indeed on my way to Hingham! My companions at first were only 2 of both sex and extremely talkative; — Poor I took my Snuff and gazed on the Nature spread around me. —

How delightful I thought was the refreshing air, and the green grass and foliage and the trees of the orchards bending beneath their loaded bows! How oft I thought of those at *home* and of my Johnny and his Maria at Charlston, and of the beloved angels of theirs, my Little Lucy and still smaller Babe Harriet; of my Lucy, my Victor and my beloved Eliza! Yet the coach proceeded on and I with it; Travellers one after another assisted in the filling of the benches, frequently the Driver stopped to exchange Letters for Letters, until at last we reached the very wharf from which a steamer is ready thrice a day to carry Passengers to Boston, and at the sound of that word, I as if by magic was conveyed there, and amid the Dear friends whom I do know in that friendly city!

But as I was bent on procuring *Names* at Hingham, I walked to the *Old Colony House*, saw my baggage safely put away, and started for the Village just a good mile off. *Chemin fesant*, I was shaved, for I really wanted it, and presently I was at the House of Ed^d Thaxter Es^gr to whom I had a letter from the Revd Mr Moore. — I dined there, but *he* did not subscribe. I called on the Revd Mr Stearns, who took immediate interest in my business, and who took me to Mr Smith — a subscriber of ours. We now perambulated through the Village and was surprised to find Mr Sturgis, and the sister of my Worthy friend Doc^t Parkman's Wife. I procured only one subscriber, took Tea at Mr Smith, Saw some very remarkable Drawings of birds (far better than any ever made by the Immortal Alex^r Wilson) by a young man named *Sprague*. Truly wonderful Drawings my Dearest friends. but this person was out shooting and I did not see him. — I however wrote a few lines on several of them the purports of which, I trust, will not displease him.

The Old Colony House here is not to me as good as the house of the same name at Plymouth. My host does not know the *treasure* now beneath his roof, but perhaps for the purpose of letting me be assured that his house was well covered, he placed me as far up as he could. Never mind, I trust I shall sleep sound and with this hope I wish you all good night. God bless thee my Lucy!

25th. My time at Mr Motley at Dedham was quite agreable, I found his wife as handsome as ever, and saw three fine children. Mrs Stuart the Mother of Mrs M. was also there. I found that the latter was a subscriber, and Mrs Motley *promissed* to subscribe before next Jan^y. — I took a good early walk, The weather quite cool, breakfasted at ½ past 6 and reached Boston again at 8., My friends of Milk Street all busy, therefore did nothing there., Was invisted to Dine at D. P. Parker, went, was pleased with all I saw, and received his name. — I gave him a card for you all, as he is desirous to see some of the small oil paintings. — No letters from home this day, and I feel much disapointed. I received 5 letters of Introduction for Lowell where I intend going tomorrow morning.

26th. I reached Lowell this morning at ½ past 8, and after having taken a room at the Merrimack House, went to M*r* John *Aiken* to whom I had a letter from Henry Hall of Boston. The letter read, the Gent. took me under his arm, introduced me to many people and ere evening had come, I had 10 names on my list. — I found Lowell very beautiful and as if New. The Streets wide and clean, the establishments called *Mills,* superior to anything of the Kind *in the World!*

Lowell Augt 27th 1840. I was more astonished and pleased yet, when I saw about four young women, all cleanly dressed, of good manners and demeanours going to & from their Labours. — I was told that the morals of these females is exemplary and I believe it! This was my second day I procured 9 more names and Instituted M*r* Bixby Bookseller as an agent there, at a commission of 5 PC*t*

Salem Masstts Sepr 18th 1840. This morning was clouded and warm, the weather indicating a change and I felt somewhat low spirited; but, thought I, to proceed on my errands is the best means of recovering from this. — Doc*r* Wheatland I called on at ½ past 7 and asked him to accompany me to Marblehead which he did. Having however missed the first train of Carrs, we called on 2 Gentlemen of Salem, but nothing could be done. We were taken to Marblehead 4 miles in 10 minutes for 12½/100 each, passing amid Salt marshes and rocky grounds almost deprived of trees. — At the Carrs going to Boston, we met with Doc*r* Pierson who gave me 2 of his Cards for 2 Persons, of wealth at Marblehead and on whom we called, but it was no go! We Sauntered about this unique Village for a while, viewing the Harbour and aridity of the rocky prospect around us and indeed beneath us for about one hour. All here indicated strongly the fact that all Marbleheaders have to depend on the products of the sea for their livelyhood, and I was glad after all that I had seen this place.

We returned to dinner at Salem, and at 5 this Afternoon I was in The Carrs underway to Boston. The sky was still very cloudy and the atmosphere somewhat cooler. While crossing an inlet of the Sea over a bridge, I saw 7 Seals laying in the grass several yards from the Water.

They were Large and all of them with a perfect *White Head* and probably each measured between 7 & 8 feet in length. As we passed them, 4 of them made for the water, dove and appeared again close by, and probably rejoined their less fearful Companions which remained in the grass. Their being thus far in the inlet, proved to me how well they knew of the change of the weather. I reached old Doc.ᵗ Shattucks at ½ passed 6, went to Doc.ᵗ Parkman for my letters, but they had been forwarded to Portsmouth.

Boston Novr 21st 1840. Breakfasted at home weather fair but cold. called on Doc.ᵗ Parkman and on Doc.ᵗ Brewer twice, but was absent. Called at the U. S. Hotel to see Daniel Webster, not in left a card. Called upon him at his office corner of Court and Tremont Streets, found him. He was greatly surprised that I have not received a Dollar yet on a/c of what he owes us for the Copy of The Large Work to which he subscribed years ago and said that he would attend to that business at once, and indeed settle it to my satisfaction by Wednesday next. Nous verrons! he bought a copy of the five volumes of my Ornithological Biographies for which he would pay me also. — he further promised to give me Several letters of Introduction, for Worcester, Springfield, Hartford, New Heaven, Northampton and Albany!

I met Mr. Truman in the street and on his saying that he wished to subscribe, I simply asked him to come along, by which I intended him to take me to some office to write down his name but he misunderstood me, and we walked nearly ¾ of a mile talking of different matters. when *he* asked me how much farther *I* was going, and here an explanation took place, we walked together to the Compting house of a Mr. Lewis, where he did subscribe! —

Boston Tuesday November 24th 1840. Met D.ˡ Webster, who shook hands with me but looked dull and uncomfortable as *I* thought. — forwarded the Cotton Cloth to Mamma by Hearden's conveyance.

Wednesday Novr 25th. Weather thick, cold and rainy. No letters from home, and therefore much disapointed. Met Mr. Isaac P. Davis, who promised to see Mr. D. Webster. Called on Mr. Skinner who was very busy. Called on Mr. H. Hall who gave me a letter for Hartford Conn.ᵗ. Called on Mr. Almy Brother in Law of M.ᵗ Page, who took me down Central Wharf where we procured 3 names and the surety of a 4.ᵗʰ. Waited on change for half an hour but had no luck. Went to Dinner at Lie.ᵘᵗ. Gov.ᵗ. Winthrop who subscribed and gave me a superb Dinner with a Company of 12 persons. his Daughter, and Grand Daughter present. Sir John Caldwell, General Miller, Mr. Pickering, Revd Messrs. Lowell, Gibson and Harris. Ho^ble Young Winthrop, Mr Gardner and 2 others names unknown. — Sat at table until ½ past 5, & went off. Called on Mr. Almy, at home 55 High St. to see Mrs. Page, found her, her Sister etc. — Raining quite hard, returned to Doc^r Shattuck. General Lyman called here and left a card for me. I would feel happy if I had heard good news from him, but I am uneasy about My Lucy, my Johny, my Babes, and my remittances. Good night & God bless you all! — Called at Doc^r. Parkman, a notice of the work by J. M. Brewster in this day Atlas.

Thursday Novr 26. Thanksgiving Day. This was 'Thanksgiving day' here, and therefore no business to do. Rec^d. a letter from home and feel quite happy! Walked a good deal. Dined at Mr. Almy's. Quite a familly party & pleasant times. My Friends the Pages present. — Spent a few minutes at Doc^r Parkman and a few minutes this evening at Mr. Francis Skinner. Wrote home but did not forward my letter. — Weather murky, snow & rain. This evening found Col^l Thayer at Doc^r. Shattuck, went over to George Shattuck and had some pleasing music from Mrs. Brown. and now good night. God bless thee my love. —

Boston Friday Novr 27th 1840. Weather Cold and rather clear. — Called on Isaac P. Davis, and was told to meet him at the Suffolk Insurance *Cos.* Office at 12. — Called on Daniel Webster twice, and finally got $100 Dollars from him on a/c of the Large Work, and a memorandum authorizing me to draw upon him at Three different dates for the balance he now owes us. To my astonishment he subscribed to the little work; and Mr. Little of Little & Brown, guaranteed me the payment thereof! He moreover, (D. Webster) promised me to send me letters of Introduction for several places by next Sunday. Nous verrons! — Procured 4 names to day. Paid Mr. Page for Oil for Mamma $29.33, for 26 Gallons and the Cask. — Sent my letter for home. — dined at Mr. H. Y. Hall, Pleasant familly, the Pages there. Called on Mr. Winthrop who wrote his name on my list, and paid me $20. — Called on D. Eckley, and Joshua Davis, and afterwards upon Mr. Almy to Tea. Put up several copies of the work in Setts of 20 N^os. — Called on Mr Bowditch, who expects to procure me a few names. This morning called on Mr. Haven at the Merchants' Bank with Doc^r. Parkman and almost procured his subscription. — The Weather perfectly clear this evening but very cold and now God Bless you all. Good night.

Novr 28th. Fair weather, but cold. Pamella Little, the servant Girl who waited upon us all at Mrs. Le Kain when we boarded with her in Pearl Street in this City, came to see me this morning and wished to go and live with us at New York. — She looks rather finely dressed I thought, however, I will write to thee my Lucy tomorrow about her. She asked $2 per week. — Went to Mr. Almy who walked with me in different parts of the City until a ¼ past 1 and we procured 12 subscribers, my self 3, he and I together the rest. I procured another at the Shop of C. Little & Brown after Dinner. — Much fatigued dined at Docr. Shattuck. Called on Docr. Parkman, not in, saw his Daughter who was playing on the Harp. — had the lock of my Green Box picked, having left the key at home or lost it. — Took 7 Copies out of it of each 1 @ 14., and carried them to Little & Brown, where the Young men assisted me in arranging them into Setts of 20 Nos. each. Went to Tea to David Eckley, and there heard of the suicide of M⸏ Prince Senior at New York, and on my return at 7 to Docr. Shattuck heard of the like act, having been commited this day in this City. Surely those men must have both been mad! Wrote home, and sent a check to Johny, value $200. I have done remarkable well today, and although I feel much fatigued, I am contented. God bless you all, Good night!

Sunday Decr 6th. Two fires last night, in this fair City, and the weather cold enough! This morning it commenced snowing and blowing a gale, but notwithstanding I went to Mr. Lawrence's Church and there heard an excellent Sermon and *excellent* music: The Pulpit which is made of Mahogany and is very ancient, is one of the finest I ever saw in my Life. — I saw there Amos Lawrence, and the Wife of Mr. Abbot Lawrence. — I went to the Post office against a tremendous gale of wind, snow and sleet sufficient to almost injure a man's eyes. No letters for me. — Dined at Doc⸏ Shattuck. Went after dinner to see Mr. Almy and Mr. Davies for a while, but the weather was so bad, (and is still) that I was glad to return home. Saw Mr. John Bruce and his wife at George Shattuck where I went for a few minutes, and now I will hope that you are all at *home*, quietly seated by a good fire and happy and that all our friends are well whether near us or far distant. God bless you. good night. Tomorrow will be a very bad day for my business I fear.

Thurs.y 10th. Beautiful day, warm & thawing fast. procured 2 names, accompanied as yesterday. P⸎ my regards to M⸏ J. Aiken, M⸏

French, Mr Booth etc. Settled accounts with D. Bixby in full, he has a *bad* cold. Dined at the Hotel in Comp.y. with a Mr Waldo, who came to Boston with me. — Had a glimpse of Abbott Lawrence as I was leaving Lowell. — Went all over Mes^{srs} Lawrence's Mill, Superior establishments! They have received an order from Baltimore to make 12 yards of Cloth for Gl. Harrison!!!. Arrived at Boston precisely in one hour. found all well. Rec^d collected for me at Mr Almy's store 44$ and at Little & Co. 61. P^d visits to Messrs Skinner, David Eckley, and the familly of W^{am} Lawrence. to the latter of whom I made a presentation of a Copy of my Ornith. Biographies. — and now that I have posted my books, I will rest my poor old bones. Oh! I received a letter from home yesterday and forwarded $300 to Johny through Doc^r Shattuck, who saved me the Premium thereupon! God bless thee and ye all, Good night.

Worcester, Masstts Decr 12th 1840 (Saturday). Weather fair and *very cold*. rose early and walked a good deal around the Village to Judge of its tout-ensemble, very handsome place, and in the summer must be quite beautiful. I felt in good spirits for a wonder, and after breakfast went to Mr. Harris, and we started in search of subscribers at once, and sure enough I have procured 12! almost all the houses are of wood, painted white and look well. I found the familly of Mr. Salisbury quite agreable, and indeed where ever we went, we were kindly received. We visited the lunatic asylum and found it kept in the very best of order; it is a large brick building standing on an eminence and commanding the view of Worcester. — Afterwards we went to the Antiquarian Library, and saw its curious old Books, paintings, etc. etc. and while here, found out that no Cars leave this place in the afternoon for Springfield, and that I must remain here until Monday morning. But I dare say, even that detention is for the best.

The Librarian told me that the famous learned Black Smith *Burritt* wished to see me and to subscribe to our Work, and off to his shop we went. he came into his office, with his sleeves turned up, his arms bare and full of sinew, his eyes sparkling bright, his forehead smooth and high, his person manly, his demeanour modesty itself! We shook hands as I am sure with sincerest good will, and talked for a while, and strange as it may appear, his opinions of our success in regard to mental improvement coincide precisely with my own; i.e. that *We are what we make ourselves*. he asked for my Autograph and I wrote a few Lines, being a very poor exchange for his Signature on my

Subscript List. — I can write a famous episode upon my friend Burritts and will do so.

After tea, M.ᵣ Harris took me to Isaac Davis a Lawyer, who has made a rapid fortune, and who took us to his Mansion, where I drank 2 glasses of good wine, found his wife, an interesting Lady, and he told me that he would let me know tomorrow evening (Sunday) whether he would purchase the Large Work, or Subscribe to the small one? I hope it may be the first. we then left and went to Mr. Haven the Librarian, but he was gone, we not having been punctual with him, and thereby have lost a subscriber. I found Mrs. Bangs a fine Lady, who had known us at Boston formerly. — and Now Good night!

Sunday 13th. Rained hard most of the Night, and until 12 to day. Then thick fog, and now a beautiful star light night. — Wrote a long letter home, walked about some, spent the evening at Mr. Harris. Rec.ᵈ a letter from Mr. Isaac Davis sending in his subscription. Last evening he talked somewhat of taking the large work. — I was astonished to see the Dinner placed on the table at our *Temperance House.* a few bits of cold meat, pies and pudding, Tea & Coffee made up the whole! What would our Southerners say to that? Not even a glass of wine can be procured at this house!! If this be not temperance with a vengeance, then indeed I know not what the value of the word is. Mr. Harris has made a list of about a dozen names, and I will remain tomorrow and try my Luck! God bless you all Good night Dearest friends.

Springfield, Masstts. Wed.y. 16th. To my surprise and pleasure, this morning almost resembled a May one. The Sun shone brightly, the air was calm, and every thing promised me a fair and prosperous day. I was out at Mr. Peabody at 9 o'clock, and we started in search of game. — We called first on a Gentleman who is President of a Bank and to whom I had a letter. He looked at the Work, said that he would subscribe, but suddenly said that he would wait until 12 o'clock when he would be pleased to see *us* at the Bank! — We then went to a paper manufacturer who amused me somewhat, by saying that should we purchase *his paper* to print our plates upon, he *might* subscribe. I saw his paper of which he gave me a sheet, but it breaks easily and is quite too smooth. — After much exertion we procured 3 names and the Banker, did not subscribe for himself but did so in C.ᵒ with a M.ᵣ Dwight in favour of the Rev.ᵈ M.ᵣ Peabody. I was highly pleased at this, and as I know that Parsons are generally (in America) none of the richest I gave my talented Friend the *Binding* that covered the first 14 N^{os} of our Work and this afternoon delivered him 8 other N^{os} making his sett complete up to N° 22 Inclusive.' I dined at his house en famille, with his five Daughters, and 4 fine looking Sons. at 4 o'clock it began suddenly to snow, and here I am doubtful whether I ought to go *to Mr. Orne's* party, but suppose I must. and now that I have actually found that my judgment of the appearance of Springfield has proved correct, I have made up my mind to proceed onward to Hartford Tomorrow morning at 8 o'clock, by stage coach, and I am told over vile muddy roads. But never mind for by 2 o'clock I hope to be 25 miles nearer to thee my beloved Wife, than I am this evening, and should Hartford prove no better than Springfield, I will yet spend Christmas day with thee. — Tomorrow night I will say what company I have found at Mr Orne's. God bless thee Good Night. —

Hartford, Connecticut, Decr 17th (Thursday) 1840. My Visit last evening to Mr Orne, was quite a pleasant one, although the snow through which I walked to his house was about ankle deep. — We had some music, and I had a good deal of conversation with Mr. Howard, the donor of the Work to the Rev^d Mr. Peabody, and as I was going away he gave me 2 letters of Intro^n, one for Hartford and the other for New York. — I forgot to say yesterday that I gave Mr. Peabody $2.50 for a pair of cloth Boots, doubled soles for Mamma, to be sent to her very soon. This was in favour of a Lady Fair. This morning at 8, the weather fair and somewhat cold, I left Springfield for Hartford in a stage, having an Irish Dyer (by trade) for my only companion. The road was very bad, but the sight of the Connecticut River, ere and there peeping, now in the distance, and again at our feet rendered the Journey pleasant. The Sun was out brightly shining, and the snow lightly wafting from the branches and twigs towards mother earth. — The valey through which we passed is beautiful during the summer months and I pictured the scenery anew as if again in my youthful days! about 2 o'clock, the several steeples of this beautiful village came to our view, and anon I was deposited at the United States Hotel.

How curious it is to me to see how eagerly the non employed loungers about Taverns peep in to the *book of names,* and again stare at the poor but honest, and I would almost say *modest* 'American Woodsman.' There are indeed times when I wish I could leave the Earth and fly away from the staring gaze of these Idlers, but as I cannot fly, I must sit still & silent and give them the fairest of chances to gratify their appetities. To Judge of success by the appearance of Cities or Villages, or of Country residences even appears to me as quite useless, for I am frequently disapointed either way. Notwith.g I could feel inclined to make my entry in this poor daily Journal *against* my wishes to procure many subscribers, for although the tout ensemble promises well, I am no longer in the Reading State of Massachusetts! — I have a very fine room here and much particular attention paid me. Strange, aye very strange!

after dinner I called on Mr. Edwin Spence at the Connecticut River Bank, found him, and he gave me 2 new names procured by himself. — We afterwards walked off, and I delivered D. Webster's letter to M.r Dwight, formerly the owner of News paper in New York, now a *writer* for Newspapers and not a rich man though 25 years older than I. — We also called on Mr. Charles Hosmer the Brother in Law of my Friend M.r H.y. Hall of Boston who promised to assist me. We met in the street Mr. Barnard whose Sister was well acquainted with my poor gone beloved child Maria, and after having sauntered about a while without doing any thing of Importance I have returned to the 'Hotel' and have scribled the above. I am very much fatigued by the rude motions of the Coach, and will to bed at once, therefore God bless thee my Lucy and all the World besides! Good night my beloved friend.

18th. Beautiful day with occasional spits of Snow, procured only 3 names and became discontented. — Saw Mr. Alden, and left at 4 for New Haven in very indifferent slow-moving, carrs. — arrived at N. Haven at 7. put up at the Tontine Coffee House a very poor concern. — and on the 19th after having sent my cards to Professor Silliman & Mr. Bakewell. left on the 19th and reached home to Dine!

OUT WEST WITH BUFFALO

AND INDIANS

UP THE MISSOURI

INTRODUCTION

IN THE fifty-eighth year of his life, and the summer of 1843, the great naturalist set out to see the West. He had been obliged to complete *The Birds of America*, and *Ornithological Biography*, without any field experience of western birds, relying upon dead specimens and the meager details furnished by exploring parties, such as the notes and skins collected by Nuttall, Townsend, Say, and Peale. Now, with *The Quadrupeds of America* advancing rapidly, the time had come when what was the greatest virgin wilderness for four-footed beasts must be seen. The plan was to reach to the Rockies, if possible, then a difficult thing to do and dependent upon some very chancy factors, such as, the temper of the Indian tribes at the time, the height of water in the Missouri, the health of the personnel of the expedition, and the morale of these *engagés*, as they were called. Steamboat captains, army officers, and fur companies, could forward or retard a private expedition. Water or weevils or mould in the food stores could bring to a halt what is now so simple a matter as a trip from St. Louis to Wyoming. And abundance or scarcity of game, and the marksmanship of the travelers, might prove decisive for very life itself.

But this expedition was better planned than any other Audubon had ever taken. He had funds, and such was the prestige of his name now that he could obtain everywhere from officials the sort of assistance that spares funds. His company consisted in his old friend Edward Harris, who had befriended him in Philadelphia with financial aid as early as 1824 and had explored the Texas and Louisiana coasts for birds with him in 1837, and John G. Bell, a celebrated taxidermist, young Lewis Squires, secretary to the expedition, and Isaac Sprague, a botanist and painter of flowers and birds. The reader will find Audubon discovering Sprague's talents in the New England journals, August 19, 1840.

Thus seconded, and with the knowledge that Doctor Bachman of Charleston would do his mammalian dissections and research the systematics for him, and that his sons would do copyist and colorist work on his pictures, and arrange for the subscriptions, sale, and editing of *The Quadrupeds*, Audubon set off for the Yellowstone country with everything in his favor — except youth and the old fire.

It is indeed chiefly when some river swallow alights upon the tedious steamer, or when Audubon sees wild swans upon a prairie slough, or, as on May 10, hears the call of an unknown bird, that he is caught up in his old enthusiasm. He is really excited over a meadowlark with a different song from the one he knew; and indeed it proves to be the western meadowlark, *Sturnella neglecta*, Audubon, 'neglected' by such predecessors as Townsend, Nuttall, Lewis and Clark, and Say.

Yet the country into which he is so slowly moving, upstream against the Missouri and its numberless sand bars, is a perfect menagerie of beasts, where elk and deer are as abundant on the prairies as ever in the woods. Where black bear calmly swim the river in front of the steamer, and bison are so plenty that their carcasses choke the thin and braided stream. Where antelopes spring and prairie dogs chitter, and wolves and foxes show themselves at any time of day. Into this great untouched prairie province, with its whooping cranes and wild swans, its inland gulls and curlews and rails and terns, its troops of cowbirds, wild parrots, wild turkeys, and prairie chickens, sails the veteran naturalist, a man now of balanced judgment in things personal and things zoölogical. How different an Audubon from the touchy, elated or alternately despondent, impoverished, ambitious, thwarted young man of 1820, sailing down the Mississippi in Captain Cummings's flatboat, all his lifework before him!

Two important personalities are mentioned casually in this text (which has been superbly edited by the distinguished naturalist, Elliott Coues). The first is Father P. J. de Smet (1801–1873), the famous Jesuit missionary to the Indians of the West. Peter John de Smet met everybody of any importance who traveled the plains, from Prince Paul of Würtemburg, riding the prairies attended by a single retainer, to

Up the Missouri

Audubon himself, and the memory of his good works is imperishable in the West. In much less complimentary terms Audubon repeatedly mentions Catlin, George Catlin (1796–1872), traveler, painter, and explorer, who had conceived the idea of establishing a gallery of Indian paintings to rescue from oblivion the fast-vanishing costumes and features, races and manners, of Indian life. In 1832 he began a series of travels extending over eight years in the wildest parts of North and South America. His most famous book told the story of his residence among the Mandan Indians, in the very country toward which Audubon was heading, and it is Catlin's pictures of the splendor of savage life on the prairies, the majesty of the scenery, the beauty of the flowers, the zest of the climate, that arouses Audubon's scorn. In particular he charges Catlin with quite misrepresenting the Indians, who appeared to the ornithologist to be the most miserable lot of dirty, begging, treacherous, and thieving human beasts he had ever encountered.

Who is right, Catlin or Audubon? The times when both of them lived are far gone by, and we cannot refer now to extant facts. It would seem to me, however, that the answer is fairly simple. Catlin saw the prairie and its Indians in his youth, and he saw them before they had had much contact with civilization. Audubon saw a people already dispirited, corrupted, diseased, drunken, beggared, prostituted. And he saw the prairie with the eyes of one fast aging. In his own youth he had idealized 'the noble red man,' and it is a James Fenimore Cooper sort of Indian that comes out to us from some of his early pages. Had Audubon seen these same Dakota scenes before Catlin, how different might have been his account! But the very fact that Catlin saw the Mandan country first is enough to stir Audubon's greatest failing, that of professional jealousy. Catlin, with his dashing pictures, right from life, in the days when life in North Dakota must have been worth living, invaded the very province that Audubon liked to consider uniquely his own. This, unconsciously, he cannot forgive his predecessor and, when he can, he catches him out in error.

1843. The 25th of April at last made its appearance, the rivers were now opened, the weather was growing warm, and every object in nature proved to us that at last the singularly lingering winter of 1842 and 1843 was over. Having conveyed the whole of our effects on board the steamer, and being supplied with excellent letters, we left St. Louis at 11.30 A.M., with Mr. Sarpy on board, and a hundred and one trappers of all descriptions and nearly a dozen different nationalities, though the greater number were French Canadians, or Creoles of this State.[1] Some were drunk, and many in that stupid mood which follows a state of nervousness produced by drinking and over-excitement. Here is the scene that took place on board the 'Omega' at our departure, and what followed when the roll was called.

First the general embarkation, when the men came in pushing and squeezing each other, so as to make the boards they walked upon fairly tremble. The Indians, poor souls, were more quiet, and had already seated or squatted themselves on the highest parts of the steamer, and were tranquil lookers-on. After about three quarters of an hour, the crew and all the trappers (these are called *engagés*) were on board, and we at once pushed off and up the stream, thick and muddy as it was. The whole of the effects and the baggage of the *engagés* was arranged in the main cabin, and presently was seen Mr. Sarpy, book in hand, with the list before him, wherefrom he gave the names of these *attachés*. The men whose names were called nearly filled the fore part of the cabin, where stood Mr. Sarpy, our captain, and one of the clerks. All awaited orders from Mr. Sarpy. As each man was called, and answered to his name, a blanket containing the apparel for the trip was handed to him, and he was ordered at once to retire and make room for the next. The outfit, by the way, was somewhat scanty, and of indifferent quality. Four men were missing, and some appeared rather reluctant; however, the roll was ended, and one hundred and one were found. In many instances their bundles were thrown to them, and they were ordered off as if slaves.

I forgot to say that as the boat pushed off from the shore, where stood a crowd of loafers, the men on board had congregated upon the hurricane deck with their rifles and guns of various sorts, all loaded, and began to fire what I should call a very disorganized sort of a salute, which lasted for something like an hour, and which has been renewed at intervals, though in a more desultory manner, at every village we have passed. However, we now find them passably good, quiet, and regularly sobered men. We have of course a motley set, even to Italians. We passed the mouth of the Missouri, and moved very slowly against the current, for it was not less than twenty minutes after four the next morning, when we reached St. Charles, distant

[1] Missouri.

forty-two miles. Here we stopped till half-past five, when Mr. Sarpy, to whom I gave my letters home, left us in a wagon.

April 29. On looking along the banks of the river, one cannot help observing the half-drowned young willows, and cotton trees of the same age, trembling and shaking sideways against the current; and methought, as I gazed upon them, of the danger they were in of being immersed over their very tops and thus dying, not through the influence of fire, the natural enemy of wood, but from the force of the mighty stream on the margin of which they grew, and which appeared as if in its wrath it was determined to overwhelm, and undo all that the Creator in His bountifulness had granted us to enjoy. The banks themselves, along with perhaps millions of trees, are ever tumbling, falling, and washing away from the spots where they may have stood and grown for centuries past.

Sunday, April 30th. At one place we passed a couple of houses, with women and children, perfectly surrounded by the flood; these houses stood apparently on the margin of a river coming in from the eastward. The whole farm was under water, and all around was the very perfection of disaster and misfortune. It appeared to us as if the men had gone to procure assistance, and I was grieved that we could not offer them any. We saw several trees falling in, and beautiful, though painful, was the sight. As they fell, the spray which rose along their whole length was exquisite; but alas! these magnificent trees had reached the day of oblivion.

May 1. When we reached Glasgow, we came in under the stern of the 'John Auld.' As I saw several officers of the United States army I bowed to them, and as they all knew that I was bound towards the mighty Rocky Mountains, they not only returned my salutations, but came on board, as well as Father de Smet. They all of them came to my room and saw specimens and skins.

May 2. It stopped raining in the night while I was sound asleep, and at about one o'clock we did arrive at Independence, distant about 379 miles from St. Louis. Here again was the 'John Auld,' putting out freight for the Santa Fe traders, and we saw many of their wagons. Of course I exchanged a handshake with Father de Smet and many of the officers I had seen yesterday.

May 3. We ran all last night and reached Fort Leavenworth at six this morning. We had an early breakfast, as we had intended to walk across the Bend; but we found that the ground was overflowed, and that the bridges across two creeks had been carried away, and reluctantly we gave up our trip. The situation of the fort is elevated and fine, and one has a view of the river up and down for some distance. Seeing a great number of Parrakeets, we went after them; Bell killed one.

After leaving this place we fairly entered the Indian country on the west side of the river, for the State of Missouri, by the purchase of the Platte River country, continues for about 250 miles further on the east side, where now we see the only settlements. We saw a good number of Indians in the woods and on the banks, gazing at us as we passed; these are, however, partly civilized, and are miserable enough.

Saturday, May 6. The wind was still high when we left our stopping place, but we progressed, and this afternoon came alongside of a beautiful prairie of some thousands of acres, reaching to the hills. Here we stopped to put out our Iowa Indians. Our Sac Indian chief started at once across the prairie towards the hills, on his way to his wigwam, and we saw Indians on their way towards us, running on foot, and many on horseback, generally riding double on skins or on Spanish saddles. Even the squaws rode, and rode well too! We counted about eighty, amongst whom were a great number of youths of different ages. I was heartily glad that our own squad of them left us here. I observed that though they had been absent from their friends and relatives, they never shook hands, or paid any attention to them.

When the freight was taken in we proceeded, and the whole of the Indians followed along the shore at a good round run; those on horseback at times struck into a gallop. I saw more of these poor beings when we approached the landing, perched and seated on the promontories about, and many followed the boat to the landing. Here the goods were received, and Major Richardson came on board, and paid freight. He told us we were now in the country of the Fox Indians as well as that of the Iowas, that the number about him is over 1200, and that his district extends about seventy miles up the river.

May 9, Tuesday. We had a famous pack of rascally Indians awaiting our landing — filthy and half-starved. We landed some cargo for the establishment, and I saw a trick of the trade which made me laugh. Eight cords of wood were paid for with five tin cups of sugar and three of coffee — value at St. Louis about twenty-five cents. We loaded some freight, and pushed off. We saw here the first ploughing of the ground we have observed since we left the lower settlements near St. Louis. We very soon reached the post of Fort Croghan. Here we found only a few soldiers, dragoons; their camp and officers having been forced to move across the prairie to the Bluffs, five miles. The soldiers assured us that their parade ground, and so-called barracks, had been four feet under water, and we saw fair and sufficient evidence of this.

May 10, Wednesday. The morning was fine, and we were under way at daylight; but a party of dragoons, headed by a lieutenant, had left their camp four miles distant from our anchorage at the same time, and reached the shore before we had proceeded far; they fired a couple of rifle shots ahead of us, and we brought to at once. The young officer came on board, and presented a letter from his commander, Captain Burgwin, from which we found that we had to have our cargo examined. Our captain was glad of it, and so were we all; for, finding that it would take several hours, we at once ate our breakfast, and made ready to go ashore. I showed my credentials and orders from the Government, Major Mitchell of St. Louis, etc., and I was therefore immediately settled comfortably. I desired to go to see the commanding officer, and the lieutenant very politely sent us there on horseback, guided by an old dragoon of considerable respectability. I was mounted on a young white horse, Spanish saddle with holsters, and we proceeded across the prairie towards the Bluffs and the camp.

My guide asked me if I 'could ride at a gallop,' to which not answering him, but starting at once at a round run, I neatly passed him ere his horse was well at the pace; on we went, and in a few minutes we entered a beautiful dell or valley, and were in sight of the encampment. We reached this in a trice, and rode between two lines of pitched tents to one at the end, where I dismounted, and met Captain Burgwin, a young man, brought up at West Point, with whom I was on excellent and friendly terms in less time than it has taken me to write this account of our meeting. I showed him my credentials, at which he smiled, and politely assured me that I was too well known throughout our country to need any letters.

While seated in front of his tent, I heard the note of a bird new to me, and as it proceeded from a tree above our heads, I looked up and saw the first Yellow-headed Troupial alive that ever came across my own migrations. The captain thought me probably crazy, as I thought Rafinesque when he was at Henderson; for I suddenly started, shot at the bird, and killed it. Afterwards I shot three more at one shot, but only one female amid hundreds of these Yellow-headed Blackbirds. They are quite abundant here, feeding on the surplus grain that drops from the horses' troughs; they walked under, and around the horses, with as much confidence as if anywhere else. When they rose, they generally flew to the very tops of the tallest trees, and there, swelling their throats, partially spreading their wings and tail, they issue their croaking note, which is a compound, not to be mistaken, between that of the Crow Blackbird and that of the Red-winged Starling.

Prairie Wolves are extremely abundant hereabouts. They are so daring that they come into the camp both by day and by night; we found their burrows in the banks and in the prairie, and had I come here yesterday I could have had a superb specimen killed here, but which was devoured by the hogs belonging to the establishment. The captain and the doctor — Madison by name — returned with us to the boat, and we saw many more Yellow-headed Troupials. Sprague killed another of the beautiful Finch. Robins are very scarce, Parrakeets and Wild Turkeys plentiful.

The officers came on board, and we treated them as hospitably as we could; they ate their lunch with us, and are themselves almost destitute of provisions. Last July the captain sent twenty dragoons and as many Indians on a hunt for Buffaloes. During the hunt they killed 51 Buffaloes, 104 Deer, and 10 Elks, within 80 miles of the camp. The Sioux Indians are great enemies to the Potowatamies, and very frequently kill several of the latter in their predatory excursions against them. This kind of warfare has rendered the Potowatamies very cowardly, which is quite a remarkable change from their previous valor and daring.

May 12, Friday. The morning was foggy, thick, and calm. We passed the river called the *Sioux Pictout*, a small stream formerly abounding with Beavers, Otters, Muskrats, etc., but now quite destitute of any of these creatures. On going along the banks bordering a long and wide prairie, thick with willows and other small brush-wood, we saw four Black-tailed Deer immediately on the bank; they trotted away without appearing to be much alarmed; after a few hundred yards, the two largest, probably males, raised themselves on their hind feet and pawed at each other, after the manner of stallions.

This afternoon the weather cleared up, and a while before sunset we passed under Wood's Bluffs, so called because a man of that name fell overboard from his boat while drunk. We saw there many Bank Swallows, and afterwards we came in view of the Blackbird Hill, where

PILEATED WOODPECKER

'It would be difficult for me to say in what part of our extensive country I have not met with this hardy inhabitant of the forest. Even now, when several species of our birds are becoming rare, destroyed as they are, either to gratify the palate of the epicure, or to adorn the cabinet of the naturalist, the Pileated Woodpecker is everywhere to be found in the wild woods, although scarce and shy in the peopled districts.' — *Ornithological Biography*, vol. 2, p. 74.

Pileated Woodpecker.

PICUS PILEATUS. Linn.

Adult Male. 1. Adult Female. 2 Young Males. 3. 4.
Raven Grape. Vitis astivalis.

the famous Indian chief of that name was buried, at his request, on his horse, whilst the animal was alive. We are now fast to the shore opposite this famed bluff. We cut good ash wood this day, and have made a tolerable run, say forty miles.

Saturday, May 13. This morning was extremely foggy, although I could plainly see the orb of day trying to force its way through the haze. While this lasted all hands were engaged in cutting wood, and we did not leave our fastening-place till seven, to the great grief of our commander. We passed many fine prairies, and in one place I was surprised to see the richness of the bottom lands.

We saw this morning eleven Indians of the Omaha tribe. They made signals for us to land, but our captain never heeded them, for he hates the red-skins as most men hate the devil. One of them fired a gun, the group had only one, and some ran along the shore for nearly two miles, particularly one old gentleman who persevered until we came to such bluff shores as calmed down his spirits. In another place we saw one seated on a log, close by the frame of a canoe; but he looked surly, and never altered his position as we passed. The frame of this boat resembled an ordinary canoe. It is formed by both sticks giving a half circle; the upper edges are fastened together by a long stick, as well as the centre of the bottom. Outside of this stretches a Buffalo skin without the hair on; it is said to make a light and safe craft to cross even the turbid, rapid stream — the Missouri. By simply looking at them, one may suppose that they are sufficiently large to carry two or three persons. On a sand-bar afterwards we saw three more Indians, also with a canoe frame, but we only interchanged the common yells usual on such occasions. They looked as destitute and as hungry as if they had not eaten for a week, and no doubt would have given much for a bottle of whiskey. I pity these poor beings from my heart!

May 16, Tuesday. We came to the establishment called that of Vermilion River, and met Mr. Cerré, called usually Pascal, the agent of the Company at this post, a handsome French gentleman, of good manners. He dined with us. After this we landed, and walked to the fort, if the place may so be called, for we found it only a square, strongly picketed, without portholes. It stands on the immediate bank of the river, opposite a long and narrow island, and is backed by a vast prairie, all of which was inundated during the spring freshet. He told me that game was abundant, such as Elk, Deer, and Bear. We passed some remarkable bluffs of blue and light limestone, towards the top of which we saw an abundance of Cliff-Swallows, and counted upwards of two hundred nests. But, alas! we have finally met with an accident. A plate of one of our boilers was found to be burned out, and we were obliged to stop on the west side of the River, about ten miles below the mouth of the Vermilion River. Here we were told that we might go ashore and hunt to our heart's content; and so I have, but shot at nothing. I started a Woodcock, and caught one of her young, and I am now sorry for this evil deed.

A dead Buffalo cow and calf passed us a few moments ago.

May 17, Wednesday. We have seen floating eight Buffaloes, one Antelope, and one Deer; how great the destruction of these animals must be during high freshets! The cause of their being drowned in such extraordinary numbers might not astonish one acquainted with the habits of these animals, but to one who is not, it may be well enough for me to describe it. Some few hundred miles above us, the river becomes confined between high bluffs or cliffs, many of which are nearly perpendicular, and therefore extremely difficult to ascend. When the Buffaloes have leaped or tumbled down from either side of the stream, they swim with ease across, but on reaching these walls, as it were, the poor animals try in vain to climb them, and becoming exhausted by falling back some dozens of times, give up the ghost, and float down the turbid stream; their bodies have been known to pass, swollen and putrid, the city of St. Louis.

The most extraordinary part of the history of these drowned Buffaloes is, that the different tribes of Indians on the shores, are ever on the lookout for them, and no matter how putrid their flesh may be, provided the hump proves at all fat, they swim to them, drag them on shore, and cut them to pieces; after which they cook and eat this loathsome and abominable flesh, even to the marrow found in the bones. In some instances this has been done when the whole of the hair had fallen off, from the rottenness of the Buffalo. Ah! Mr. Catlin, I am now sorry to see and to read your accounts of the Indians *you* saw — how very different they must have been from any that I have seen! We saw here no 'carpeted prairies,' no 'velvety distant landscape'; and if these things are to be seen, why, the sooner we reach them the better.

May 18, Thursday. Our good captain called us all up at a quarter before four this fair morning, to tell us that four barges had arrived from Fort Pierre, and that we might write a few letters, which Mr.

Laidlaw, one of the partners, would take to St. Louis for us. The names of these four boats are 'War Eagle,' 'White Cloud,' 'Crowfeather,' and 'Red-fish.' We went on board one of them, and found it comfortable enough. They had ten thousand Buffalo robes on the four boats; the men live entirely on Buffalo meat and pemmican. We gave them six bottles of whiskey, for which they were very thankful; they gave us dried Buffalo meat, and three pairs of moccasins. They breakfasted with us, preferring salt meat to fresh venison. They departed soon after six o'clock, and proceeded rapidly down-stream in Indian file. These boats are strong and broad; the tops, or roofs, are supported by bent branches of trees, and these are covered by water-proof Buffalo hides; each has four oarsmen and a steersman, who manages the boat standing on a broad board; the helm is about ten feet long, and the rudder itself is five or six feet long. They row constantly for sixteen hours, and stop regularly at sundown.

May 19, Friday. I forgot to say yesterday two things which I should have related, one of which is of a dismal and very disagreeable nature, being no less than the account given us of the clerks of the Company having killed one of the chiefs of the Blackfeet tribe of Indians, at the upper settlement of the Company, at the foot of the great falls of the Missouri, and therefore at the base of the Rocky Mountains, and Mr. Laidlaw assured us that it would be extremely dangerous for us to go that far towards these Indians. The other thing is that Mr. Laidlaw brought down a daughter of his, a half-breed of course, whom he is taking to St. Louis to be educated.

May 20, Saturday. We saw three Deer in the flat of one of the prairies, and just before our dinner we saw, rather indistinctly, a number of Buffaloes, making their way across the hills about two miles distant; after which, however, we saw their heavy tracks in a well and deep cut line across the said hills. Therefore we are now in what is pronounced to be the 'Buffalo country,' and may expect to see more of these animals to-morrow. We have stopped for wood no less than three times this day, and are fast for the night. Three of our Indian rascals left us at our last wooding-ground, and have gone towards their miserable village. We have now only one Sioux with us, who will, the captain says, go to Fort Pierre in our company. They are, all that we have had as yet, a thieving and dirty set, covered with vermin.

May 22, Monday. We began seeing Buffaloes again in small gangs, but this afternoon and evening we have seen a goodly number, probably more than a hundred. We also saw fifteen or twenty Antelopes. I saw ten at once, and it was beautiful to see them running from the top of a high hill down to its base, after which they went round the same hill, and were lost to us. We have landed three times to cut wood, and are now busy at it on Cedar Island. At both the previous islands we saw an immense number of Buffalo tracks, more, indeed, than I had anticipated. The whole of the prairies as well as the hills have been so trampled by them that I should have considered it quite unsafe for a man to travel on horseback. The ground was literally covered with their tracks, and also with bunches of hair, while the bushes and the trunks of the trees, between which they had passed, were hanging with the latter substance. I collected some, and intend to carry a good deal home.

We found here an abundance of what is called the White Apple,[1] but which is anything else but an apple. The fruit grows under the ground about six inches; it is about the size of a hen's egg, covered with a woody, hard pellicle, a sixteenth of an inch thick, from which the fruit can be drawn without much difficulty; this is quite white; the exterior is a dirty, dark brown. The roots are woody. The flowers were not in bloom, but I perceived that the leaves are ovate, and attached in fives. This plant is collected in great quantities by the Indians at this season and during the whole summer, and put to dry, which renders it as hard as wood; it is then pounded fine, and makes an excellent kind of mush, upon which the Indians feed greedily.

Could we have remained on shore at several places that we passed, we should have made havoc with the Buffaloes, no doubt; but we shall have enough of that sport ere long. They all look extremely poor and shabby; we see them sporting among themselves, butting and tearing up the earth, and when at a gallop they throw up the dust behind them. We saw their tracks all along both shores; where they have landed and are unable to get up the steep cliffs, they follow along the margin till they reach a ravine, and then make their way to the hills, and again to the valleys; they also have roads to return to the river to drink. They appear at this season more on the west side of the Missouri. The Elks, on the contrary, are found on the islands and low bottoms, well covered with timbers; the common Deer is found indifferently everywhere. All the Antelopes we have seen were on the west side.

---

[1] The *pomme blanche* or *pomme de prairie* of the voyageurs, the starchy root of *Psoralea esculenta*, a member of the legume family.

Up the Missouri

After we had left our first landing-place a few miles, we observed some seven or eight Indians looking at us, and again retiring to the woods, as if to cover themselves; when we came nearly opposite them, however, they all came to the shore, and made signs to induce us to land. The boat did not stop for their pleasure, and after we had fairly passed them they began firing at us, not with blank cartridges, but with well-directed rifle-balls, several of which struck the 'Omega' in different places. I was standing at that moment by one of the chimneys, and saw a ball strike the water a few feet beyond our bows; and Michaux, the hunter, heard its passing within a few inches of his head. A Scotchman, who was asleep below, was awakened and greatly frightened by hearing a ball pass through the partition, cutting the lower part of his pantaloons, and deadening itself against a trunk. Fortunately no one was hurt. Those rascals were attached to a war party, and belong to the Santee tribes which range across the country from the Mississippi to the Missouri. I will make no comment upon their conduct, but I have two of the balls that struck our boat; it seems to be a wonder that not one person was injured, standing on deck as we were to the number of a hundred or more.

Our captain has just sent out four hunters this evening, who are to hunt early to-morrow morning, and will meet the boat some distance above; Squires has gone with them. How I wish I were twenty-five years younger! I should like such a tramp greatly; but I do not think it prudent now for me to sleep on the ground when I can help it, while it is so damp.

May 23, Tuesday. The wind blew from the south this morning and rather stiffly. We rose early, and walked about this famous Cedar Island, where we stopped to cut large red cedars for one and a half hours; we started at half-past five, breakfasted rather before six, and were on the lookout for our hunters. One was Michaux; the other a friend of his, whose name I do not know. It happened, by hook or by crook, that these two managed to kill four Buffaloes; but one of them was drowned, as it took to the river after being shot. Only a few pieces from a young bull, and its tongue, were brought on board, most of the men being too lazy, or too far off, to cut out even the tongues of the others; and thus it is that thousands multiplied by thousands of Buffaloes are murdered in senseless play, and their enormous carcasses are suffered to be the prey of the Wolf, the Raven and the Buzzard.

Bell and Sprague saw several Meadow-larks, which I trust will prove new, as these birds have quite different notes and songs from those of our eastern birds. They brought a curious cactus, some handsome well-scented dwarf peas, and several other plants unknown to me. On the island I found abundance of dwarf wild-cherry bushes in full blossom, and we have placed all these plants in press.

May 24, Wednesday. A boat from Fort Pierre containing two men, passed us, bound for Fort Vermilion; one of them was Mr. Charity, one of the Company's associate traders. The boat was somewhat of a curiosity, being built in the form of a scow; but instead of being made of wood, had only a frame, covered with Buffalo skins with the hair on. They had been nine days coming 150 miles, detained every day, more or less, by Indians. We landed for the night on an island so thick with underbrush that it was no easy matter to walk through; perhaps a hundred Buffalo calves were dead in it, and the smell was not pleasant, as you may imagine. We have seen more White Wolves this day, and few Antelopes. The whole country is trodden down by the heavy Buffaloes, and this renders the walking both fatiguing and somewhat dangerous. The garlic of this country has a red blossom, otherwise it looks much like ours; when Buffalo have fed for some time on this rank weed, their flesh cannot be eaten.

May 26, Friday. The weather was fine, but we moved extremely slowly, not having made more than ten miles by twelve o'clock. The captain arranged all his papers for Fort Pierre. Three of the best walkers, well acquainted with the road, were picked from among our singularly mixed crew of *engagés*, and were put ashore at Big Bend Creek, on the banks of a high cliff on the western side; they ascended through a ravine, and soon were out of sight. We ourselves landed of course, but found the prairie so completely trodden by Buffaloes that it was next to impossible to walk. Notwithstanding this, however, a few birds were procured. The boat continued on with much difficulty, being often stopped for the want of water. At one place we counted over a hundred dead Buffalo calves; we saw a great number, however, that did reach the top of the bank, and proceeded to feeding at once.

There now was heard on board some talk about the *Great Bend*, and the captain asked me whether I would like to go off and camp, and await his arrival on the other side to-morrow. I assured him that nothing would give us more pleasure, and he gave us three stout young men to go with us to carry our blankets, provisions, etc., and to act as guides and hunters. All was ready by about five of the afternoon, when Harris, Bell, Sprague, and I, as well as the three men, were put ashore; and off we went at a brisk walk across a beautiful, level prairie, whereon in sundry directions we could see small groups of Buffaloes, grazing at leisure. We saw a great number of Cactus, some Bartram Sandpipers, and a Long-billed Curlew.

We proceeded on, being somewhat anxious to pitch our camp for the night before dark. The walk from our landing crossing the prairies was quite four miles, whilst the distance by water is computed to be twenty-six. From the pinnacle we stood on, we could see the movements of our boat quite well, and whilst the men were employed cutting wood for her engines, we could almost count every stroke of their axes, though fully two miles distant, as the crow flies. As we advanced we soon found ourselves on the ridges leading us across the Bend, and plainly saw that we were descending towards the Missouri once more.

Chemin faisant, we saw four Black-tailed Deer, a shot at which Michaux or Bell, who were in advance, might perhaps have had, had not Harris and Sprague taken a route across the declivity before them, and being observed by these keen-sighted animals, the whole made off at once. I had no fair opportunity of witnessing their movements; but they looked swiftness itself, combined with grace. They were not followed, and we reached the river at a spot which evidently had been previously camped on by Indians; here we made our minds up to stop at once, and arrange for the night, which now promised to be none of the fairest.

One man remained with us to prepare the camp, whilst Michaux and the others started in search of game, as if blood-hounds. Meantime we lighted a large and glowing fire, and began preparing some supper. In less than half an hour Michaux was seen to return with a load on his back, which proved to be a fine young buck of the Black-tailed Deer. This produced animation at once. I examined it carefully, and Harris and Sprague returned promptly from the point to which they had gone.

The darkness of the night, contrasting with the vivid glare of our fire, which threw a bright light on the skinning of the Deer, and was reflected on the trunks and branches of the cottonwood trees, six of them in one clump, almost arising from the same root, gave such superb effect that I retired some few steps to enjoy the truly fine picture. Some were arranging their rough couches, whilst others were engaged in carrying wood to support our fire through the night; some brought water from the great, muddy stream, and others were busily at work sharpening long sticks for skewers, from which large pieces of venison were soon seen dropping their rich juices upon the brightest of embers. The very sight of this sharpened our appetites, and it must have been laughable to see how all of us fell to, and ate of this first-killed Black-tailed Deer.

After a hearty meal we went to sleep, one and all, under the protection of God, and not much afraid of Indians, of whom we have not seen a specimen since we had the pleasure of being fired on by the Santees. We slept very well for a while, till it began to sprinkle rain; but it was only a very slight shower, and I did not even attempt to shelter myself from it. Our fires were mended several times by one or another of the party, and the short night passed on, refreshing us all as only men can be refreshed by sleep under the sky, breathing the purest of air, and happy as only a clear conscience can make one.

May 27, Saturday. At half-past three this morning my ears were saluted by the delightful song of the Red Thrush, who kept on with his strains until we were all up. Our boat made its appearance at two o'clock. At three our camp was broken up, our effects removed, our fire left burning, and our boat having landed for us, and for cutting cedar trees, we got on board, highly pleased with our camping out.

We had not proceeded very far when the difficulties of navigation increased so much that we grounded several times, and presently saw a few Indians on the shore; our yawl was out sounding for a passage amid the many sand-bars in view; the Indians fired, not balls, but a salute, to call us ashore. We neared shore, and talked to them; for, they proving to be Sioux, and our captain being a good scholar in that tongue, there was no difficulty in so doing. He told them to follow us, and that he would come-to. They ran to their horses on the prairie, all of which stood still, and were good-looking, comparatively speaking, leaped on their backs without saddles or stirrups, and followed us with ease at a walk. They fired a second salute as we landed; there were only four of them, and they are all at this moment on board. They are fine-looking fellows; the captain introduced Harris and me to the chief, and we shook hands all round. They are a poor set of beggars after all. The captain gave them supper, sugar and coffee, and about one pound of gunpowder, and the chief coolly said: 'What is the use of powder, without balls?'

It is quite surprising that these Indians did not see us last night, for

I have no doubt our fire could have been seen up and down the river for nearly twenty miles. But we are told their lodges are ten miles inland, and that may answer the question. I shall not be sorry now to go to bed. Our camp of the *Six Trees* is deserted and silent.

Sunday, May 28. This morning was beautiful, though cool. Our visiting Indians left us at twelve last night, and I was glad enough to be rid of these beggars by trade. Both shores were dotted by groups of Buffaloes as far as the eye could reach, and although many were near the banks they kept on feeding quietly till we nearly approached them; those at the distance of half a mile never ceased their avocations. The prairies appear better now, the grass looks green, and probably the poor Buffaloes will soon regain their flesh. We have seen more than 2,000 this morning up to this moment — twelve o'clock.

We reached Fort George at about three this afternoon. This is what is called the 'Station of the Opposition line'; some Indians and a few lodges are on the edge of the prairie. Sundry bales of Buffalo robes were brought on board, and Major Hamilton, who is now acting Indian agent here until the return of Major Crisp, came on board also. I knew his father thirty-five years ago. He pointed out to us the cabin on the opposite shore, where a partner of the 'Opposition line' shot at and killed two white men and wounded two others, all of whom were remarkable miscreants.

We are about thirty miles below Fort Pierre. Indians were seen on both sides the river, ready to trade both here and at Fort Pierre, where I am told there are five hundred lodges standing. We entered the lodge of a trader attached to our company, a German, who is a clever man, has considerable knowledge of botany, and draws well. There were about fifteen lodges, and we saw a greater number of squaws and half-breed children than I had expected. But as every clerk and agent belonging to the companies has 'a wife,' as it is *called*, a spurious population soon exhibits itself around the wigwams. I will not comment upon this here. We returned before dark to our boat, and I am off to bed.

Monday, May 29. Bell, Harris, Squires, and myself went off to shoot some Prairie-dogs, as the *Arctomys ludovicianus* is called. After walking over the hills for about one mile, we came to the 'village,' and soon after heard their cries but not their barkings. The sound they make is simply a 'chip, chip, chip,' long and shrill enough, and at every cry the animal jerks its tail, without however erecting it upright, as I have seen them represented. Their holes are not perpendicular, but oblique, at an angle of about forty degrees, after which they seem to deviate; but whether sideways or upwards, I cannot yet say. I shot at two of them, which appeared to me to be standing, not across their holes, but in front of them. The first one I never saw after the shot; the second I found dying at the entrance of the burrow, but at my appearance it worked backwards. I drew my ramrod and put the end in its mouth; this it bit hard but kept working backwards, and notwithstanding my efforts, was soon out of sight and touch.

Bell saw two enter the same hole, and Harris three. Bell saw some standing quite erect and leaping in the air to see and watch our movements. I found, by lying down within twenty or thirty steps of the hole, that they reappeared in fifteen or twenty minutes. This was the case with me when I shot at the two I have mentioned. Harris saw one that, after coming out of its hole, gave a long and somewhat whistling note, which he thinks was one of invitation to its neighbors, as several came out in a few moments. I have great doubts whether their cries are issued at the appearance of danger or not. I am of opinion that they are a mode of recognition as well as of amusement.

Buffalo cows at this season associate together, with their calves, but if pursued, leave the latter to save themselves. The hides at present are not worth saving, and the Indians as well as the white hunters, when they shoot a Buffalo, tear off the hide, cut out the better portions of the flesh, as well as the tongue, and leave the carcass to the Wolves and Ravens.

Fort Pierre, May 31, Wednesday. We were forced to come-to about a quarter of a mile above Fort Pierre, after having passed the steamer 'Trapper' of our Company. Bell, Squires, and myself walked to the Fort as soon as possible, and found Mr. Picotte and Mr. Chardon there. More kindness from strangers I have seldom received. I was presented with the largest pair of Elk horns I ever saw, and also a skin of the animal itself, most beautifully prepared, which I hope to give to my beloved wife. I was also presented with two pairs of moccasins, an Indian riding-whip, one collar of Grizzly Bear's claws, and two long strings of dried white apples, as well as two Indian dresses.

We are about one and a half miles above the Teton River, or, as it is now called, the Little Missouri, a swift and tortuous stream that finds its source about 250 miles from its union with this great river, in what are called the Bad Lands of Teton River, where it seems, from what we hear, that the country has been at one period greatly convulsed, and is filled with fossil remains. I saw the young Elk belonging to our captain, looking exceedingly shabby, but with the most beautiful eyes I ever beheld in any animal of the Deer kind.

June 5, Monday. In the course of the morning we passed Cannon Ball River, and the very remarkable bluffs about it, of which we cannot well speak until we have stopped there and examined their nature. We saw two Swans alighted on the prairie at a considerable distance. We stopped to take wood at Bowie's settlement, at which place his wife was killed by some of the Riccaree Indians, after some Gros Ventres had assured him that such would be the case if he suffered his wife to go out of the house. She went out, however, on the second day, and was shot with three rifle-balls. The Indians took parts of her hair and went off. She was duly buried; but the Gros Ventres returned some time afterwards, took up the body, and carried off the balance of her hair. They, however, reburied her; and it was not until several months had elapsed that the story came to the ears of Mr. Bowie.

June 6, Tuesday. This morning was quite cold, and we had a thick white frost on our upper deck. It was also extremely cloudy, the wind from the east, and all about us looked dismal enough. The hands on board seemed to have been busy the whole of the night, for I scarcely slept for the noise they made. We soon came to a very difficult part of the river, and had to stop full three hours. Meanwhile the yawl went off to seek and sound for a channel, whilst the wood-cutters and the carriers — who, by the way, are called 'charrettes' — followed their work, and we gathered a good quantity of driftwood, which burns like straw. Our hopes of reaching the Mandan Village were abandoned, but we at last proceeded on our way and passed the bar; it was nearly dinner-time.

The place where we landed showed many signs of Deer, Elk, and Buffaloes. I saw trees where the latter had rubbed their heavy bodies against the bark, till they had completely robbed the tree of its garment. The Buffalo, when hunted on horseback, does *not* carry its tail erect, as has been represented in books, but close between the legs; but when you see a Buffalo bull work its tail sideways in a twisted rolling fashion, *then* take care of him, as it is a sure sign of his intention to rush against his pursuer's horse, which is very dangerous, both to hunter and steed.

Immediately upon the breaking up of the ice about the Mandan Village, three Buffaloes were seen floating down on a large cake; they were seen by Mr. Primeau from his post, and again from Fort Pierre.

How much further the poor beasts travelled, no one can tell. It happens not infrequently, when the river is entirely closed in with ice, that some hundreds of Buffaloes attempt to cross; their aggregate enormous weight forces the ice to break, and the whole of the gang are drowned, as it is impossible for these animals to climb over the surrounding sharp edges of the ice.

June 7, Wednesday. We reached Fort Clark and the Mandan Villages at half-past seven this morning. Great guns were fired from the fort and from the 'Omega,' as our captain took the guns from the 'Trapper' at Fort Pierre. The site of this fort appears a good one, though it is placed considerably below the Mandan Village. We saw some small spots cultivated, where corn, pumpkins, and beans are grown. The fort and village are situated on the high bank, rising somewhat to the elevation of a hill. The Mandan mud huts are very far from looking poetical, although Mr. Catlin has tried to render them so by placing them in regular rows, and all of the same size and form, which is by no means the case. But different travellers have different eyes! We saw more Indians than at any previous time since leaving St. Louis; and it is possible that there are a hundred huts, made of mud, all looking like so many potato winter-houses in the Eastern States.

As soon as we were near the shore, every article that could conveniently be carried off was placed under lock and key, and our division door was made fast, as well as those of our own rooms. Even the axes and poles were put by. Our captain told us that last year they stole his cap and his shot-pouch and horn, and that it was through the interference of the first chief that he recovered his cap and horn; but that a squaw had his leather belt, and would not give it up.

The appearance of these poor, miserable devils, as we approached the shore, was wretched enough. There they stood in the pelting rain and keen wind, covered with Buffalo robes, red blankets, and the like, some partially and most curiously besmeared with mud; and as they came on board, and we shook hands with each of them, I felt a clamminess that rendered the ceremony most repulsive. Their legs and naked feet were covered with mud. They looked at me with apparent curiosity, perhaps on account of my beard, which produced the same effect at Fort Pierre. They all looked very poor; and our captain says they are the *ne plus ultra* of thieves. It is said there are nearly three thousand men, women, and children that, during winter, cram themselves into their miserable hovels.

[292]

Up the Missouri

Harris and I walked to the fort about nine o'clock. The walking was rascally, passing through mud and water the whole day. The yard of the fort itself was as bad. We entered Mr. Chardon's own room, crawled up a crazy ladder, and in a low garret I had the great pleasure of seeing alive the Swift or Kit Fox which he has given to me. It ran swiftly from one corner to another, and, when approached, growled somewhat in the manner of a common Fox. Mr. Chardon told me that good care would be taken of it until our return, that it would be chained to render it more gentle, and that I would find it an easy matter to take it along. I sincerely hope so. Seeing a remarkably fine skin of a large Cross Fox which I wished to buy, it was handed over to me.

After this, Mr. Chardon asked one of the Indians to take us into the village, and particularly to show us the 'Medicine Lodge.' We followed our guide through mud and mire, even into the Lodge. We found this to be, in general terms, like all the other lodges, only larger, measuring twenty-three yards in diameter, with a large squarish aperture in the centre of the roof, some six or seven feet long by about four wide. We had entered this curiosity shop by pushing aside a wet Elk skin stretched on four sticks. Looking around, I saw a number of calabashes, eight or ten Otter skulls, two very large Buffalo skulls with the horns on, evidently of great age, and some sticks and other magical implements with which none but a 'Great Medicine Man' is acquainted.

During my survey there sat, crouched down on his haunches, an Indian wrapped in a dirty blanket, with only his filthy head peeping out. Our guide spoke to him; but he stirred not. Again, at the foot of one of the posts that support the central portion of this great room, lay a parcel that I took for a bundle of Buffalo robes; but it moved presently, and from beneath it half arose the emaciated body of a poor blind Indian, whose skin was quite shrivelled; and our guide made us signs that he was about to die. We all shook both hands with him; and he pressed our hands closely and with evident satisfaction. He had his pipe and tobacco pouch by him, and soon lay down again.

We left this abode of mysteries, as I was anxious to see the interior of one of the common huts around; and again our guide led us through mud and mire to his own lodge, which we entered in the same way as we had done the other. All these lodges have a sort of portico that leads to the door, and on the tops of most of them I observed Buffalo skulls. This lodge contained the whole family of our guide — several women and children, and another man, perhaps a son-in-law or a brother. All these, except the man, were on the outer edge of the lodge, crouching on the ground, some suckling children; and at nearly equal distances apart were placed berths, raised about two feet above the ground, made of leather, and with square apertures for the sleepers or occupants to enter. The man of whom I have spoken was lying down in one of these, which was all open in front. I walked up to him, and, after disturbing his happy slumbers, shook hands with him; he made signs for me to sit down; and after Harris and I had done so, he rose, squatted himself near us, and, getting out a large spoon made of boiled Buffalo horn, handed it to a young girl, who brought a great rounded wooden bowl filled with pemmican, mixed with corn and some other stuff. I ate a mouthful or so of it, and found it quite palatable; and Harris and the rest then ate of it also. Bell was absent; we had seen nothing of him since we left the boat.

This lodge, as well as the other, was dirty with water and mud; but I am told that in dry weather they are kept cleaner, and much cleaning do they need, most truly. A round, shallow hole was dug in the centre for the fire; and from the roof descended over this a chain, by the aid of which they do their cooking, the utensil being attached to the chain when wanted. As we returned towards the fort, I gave our guide a piece of tobacco, and he appeared well pleased. He followed us on board, and as he peeped in my room, and saw the dried and stuffed specimens we have, he evinced a slight degree of curiosity.

The whole country around was overgrown with 'Lamb's quarters' (*Chenopodium album*), which I have no doubt, if boiled, would take the place of spinach in this wild and, to my eyes, miserable country, the poetry of which lies in the imagination of those writers who have described the 'velvety prairies' and 'enchanted castles' (of mud), so common where we now are. We observed a considerable difference in the color of these Indians, who, by the way, are almost all Riccarees; many appeared, and in fact are, redder than others; they are lank, rather tall, and very alert, but, as I have said before, all look poor and dirty. After dinner we went up the muddy bank again to look at the cornfields, as the small patches that are meanly cultivated are called. We found poor, sickly looking corn about two inches high, that had been represented to us this morning as full six inches high.

Up the Missouri

Not a drop of spirituous liquor has been brought to this place for the last two years; and there can be no doubt that on this account the Indians have become more peaceable than heretofore, though now and then a white man is murdered, and many horses are stolen. As we walked over the plain, we saw heaps of earth thrown up to cover the poor Mandans who died of the small-pox. These mounds in many instances appear to contain the remains of several bodies and, perched on the top, lies, pretty generally, the rotting skull of a Buffalo. Indeed, the skulls of the Buffaloes seem as if a kind of relation to these most absurdly superstitious and ignorant beings. Our boat has been thronged with Indians ever since we have tied to the shore; and it is with considerable difficulty and care that we can stop them from intruding into our rooms when we are there. Our captain tells us that no matter what weather we may have to-morrow, he will start at daylight, even if he can only go across the river, to get rid of these wolfish-looking vagabonds of Indians. I sincerely hope that we may have a fair day and a long run, so that the air around us may once more be pure and fresh from the hand of Nature.

After the Riccarees had taken possession of this Mandan Village, the remains of that once powerful tribe removed about three miles up the river, and there have now fifteen or twenty huts, containing, of course, only that number of families. During the worst periods of the epidemic which swept over this village with such fury, many became maniacs, rushed to the Missouri, leaped into its turbid waters, and were seen no more.

Mr. Primeau, wife, and children, as well as another half-breed, have gone to the fort, and are to remain there till further orders. The fort is in a poor condition, roofs leaking, etc. One of the agents arrived this afternoon from the Gros Ventre, or Minnetaree Village, about twelve miles above us. He is represented as a remarkably brave man, and he relates some strange adventures of his prowess. Several *great warriors* have condescended to shake me by the hand; their very touch is disgusting — it will indeed be a deliverance to get rid of all this 'Indian poetry.' We are, nevertheless, to take a few to the Yellowstone. Alexis has his wife, who is, in fact, a good-looking young woman; an old patron, Provost, takes one of his daughters along; and we have, besides, several red-skinned single gentlemen.

It is now nine o'clock, but before I go to rest I cannot resist giving you a description of the curious exhibition that we have had on board, from a numerous lot of Indians of the first class, say some forty or fifty. They ranged themselves along the sides of the large cabin, squatting on the floor. Coffee had been prepared for the whole party, and hard sea-biscuit likewise. The coffee was first given to each of them, and afterwards the biscuits, and I had the honor of handing the latter to the row on one side of the boat; a box of tobacco was opened and laid on the table. The man who came from the Gros Ventres this afternoon proved to be an excellent interpreter; and after the captain had delivered his speech to him, he spoke loudly to the group, and explained the purport of the captain's speech. They grunted their approbation frequently, and were, no doubt, pleased.

Two individuals (Indians) made their appearance highly decorated, with epaulets on the shoulders, red clay on blue uniforms, three cocks' plumes in their head-dress, rich moccasins, leggings, etc. These are men who, though in the employ of the Opposition company, act truly as friends; but who, meantime, being called 'Braves,' never grunted, bowed, or shook hands with any of us. Supper over and the tobacco distributed, the whole body arose simultaneously, and each and every one of these dirty wretches we had all to shake by the hand. The two braves sat still until all the rest had gone ashore, and then retired as majestically as they had entered, not even shaking hands with our good-humored captain.

I am told that this performance takes place once every year, on the passing of the Company's boats. I need not say that the coffee and the two biscuits apiece were gobbled down in less than no time. The tobacco, which averaged about two pounds to each man, was hid in their robes or blankets for future use. Two of the Indians, who must have been of the highest order, and who distributed the 'rank weed,' were nearly naked; one had on only a breech-clout and one legging, the other was in no better case. They are now all ashore except one or more who are going with us to the Yellowstone; and I will now go to my rest.

Though I have said 'Good-night,' I have arisen almost immediately, and I must write on, for we have other scenes going on both among the trappers below and some of the people above. Many Indians, squaws as well as men, are bartering and trading, and keep up such a babble that Harris and I find sleep impossible; needless to say, the squaws who are on board are of the lowest grade of morality.

June 8, Thursday. This morning was fair and cold, as you see by the range of the thermometer, 37° to 56°. We started at a very early hour, and breakfasted before five, on account of the village of Gros Ventres, where our captain had to stop. We passed a few lodges belonging to the tribe of the poor Mandans, about all that remained. I only counted eight, but am told there are twelve. The village of the Gros Ventres (Minnetarees) has been cut off from the bank of the river by an enormous sand-bar, now overgrown with willows and brush, and we could only see the American flag flying in the cool breeze.

Two miles above this, however, we saw an increasing body of Indians, for the prairie was sprinkled with small parties, on horse and on foot. The first who arrived fired a salute of small guns, and we responded with our big gun. They had an abundance of dogs harnessed to take wood back to the village, and their yells and fighting were severe upon our ears. Some forty or more of the distinguished black-guards came on board; and we had to close our doors as we did yesterday. After a short period they were feasted as last evening; and speeches, coffee, and tobacco, as well as some gunpowder, were given them, which they took away in packs, to be divided afterward. We took one more passenger, and lost our interpreter, who is a trader with the Minnetarees. The latter are by no means as fine-looking a set of men as those we have seen before, and I observed none of that whiteness of skin among them.

June 9, Friday. We landed at four o'clock, and Sprague and I went up to the top of the hills, bounding the beautiful prairie, by which we had stopped to repair something about the engine. We gathered some handsome lupines, of two different species, and many other curious plants. From this elevated spot we could see the wilderness to an immense distance; the Missouri looked as if only a brook, and our steamer a very small one indeed. At this juncture we saw two men running along the shore upwards, and I supposed they had seen an Elk or something else, of which they were in pursuit. Meantime, gazing around, we saw a large lake, where we are told that Ducks, Geese, and Swans breed in great numbers; this we intend also to visit when we come down.

At this moment I heard the report of a gun from the point where the men had been seen, and when we reached the steamboat, we were told that a Buffalo had been killed. From the deck I saw a man swimming round the animal; he got on its side, and floated down the stream with it. The captain sent a parcel of men with a rope; the swimmer fastened this round the neck of the Buffalo, and with his assistance, for he now swam all the way, the poor beast was brought alongside; and as the tackle had been previously fixed, it was hauled up on the fore deck. The head is so full of symmetry, and so beautiful, that I shall have a drawing of it to-morrow, as well as careful ones of the feet.

Whilst the butchers were at work, I was highly interested to see one of our Indians cutting out the milk-bag of the cow and eating it, quite fresh and raw, in pieces somewhat larger than a hen's egg. One of the stomachs was partially washed in a bucket of water, and an Indian swallowed a large portion of this. Mr. Chardon brought the remainder on the upper deck and ate it uncleaned. I had a piece well cleaned and tasted it; to my utter astonishment, it was very good, but the idea was repulsive to me; besides which, I am not a meat-eater, as you know, except when other provisions fail. The animal was in good condition; and the whole carcass was cut up and dispersed among the men below, reserving the nicer portions for the cabin. This was accomplished with great rapidity; the blood was washed away in a trice, and half an hour afterwards no one would have known that a Buffalo had been dressed on deck.

I have been hearing much of the prevalence of scurvy, from living so constantly on dried flesh, also about the small-pox, which destroyed such numbers of the Indians. Among the Mandans, Riccarées, and Gros Ventres, hundreds died in 1837, only a few surviving; and the Assiniboins were nearly exterminated. Indeed it is said that in the various attacks of this scourge 52,000 Indians have perished. This last visitation of the dread disease has never before been related by a traveller, and I will write more of it when at Fort Union.

June 11, Sunday. This day has been tolerably fine, though windy. We have seen an abundance of game, a great number of Elks, common Virginian Deer, Mountain Rams in two places, and a fine flock of Sharp-tailed Grouse. We have seen much remarkably handsome scenery, but nothing at all comparing with Catlin's descriptions; his book must, after all, be altogether a humbug. Poor devil! I pity him from the bottom of my soul; had he studied, and kept up to the old French proverb that says, 'Bon renommé vaut mieux que ceinture doré,' he might have become an 'honest man' — the quintessence of God's works.

ON THE DAKOTA PRAIRIES

INTRODUCTION

THE Audubon journals of 1843, as edited and originally published by Elliott Coues and Maria Audubon, flow on without break or change of title, whether Audubon is going upstream into country new to him, remaining stationary for weeks at Fort Union, or descending as swiftly as possible through territory now well explored. I have chosen to assign to the period of his stay of two months at Fort Union a separate title, for the accidents and fatigues of travel, and constant fresh scenes, are not now his daily lot. He and his assistants are engaged in collecting, dissecting, drawing, and study, and we have a full-fledged scientific expedition now in operation at field base, from which short excursions are made.

The intention had been to go on to the Rockies, but various obstacles seem to have prevented this, and consequently Audubon got only two hundred miles farther up the Missouri than the first winter's halt of Lewis and Clark, some forty years earlier. Near Fort Union the naturalist Prince Maximilian of Neuwied had also remained some time, and this had been Catlin's country. It was still, however, some four hundred miles from what is now Yellowstone Park, and even the Big Horns, two hundred and fifty miles distant, were not visible, though the younger hunters ranged that far after mountain goats and sheep and antelope. Fort Union, where Audubon found his expedition at a halt, was not an army fort, but a fortified trading post of the American Fur Company, under the administration at that time of a *bourgeois* (that is, 'head man'), Mr. Alexander Culbertson, who had taken to wife an Indian princess. It was then considered one of the handsomest trading posts on the Missouri, was located on the north bank of the river, opposite the junction of the Yellowstone and the Missouri, and not far from what is now Williston, North Dakota, on the borders of Montana. The fort had been begun in 1829 by Kenneth McKenzie, a Scotch trader, and it now enclosed an area two hundred and twenty by two hundred forty feet in extent, and was defended by palisades, bastions, cannon, and swivel guns. There was a handsome piazza with the unheard-of elegance, for the wilderness, of turned pillars painted white; within, the principal building boasted wallpaper and framed pictures, offices and mess-room, saddlery, and tailor shop, while outside there were ranges of buildings including such luxuries as an ice house and such an advanced form of press room or peltry that it was absolutely waterproof. There were stables, pens for wild and domestic beasts, blacksmith shop, Indian reception room quite separate from access to the fort, trading shops, and powder magazine. A garden provided peas, turnips, radishes, lettuce, beets, onions, etc., and outside the fort were patches for the growing of corn and potatoes. In this self-sustaining outpost of civilization did Audubon and his assistants settle down for the last great scientific field work of the old master's life.

Audubon's journal of these days at Fort Union gives us the glamor and the squalor of the frontier, the sense of vasty space and abundance, the howling of the wolves at night, the mountains of decaying buffalo, the waste of natural resources, the decadence of the Indians; his journal is like a great panorama, sweeping around three hundred and sixty degrees of the level horizon. It was the last wilderness he saw, and his powers to describe it were at their full.

Fort Union, June 12, Monday [1843]. We had a cloudy and showery day, and a high wind besides. We saw many Wild Geese and Ducks with their young. We took in wood at two places, but shot nothing. I saw a Wolf giving chase, or driving away four Ravens from a sandbar; but the finest sight of all took place shortly before we came to the mouth of the Yellowstone, and that was no less than twenty-two Mountain Rams and Ewes mixed, and amid them one young one only. We came in sight of the fort at five o'clock, and reached it at seven. We passed the Opposition fort three miles below this; their flags were hoisted, and ours also. We were saluted from Fort Union, and we fired guns in return, six in number. The moment we had arrived, the gentlemen of the fort came down on horseback, and appeared quite a cavalcade. I was introduced to Mr. Culbertson and others, and, of course, the introduction went the rounds. We walked to the fort and drank some first-rate port wine, and returned to the boat at half-past nine o'clock.

Our trip to this place has been the quickest on record, though our boat is the slowest that ever undertook to reach the Yellowstone. Including all stoppages and detentions, we have made the trip in forty-eight days and seven hours from St. Louis. We left St. Louis April 25th, at noon; reaching Fort Union June 12th, at seven in the evening.

June 14, Wednesday. After dinner Mr. Culbertson told us that if a Wolf made its appearance on the prairie near the fort, he would give it chase on horseback, and bring it to us, alive or dead; and he was as good as his word. It was so handsomely executed, that I will relate the whole affair.

When I saw the Wolf (a white one), it was about a quarter of a mile off, alternately standing and trotting; the horses were about one-half the distance off. A man was started to drive these in; and I thought the coursers never would reach the fort, much less become equipped so as to overhaul the Wolf. We were all standing on the platform of the fort, with our heads only above the palisades; and I was so fidgety that I ran down twice to tell the hunters that the Wolf was making off. Mr. Culbertson, however, told me he would see it did not make off; and in a few moments he rode out of the fort, gun in hand, dressed only in shirt and breeches.

He threw his cap off within a few yards, and suddenly went off with the swiftness of a jockey bent on winning a race. The Wolf trotted on, and ever and anon stopped to gaze at the rider and the horse; till, finding out the meaning (too late, alas! for him), he galloped off with all his might; but the horse was too swift for the poor cur, as we saw the rider gaining ground rapidly. Mr. Culbertson fired his gun off as a signal, I was told, that the Wolf would be brought in; and the horse, one would think, must have been of the same opinion, for although the Wolf had now reached the hills, and turned into a small ravine, the moment it had entered it, the horse dashed after, the sound of the gun came on the car, the Wolf was picked up by Mr. Culbertson without dismounting, hardly slackening his pace, and thrown across the

Audubon's America

saddle. The rider returned as swiftly as he had gone, wet through with a smart shower that had fallen meantime; and the poor Wolf was placed at my disposal. The time taken from the start to the return in the yard did not exceed twenty minutes, possibly something less.

Two other men who had started at the same time rode very swiftly also, and skirted the hills to prevent the Wolf's escape; and one of them brought in Mr. C.'s gun, which he had thrown on the ground as he picked up the Wolf to place it on the saddle. The beast was not quite dead when it arrived, and its jaws told of its dying agonies; it scratched one of Mr. C.'s fingers sorely; but we are assured that such things so often occur that nothing is thought of it.

And now a kind of sham Buffalo hunt was proposed, accompanied by a bet of a suit of clothes, to be given to the rider who would load and fire the greatest number of shots in a given distance. The horses were mounted as another Wolf was seen trotting off towards the hills, and Mr. Culbertson again told us he would bring it in. This time, however, he was mistaken; the Wolf was too far off to be overtaken, and it reached the hill-tops, made its way through a deep ravine full of large rocks, and was then given up. Mr. Culbertson was seen coming down without his quarry. He joined the riders, started with his gun empty, loaded in a trice, and fired the first shot; then the three riders came on at full speed, loading and firing first on one side, then on the other of the horse, as if after Buffaloes. Mr. C. fired eleven times before he reached the fort, and within less than half a mile's run; the others fired once less, each. We were all delighted to see these feats. No one was thrown off, though the bridles hung loose, and the horses were under full gallop all the time. Mr. Culbertson's mare, which is of the full Blackfoot Indian breed, is about five years old, and could not be bought for four hundred dollars. I should like to see some of the best English hunting gentlemen hunt in the like manner.

We are assured that after dusk, or as soon as the gates of the fort are shut, the Wolves come near enough to be killed from the platform, as these beasts oftentimes come to the trough where the hogs are fed daily. We have seen no less than eight this day from the fort, moving as leisurely as if a hundred miles off. This day has been spent altogether in talking, sight-seeing, and enjoyment. Our room was small, dark, and dirty, and crammed with our effects. Mr. Culbertson saw this, and told me that to-morrow he would remove us to a larger, quieter, and better one. I was glad to hear this, as it would have been very difficult to draw, write, or work in; and yet it is the very room where the Prince de Neuwied resided for two months, with his secretary and bird-preserver.

The evening was cloudy and cold; we had had several showers of rain since our bath in the bushes this morning, and I felt somewhat fatigued. Harris and I made our beds up; Squires fixed some Buffalo robes, of which nine had been given us, on a long old bedstead, never knowing it had been the couch of a foreign prince; Bell and Sprague settled themselves opposite to us on more Buffalo skins, and night closed in. Now clarionets, fiddles, and a drum were heard in the dining-room, where indeed they had been playing at different times during the afternoon. We had retired for the night; but an invitation was sent us to join the party in the dining-room. Squires was up in a moment, and returned to say that a ball was on foot, and that 'all the beauty and fashion' would be skipping about in less than no time. There was no alternative; we all got up, and in a short time were amid the *beau monde* of these parts. Several squaws, attired in their best, were present, with all the guests, *engagés*, clerks, etc. Mr. Culbertson played the fiddle very fairly; Mr. Guèpe the claronet, and Mr. Chouteau the drum, as if brought up in the army of the great Napoleon. Cotillions and reels were danced with much energy and apparent enjoyment, and the company dispersed about one o'clock.

June 19, Monday. Harris and Bell have returned, and, to my delight and utter astonishment, have brought two new birds: one a Lark, small and beautiful; the other like our common Gold-winged Woodpecker, but with a red mark instead of a black one along the lower mandible running backward.

June 20, Tuesday. To fill the time on this dreary day, I asked Mr. Chardon to come up to our room and give us an account of the small-pox among the Indians, especially among the Mandans and Riccarees, and he related as follows: Early in the month of July, 1837, the steamer 'Assiniboin' arrived at Fort Clark with many cases of small-pox on board. Mr. Chardon, having a young son on the boat, went thirty miles to meet her, and took his son away. The pestilence, however, had many victims on the steamboat, and seemed destined to find many more among the helpless tribes of the wilderness. An Indian stole the blanket of one of the steamboat's watchmen (who lay at the point of death, if not already dead), wrapped himself in it, and carried it off, unaware of the disease that was to cost him his life, and that of many of his tribe — thousands, indeed. Mr. Chardon offered a reward immediately for the return of the blanket, as well as a new one in its stead, and promised that no punishment should be inflicted. But the robber was a great chief; through shame, or some other motive, he never came forward, and, before many days, was a corpse.

Most of the Riccarees and Mandans were some eighty miles in the prairies, hunting Buffaloes and saving meat for the winter. Mr. Chardon despatched an express to acquaint them all of the awful calamity, enjoining them to keep far off, for that death would await them in their villages. They sent word in return, that their corn was suffering for want of work, that they were not afraid, and would return; the danger to them, poor things, seemed fabulous, and doubtless they thought other reasons existed, for which this was an excuse. Mr. Chardon sent the man back again, and told them their crop of corn was nothing compared to their lives; but Indians are Indians, and, in spite of all entreaties, they moved *en masse*, to confront the awful catastrophe that was about to follow.

When they reached the villages, they thought the whites had saved the Riccarees, and put the plague on them alone (they were Mandans). Moreover, they thought, and said, that the whites had a preventive medicine, which the whites would not give them. Again and again it was explained to them that this was not the case, but all to no purpose; the small-pox had taken such a hold upon the poor Indians, and in such malignant form, that they died oftentimes within the rising and setting of a day's sun. They died by hundreds daily; their bodies were thrown down beneath the high bluff, and soon produced a stench beyond description. Men shot their wives and children, and afterwards, driving several balls in their guns, would place the muzzle in their mouths, and, touching the trigger with their feet, blow their brains out.

The mortality, as taken down by Major Mitchell, was estimated by that gentleman at 150,000 Indians, including those from the tribes of the Riccarees, Mandans, Sioux, and Blackfeet. The small-pox was in the very fort from which I am now writing this account, and its ravages here were as awful as elsewhere. Mr. Chardon had the disease, and was left for dead; but one of his clerks saw signs of life, and forced him to drink a quantity of hot whiskey mixed with water and nutmeg; he fell into a sound sleep, and his recovery began from that hour. He says that with him the pains began in the small of the back, and on the back part of his head, and were intense. He concluded by assuring us all that the small-pox had never been known in the civilized world, as it had been among the poor Mandans and other Indians. Only *twenty-seven* Mandans were left to tell the tale; they have now augmented to ten or twelve lodges in the six years that have nearly elapsed since the pestilence.

June 22, Thursday. The little new Lark that I have named after Sprague has almost all the habits of the Skylark of Europe. Whilst looking anxiously after it, on the ground where we supposed it to be singing, we discovered it was high over our heads, and that sometimes it went too high for us to see it at all. We have not yet been able to discover its nest.

June 24, Saturday. This afternoon I thought would be a fair opportunity to examine the manners of Sprague's Lark on the wing. Bell drove Peter for me, and I killed four Larks; we then watched the flight of several. The male rises by constant undulations to a great height, say one hundred yards or more; and whilst singing its sweet-sounding notes, beats its wings, poised in the air like a Hawk, without rising at this time; after which, and after each burst of singing, it sails in divers directions, forming three quarters of a circle or thereabouts, then rises again, and again sings; the intervals between the singing are longer than those which the song occupies, and at times the bird remains so long in the air as to render it quite fatiguing to follow it with the eye. Sprague thought one he watched yesterday remained in the air about one hour. Bell and Harris watched one for more than half an hour, and this afternoon I gazed upon one, whilst Bell timed it, for thirty-six minutes.

July 6, Thursday. Whilst we were sitting at the back gate of the fort, we saw a parcel of Indians coming towards the place, yelling and singing what Mr. Culbertson told me was the song of the scalp dance; we saw through the telescope that they were fourteen in number, with their faces painted black, and that it was a detachment of a war party. When within a hundred yards they all stopped, as if awaiting an invitation; we did not hurry as to this, and they seated themselves on the ground and looked at us, while Mr. Culbertson sent Mr. Denig to ask them to come in by the front gate of the fort, and put them in the Indian house, a sort of camp for the fellows. They all looked miserably poor, filthy beyond description, and their black faces and foully smelling Buffalo robes made them appear to me like so many devils. The leader, who was well known to be a famous rascal, and was painted red, was a tall, well-formed man. The party had only three poor guns, and a few had coarse, common lances; every man had a knife, and the leader was armed with a stick in which were inserted three blades of butcher's-knives; a blow from this weapon would doubtless kill a man. Some of the squaws of the fort, having found that they were Assiniboins, went to meet them; they took one of these, and painted her face black, as a sign of friendship. Most of these mighty warriors had a lump of fresh Buffalo meat slung on his back, which was all traded for by Mr. Larpenteur, who gave them in exchange some dried meat, not worth the notice of Harris's dog, and some tobacco.

July 7, Friday. This morning the dirty Indians, who could have washed had they so minded, were beating the tambour and singing their miserable scalp song, until Mr. Culbertson ordered the drum taken away, and gave them more tobacco and some vermilion to be-daub their faces. They were permitted to remain about the fort the remainder of the day, and the night coming they will again be sheltered; but they must depart to-morrow morning. After breakfast Sprague worked on the view of the fort. I went on with the portrait of Mr. Culbertson, who is about as bad a sitter as his wife, whose portrait is very successful, notwithstanding her extreme restlessness.

After dinner Harris, Bell, and I started on foot, and walked about four miles from the fort; the day was hot, and horseflies and mosquitoes pretty abundant, but we trudged on, though we saw nothing; we had gone after Rabbits, the tracks of which had been seen previously. On our way we passed through some grasses with bearded shafts, so sharp that they penetrated our moccasins and entered our feet and ankles, and in the shade of a stumpy ash-tree we took off our moccasins and drew the spines out. The Lazuli Finches and Arctic Bluebirds sang in our view; but though we beat all the clumps of low bushes where the Rabbits must go in, whether during night or day, we did not start one.

We saw a patch of wood called in these regions a 'Point'; we walked towards it for the purpose of shooting Deer. I was sent to the lower end, Bell took one side, and Harris the other, and the hound we had with us was sent in; no Deer there, however, and we made for the fort, which we reached hot and thirsty enough after our long walk. As soon as I was cooled I took a good swim. I think the Indians hereabouts poor swimmers; they beat the water with their arms, attempting to 'nage a la brasse'; but, alas! it is too bad to mention. I am told, however, that there are no good specimens to judge from at the fort, so this is

AMERICAN BISON

'Whether we consider this noble animal as an object of the chase, or as an article of food for man, it is decidedly the most important of all our contemporary American quadrupeds; and as we can no longer see the gigantic mastodon passing over the broad savannas, or laving its enormous sides in the deep rivers of our wide-spread land, we will consider the Buffalo as a link, (perhaps sooner to be forever lost than is generally supposed,) which to a slight degree yet connects us with larger American animals, belonging to extinct creations.' — *The Quadrupeds*, vol. 2, p. 35.

Drawn from Nature by J.J.Audubon.F.R.S.F.L.S.

BOS AMERIC.

AMERICAN BISON OR

½ Natural Size
MALE.

US, GMEL

FFALO.

Lith.ᵈ Printed & Col.ᵈ by J. T. Bowen. Philad.ᵃ 1845.

not much of an opinion. It is strange how very scarce snakes of every description are, as well as insects, except mosquitoes and horseflies.

July 8, Saturday. When I came down this morning early, I was delighted to see the dirty and rascally Indians walking off to their lodge on the other side of the hills, and before many days they will be at their camp enjoying their merriment (rough and senseless as it seems to me), yelling out their scalp song, and dancing. Now this dance, to commemorate the death of an enemy, is a mere bending and slackening of the body, and patting of the ground with both feet at once, in very tolerable time with their music. Our squaws yesterday joined them in this exemplary ceremony; one was blackened, and all the others painted with vermilion. The art of painting in any color is to mix the color desired with grease of one sort or another; and when well done, it will stick on for a day or two, if not longer. Indians are not equal to the whites in the art of dyeing Porcupine quills; their ingredients are altogether too simple and natural to equal the knowledge of chemicals.

July 13, Thursday. We have had a fine opportunity of witnessing the agility and extreme strength of a year-old Buffalo bull belonging to the fort. Our cook, who is an old Spaniard, threw his lasso over the Buffalo's horns, and all the men in the fort at the time, hauled and pulled the beast about, trying to get him close to a post. He kicked, pulled, leaped sideways, and up and down, snorting and pawing until he broke loose, and ran, as if quite wild, about the enclosure. He was tied again and again, without any success, and at last got out of the fort, but was soon retaken, the rope being thrown round his horns, and he was brought to the main post of the Buffalo-robe press. There he was brought to a standstill, at the risk of breaking his neck, and the last remnant of his winter coat was removed by main strength, which was the object for which the poor animal had undergone all this trouble.

July 14, Friday. After dinner we had a curious sight. Squires put on my Indian dress. McKenzie put on one of Mr. Culbertson's, Mrs. Culbertson put on her own *superb* dress, and the cook's wife put on the one Mrs. Culbertson had given me. Squires and Owen were painted in an awful manner by Mrs. Culbertson, the *Ladies* had their hair loose, and flying in the breeze, and then all mounted on horses with Indian saddles and trappings. Mrs. Culbertson and her maid rode astride like men, and all rode a furious race, under whip the whole way, for more than one mile on the prairie; and how amazed would have been any

European lady, or some of our modern belles who boast their equestrian skill, at seeing the magnificent riding of this Indian princess — for that is Mrs. Culbertson's rank — and her servant.

Mr. Culbertson rode with them, the horses running as if wild, with these extraordinary Indian riders, Mrs. Culbertson's magnificent black hair floating like a banner behind her. As to the men (for two others had joined Squires and McKenzie), I cannot compare them to anything in the whole creation. They ran like wild creatures of unearthly compound. Hither and thither they dashed, and when the whole party had crossed the ravine below, they saw a fine Wolf and gave the whip to their horses, and though the Wolf cut to right and left Owen shot at him with an arrow and missed, but Mr. Culbertson gave it chase, overtook it, his gun flashed, and the Wolf lay dead.

They then ascended the hills and away they went, with our princess and her faithful attendant in the van, and by and by the group returned to the camp, running full speed till they entered the fort, and all this in the intense heat of this July afternoon. Mrs. Culbertson, herself a wonderful rider, possessed of both strength and grace in a marked degree, assured me that Squires was equal to any man in the country as a rider, and I saw for myself that he managed his horse as well as any of the party, and I was pleased to see him in his dress, ornaments, etc., looking, however, I must confess, after Mrs. Culbertson's painting his face, like a being from the infernal regions.

Mr. Culbertson presented Harris with a superb dress of the Blackfoot Indians, and also with a Buffalo bull's head, for which Harris had in turn presented him with a gun-barrel of the short kind, and well fitted to shoot Buffaloes.

July 16, Sunday. At half-past three this afternoon we were travelling towards Fort Union. But hours previous to this, and before our scanty dinner, Owen had seen another bull, and Harris and Bell joined us in the hunt. The bull was shot at by McKenzie, who stopped its career, but as friend Harris pursued it with two of the hunters and finished it I was about to return, and thought sport over for the day. However, at this stage of the proceedings Owen discovered another bull making his way slowly over the prairie towards us. I was the only one who had balls, and would gladly have claimed the privilege of running him, but fearing I might make out badly on my slower steed, and so lose meat which we really needed, I handed my gun and balls to Owen McKenzie, and Bell and I went to an eminence to view the chase.

On the Dakota Prairies

Owen approached the bull, which continued to advance, and was now less than a quarter of a mile distant; either it did not see, or did not heed him, and they came directly towards each other, until they were about seventy or eighty yards apart, when the Buffalo started at a good run, and Owen's mare, which had already had two hard runs this morning, had great difficulty in preserving her distance. Owen, perceiving this, breathed her a minute, and then applying the whip was soon within shooting distance, and fired a shot which visibly checked the progress of the bull, and enabled Owen to soon be alongside of him, when the contents of the second barrel were discharged into the lungs, passing through the shoulder blade. This brought him to a stand.

Bell and I now started at full speed, and as soon as we were within speaking distance, called to Owen not to shoot again. The bull did not appear to be much exhausted, but he was so stiffened by the shot on the shoulder that he could not turn quickly, and taking advantage of this we approached him; as we came near he worked himself slowly round to face us, and then made a lunge at us; we then stopped on one side and commenced discharging our pistols with little or no effect, except to increase his fury with every shot. His appearance was now one to inspire terror had we not felt satisfied of our ability to avoid him. However, even so, I came very near being overtaken by him. Through my own imprudence, I placed myself directly in front of him, and as he advanced I fired at his head, and then ran *ahead* of him, instead of veering to one side, not supposing that he was able to overtake me; but turning my head over my shoulder, I saw to my horror, Mr. Bull within three feet of me, prepared to give me a taste of his horns. The next instant I turned sharply off, and the Buffalo being unable to turn quickly enough to follow me, Bell took the gun from Owen and shot him directly behind the shoulder blade. He tottered for a moment, with an increased jet of blood from the mouth and nostrils, fell forward on his horns, then rolled over on his side, and was dead.

July 21, Friday. We were up at sunrise, and had our coffee, after which Lafleur a mulatto, Harris, and Bell went off after Antelopes, for we cared no more about bulls; where the cows are, we cannot tell. Cows run faster than bulls, yearlings faster than cows, and calves faster than any of these.

As we came near Fox River, we thought of the horns of our bulls, and Mr. Culbertson, who knows the country like a book, drove us first to Bell's, who knocked the horns off, then to Harris's, which was served in the same manner; this bull had been eaten entirely except the head, and a good portion of mine had been devoured also; it lay immediately under 'Audubon's Bluff' (the name Mr. Culbertson gave the ridge on which I stood to see the chase), and we could see it when nearly a mile distant. Bell's horns were the handsomest and largest, mine next best, and Harris's the smallest, but we are all contented.

Mr. Culbertson tells me that Harris and Bell have done wonders, for persons who have never shot at Buffaloes from on horseback. Harris had a fall too, during his second chase, and was bruised in the manner of Squires, but not so badly. I have but little doubt that Squires killed his bull, as he says he shot it three times, and Mr. Culbertson's must have died also.

What a terrible destruction of life, as it were for nothing, or next to it, as the tongues only were brought in, and the flesh of these fine animals was left to beasts and birds of prey, or to rot on the spots where they fell. The prairies are literally *covered* with the skulls of the victims, and the roads the Buffalo make in crossing the prairies have all the appearance of heavy wagon tracks.

July 23, Sunday. When the sun had fairly risen, some one came and told me the hilltops were covered with Indians, probably Blackfeet. I walked to the back gate, and the number had dwindled, or the account been greatly exaggerated, for there seemed only fifty or sixty, and when, later, they were counted, there were found to be exactly seventy. They remained a long time on the hill, and sent a youth to ask for whiskey. But whiskey there is none for them, and very little for any one.

By and by they came down the hill leading four horses, and armed principally with bows and arrows, spears, tomahawks, and a few guns. They have proved to be a party of Crees from the British dominions on the Saskatchewan River, and have been fifteen days in travelling here. They had seen few Buffaloes, and were hungry and thirsty enough. They assured Mr. Culbertson that the Hudson's Bay Company supplied them all with abundance of spirituous liquors, and as the white traders on the Missouri had none for them, they would hereafter travel with the English. Now ought not this subject to be brought before the press in our country and forwarded to England? If our Congress will not allow our traders to sell whiskey or rum to the Indians, why should not the British follow the same rule? Surely the British, who are so anxious about the emancipation of the blacks, might as well take care of the souls and bodies of the redskins.

After a long talk and smoking of pipes, tobacco, flints, powder, gun-screws and vermilion were placed before their great chief (who is tattooed and has a most rascally look), who examined everything minutely, counting over the packets of vermilion; more tobacco was added, a file, and a piece of white cotton with which to adorn his head; then he walked off, followed by his son, and the whole posse left the fort. They passed by the garden, pulled up a few squash vines and some turnips, and tore down a few of the pickets on their way elsewhere.

We all turned to, and picked a quantity of peas, which with a fine roast pig, made us a capital dinner. After this, seeing the Assiniboins loitering about the fort, we had some tobacco put up as a target, and many arrows were sent to enter the prize, but I never saw Indians — usually so skilful with their bows — shoot worse in my life. Presently some one cried there were Buffaloes on the hill, and going to see we found that four bulls were on the highest ridge standing still. The horses being got in the yard, the guns were gathered, saddles placed, and the riders mounted, Mr. C., Harris, and Bell; Squires declined going, not having recovered from his fall, Mr. C. led his followers round the hills by the ravines, and approached the bulls quite near, when the affrighted cattle ran down the hills and over the broken grounds, out of our sight, followed by the hunters. When I see game chased by Mr. Culbertson, I feel confident of its being killed, and in less than one hour he had killed two bulls, Harris and Bell each one. Thus these poor animals which two hours before were tranquilly feeding are now dead; short work this.

July 24, Monday. I had a fine sleep last night, and this morning early a slight sprinkling of rain somewhat refreshed the earth. After breakfast we talked of going to see if Mr. Culbertson's bull had been injured by the Wolves. Mr. C., Harris, and I went off to the spot by a roundabout way, and when we reached the animal it was somewhat swollen, but untouched, but we made up our minds to have it weighed, *coute qui coute.* Harris proposed to remain and watch it.

We returned first to the fort, and mustered three men and Bell, for Sprague would not go, being busy drawing a plant, and finding the heat almost insupportable. We carried all the necessary imple-ments, and found Harris quite ready to drink some claret and water which we took for him. To cut up so large a bull, and one now with so dreadful an odor, was no joke; but with the will follows the success, and in about one hour the poor beast had been measured and weighed, and we were once more *en route* for the fort. This bull measured as follows: from end of nose to root of tail, 131 inches; height at shoulder, 67 inches; at rump, 57 inches; tail vertebrae, 15½ inches, hair in length beyond it 11 inches. We weighed the whole animal by cutting it in parts and then by addition found that this Buffalo, which was an old bull, weighed 1777 lbs. avoirdupois.

I lost the head of my first bull because I forgot to tell Mrs. Culbertson that I wished to save it, and the princess had its skull broken open to enjoy its brains. Handsome, and really courteous and refined in many ways, I cannot reconcile to myself the fact that she partakes of raw animal food with such evident relish.

Before our departure, in came six half-breeds, belonging, or attached to Fort Mortimer; and understanding that they were first-rate hunters, I offered them ten dollars in goods for each Bighorn up to eight or ten in number. They have promised to go to-morrow, but, alas! the half-breeds are so uncertain I cannot tell whether they will move a step or not. Mrs. Culbertson, who has great pride in her pure Indian blood, told me with scorn that 'all such no-color fellows are lazy.' Mrs. Culbertson was good enough to give me six young Mallards, which she had caught by swimming after them in the Missouri; she is a most expert and graceful swimmer, besides being capable of remaining under water a long time; all the Blackfoot Indians excel in swimming and take great pride in the accomplishment.

We found three of the Assiniboins had remained, one of whom wanted to carry off a squaw, and probably a couple of horses too. He strutted about the fort in such a manner that we watched him pretty closely. Mr. Culbertson took his gun, and a six-barrelled pistol in his pocket; I, my double-barrelled gun, and we stood at the back gate. The fellow had a spear made of a cut-and-thrust sword, planted in a good stick covered with red cloth, and this he never put down at any time; but no more, indeed, do any Indians, who carry all their goods and chattels forever about their persons. The three gentlemen, however, went off about dusk, and took the road to Fort Mortimer, where six half-breeds from the Northeast brought to Fort Mortimer eleven head of cattle, and came to pay a visit to their friends here.

July 30, Sunday. Weather cool and pleasant. After breakfast we despatched La Fleur and Provost after Antelopes and Bighorns. We then went off and had a battle for Rabbits, and although we were nine in number, and all beat the rose bushes and willows for several hundred yards, not one did we see, although their traces were apparent in several places. We saw tracks of a young Grizzly Bear near the river shore. After a good dinner at Buffalo meat, green peas, and a pudding, Mr. C., Owen, Mr. Pike, and I went off to Fort Mortimer. We had an arrival of five squaws, half-breeds, and a gentleman of the same order, who came to see our fort and our ladies. The princess went out to meet them covered with a fine shawl, and the visitors followed her to her own room. These ladies spoke both the French and Cree languages.

At Fort Mortimer we found the hunters from the north, who had returned last evening and told me they had seen nothing. I fear that all my former opinions of the half-breeds are likely to be realized, and that they are all more *au fait* at telling lies, than anything else; and I expect now that we shall have to make a regular turn-out ourselves, to kill both Grizzly Bears and Bighorns. As we were riding along not far from this fort, Mr. Culbertson fired off the gun given him by Harris, and it blew off the stock, lock, and breech, and it was a wonder it did not kill him, or me, as I was sitting by his side.

After we had been at home about one hour, we were all called out of a sudden by the news that the *Horse Guards* were coming, full gallop, driving the whole of their charge before them. We saw the horses, and the cloud of dust that they raised on the prairies, and presently, when the Guards reached the gates, they told us that they had seen a party of Indians, which occasioned their hurried return. It is now more than one hour since I wrote this, and the Indians are now in sight, and we think they were frightened by three or four squaws who had left the fort in search of 'pommes blanches.'

This evening five Indians arrived, among whom is the brother of the man who died a few days ago; he brought a horse, and an Elk skin, which I bought, and he now considers himself a rich man. He reported Buffaloes very near, and to-morrow morning the hunters will be after them.

When Buffaloes are about to lie down, they draw all their four feet together slowly, and balancing the body for a moment, bend their fore legs, and fall on their knees first, and the hind ones follow. In young animals, some of which we have here, the effect produced on their tender skin is directly seen, as callous round patches without hair are found; after the animal is about one year old, these are seen no more.

I am told that Wolves have not been known to attack men and horses in these parts, but they do attack mules and colts, always making choice of the fattest. We scarcely see one now-a-days about the fort, and yet two miles from here, at Fort Mortimer, Mr. Collins tells me it is impossible to sleep, on account of their howlings at night.

When Assiniboin Indians lose a relative by death, they go and cry under the box which contains the body, which is placed in a tree, cut their legs and different parts of the body, and moan miserably for hours at a time. This performance has been gone through with by the brother of the Indian who died here.

August 1, Tuesday. The weather fine, and warmer than yesterday. We sent off four Indians after Rabbits, but as we foolishly gave them powder and shot, they returned without any very soon, having, of course, hidden the ammunition. After breakfast Mr. C. had a horse put in the cart, and three squaws went off after 'pommes blanches,'[1] and Sprague and I followed in the wagon, driven by Owen. These women carried sticks pointed at one end, and blunt at the other, and I was perfectly astonished at the dexterity and rapidity with which they worked. They place the pointed end within six inches of the plant, where the stem enters the earth, and bear down upon the other end with all their weight and move about to the right and left of the plant until the point of the stick is thrust in the ground to the depth of about seven inches, when acting upon it in the manner of a lever, the plant is fairly thrown out, and the root procured. Sprague and I, who had taken with us an instrument resembling a very narrow hoe, and a spade, having rather despised the simple instruments of the squaws, soon found out that these damsels could dig six or seven, and in some cases a dozen, to our *one*.

August 2, Wednesday. I have been examining the fawn of the Long-tailed Deer of this country, belonging to old Baptiste; the man feeds it regularly, and the fawn follows him everywhere. It will race backwards and forwards over the prairie back of the fort, for a mile or more, running at the very top of its speed; suddenly it will make for the gate, rush through and overwhelm Baptiste with caresses, as if it had actually lost him for some time. If Baptiste lies on the ground pretending to sleep, the fawn pushes with its nose, and licks his face as a dog would, till he awakens.

August 5, Saturday. Provost tells me that Buffaloes become so very

[1] See footnote on page 284.

poor during hard winters, when the snows cover the ground to the depth of two or three feet, that they lose their hair, become covered with scabs, on which the Magpies feed, and the poor beasts die by hundreds. One can hardly conceive how it happens, notwithstanding these many deaths and the immense numbers that are murdered almost daily on these boundless wastes called prairies, besides the hosts that are drowned in the freshets, and the hundreds of young calves who die in early spring, so many are yet to be found. Daily we see so many that we hardly notice them more than the cattle in our pastures about our homes. But this cannot last; even now there is a perceptible difference in the size of the herds, and before many years the Buffalo, like the Great Auk, will have disappeared; surely this should not be permitted.

August 6, Sunday. Antelopes often die from the severity of the winter weather, and are found dead and shockingly poor, even in the immediate vicinity of the forts. These animals are caught in pens in the manner of Buffaloes, and are despatched with clubs, principally by the squaws. In 1840, during the winter, and when the snow was deep on the prairies and in the ravines by having drifted there, Mr. Laidlow, then at Fort Union, caught four Antelopes by following them on horseback and forcing them into these drifts, which were in places ten or twelve feet deep. They were brought home on a sleigh, and let loose about the rooms. They were so very gentle that they permitted the children to handle them, although being loose they could have kept from them. They were removed to the carpenter's shop, and there one broke its neck by leaping over a turning-lathe. The others were all killed in some such way, for they became very wild, and jumped, kicked, etc., till all were dead.

The Antelopes cannot be tamed except when caught young, and then they can rarely be raised. Mr. Wm. Sublette, of St. Louis, had one however, a female, which grew to maturity, and was so gentle that it would go all over his house, mounting and descending steps, and even going on the roof of the house. It was alive when I first reached St. Louis, but I was not aware of it, and before I left, it was killed by an Elk belonging to the same gentleman.

August 8, Tuesday. Another sultry day. Immediately after breakfast Mr. Larpenteur drove Harris and myself in search of geological specimens, but we found none worth having. We were told that a few minutes after our departure the roarings and bellowings of Buffalo were heard across the river, and that Owen and two men had been despatched with a cart to kill three fat cows but *no more*; so my remonstrances about useless slaughter have not been wholly unheeded.

August 10, Thursday. Although I have said much about Buffalo running, and butchering in general, I have not given the particular manner in which the latter is performed by the hunters of this country — I mean the white hunters — and I will now try to do so. The moment that the Buffalo is dead, three or four hunters, their faces and hands often covered with gunpowder, and with pipes lighted, place the animal on its belly, and by drawing out each fore and hind leg, fix the body so that it cannot fall down again; an incision is made near the root of the tail, immediately above the root in fact, and the skin cut to the neck, and taken off in the roughest manner imaginable, downwards and on both sides at the same time.

The knives are going in all directions, and many wounds occur to the hands and fingers, but are rarely attended to at this time. The pipe of one man has perhaps given out, and with his bloody hands he takes the one of his nearest companion, who has his own hands equally bloody. Now one breaks in the skull of the bull, and with bloody fingers draws out the hot brains and swallows them with peculiar zest; another has now reached the liver, and is gobbling down enormous pieces of it; whilst, perhaps, a third, who has come to the paunch, is feeding luxuriously on some — to me — disgusting-looking offal. But the main business proceeds. The flesh is taken off from the sides of the boss, or hump bones, from where these bones begin to the very neck, and the hump itself is thus destroyed. The hunters give the name of 'hump' to the mere bones when slightly covered by flesh; and it is cooked, and very good when fat, young, and well broiled. The pieces of flesh taken from the sides of these bones are called *filets*, and are the best portion of the animal when properly cooked. The fore-quarters, or shoulders, are taken off, as well as the hind ones, and the sides, covered by a thin portion of flesh called the *depouille*, are taken out. Then the ribs are broken off at the vertebrae, as well as the boss bones. The marrow-bones, which are those of the fore and hind legs only, are cut out last. The feet usually remain attached to these; the paunch is stripped of its covering of layers of fat, the head and the backbone are left to the Wolves, the pipes are all emptied, the hands, faces, and clothes all bloody, and now a glass of grog is often enjoyed, as the stripping off the skins and flesh of three or four animals is truly very hard work.

[316]

On the Dakota Prairies

In some cases when no water was near, our supper was cooked without our being washed, and it was not until we had travelled several miles the next morning that we had any opportunity of cleaning ourselves; and yet, despite everything, we are all hungry, eat heartily, and sleep soundly. When the wind is high and the Buffaloes run towards it, the hunter's guns very often snap, and it is during their exertions to replenish their pans, that the powder flies and sticks to the moisture every moment accumulating on their faces; but nothing stops these daring and usually powerful men, who the moment the chase is ended, leap from their horses, let them graze, and begin their butcher-like work.

August 11, Friday. The activity of Buffaloes is almost beyond belief; they can climb the steep defiles of the Mauvaises Terres in hundreds of places where men cannot follow them, and it is a fine sight to see a large gang of them proceeding along these defiles four or five hundred feet above the level of the bottoms, and from which pathway if one of the number makes a mis-step or accidentally slips, he goes down rolling over and over, and breaks his neck ere the level ground is reached. The thing that troubles them most is crossing rivers on the ice; their hoofs slip from side to side, they become frightened, and stretch their four legs apart to support the body, and in such situations the Indians and white hunters easily approach, and stab them to the heart, or cut the ham-strings, when they become an easy prey. When in large gangs those in the centre are supported by those on the outposts, and if the stream is not large, reach the shore and readily escape.

Indians of different tribes hunt the Buffalo in different ways; some hunt on horseback, and use arrows altogether; they are rarely expert in reloading the gun in the close race. Others hunt on foot, using guns, arrows, or both. Others follow with patient perseverance, and kill them also. But I will give you the manner pursued by the Mandans. Twenty to fifty men start, as the occasion suits, each provided with two horses, one of which is a pack-horse, the other fit for the chase. They have quivers with from twenty to fifty arrows, according to the wealth of the hunter. They ride the pack horse bareback, and travel on, till they see the game, when they leave the pack-horse, and leap on the hunter, and start at full speed and soon find themselves amid the Buffaloes, on the flanks of the herd, and on both sides. When within a few yards the arrow is sent, they shoot at a Buffalo somewhat ahead of them, and send the arrow in an oblique manner, so as to pass through the lights. If the blood rushes out of the nose and mouth the animal

[317]

is fatally wounded, and they shoot at it no more; if not, a second, and perhaps a third arrow, is sent before this happens.

The Buffaloes on starting carry the tail close in between the legs, but when wounded they switch it about, especially if they wish to fight, and then the hunter's horse shies off and lets the mad animal breathe awhile. If shot through the heart, they occasionally fall dead on the instant; sometimes, if not hit in the right place, a dozen arrows will not stop them. When wounded and mad they turn suddenly round upon the hunter, and rush upon him in such a quick and furious manner that if horse and rider are not both on the alert, the former is overtaken, hooked and overthrown, the hunter pitched off, trampled and gored to death. Although the Buffalo is such a large animal, and to all appearance a clumsy one, it can turn with the quickness of thought, and when once enraged, will rarely give up the chase until avenged for the wound it has received. If, however, the hunter is expert, and the horse fleet, they outrun the bull, and it returns to the herd. Usually the greater number of the gang is killed, but it very rarely happens that some of them do not escape.

This however is not the case when the animal is pounded, especially by the Gros Ventres, Black Feet, and Assiniboins. These pounds are called 'parks,' and the Buffaloes are made to enter them in the following manner: The park is sometimes round and sometimes square, this depending much on the ground where it is put up; at the end of the park is what is called a *precipice* of some fifteen feet or less, as may be found. It is approached by a funnel-shaped passage, which like the park itself is strongly built of logs, brushwood, and pickets, and when all is ready a young man, very swift of foot, starts at daylight covered over with a Buffalo robe and wearing a Buffalo headdress. The moment he sees the herd to be taken, he bellows like a young calf, and makes his way slowly towards the contracted part of the funnel, imitating the cry of the calf, at frequent intervals. The Buffaloes advance after the decoy; about a dozen mounted hunters are yelling and galloping behind them, and along both flanks of the herd, forcing them by these means to enter the mouth of the funnel.

Women and children are placed behind the fences of the funnel to frighten the cattle, and as soon as the young man who acts as decoy feels assured that the game is in a fair way to follow to the bank or 'precipice,' he runs or leaps down the bank, over the barricade, and either rests, or joins in the fray. The poor Buffaloes, usually headed by a large bull, proceed, leap down the bank in haste and confusion, the Indians all yelling and pursuing till every bull, cow, and calf is impounded. Although this is done at all seasons, it is more general in October or November, when the hides are good and salable.

Now the warriors are all assembled by the pen, calumets are lighted, and the chief smokes to the Great Spirit, the four points of the compass, and lastly to the Buffaloes. The pipe is passed from mouth to mouth in succession, and as soon as this ceremony is ended, the destruction commences. Guns shoot, arrows fly in all directions, and the hunters being on the outside of the enclosure, destroy the whole gang, before they jump over to clean and skin the murdered herd. Even the children shoot small, short arrows to assist in the destruction.

It happens sometimes however, that the leader of the herd will be restless at the sight of the precipices, and if the fence is weak will break through it, and all his fellows follow him, and escape. The same thing sometimes takes place in the pen, for so full does this become occasionally that the animals touch each other, and as they cannot move, the very weight against the fence of the pen is quite enough to break it through; the smallest aperture is sufficient, for in a few minutes it becomes wide, and all the beasts are seen scampering over the prairies, leaving the poor Indians starving and discomfited.

Mr. Kipp told me that while travelling from Lake Travers to the Mandans, in the month of August, he rode in a heavily laden cart for six successive days through masses of Buffaloes, which divided for the cart, allowing it to pass without opposition. He has seen the immense prairie back of Fort Clark look black to the tops of the hills, though the ground was covered with snow, so crowded was it with these animals; and the masses probably extended much further. In fact it is *impossible to describe or even conceive* the vast multitudes of these animals that exist even now, and feed on these ocean-like prairies.

ENVOI

AUDUBON and his companions returned in August, in a Mackinaw barge, forty feet long, which they built, and this bore them swiftly to St. Louis which they reached about the middle of October. Everything of value was sent for storage to the warehouse of faithful old Nicholas Berthoud, except some live animals which Audubon was bringing home (foxes, a badger, and a Rocky Mountain doe), and at last the old wanderer walked up to his own gates, to the house above the Hudson.

His daughter-in-law, sitting with Captain Cummings of the flatboat that had borne Audubon down the Mississippi on his first great trip to Nature in 1821, saw him approach. In his green blanket coat with fur cuffs and collar, his hair and beard long as a patriarch's, his gun in his arm, he came marching home with a firm tread and a glowing face. So we see him, plainly, for the last time.

THE END

INDEX

INDEX

By Francis H. Allen

Index

Index

Index

Lawrence, Amos, 266
Lawrence, Sir Thomas, 20
Lawrence, Rev. William, 266, 267
Lawson, Alexander, 18, 19, 35
Lecorgne, Mr., 156
Lehman, George, 20, 25; Florida cruise with A., 178; his backgrounds to A.'s drawings, 178, 182
Le Kain, Mr., 266
Le Sueur, Charles Alexandre, 18, 19
Les Cayes, Haiti, 5, 7
Lewis, Mr., of Boston, 264
Lewis, Meriwether, 95
Liautaud, A., 168, 169
Lincoln, Abraham, 159
Lincoln, Thomas, Jr., on Labrador trip, 225, 229, 230, 234
Lion, mountain. See Cougar
Little, Mr., of Little & Brown, 265
Little, C. C., & Co., 267
Little, Pamela, 266
Little & Brown, 265, 266
Little Mecattina, 244
Little Missouri River, 290
Liverpool, 20
Lizars, William H., 21
Lobsters, in Labrador, 251
London, Audubon in, 20
Loon, common, or imber diver, or black-necked diver, 240, 242; drawing, 166; tolling, 240, 241
Loon, red-throated, or red-necked diver, 240, 242
Louaillier, Mr., 165
Louis Philippe, Duke of Orleans, 20
Louise, Miss, 177
Louisiana, Audubon in, 15–18, 20, 118–23, 159–77; a bear hunt in, 81–83
Louisville, Ky., 11, 20, 33–40, 106
Lovelace, Mr., 138, 143
Lowell, Mass., 259, 263, 266, 267
Lowell, Rev. Charles, 265
Lucin, young and Mrs., 165
Lupines, 297
Lyman, Gen. Theodore, 265
Lynx, 238

MacGillivray, William, 22, 23, 29, 117
McKenzie, Kenneth, 300
McKenzie, Owen, 307–09, 313, 314, 315
Maddis, Mrs., 142
Madison, Dr. Thomas C., 280
Magdalen Islands, 228, 229
Magpie, black-billed, 315
Mallard, 144, 152, 161, 166, 312

Manatees, 181
Mandan Village, 291–98
Mangrove, 188
Man-o'-war-bird, or frigate pelican, 183, 185
Marblehead, Mass., 263
Marion, U.S. revenue cutter, cruise on, 178–89
Marten, pine, 238, 246
Martin, purple, 166
Mason, Joseph, 15, 18, 25; sketch of, 135; on the trip down the Ohio and Mississippi, 136–58; in New Orleans, 161–64, 167, 170, 173, 177; death of his father, 174
Mason, Samuel, 100–04, 139
Mason, Setton, 101
Masonic initiation, a, 169
Massachusetts, A. in, 260–69
Mathewson, Mr., 152
Meadow lark, eastern, 146
Meadow lark, western, 274, 285, 286
Meadville, Pa., 112–16
Memphis, Tenn., 144
Merganser, red-breasted, 244
Mergansers, 161
Michaux, Jean-Baptiste, 285, 287
Mill Grove, Pa., 7
Miller, Gen., 265
Minnie's Land, 26
Missingsat, 175
Mississippi, State of, cougar-hunting in, 73–78
Mississippi River, 14, 15; squatters on, 124–29; voyage down, 140–58; entering the, 140
Missouri River, expedition up, 273–320; banks, 277
Mitchell, Major, 279, 304
Mitchell, Dr. Samuel, 9
Mockingbird, 153; A.'s picture of, 27; tameness, 157; in New Orleans, 167
Moncrévier, Jean-Baptiste, 313
Montgomery, Mrs., 146
Moore, Rev. Josiah, 261, 262
Moss, sphagnum, 241
Motley, Mr., of Dedham, 262
Motley, Mrs., 262
Mud Islands, 226
Mule keys, 189
Murre, common, or foolish guillemot, 231, 232, 239, 247; robbed by eggers, 255–57
Musignano, Prince of. See Bonaparte, Charles Lucien

Nantes, 6
Natasquan River, 233, 235
Natchez, Miss., 18, 150–54
Neuwied, Maximilian Prince de, 299, 303

New England, Audubon in, 258–70
New Haven, Conn., 270
New Madrid, Mo., 101, 141, 142
New Orleans, 9–11; Audubon in, 15–18, 20, 160–77; in 1821, 159, 160
New York, Audubon in, 9, 19
Newfoundland, 250
Nighthawk, 96, 173
Nolte, Vincent, 176
North, Christopher, 20
Northeast Fur and Fish Company, 235, 236
Nova Scotia, coasting, 227; Pictou, 251, 252
Nuttall, Thomas, 24, 147; his Manual of the Ornithology of the United States and Canada, 211

Oakley, 16
Ohio River, 44; flatboats on, 44, 45; a bear killed in, 84; voyage down, 133–41; its water entering the Mississippi, 140
Omega, steamer, Missouri River trip on, 276–98
Opossum, 62, 140; habits, 69–72; flesh of, 72
Orange trees, 152, 154
Orbigny, Charles d', 9
Ord, George, 18, 19, 21, 34–36; strictures on A., 27, 28
Oriole, Baltimore, plate of, 135
Oriole, orchard, 173
Orne, William W., 269
Otter, 238, 246
Owl, barred, 161
Owl, great gray, 242

Page, Mr., of Boston, 264, 265
Page, Mrs., of Boston, 265
Pamar, R., 163, 164, 168, 169, 173, 176
Panther, American. See Cougar
Paper manufacturer, a, 268
Parakeet, Carolina. See Paroquet, Carolina
Paris, Audubon in, 20
Parker, Daniel P., 263
Parkman, Dr. George, 260, 262, 265, 266
Paroquet, Carolina, or Carolina parrot, or Carolina parakeet, history and natural history of, 217–22
Paroquet, Louisiana (western race of Carolina paroquet), 143; poisonous effect of heart of, 148; on the Missouri River, 278, 280
Parrot, Carolina. See Paroquet, Carolina
Partridge. See Bob-white

[327]

Index

Index